REPRESENTATION
AND
MEANING

**Prentice-Hall
Series in Automatic Computation**

George Forsythe, editor

AHO AND ULLMAN, *Theory of Parsing, Translation, and Compiling*, Volume I: *Parsing*
(ANDREE),[3] *Computer Programming: Techniques, Analysis, and Mathematics*
ANSELONE, *Collectively Compact Operator Approximation Theory
　and Applications to Integral Equations*
ARBIB, *Theories of Abstract Automata*
BATES AND DOUGLAS, *Programming Language/One*, 2nd ed.
BLUMENTHAL, *Management Information Systems*
BOBROW AND SCHWARTZ, *Computers and the Policy-Making Community*
BOWLES, editor, *Computers in Humanistic Research*
CESCHINO AND KUNTZMAN, *Numerical Solution of Initial Value Problems*
CRESS, et al., *FORTRAN IV with WATFOR and WATFIV*
DANIEL, *The Approximate Minimization of Functionals*
DESMONDE, *A Conversational Graphic Data Processing System*
DESMONDE, *Computers and Their Uses*, 2nd ed.
DESMONDE, *Real-Time Data Processing Systems*
EVANS, et al., *Simulation Using Digital Computers*
FIKE, *Computer Evaluation of Mathematical Functions*
FIKE, *PL/1 for Scientific Programmers*
FORSYTHE AND MOLER, *Computer Solution of Linear Algebraic Systems*
GAUTHIER AND PONTO, *Designing Systems Programs*
GEAR, *Numerical Initial Value Problems in Ordinary Differential Equations*
GOLDEN, *FORTRAN IV Programming and Computing*
GOLDEN AND LEICHUS, *IBM/360 Programming and Computing*
GORDON, *System Simulation*
GREENSPAN, *Lectures on the Numerical Solution of Linear, Singular, and
　Nonlinear Differential Equations*
GRUENBERGER, editor, *Computers and Communications*
GRUENBERGER, editor, *Critical Factors in Data Management*
GRUENBERGER, editor, *Expanding Use of Computers in the 70's*
GRUENBERGER, editor, *Fourth Generation Computers*
HARTMANIS AND STEARNS, *Algebraic Structure Theory of Sequential Machines*
HULL, *Introduction to Computing*
JACOBY, et al., *Iterative Methods for Nonlinear Optimization Problems*
JOHNSON, *System Structure in Data, Programs, and Computers*
KANTER, *The Computer and the Executive*
KIVIAT, et al., *The SIMSCRIPT II Programming Language*
LORIN, *Parallelism in Hardware and Software: Real and Apparent Concurrency*
LOUDEN AND LEDIN, *Programming the IBM 1130*, 2nd ed.
MARTIN, *Design of Real-Time Computer Systems*
MARTIN, *Future Developments in Telecommunications*
MARTIN, *Man-Computer Dialogue*
MARTIN, *Programming Real-Time Computing Systems*

MARTIN, *Systems Analysis for Data Transmission*
MARTIN, *Telecommunications and the Computer*
MARTIN, *Teleprocessing Network Organization*
MARTIN AND NORMAN, *The Computerized Society*
MATHISON AND WALKER, *Computers and Telecommunications: Issues in Public Policy*
MCKEEMAN, et al., *A Compiler Generator*
MINSKY, *Computation: Finite and Infinite Machines*
MOORE, *Interval Analysis*
PLANE AND MCMILLAN, *Discrete Optimization: Integer Programming and Network Analysis for Management Decisions*
PRITSKER AND KIVIAT, *Simulation with GASP II: a FORTRAN-Based Simulation Language*
PYLYSHYN, editor, *Perspectives on the Computer Revolution*
RICH, *Internal Sorting Methods Illustrated with PL/1 Programs*
RUSTIN, editor, *Algorithm Specification*
RUSTIN, editor, *Computer Networks*
RUSTIN, editor, *Debugging Techniques in Large Systems*
RUSTIN, editor, *Formal Semantics of Programming Languages*
SACKMAN AND CITRENBAUM, editors, *On-Line Planning: Towards Creative Problem-Solving*
SALTON, editor, *The SMART Retrieval System: Experiments in Automatic Document Processing*
SAMMET, *Programming Languages: History and Fundamentals*
SCHULTZ, *Digital Processing: A System Orientation*
SCHULTZ, *Finite Element Analysis*
SCHWARZ, et al., *Numerical Analysis of Symmetric Matrices*
SHERMAN, *Techniques in Computer Programming*
SIMON AND SIKLÓSSY, *Representation and Meaning: Experiments with Information Processing Systems*
SNYDER, *Chebyshev Methods in Numerical Approximation*
STERLING AND POLLACK, *Introduction to Statistical Data Processing*
STOUTMEYER, *PL/1 Programming for Engineering and Science*
STROUD, *Approximate Calculation of Multiple Integrals*
STROUD AND SECREST, *Gaussian Quadrature Formulas*
TAVISS, editor, *The Computer Impact*
TRAUB, *Iterative Methods for the Solution of Polynomial Equations*
VAN TASSEL, *Computer Security Management*
VARGA, *Matrix Iterative Analysis*
VAZSONYI, *Problem Solving by Digital Computers with PL/1 Programming*
WAITE, *Implementing Software for Non-Numeric Application*
WILKINSON, *Rounding Errors in Algebraic Processes*
ZIEGLER, *Time-Sharing Data Processing Systems*

REPRESENTATION AND MEANING
Experiments with Information Processing Systems

Edited by

HERBERT A. SIMON
Carnegie-Mellon University

and

LAURENT SIKLÓSSY
University of Texas

PRENTICE-HALL, INC., Englewood Cliffs, New Jersey

© 1972 by Prentice-Hall, Inc.
Englewood Cliffs, N. J.

All rights reserved. No part of this book
may be reproduced in any form or by any
means without permission in writing from
the publisher.

10 9 8 7 6 5 4 3 2 1

ISBN: 0-13-773549-9

Library of Congress Catalog Card No. 71-167787

Printed in the United States of America

PRENTICE-HALL, INTERNATIONAL, INC., *London*
PRENTICE-HALL OF AUSTRALIA, PTY. LTD., *Sydney*
PRENTICE-HALL OF CANADA, LTD., *Toronto*
PRENTICE-HALL OF INDIA PRIVATE LIMITED, *New Delhi*
PRENTICE-HALL OF JAPAN, INC., *Tokyo*

CONTENTS

GENERAL INTRODUCTION, 1

Part I
SEMANTICS IN INFORMATION PROCESSING SYSTEMS, 7

Chapter 1 THE HEURISTIC COMPILER, 9
Herbert A. Simon

  1 Experiments with a Heuristic Compiler, 10
    1.1 Theory of Problem Solving, 10
    1.2 Program Writing as Problem Solving, 11
    1.3 Outline of a Heuristic Compiler for IPL-V, 12
    1.4 Some Characteristics of IPL-V, 13
    1.5 State Description Compiler, 13
    1.6 Functional Description Compiler, 16
    1.7 General Compiler, 18
    1.8 Relation of the Heuristic Compiler to the General Problem Solver, 21
    1.9 Flow Diagrams, 21
    1.10 Summary, 24

  2 General Implications for Representations, 25
    2.1 Language and Representations in the Compiler, 25
    2.2 The Design of Representations, 28

3 Experiments with Representations, 31

    3.1 Generalized Processes, 32
    3.2 Definite Descriptions, 37
    3.3 Compilation of Routines from Partial Descriptions, 40

Chapter 2 SOME SEMANTIC METHODS FOR LANGUAGE PROCESSING, 44
Laurent Siklóssy and H. A. Simon

1 Introduction, 44

    1.1 Semantics, 45
    1.2 The Point of View, 46
    1.3 Hearer, Speaker, and Learner, 47
    1.4 Ambiguity and Synonymy, 47
    1.5 Syntax and Generality, 48
    1.6 The Programs, 49

2 Hearer Programs, 51

    2.1 Organization of the Processing, 51
    2.2 Structuring the Input, 52
    2.3 Using the Structured Input, 54
    2.4 Types of Stored Knowledge, 59
    2.5 Inference and Response, 60

3 Speaker Programs, 61

4 A Learner Program, 63

5 Conclusion, 64

Part II
GENERATING INTERNAL REPRESENTATIONS, 67

Chapter 3 SOME STUDIES IN GAME PLAYING WITH A DIGITAL COMPUTER, 71
Thomas G. Williams

1 Introduction, 71

    1.1 A Brief Survey of Game-Playing Programs, 71
    1.2 Definition of the Problem, 72

2 GGPP and Human Behavior, 73

2.1 General Information and Experience, 74
2.2 Form and Interrelations of Objects, 74
2.3 The Rules of the Game, 75

3 Use of the System, 75

3.1 The Programming System, 75
3.2 Basic Forms of GPL Data, 76
3.3 Interpretation of Statements and Programs, 81
3.4 Input Card Format, 83
3.5 Special Facilities of GPL, 84

4 Examples of Games, 99

4.1 Tic-Tac-Toe, 99
4.2 Checkers, 103
4.3 Eights, 107
4.4 Hearts, 111
4.5 Conclusions, 116

5 Internal Representation, 117

5.1 Specifications for an Internal Representation, 117
5.2 Evaluation of the Internal Representation, 118
5.3 Some Conclusions about the Representation, 122
5.4 Some Other Representations, 123

6 Problems in Learning and Generalization, 124

6.1 Move Selection, 124
6.2 Subgoal Generation, 125

7 Generality, 127

7.1 Trick-Winning Card Games, 128
7.2 Stops, 130
7.3 Poker and Rummy, 130
7.4 Other Card Games, 132
7.5 Board Games, 133
7.6 Conclusions, 133

8 Conclusions, 133

Appendix   Primitive Routines, 134

Chapter 4 COMPUTER PROGRAM ORGANIZATION INDUCED FROM PROBLEM EXAMPLES, 143
Donald S. Williams

1 The Aptitude Test Taker, 143

    1.1 Antecedents, 144
    1.2 Procedure, 145
    1.3 Structure, 145
    1.4 Organization of this Study, 146

2 Data Representation, 147

    2.1 Test Item Representation, 147
    2.2 Task Form Specification, 148
    2.3 Test Item Taker, 151
    2.4 Test Item Description, 152

3 Implementation, 155

    3.1 Test Form Analyzer, 155
    3.2 Forming the Test Item Taker, 159
    3.3 Operation of the TIT, 161

4 Comparison, 166

    4.1 Test Selection, 167
    4.2 Test Battery, 169
    4.3 Aptitude Tests, 171
    4.4 Test Items, 176

5 Other Approaches, 185

    5.1 Transformation Graphs, 186
    5.2 Catalog of Operations, 188
    5.3 Program Organization, 190

6 Problem Solvers, 191

    6.1 The Concept Former, 191
    6.2 The General Problem Solver, 194
    6.3 Sequence Prediction Program, 196

7 Summary, 197

    7.1 Method, 197
    7.2 Results, 198

Appendix Description of Aptitude Tests Used with the Aptitude Test Taker, 199

Part III
USE OF CONTEXT IN DETERMINING MEANING, 207

Chapter 5   SYNTAX DIRECTED INTERPRETATION OF NATURAL LANGUAGE, 211
L. Stephen Coles

1   Introduction, 211

     1.2   Definition of the Problem, 211
     1.2   Reasons for Wanting Natural Language and Picture Input, 213
     1.3   Related Systems, 216

2   An Integrated Linguistic Description, 223

     2.1   The Syntactic Component, 224
     2.2   The Semantic Company, 225
     2.3   Relation Between Syntax and Semantics, 227
     2.4   The Pragmatic Component, 229
     2.5   Productions, 231
     2.6   Natural Inference Systems, 232

3   GRANIS, A Computer Model, 241

     3.1   Program Structure, 242
     3.2   Results, 255

4   Extensions, 261

     4.1   Habitability, 261
     4.2   Inferential Power, 265
     4.3   Knowledge Acquisition, 273
     4.4   Adaptive Properties, 275

5   Conclusions, 278

Chapter 6   NATURAL LANGUAGE LEARNING BY COMPUTER, 288
Laurent Siklóssy

1   Introduction, 288

2   The Program and Representation, 290

     2.1   The Functional Language, FL, 290
     2.2   The Program's Internal Representation, 292
     2.3   The Program's Organization, 296

3 Learning Russian, 304

4 A Critical Look at ZBIE, 319

5 Envoi, 322

Appendix Evolutionary Learning, 323

Part IV
REPRESENTATION BY DESCRIPTION AND MODELING, 329

Chapter 7 A GOAL-ORIENTED LANGUAGE FOR THE COMPUTER, 331
Harry E. Pople, Jr.

1 Introduction, 331

    1.1 Description vs. Model in Problem Solving, 332
    1.2 A Descriptive Formulation of the Task, 333
    1.3 A Model Formulation of the Task, 338
    1.4 Representation and Process, 339
    1.5 A Synthesis of Description and Model, 341

2 The GOL Programming System, 343

    2.1 Overview, 343
    2.2 Syntax of GOL Expressions, 347
    2.3 Semantics of GOL Expressions, 350
    2.4 Pragmatics of the Language, 352
    2.5 Use of Recursive GOL Expressions, 360
    2.6 Summary, 367

3 Examples of GOL Programming, 368

    3.1 The Maze Examples Revisited, 368
    3.2 The GOL Advice Taker, 369
    3.3 Critique of the Advice Taker, 376
    3.4 The GOL General Problem Solver, 378
    3.5 The Revised Monkey Problem, 381
    3.6 The Logic Theorist in GOL, 387

4 Summary and Conclusions, 393

    4.1 Proposed Revisions and Extensions of the GOL System, 393
    4.2 Areas for Further Research, 396

Appendix A Relation to Contemporary Work, 397

- A.1 Green's System QA3, 397
- A.2 Fikes' System REF, 400

Appendix B The GOL Compiler and Evaluation Routines, 403

- B.1 Primitive Generators, 403
- B.2 Composite Generators, 404
- B.3 Conjunctive Expressions and Cascaded Generators, 405
- B.4 The GOL Executive and GOLIST, 407
- B.5 Disjunctive Expressions and Parallel Generators, 409
- B.6 Implicative Expressions and the Universal Quantifier, 409
- B.7 Run-Time Routines, 411
- B.8 Termination of Search, 411

Chapter 8 ON REASONING ABOUT ACTIONS, 414
Herbert A. Simon

1. Actions, 415
2. Models, 415
3. Proofs, 416
4. Incomplete Descriptions, 417
5. The Monkey-Banana Problem, 420
6. Comments on Models, 421
7. Symmetries, 422
8. Hereditary Properties, 423
   - 8.1 Cube-brick Problem, 424
   - 8.2 Rule of the Square, 425
   - 8.3 NIM, 425
9. Model Subspaces, 426
10. Non-Independence, 427
    - 10.1 Resource Limitation, 427
    - 10.2 Specific Requirements, 428
    - 10.3 Temporal Interdependence, 429
    - 10.4 Analysis in Chess, 430

Index, 431

PREFACE

This volume brings together some studies of how an information processing system—computer or human—can represent, internally, information gathered from the outside world, and can employ such information to bring about desired actions in that world. In the literature of artificial intelligence and cognitive psychology, a variety of different labels have been applied to these topics. At one time or another, they have been called questions of representation, semantics, natural language processing, pattern recognition, and learning.

Some notion of what these labels mean can be gained from the research reported in this book. Thomas and Donald Williams (no relation) seek to explain how an information processing system, provided with information about a task, can learn to perform that task. In their respective studies, they treat, however, two quite different kinds of external information: Thomas Williams, instructions of the sort that one might find in Hoyle's book of games or a cookbook; Donald Williams, worked-out examples of the task.

Coles and Siklóssy consider how to extract meaning from combinations of pictures and natural language sentences describing the pictures. Coles uses information from the pictures to remove syntactic ambiguity from natural language, while Siklóssy's system learns to produce grammatically correct natural language sentences that describe corresponding pictures.

Finally, Pople describes a problem-solving system incorporating two different kinds of internal representations. One uses explicit propositions to describe situations, the other represents them by modeling them.

These five studies, all undertaken as doctoral research projects at Carnegie-Mellon University, were completed in the years 1965 through 1969. Some of the problems that gave rise to them are explored in the introductory chapter, on the Heuristic Compiler, written by Simon between 1960 and

1962, which aims at building a bridge between the sorts of internal representations that were used in the General Problem Solver and external situations described in natural language. The first portion of this essay has been published previously. A survey by Siklóssy and Simon of semantic methods in language processing completes Part I, and provides some common framework for the essays of the two following parts. Finally, some of the issues central to Pople's research in Part IV are discussed in Simon's unpublished working paper, "On Reasoning About Actions," which also examines the relative merits of descriptions and models as internal representations.

All of these studies are reproduced here in essentially their original forms, with changes only of an editorial nature. In particular, no attempt has been made to update them by reference to subsequent research in this rapidly moving field. They have lost none of their relevance in the short time since their completion.

A good deal of closely related work in artificial intelligence has been brought together in two earlier volumes. In Feigenbaum's and Feldman's *Computers and Thought* are found a report on the BASEBALL program of Bert Green and his colleagues, and Lindsay's paper on "Inferential Memory as the Basis of Machines Which Understand Natural Language." Studies by Minsky, Raphael, Bobrow, Quillian, Evans, Black, and McCarthy are assembled in a volume titled *Semantic Information Processing*, under the editorship of Marvin Minsky. In the bibliographies appended to the chapters of this volume, references that are reprinted in these two earlier volumes are marked [FF] and [M], respectively, and those appearing elsewhere in this volume are marked [SS].

Herbert A. Simon
Laurent Siklóssy

ACKNOWLEDGMENTS

HERBERT A. SIMON. *The Heuristic Compiler*

Most of this research was carried out as part of the RAND Corporation's research on complex information processing under Air Force Project RAND. The author acknowledges the assistance of H. S. Kelly.

L. SIKLÓSSY and H. A. SIMON. *Some Semantic Methods for Language Processing*.

This work was supported in part by Public Health Service Research Grant MH-07722 from the National Institute of Mental Health, and in part by the Advanced Research Projects Agency of the Office of the Secretary of Defense (SD-146). The authors thank D. G. Bobrow, N. Chomsky, E. Clark, H. Clark, and W. C. Watt for comments on an earlier draft.

THOMAS G. WILLIAMS. *Some Studies in Game Playing With a Digital Computer*

This research was partially supported by the Advanced Research Projects Agency of the Office of the Secretary of Defense under contract SD-146 to the Carnegie Institute of Technology. The author acknowledges the assistance of H. A. Simon (thesis supervisor), A. Newell, A. Lavi, D. Cooper, J. Rubenfeld, R. Bushyager, and G. Williams.

DONALD S. WILLIAMS. *Computer Program Organization Induced From Problem Examples*

This research was supported by Public Health Service Research Grant MH-07722 from the National Institute of Mental Health to Carnegie–Mellon University. The author thanks the Aptitude Research Project of the University of Southern California Psychological Laboratories and Dr. J. P. Guilford for supplying the aptitude tests used in the research; Dr. A. W. Winikoff for making the eye-motion films; and the University of Pittsburgh

Computer Center for the use of their IBM 7090 computer. He acknowledges the assistance of H. A. Simon (thesis supervisor), T. van Wormer, L. W. Gregg, B. F. Green, Jr., and A. Newell.

L. STEPHEN COLES. *Syntax Directed Interpretation of Natural Language*

This work was supported by the Advanced Research Projects Agency of the Office of the Secretary of Defense under contract SD-146 to the Carnegie Institute of Technology. The author acknowledges the assistance of H. A. Simon (thesis supervisor), A. J. Perlis, R. Iturriaga, R. Krutar, and T. Standish.

LAURENT SIKLÓSSY. *Natural Language Learning by Computer*

This work was supported in part by the Danforth Foundation and in part by the Advanced Research Projects Agency of the Office of the Secretary of Defense under contract SD-146 to Carnegie–Mellon University. The author acknowledges the assistance of H. A. Simon (thesis supervisor), G. Berglass, R. Fikes, P. Freeman, R. Grove, R. Bushyager, and T. Cunningham.

HARRY E. POPLE, JR. *A Goal-Oriented Language for the Computer*

The author acknowledges the assistance of H. A. Simon (thesis supervisor), P. Andrews, A. Newell, S. Amarel, and R. Floyd.

HERBERT A. SIMON. *On Reasoning About Actions*

The author thanks A. Newell and S. Amarel with whom he participated in a seminar on representation. This research was supported in part by the Public Health Service Research Grant MH-07722 from the National Institute of Mental Health.

REPRESENTATION AND MEANING

GENERAL INTRODUCTION

During the early years of research on artificial intelligence and simulation of cognitive processes, that is to say, until about 1960, most work focused on one or another of three main areas: problem solving by heuristic search methods, pattern recognition, and learning (including learning by perceptrons and other self-organizing networks). The first of these areas showed the most rapid progress, but each successful exploration revealed limitations in these early problem-solving programs, and posed new conceptual problems.

REPRESENTATION

By 1960, the rubrics "representation" and "semantics" began to be applied to two of the most prominent issues that were emerging from the research. Representation has to do with the kinds of symbol structures that are used inside a computer (or a human brain) to represent the external task situation confronting it. Most early problem-solving systems used a fixed form of problem representation, tailored to a single, specific task domain and requiring that task information be provided in a particular definite format adapted to the internal representation. The General Problem Solver attained a certain measure of independence from a specific task domain, but still required its problems to be specified in a rigid format.

There was a strong contrast between these task-restricted, format-constricted artificial intelligence systems, and the human problem solver with his *relative* versatility and ability to accept tasks expressed, often elliptically, in natural language. Clearly, progress toward a fuller understanding of problem solving required an ability to design representations of broader compass and representations that could "interface" more flexibly with information—whether pictorial or in natural language—coming into the system from its external environment.

SEMANTICS

Semantics has to do with the extraction of meanings from symbol structures and the use of these meanings to aid problem solving. Again, most early problem-solving programs manipulated symbols solely on the basis of "external" characteristics. The programs moved symbols, shaped them, copied them, joined them, divided them as though they were so many pieces of wood or metal. The *Logic Theorist* discovered proofs for theorems in elementary symbolic logic without knowing—or needing to know—that a wedge-shaped symbol ($\vee$) stood for "or," or a dot ($\cdot$) for "and." It operated by formal transformations upon axioms, themselves expressed as formal strings of symbols. The earliest problem solver having a semantic component was Gelernter and Rochester's *Geometry Theorist*, which had access to a geometric diagram, usable both as a source of hypotheses about possibly provable statements and as a quick check of the (empirical) validity of conjectures.

Schemes for automatic language translation that were developed during this period also relied solely on syntactic information to transform source-language into target-language statements. But it became increasingly clear that it was impractical to resolve ambiguity entirely by syntactic means—that correct readings could often be chosen only on the basis of intended meanings. In the decade since 1960, partly from the stimulus of these obvious inadequacies in automatic translation schemes, modern theoretic linguistics has been moving steadily toward a concern with the relation of semantics to syntax.

AN EXPERIMENTAL APPROACH

The studies collected in this volume exemplify the method that has proved most fruitful in research on complex information processing: to investigate a phenomenon, choose a task domain where that phenomenon is prominent and design an information processing system that is able to perform tasks from that domain. Any such study is *theoretical* in its concern with specifying a particular artificial information processing system, but is *experimental* in studying the system's properties and behavior by actually programming it and testing it. Very little of the research has to do with proving theorems about the systems that are constructed. It has, over all, much more the flavor of experimental natural science than of mathematics or theoretical physics, say. Most of what we know today about artificial intelligence and cognitive simulation is embedded in a series of experiments of this kind.

INDUCTION WITHOUT TEARS (or STATISTICS)

Several of the programs described in this book perform inductions, that is to say, make use of context in order to arrive at specific interpretations of input information. The Heuristic Compiler induces meanings of input sentences by matching them against archetypal forms stored in memory. D. Williams' program generates test-taking programs from examples, by using context previously stored in modular form; Coles' program uses pictorial context to resolve syntactic ambiguities; while Siklóssy's builds up translational schemes from examples.

In most previous artificial intelligence attempts at induction, a probabilistic and statistical approach has been taken. Experience is accumulated in terms of the frequencies or probabilities of co-occurrence of certain inputs with the corresponding possible interpretations. Some analog of Bayes' principle is used to winnow out gradually the correct interpretation from the wrong ones.

This kind of statistical apparatus is strikingly absent from the inductive schemes described in this book. Instead, a radically different approach is explored, the central idea of which is that the real world is highly redundant. In a highly redundant world, coincidences never happen (or hardly ever happen!). If two structures match, and match redundantly, it can be assumed safely that they are related. Hence, a system can proceed on the assumption that it has detected a correct match whenever such redundant matching is present. Learning can be embodied in structures that are then built to facilitate future matching. As a further safeguard, the system may be provided with a little back-off capability and ability to explore a modest number of alternatives. It does not, however, have to be provided with the ability to keep elaborate, nearly complete records of its past experience, most of which is irrelevant to future performance.

The demonstrations here of the effectiveness of induction without statistics and elaborate record keeping have implications for artificial intelligence that go well beyond the specific tasks handled by these particular systems.

COMPLEXITY AND SIMPLICITY

In one sense, information processing systems of the sort discussed in this volume are highly complex, so complex that it is seldom possible to deduce their properties by mathematical means. Instead, as indicated earlier, we must resort to experiment in order to understand them.

Once we understand one of these systems, however, we often find it to be disappointingly simple. Abstracting from details of programming, a problem solver like GPS, for example, can be described in terms of just a handful of simple, commonsensical, heuristic devices. GPS is little more than a scheme for finding differences between an actual present and a desired future, retrieving from memory operators that are relevant to reducing such differences, and applying the operators. What could be more obvious? The programs described in this volume are, in their essentials, equally transparent.

The task of science is not to bedazzle, but to explain—to show that what we thought complex is, when viewed from the proper vantage point, trivially simple. We may well apply to our scientific ventures the rule that Mies van der Rohe thought fundamental to good architecture:

"*Least is Most.*"

Following that rule, we will not try to impress on readers the complexity of the programs described here, but rather their fundamental simplicity. They demonstrate what a small amount of machinery is needed to perform information processing tasks of considerable apparent difficulty.

Part I

SEMANTICS IN INFORMATION PROCESSING SYSTEMS

The two chapters of this part are included primarily to provide a setting for the more specific studies of the remaining three parts of the book.

The research reported in Chapter 1, on the Heuristic Compiler, was not aimed at the construction of a specific compiler, but was directed toward deepening our understanding of the kinds of problem-solving activity that are involved in computer programming, and the kinds of language and representational means that are needed to produce more sophisticated compilers. This chapter takes the form of a series of illustrative problems of compiler design, with proposals, worked out in varying degrees of detail, for their solution.

The decade of the 1950's saw great progress in the development of higher-level programming languages for instructing computers. Through the invention of algebraic compilers, like FORTRAN, IT, and ALGOL, data processing languages like COBOL, and list-processing languages like IPL, LISP, and COMIT, the labor of programming was reduced several orders of magnitude. Yet, with all this progress, programming a computer to perform a complex task remained much more intricate and tedious than instructing an intelligent and trained human being for that task.

First of all, the human does not have the literalness of mind that is so characteristic of the computer when we communicate with it through languages like these. From his own store of knowledge, he supplies facts that we neglect to give him; given statements of objectives in broad functional terms, he applies his problem-solving powers to filling in the detail of method; confronted with the vagueness and informality of natural language, he interprets meaning and intent.

The experiments reported in the chapter on the Heuristic Compiler aimed toward bridging the gap between the explicitness of computer programming languages and the freedom and flexibility of human communication. A number of the ideas sketched in this chapter are developed further and implemented in later chapters, e.g., those by Tom Williams and Donald Williams. It is also interesting to compare these ideas with recent developments in automated definitional facilities as described, for example, in B. A. Galler and A. J. Perlis, *A View of Programming Languages* (Addison–Wesley, 1970), Chapter 4.

Chapter 2, by Siklóssy and Simon, is a review and commentary on progress made during the first seven years of the 1960's toward achieving some of the flexibility of natural-language communication in computers by introducing semantics into the processing. Some eleven programs are discussed that make use of "meanings," in some sense of that word, to aid in natural language processing. The comparisons of these eleven programs serve to illustrate the multitudinous meanings of "meaning," the variety of artificial intelligence tasks to which natural language processing is relevant, and the many ways in which semantic procedures can be employed in performing these tasks.

Since semantic information processing is one of the liveliest areas of research today, not only in artificial intelligence but also in linguistics and in cognitive psychology, the chapter, written in 1968, does not cover all recent developments. The reader who is interested in carrying the story further may wish to consult, for example, the *Proceedings* of the First International Joint Conference on Artificial Intelligence, and Volumes 3, 4, and 5 of *Machine Intelligence*, where several pieces of later work are described. But the issues outlined in this chapter are still the issues that must be addressed in research on semantic information processing.

Chapter 1

THE HEURISTIC COMPILER

HERBERT A. SIMON

Two major themes run through the topics discussed in this chapter. The first is that more of the programming burden can be shifted from programmer to computer if the computer is given some problem-solving powers. In a previous work [1] it has been shown how a computer program, the General Problem Solver, can simulate the kinds of means-end analysis that humans use to solve problems. Section 1 of this chapter shows how a compiler can be designed, one that makes use of heuristic problem-solving techniques like those incorporated in the General Problem Solver (GPS). Such a scheme permits a desired program to be specified in general terms, with the compiler using means-end analysis and selective trial-and-error search to work out the exact "how" of it.

The second main theme is that if we are to have flexibility in a compiler language commensurate with the flexibility of natural language, we must first gain an understanding of the ways in which meanings are represented in natural language, and then devise representations of corresponding power (and ambiguity) for compiling languages. Sections 2 and 3 are devoted primarily to questions of language and representation. They provide a number of suggestions for increasing the generality and flexibility of compiler languages.

The boundaries between the three parts are largely chronological. Section 1 represents work completed during the winter of 1960–1961; Section 2, work done during the spring of 1961; Section 3, work done since the summer of 1961, particularly during the summer and autumn of 1962.

SECTION 1
EXPERIMENTS WITH A HEURISTIC COMPILER

Section 1 describes some experiments in constructing a compiler that makes use of heuristic problem-solving techniques such as those incorporated in the General Problem Solver (GPS) [1]. The experiments were aimed at the dual objectives of throwing light on some of the problems of constructing more powerful programming languages and compilers, and of testing whether the task of writing a computer program can be regarded as a "problem" in the sense in which that term is used in GPS. The present section is concerned primarily with the second objective—with analyzing some of the problem-solving processes that are involved in writing computer programs. At the present stage of their development, no claims will be made for the heuristic programming procedures described here as practical approaches to the construction of compilers. Their interest lies in what they teach us about the nature of the programming task.

1.1 Theory of Problem Solving

The motivation for the compiler is supplied by a theory of problem solving that also provides the basic framework for GPS [1]. By a problem, a situation of the following kind is meant:

1. We are given a (partial) description of a *present situation* and a *desired situation*. These situations are described in a language that we may call the *state language*. The state language is sufficiently rich to permit us to describe situations (we shall call such descriptions *objects*) and to describe *differences* between pairs of situations.

2. We are given a list of *operators* which can be applied to situations to transform them into new situations. Operators are named in a language that we may call the *process language*. Any sequence of operators in the process language also is an operator—the compound operator corresponding to the application, in order, of the elementary operators belonging to the sequence.

3. A problem *solution* is a (compound) operator in the process language which will transform the object describing the present situation into the object describing the desired situation.

Example. Take as the objects in the state language the integers 1, 2, ... Take as the elementary operator the successor operation, which we shall designate as ′ in the process language. Then ‴ and ′′′′′ are examples of compound operators. Consider the problem of transforming the present object 5 into the goal object 8. The solution is the operator ‴, for 5‴ = 8. More generally, ‴ is the operator that removes the difference +3 between any two objects, x and y; for if $y - x = +3$, then $x''' = y$. Here +3 is a difference, in the state language; ‴ is the operator *relevant to that difference*, in the process language. We may construct a *table of connections* to associate with each difference the operator or operators relevant to it.

The distinction between state language and process language derives from the problem solver's dual relation with his environment. On the one hand, he perceives objects in the environment and represents them internally —in the state language. On the other hand, he acts upon the environment, and needs a language, the process language, to represent his actions. There may be more than one way of representing environmental objects—more than one state language. There also may be several process languages. In this section we introduce several state languages in which programming problems may be expressed. (The most important of these will be called the "state description" language and "functional description" language, respectively.) Our process language will be a particular interpretive language, IPL-V.[1]

With this explication of the concept of "problem," many techniques of problem solving can be subsumed under the following general paradigm:

Means-End Analysis. Given the present and desired objects, find a difference between them. Next, find an operator relevant to the difference; determine if the operator can be applied to the present object. If so, apply it. (If not, describe the objects to which it would apply and transform the present object into an object of that kind—a new "desired object.") Take the new object thus obtained as the present object and repeat the process.

The General Problem Solver is a program that uses this scheme of means-end analysis to attempt the solution of any problem cast into the form described.[2]

1.2 Program Writing as Problem Solving

The task of proving a theorem can be formulated as a problem for GPS. The desired object is the theorem to be proved. The present object is the set of axioms and already-proved theorems. The operators are the legitimate processes for transforming a subset of axioms and/or theorems into a new theorem. We have a proof when we have a sequence of operators

---

[1] IPL-V is described only to the extent necessary for this exposition. A complete description will be found in [3].
[2] This is a bare-bone description of GPS, but it will suffice for present purposes. Reference [1] gives a fuller description.

that transforms the present object into the desired object. (What we call a proof here is usually regarded as the *justification* for the proof steps; the proof as usually written out consists of the sequence of successive transformations of the axioms and given theorems.)

The sequence of operators constituting a proof can also be interpreted as a *program* which generates the desired object from the given object; for if we apply the operators of the proof, in sequence, to the present object (the axioms and previous theorems), we obtain precisely the desired object —the theorem to be proved. Thus a theorem-proving system can be regarded, at least formally, as a program-writing system. Conversely, if we can formulate a programming goal as a difference between a present and a desired object, we can presumably use the same processes, which in the other context will generate the proof of a theorem, to generate a program.

1.3 Outline of a Heuristic Compiler for IPL-V

In the remainder of this section we describe a number of routines for compiling programs in Information Processing Language V (IPL-V), an interpretive list processing language. What is common to all of these compiling procedures is that they embody the problem-solving notions discussed in the preceding paragraphs. That is, each of the compiling routines accepts the task of writing programs in IPL-V on the basis of certain information provided to it. The task is accomplished by the application of the means-end analysis described. The several compiling routines differ with respect to their methods of formulating or representing the problem—that is, each operates with a different state language. At present, there are three compiling routines:

1. *State Description Compiler*. This routine takes as its input a description (state description) of the contents of the relevant computer cells before and after the routine to be compiled has been executed. It produces an IPL-V routine that will transform the input state description into the output state description.

2. *Functional Description Compiler*. This routine takes as its input a verbal definition (in the form of an imperative sentence) of the routine to be compiled. It produces an IPL-V routine that is the translation, in the interpretive language, of that definition.

3. *General Compiler*. This is an executive routine that can use the state description compiler, the functional description compiler, and others as subroutines. It takes as its input information about the routine to be compiled; the information can be stated in any one of several representations (e.g., those appropriate to either of the component compilers). The routine

then selects subroutines that can use this information to produce the desired IPL-V code.

From a logical standpoint, we could describe the Heuristic Compiler as a single program whose executive routine is the General Compiler, and which contains the State Description Compiler and the Functional Description Compiler as subroutines. For clarity of exposition, it will be better to describe the two parts first as independent programs, and then show how they are imbedded in the General Compiler.

1.4 Some Characteristics of IPL-V

Before we begin, it will be useful to mention a few of the features of IPL-V that will be referred to in our discussion. In IPL-V, cells may have lists (pushdown lists) associated with them. The primitive processes of IPL-V find their operands in a *communication cell* and its pushdown list. We shall call this cell the "accumulator," because it has many of the functions of the accumulator in a standard computer. Processes (except tests) put their outputs in the accumulator and its pushdown list. Tests in IPL record their result by placing a PLUS or a MINUS in a special cell called the Signal Cell.

Lists in the IPL memory may have *description lists* associated with them. A description list is simply a list having a special format. It consists of pairs of symbols; the first symbol of each pair designating an attribute, the second symbol designating the value of that attribute. The value may be a simple symbol or it may itself be a list. Thus, we might have in memory a representation of a class of objects called "apples." The description list associated with this class might contain the attribute "color" with the value "red." Another attribute of "apple" could be "type," having the list of values "Winesap," "Delicious," and so on.

Values of attributes of objects may themselves have descriptions. Thus, in the compiler we shall have occasion to store representations of *routines* or programs in memory. These representations will take the form of description lists, each routine having one or more of the attributes "IPL name," "IPL-V definition," "Functional Description," "State Description," and "Flow Diagram." The values of these attributes will themselves be described —will have description lists associated with them. Thus, for example, the state description of a routine will be given by a description list having the attribute "list of affected cells." The value of that attribute will be a list, each item of which will again have a description list associated with it.

1.5 State Description Compiler

A computer routine can be defined by specifying the changes it produces in the contents of the storage locations it affects, or, what amounts to almost the same thing, by specifying the before-and-after conditions of these storage locations. A definition of this kind is not, of course, univocal, for programming is a synthetic, not an analytic task; generally there will be many programs (not all equally efficient or elegant) that will do the same work. As presently constituted, the State Description Compiler attempts to find one routine to accomplish a given task.

Example. In IPL-V there is a process, "Put symbol MINUS in Signal Cell," which affects a single memory location, the Signal Cell. This process has the following state description: *before* the process is executed, the Signal Cell contains a symbol, call it SYMB1, followed by an indeterminate list of symbols, PUSHDOWN1 (call this the pushdown list associated with the Signal Cell); *after* the process has been executed, the Signal Cell contains the symbol MINUS followed by the same list of symbols PUSHDOWN1, as before. The token of symbol SYMB1 previously in the Signal Cell has been destroyed.

Notice that it is implicit in this definition of SET SIGNAL MINUS that the content of no cell other than the Signal Cell has been altered by the routine. We can depict the state description diagrammatically as follows:

State Description of SET SIGNAL MINUS
Affected Cells: Signal Cell
Input   SYMB1, PUSHDOWN1
Output   MINUS, PUSHDOWN1

Generalizing, the state description of a routine consists of a *list of affected cells*. For each affected cell on the list, the state description specifies its *input state* and its *output state*.

To compile the IPL-V code for SET SIGNAL MINUS, the Compiler proceeds as follows:

1. It matches the input states with the output states of the affected cells until it *finds a difference*. In the example cited, the difference between the input and output states of the Signal Cell may be called a *replacement in the Signal Cell*.

2. It searches a *table of connections* which associates with each difference a list of *operators* (compiled IPL-V routines) relevant to that difference. In the example, the table of connections contains, associated with the replacement difference, the IPL-V routine REPLACE [(CELL)] BY (ACCUMULATOR).[3]

REPLACE [(CELL1)] BY (ACCUMULATOR) replaces the symbol in cell CELL1, a variable, with the symbol in the accumulator. Thus, the "Replace" process has the following state description:

State Description of REPLACE [(CELL1)] BY (ACCUMULATOR)
Affected Cells: Accumulator   Cell
Input   SYMB2, PUSHDOWN1   SYMB1, PUSHDOWN2
Output   PUSHDOWN1   SYMB2, PUSHDOWN2

[3] We adopt the usual convention that parentheses mean "the contents of."

3. It tentatively applies the relevant operator it has found to the input state of the state description to be compiled, and determines the resulting output state. In applying the operator, it makes appropriate substitutions for the variables in the operator. Thus, applying REPLACE [(CELL1)] to the input of SET SIGNAL MINUS, we find, by matching, that we should set CELL1 = SIGNAL and SYMB2 = MINUS, giving:

> State Description of REPLACE (SIGNAL) BY (ACCUMULATOR)
> *Affected Cells:*   Accumulator   Signal
> Input   MINUS, PUSHDOWN1   SYMB1, PUSHDOWN2
> Output   PUSHDOWN1   MINUS, PUSHDOWN2

4. The application of the operator creates two new subproblems: Let I_a represent the input state of the routine to be compiled, O_a its output state, I_b the input state of the operator, and O_b its output state. The original problem was to transform I_a into O_a. The new problems are: (1) to transform I_a into I_b (i.e., to establish the input conditions for application of the operator), and (2) to transform O_a into O_b (i.e., to transform the output state of the operator into the desired output state of the routine to be compiled). Either of these new problems may reduce to the identity transformation, in which case that part of the problem is solved. If this reduction does not occur, then the same steps 1, 2, 3 are applied to the new subproblem.

In the example at hand, O_b is identical with O_a; hence the remaining subproblem is to transform I_a into I_b, that is, to compile a routine with state description:

> Accumulator
> Input   PUSHDOWN1
> Output   MINUS, PUSHDOWN1

The repetition of step 1 for this subproblem discovers a new difference, an addition to the contents of the accumulator. Step 2 finds the relevant operator, LOAD [S] INTO ACCUMULATOR, which adds to the symbol list in the accumulator the symbol s. Applying, in step 3, the operator LOAD [MINUS], the input state of the accumulator is transformed into the desired output state. Hence the solution to the original problem of compiling SET SIGNAL MINUS is obtained by the sequence LOAD MINUS, REPLACE (SIGNAL) or, in the usual IPL-V format,[4]

> Set signal minus   J3   10J3   Load MINUS
>   20H5   0.   Replace (SIGNAL), Terminate

We see that for the state description compiler to operate, it must be provided with a set of differences and matching tests for noticing differences, a set of already-compiled operators, and a table of connections between

---

[4] The standard IPL-V notation for the routine is shown in the center, with its translation in the left- and right-hand columns. Thus J3 is the IPL name for SET SIGNAL MINUS and also for the symbol MINUS. 10 means LOAD, 20 means REPLACE. H5 is the name for SIGNAL, 0 for TERMINATE.

differences and operators. Further, when it has compiled a new routine, the compiler can annex this routine to its set of available operators and use it in compiling subsequent routines.

1.6 Functional Description Compiler

Let us now consider an alternative compiling scheme for the same routine, SET SIGNAL MINUS. Instead of specifying the before-and-after condition of the computer cells, we define the routine in terms of the function it performs: "Replace the symbol in the Signal Cell by MINUS." This definition (functional description) resembles more closely than the previous one the manner in which routines are defined for conventional compilers like FORTRAN or LISP. What distinguishes the present scheme from these is the use of heuristic means-end analysis for working from the definition to the compiled routine.

The first step in the Functional Description Compiler is to search a list of available (compiled) routines to find one whose functional description is as similar as possible to the functional description of the routine to be compiled. In the case at hand, we would find the routine REPLACE (CELL1): "Replace the symbol in CELL1 by the top symbol of the pushdown list in the accumulator."

At the second step, means-end analysis is performed to transform the compiled routine into the new routine. The transformations are performed on the functional descriptions. Thus, in the present example there are two differences between REPLACE [(CELL1)] BY (ACCUMULATOR) and REPLACE (SIGNAL) BY MINUS. The former refers to the cell, CELL1, the latter to the Signal Cell; the former refers to the symbol that is contained in the accumulator, the latter to the symbol MINUS.

The compiler notices these differences (in a sequence), and searches for an operator relevant to removing the differences. In this case, CELL1 can be transformed to SIGNAL by a *substitution* operator. (ACCUMULATOR) can be changed to MINUS by an *addition* operator ("Make (ACCUMULATOR) equal to MINUS by addition"). The application of these operators to the functional description of REPLACE [(CELL1)] would compile the desired routine in the following stages:

REPLACE [(CELL1)]	Replace the symbol in CELL1 by (ACCUMULATOR)
Apply *substitution*	Replace the symbol in SIGNAL by (ACCUMULATOR)
Apply *addition*	Replace the symbol in ACCUMULATOR BY MINUS

The resulting program in this case is identical with that obtained by the State Description Compiler.

A somewhat more complex routine compiled by the Functional Description Compiler is[5] INSERT 1ACCUMULATOR AT THE END OF (THE VALUE OF ATTRIBUTE 0ACCUMULATOR OF 2ACCUMULATOR). The list of available IPL routines includes INSERT 0ACCUMULATOR AT THE END OF 1ACCUMULATOR.

The differences between these two functional descriptions are in their arguments. The latter has the argument 0ACCUMULATOR where the former has the argument 1ACCUMULATOR; the latter has the argument 1ACCUMULATOR where the former has the argument THE VALUE OF ATTRIBUTE 0ACCUMULATOR OF 2ACCUMULATOR. Since it is not easy in IPL-V to rearrange arguments located in the pushdown list of the accumulator, the compiler facilitates matters by incorporating in the compiled routine an algorithm that moves the inputs of the routine to be compiled into known working storage locations, then puts these inputs back into the accumulator pushdown list in the order in which they are needed for the subprocesses. That is, the compiler first transforms INSERT AT END OF VALUE LIST into another routine, which it then compiles. The functional description of this intermediary routine[6] is INSERT 1WORKING AT THE END OF THE VALUE OF ATTRIBUTE 0WORKING OF 2WORKING. The code for INSERT AT END OF VALUE LIST may be written as:

Insert at end of value list:
    J13   J52   Put symbols in working storage
            K13   Execute intermediary routine
            J32   0.   Restore working storage, Terminate

Now the intermediary routine is to be compiled with the aid of INSERT AT END OF LIST. Comparing the corresponding arguments of the two routines, we see that this involves finding the value of attribute 0WORKING of 2WORKING, placing the value in the accumulator, bringing 1WORKING into the accumulator, and then performing INSERT AT END OF LIST. That is to say the intermediary routine will have the general form:

Insert at end of value list:
        K13   Find V(0w, 2w)   Find value list of attribute
                                                 0WORKING OF 2WORKING
               11W1   Add 1WORKING
               J65   Insert 0ACCUMULATOR AT END OF
                                             1ACCUMULATOR

---

[5] We shall use, from now on, the following abbreviations: 0ACCUMULATOR is the symbol in the accumulator, 1ACCUMULATOR is the first symbol of the pushdown list of the accumulator, 2ACCUMULATOR the second symbol, and so on. In IPL-V, the operands for processes are held in the accumulator and its pushdown list.

[6] 0WORKING, 1WORKING, etc., are abbreviations for the contents of a set of working cells available in IPL-V.

18 The Heuristic Compiler

In the list of available routines, the compiler finds FIND THE VALUE OF ATTRIBUTE 0ACCUMULATOR OF 1ACCUMULATOR, which may be abbreviated "Find V(0A, 1A)." Comparing its arguments with those of V(0w, 2w), we see that 1ACCUMULATOR must be set equal to 2WORKING and 0ACCUMULATOR to 0WORKING. Hence V(0w, 2w) is equivalent to

11W2	Add 2WORKING
11W0	Add 0WORKING
J10	Find value of 0ACCUMULATOR of 1ACCUMULATOR

Hence, the complete code for the intermediary routine is

11W2	Add 2w
11W0	Add 0w
J10	Find value of 0A of 1A
11W1	Add 1w
J65	Insert 0A at end of 1A

and the complete code for the desired routine[7] is

Insert 0A at end of value list of 1A of 2A:

J13	J52		Put symbols in working storage
	11W2		Add 2w
	11W0		Add 0w
	J10		Find value of 0A of 1A
	11W1		Add 1w
	J65		Insert 0A at end of 1A
	J32	0.	Restore working storage, Terminate

1.7 General Compiler

The General Compiler is an executive routine whose task is to compile a routine from information in any of the forms already discussed (state description or functional description) or in other forms that may be described. It takes as its input the internal name of the routine to be compiled. Associated with this routine (on its description list) is the information to be used in the compilation. More formally:

A *routine* is a description list containing values of some subset of the following attributes:

---

[7] Readers familiar with IPL-V will see that we are simplifying for purposes of illustration. The routine as written does not taken care of the case where the attribute value in question does not exist.

1. *IPL name.* The value of this attribute is a description list naming a region and a location in the region—e.g., J60, R149, J3.

2. *IPL-V definition.* The value of this attribute is a list of IPL-V instructions, each in the form of a description list describing the corresponding IPL-V word, defining an IPL-V routine with the specified name. For example, the routine with IPL name J3 might have the following IPL-V definition:

    J3 10J3
        20H5 0.

3. *Functional description.* The value of this attribute is an imperative sentence (encoded as a list structure) describing the process defined by the IPL-V definition. For example, the routine with name J3 has, as already explained, the functional description: REPLACE THE SYMBOL IN SIGNAL BY MINUS.

4. *State description.* The value of this attribute is a list structure describing the state of the IPL computer before and after the routine in question has been executed. Only changes are mentioned explicitly. Thus the state description of J3, SET SIGNAL MINUS, is: Affected cell, SIGNAL; Input, SYMB1, PUSHDOWN1; Output, MINUS, PUSHDOWN1.

5. *Flow diagram.* The value of this attribute is a list structure giving the flow diagram corresponding to the IPL-V definition. This list structure will be described in more detail later.

A compiled routine is a routine having an IPL-V definition. Now we can state the problem of compiling a routine as follows: given a routine

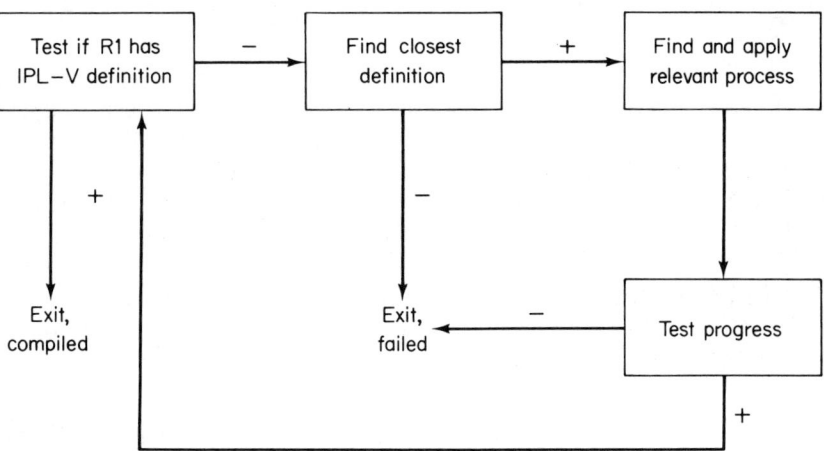

Figure 1 Flow diagram for Compile Routine R1

without a definition (the present object), find the corresponding routine with a definition (the goal object). "Corresponding" means that the compiled routine has the same state description or functional description as the given routine. Figure 1 presents the flow diagram of a compiler using means-end analysis to accomplish this compilation.

Let us translate this flow diagram into the language of means-end analysis.

1. *Test whether the routine has an IPL-V definition.* This test determines whether the present object has the characteristics of the desired object. If so, the compilation is complete.

2. *Find the closest definition.* This process corresponds to finding a difference between the present and desired objects. However, we generalize this notion to mean: look for a *characteristic* of the present object that will suggest a relevant operator. If the object possesses a functional description, then an attempt could be made to compile the IPL-V definition from the functional description; if it possesses a state description, an attempt could be made to compile the IPL-V definition from the state description. The attributes the routine could possess are listed in an order reflecting the relative ease of compiling an IPL-V definition from them. The process then finds the first attribute on this list possessed by the routine to be compiled. In the present form of the compiler, it is assumed that it is easier to compile from a functional description than from a state description; hence the attributes are listed in this order. If the routine possesses no attribute that could be used as a basis for compilation, the compiler reports a failure.

3. *Find and apply the relevant process.* The input to this process is the "closest definition" just found. A table of connections is searched to find a process relevant to compiling the IPL-V definition from the closest definition. If one is found, it is applied (in a manner to be described later).

4. *Test progress.* If the operator has been applied successfully, the routine will now possess at least one attribute (an IPL-V definition or another) not previously possessed. If the progress test detects that it now has a definition closer to the IPL-V definition than any it had previously, it initiates a new compilation cycle; if not, it reports a failure and quits.

The present list of "closest definitions" is very short, consisting only of the functional description and state description. The present table of connections is also brief:

1. If the routine possesses a functional description, apply the operator, COMPILE IPL-V DEFINITION FROM FUNCTIONAL DESCRIPTION.

2. If the routine possesses only a state description, apply the operator, COMPILE IPL-V DEFINITION FROM STATE DESCRIPTION.

1.8 Relation of the Heuristic Compiler to the General Problem Solver

Since each of the major components of the Heuristic Compiler is a system of means-end analysis, each of these components can be viewed as a rudimentary General Problem Solver. It should therefore be feasible, by modifying the top level programs, to bring the Heuristic Compiler into a form which would allow its problem-solving processes to be governed by GPS. The programs for detecting differences, the tables of connections, and the operators would provide definitions of task environments for GPS. To accomplish this, GPS would have to be arranged so that a subproblem could involve applying GPS to a new task environment. That is, GPS would first be applied to the task environment of the General Compiler; applying an operator in this environment would consist in applying GPS to the task environment of the functional descriptions or the state descriptions, as the case may be.

1.9 Flow Diagrams

Up to this point we have considered only very simple programs requiring no branches or loops. Each program is a list of instructions; each instruction, an IPL word represented as a description list with these attributes: type, name, sign, P, Q, symbol, and link.

To represent a program with branches and loops, we divide the program into segments. Each entry point to a loop (an instruction with a local name) begins a new segment; each branch instruction (branches are indicated by $P = 7$) ends a segment. Each segment has the same attributes as an IPL word—specifically: name, P, symbol, link, and an additional attribute, IPL-V definition, whose value is the list of IPL instructions for the segment. The name of the first instruction of the segment is assigned as the name of the segment; if the segment ends in a branch instruction, it is assigned $P = 7$, and its symbol and link are set equal to the symbol and link of the branch instruction. If the segment does not end in a branch, it is assigned $P = 0$ and SYMB $= 0$, and its LINK is set equal to the link of its last instruction. Under these conventions, the list of segments is a flow diagram of the routine with the detail of the routine segments appended.

To illustrate the format of a flow diagram, we show below the code for the IPL routine named J77 followed by its flow diagram. The functional

22 The Heuristic Compiler

description of J77 is: TEST WHETHER THERE IS A SYMBOL EQUAL TO 0ACCU-
MULATOR ON LIST 1ACCUMULATOR.

IPL-V Code for J77

Name	P Q Symb	Link	
J77	J50	90	Segment I: Put 0ACCUM in 0WORKING
90	J60		Segment II: Find next location on list 1ACCUM;
	7 0 91	92	if end of list, go to 91
92	1 2 H0		Segment III: Test if symbol at location is equal
	1 1 W0		to 0ACCUM. If equal, go to 91; if not, go to 90
	J2		
	7 0 90	91	
91	3 0 H0		Segment IV: Clean up and exit
	J30	0	

Flow Diagram for J77

Name	P	Symb	Link
J77	0		90
90	7	91	92
92	7	90	91
91	0		0

From the description of the flow diagram, it is easy to provide a program that will construct a flow diagram from an IPL routine, and a program that will compile an IPL routine from the flow diagram and appended code segments. In this way the task of compiling an IPL routine is reduced to the problem of compiling its flow diagram and compiling the code for each of the segments of the flow diagram.

The program for compiling such a routine from its functional description has not yet been written, but examination of the structure of the routine itself shows what is involved. The test involves a quantifier—whether *there exists* on a particular list of symbols a symbol having a certain property. In IPL-V, such existence tests are performed by means of a loop or a generator; the members of the set in question are produced one by one and tested for their possession of the property. If a test result is positive, the process stops and the symbol PLUS is stored in the signal cell. If the set is exhausted, the symbol MINUS is stored in the signal cell. Thus a standard flow diagram can be used for all routines of this kind:

A   Perform required setup
B   Locate another member of set
    (If none, exit via D)
C   Perform test on member
    (If it succeeds, exit via E;
    if it fails, return to B)
D   Exit with signal MINUS
E   Exit with signal PLUS

Except for the provision of two distinct exits, this is identical with the flow diagram previously shown for J77 (Set A = J77, B = 90, C = 92, D = E = 91). Now, we can compile for each segment of the flow diagram a routine that corresponds to the functional description of that segment. For example, FIND ANOTHER MEMBER OF 1ACCUMULATOR becomes LOCATE NEXT, J60 (after appropriate recognition of the changed location of 1ACCUMULATOR); PERFORM TEST ON MEMBER becomes:

12H0
11W0
J2   Test 0ACCUM and 1ACCUM for equality

The only complications lie in moving the inputs for the various processes (J60, LOCATE NEXT, and J2, TEST IF EQUAL) in appropriate ways. The compiler can do this in a straightforward, if inefficient, way by using the working storages. Thus, an unedited compiled version of J77 might look like this:

Test if 0A is on 1A	J77	J51	90	Put inputs in working storage
Locate next on 1A	90	11W1		Bring in 1w (list location)
		J60		Locate next
		20W1		Store location again
If none, exit		7091	92	
Compare next symbol with 0A	92	12W1		Bring in located symbol [(1w)]
		11W0		Bring in comparison symbol, 0w
		J2		Test for equality
Branch on test		7090	93	
	91	J31	0	Clean up working storage and
	93	J30	0.	terminate

The same flow diagram would be used in the compilation of LOCATE ON 1ACUMULATOR AN X SUCH THAT (X) = 0ACCUMULATOR. In fact, this routine is identical with the one just discussed, except that it requires 11W1

(LOAD 1WORKING INTO 0ACCUMULATOR) before the exit. It should be observed that the indefinite article "an" plays the same role in the functional description of this routine as the quantifier "there is a" in the previous one. The compiler, therefore, would be provided with the knowledge that the above flow diagram, using J60 (LOCATE NEXT SYMBOL) in the second segment, is the appropriate means for translating this quantifier.

Declarative and interrogative sentences in a functional description correspond to tests in the compiled routine. Thus, the phrase "such that SYMB1 = (ACCUMULATOR)" leads to the question, "Does SYMB1 equal (ACCUMULATOR)?" and thence to the test J2[SYMB1, (ACCUMULATOR)].

1.10 Summary

The experiments described in this section demonstrate that compiling tasks—at least simple compiling tasks—can fruitfully be viewed as problem-solving tasks, and can be performed by a program having the general organization and capabilities of the General Problem Solver.[8]

The explorations have followed two main lines. The state description compiler illustrates how the state of a computer before and after the execution of a process can be described, and how this description can be used to define and solve a compiling problem. The compiler would require substantial further development before it could be used as a practical compiling device, but, besides providing guideposts for such development, it casts light on two important topics: (1) the nature of the problem-solving processes involved in programming—particularly machine-language programming; (2) the use of description lists in IPL-V as an expository language having expressive capabilities not readily available in more usual computer command languages. In the state description compiler the declarative mode, rather than the imperative mode, bears the main burden of information storage and communication.

The functional description compiler follows more traditional lines. Apart from its heuristic organization, it closely resembles compilers like FORTRAN, ALGOL, and LISP. Its language is primarily a language of imperatives, of processes. The functional description compiler illustrates how means-end analysis, like that employed in the General Problem Solver, can be used to translate requests for general, functionally defined processes into programs. Like the state description compiler, it gives us a great deal of information about the problem-solving processes required for programming. Further experiments, to be reported subsequently, suggest that it can be

---

[8] Some further discussion of language and representations in the Heuristic Compiler together with a listing of the program as of June 1961, will be found in [2].

a tool in exploring the relation between problem statements in natural language and in formalized computer languages.

The investigation described here stimulated a certain amount of introspection about my own programming processes and inquiries about the processes of my fellow programmers. From these informal inquiries I am persuaded that programmers employ, in their problem-solving processes, both a language like that of the state description compiler and a language like that of the functional description compiler. The former becomes essential in designating machine representations and in writing programs depending on the detail of machine representation—processes of packing and unpacking words that are intimately dependent on word structure. On the other hand, at the higher levels often represented by flow diagrams, a language of functions appears generally the more natural and powerful. In general, the mappings from functional descriptions to process language are simpler and more direct than the mappings from state descriptions—a possible explanation of why most existing compilers use a functional source language. The Heuristic Compiler is an exploratory tool that is beginning to reveal to us something of the role played by these and other representations in the programming process.

SECTION 2
GENERAL IMPLICATIONS FOR REPRESENTATIONS

Our examination of flow diagrams has already led us to consider how some syntactical devices of English (e.g., the definite and indefinite articles) are to be rendered in the compiler. In this part, we raise at a more general level the question of the syntactical flexibility and range of the compiler languages. In Sec. 2.1, we ask what forms of English expressions are handled naturally and simply by functional description and state description languages, respectively. In Sec. 2.2, we ask how we would go about formalizing the notion of representation so that a problem-solving compiler could be given the task of designing its own representations.

2.1 Language and Representations in the Compiler

We can ask appropriately about any compiler, "What range of source statements can it accept?" In Sec. 1, we have discussed two kinds of source statements, functional descriptions and state descriptions. Let us now consider in a little more detail the range of English language expressions that these compilers can handle. We take up the two languages in turn.

2.1.1 Functional Descriptions. The functional descriptions are particularly interesting because they take the form of English sentences—imperatives, or, as we have just shown, declaratives and interrogatives. How restricted is the language in relation to the whole class of grammatical English sentences?

Consider the sentence, "What is the color of that apple?" The answer might be "Its color is red," or even "It is red." In the original sentence, "that apple" denotes a particular object; "the color," an attribute of that object; and "what," the unknown value of the attribute. In the replies, "it" denotes the same object as "that apple"; "red," the (now known) value of the attribute. Thus, we might represent the question and the first answer, respectively, as:

$$? = \text{Color (that apple)}$$
$$\text{Red} = \text{Color (it)}.$$
$$\text{Red} = \text{Value (it)}.$$

The second answer can be interpreted as synonymous with the first if we stipulate that "red" can be a value only of the function "color."

The process in IPL-V that provides the answer to such questions is FIND THE VALUE OF ATTRIBUTE (0) OF (1). In terms of our example, this is: "Find the value of attribute 'color' of that apple." Thus, the process that answers the question takes two inputs—the names of the attribute and the object—and produces the value as its output. It defines a function, in the mathematical sense of the term. In the statement of the process, "attribute" is in apposition with "color," the former term specifying the genus to which the argument belongs. We could equally (though not quite grammatically) have said "of the object, 'that apple'." Likewise, the phrase, "Find the value of the color," is synonymous with, "Find the color," "value" being in apposition with the (implicit) "?". That is, in English, we abridge, "The value of the attribute, the color, of the object, that apple, is red," to, "The color of that apple is red," or, "That apple is red." We can do this because "color" is an attribute, "that apple" is an object, and "red" is a value—nothing is added to meaning by making these classifications explicit.

This example shows how, in general, we can handle a wide class of grammatical forms within the framework of the functional descriptions. Interrogatives are unknowns, like the x's of algebra, whose genera may be specified, in part or full, to identify them. The couple "the...of..." signals a *determiner*—a phrase that names something by giving enough of its properties to tag it uniquely. Pronouns (e.g., "it") and pronominal adjectives ("that") identify by reference to terms that have occurred in previous phrases or sentences. "Find" is a general process that replaces a determiner by the object determined. Appositive phrases and relative clauses provide additional identifying information about the object to which they refer. Adjectives, adverbs, prepositional phrases (other than "of" phrases), and adjectival nouns have the same function—identification or description. Quantifiers ("there is," "all," "a," "some," etc.) require special treatment—several of them have already been discussed.

The present functional description compiler was constructed specifically to handle verbs (processes), determiners (especially those involving "the ... of..."), and proper names (in IPL-V these are always locations). Essentially, what the compiler does is replace determiners by the appropriate proper names, using the FIND processes for the compilation. In the previous section, we indicated how loops and flow diagrams could be used to handle quantifiers and conjunctions, including "and," "but," and "if...then." Pronouns could be handled in a manner similar to that used for determiners. Appositive and modifying words, phrases, and clauses could be used as aids in identifying proper names. It appears that with these extensions, the format would encompass many forms of grammatical English sentences. Only programming, of course, can determine to what extent this claim is correct.

2.1.2 State Descriptions. Just as the functional description language admits of considerable flexibility in representing English sentences, so the state description language admits of broad flexibility in representing information storage in the computer. This flexibility is achieved by using description lists as the holders of information. Each computer address referred to in the state description is represented by a cell having a description list. On the description list are the attributes NAME, TYPE, P, Q, SIGN, SYMBOL, LINK—i.e., precisely the attributes that name the fields in an IPL word (and the name of that word) and that appear on the coding sheet. Since the state descriptions make these attributes explicit, the program that uses the descriptions need not be provided with this information in any format more specialized than the description list format itself. Moreover, additional attributes and their values can be added, ad lib, to the description list.

By introducing attributes that refer to a particular machine representation of IPL, the state description language is readily extended to admit statements about the relation between IPL and its particular representations. For example, suppose the fields in the words of a particular computer were designated by the attributes DECREMENT, ADDRESS, etc. We could then *define* a machine language representation of IPL by setting up appropriate correspondences between IPL attributes and machine language attributes. (For example, we might specify SYMB = DECREMENT, LINK = ADDRESS, etc.) We shall indicate in the next section how this technique can be used to give the Heuristic Compiler the capability of designing appropriate representations—hence how the compiler itself might choose an appropriate machine language representation of IPL prior to undertaking the task of compiling IPL into a machine language program.

Also, each description list is not necessarily limited to describing the contents of a *single* computer address; it may also describe the contents of an entire list. Suppose, for example, we wish to represent the fact that the symbol in cell H5 is J3, and that H5 is linked to a pushdown list having unknown contents. All of this information can be given in two description lists:

	NAME	SYMB	LINK	KIND OF OBJECT
1.	H5	J3	R0	Pushdown cell
2.	NAME			KIND OF OBJECT
	R0			List

We have already illustrated how this flexibility is used to represent segments of instructions in flow diagrams.

2.2 The Design of Representations

One distinction between the restricted, relatively simple tasks we call "coding," and the broader, more difficult tasks we call "programming," is that the latter may encompass the selection or design of an appropriate problem representation, while the former do not. Our discussion of languages now enables us to see what is involved in designing or selecting a representation, and what we would need to do in order to give the Heuristic Compiler the capacity to cope with such design and selection tasks. We shall illustrate this point with an example of a representation problem within the structure of IPL-V itself.

Let us suppose that we had an operating "basic" IPL system, quite like the language defined in the IPL-V Manual, except that the description list processes were omitted. We now give a programmer the task of introducing description lists into the language, using the basic system itself to define them, without writing any new machine code.

What do we mean by "introducing description lists"? We mean that we wish to be able to associate with the name of an object (which in IPL is always an address) a description of that object. The description consists of a set of pairs: one member of each pair is an attribute; the other member of the pair is the value of that attribute for the object to which the description belongs. Moreover, we wish to be able to store and retrieve descriptive information about objects. That is, we wish to be able to add new pairs to descriptions, and when we are given the name of an object and an attribute, we wish to be able to find the value of that attribute for that object. Stated formally:

With every object A_i, we associate a set of pairs (B_j, C_{ij}). The number of pairs is to be arbitrary and variable, and we want a process that will answer questions of the form: $? = B_j(A_i)$.

How could a programmer solve this problem? By the basic conventions of IPL-V, "object" already means "address." Thus, he must find some way of associating a set with each address. Again, in IPL, the standard way to represent a set is by a list. The question then becomes: What list can we associate with an address? The basic relations that are represented in IPL-V are CONTENT OF and NEXT. The CONTENT OF a cell is the SYMB of that cell, and the NEXT of the cell is its LINK. Moreover, basic processes exist for FIND CONTENT and FIND NEXT. Thus, the set we associate with an address can be taken to be the list whose name is the SYMB (or, alternatively, the LINK) at that address. Let us call this list (pursuing the first alternative) the *description list* associated with the address.

We must next define a format for description lists that will represent the pairing of attributes and values. One method would be to associate a pair of words with each element of the description list, again using the relations CONTENT and NEXT. Thus, if S_j is the content of the jth member of the description list, we could define $B_j =$ CONTENT OF S_j, and $C_{ij} =$ CONTENT OF NEXT OF S_j. (This is substantially the representation that was used in an earlier version of IPL. An even simpler representation would make $C_{ij} =$ LINK OF S_j.) Now, to add a pair (B_j, C_{ij}) to the description list of A_i, we add a cell to the description list, assign it a SYMB (S_j), assign B_j as the SYMB of S_j, and assign C_{ij} as the SYMB of the LINK of S_j. Similarly, if we are given A_i and B_j, in order to find C_{ij}, we first find the description list, CONTENT OF A_i, and we go down this list comparing B_j with the CONTENT of the CONTENT of each location on the list. When we obtain a match, we find the CONTENT of the cell NEXT to the matched cell, and this is the desired value. These processes follow from the representation.

An alternative representation is obtained by dividing the members of the description list into two subsets—its ODDS and its EVENS. We then take the ODDS as the attributes; the value of an attribute is simply the EVEN that follows it. These definitions, again, make use only of the relations CONTENT and NEXT. Thus, an ODD of a list is the FIRST of the list or the NEXT of the NEXT of an ODD.

This definition allows us to construct a loop that will find, in sequence, all the attributes on the list. Given the location of an attribute, a FIND CONTENT OF NEXT finds its value. This representation is, of course, the one actually adopted in IPL-V.

It will be instructive to see what the program for FIND THE VALUE OF ATTRIBUTE (0) OF (1) looks like in each of these representations. We write the two programs side by side:

30 The Heuristic Compiler

Representation 1	Representation 2	Comment
FIND CONTENT OF (1);	FIND CONTENT OF (1);	Find description list
92 FIND NEXT,	92 FIND NEXT,	Find next attribute
IF NONE, EXIT;	IF NONE, EXIT;	
STORE IN (1);	STORE IN (1);	(Keep place in list)
FIND CONTENT;	FIND CONTENT;	
FIND CONTENT;		
COMPARE WITH (0),	COMPARE WITH (0),	Test if it is
IF ≠, GOTO 91;	IF ≠, GOTO 91	equal to (0)
FIND NEXT;	FIND NEXT;	If so, find and
FIND CONTENT, EXIT.	FIND CONTENT, EXIT.	report value
91 FIND (1);	91 FIND (1);	If not, proceed
GOTO 92.	FIND NEXT,	down description
	GOTO 92.	list

We see from this example that designing a suitable representation amounts to finding an isomorphism. A description was defined in terms of certain elements (objects, attributes, values), relations between elements (e.g., the attributes of an object), and processes (e.g., FIND THE VALUE OF (0) OF (1)). The programmer had to find a set of elements, relations, and processes defined in IPL-V that were isomorphic with the required elements, relations, and processes. I have not worked out how such a search could be automated, but the main requirements are clear. In particular, to enable the Heuristic Compiler to perform this search, it would have to be provided with lists of the available elements, relations, and processes, or it would have to be able to recognize such things when they were described. For example, it would have to recognize that every determiner (e.g., "the ... of ...") defines a relation.

As a second example of what is involved in designing a representation, let us consider the representation of IPL-V words in the state description language. Since each word consists of a number of symbols belonging to different fields, we can again use the description list format, in which we equate "field" with "attribute" and "symbol in field" with "value of attribute." But the symbols in the NAME, SYMB, and LINK fields themselves contain encoded information, for they are in the form ANNNN, where A is an alphameric symbol, and NNNN is a number. Hence, we represent each of these symbols by an object with a description list containing the attributes REGION and LOCATION. The value of REGION is the alphameric symbol A; the value of LOCATION, the number NNNN. Therefore, the information that a *local symbol* is one with A = 9 can be represented. Again, the lesson here is that we must create an isomorphism between the elements of the representation, their relations, and the structure to be represented.

Suppose, as a third example, that we set ourselves the task of writing a program to sort a bridge hand. To accomplish this task, the meanings of "sort" and "bridge hand" must be known. A bridge hand is a set of (13) elements, each characterized by a primary characteristic, suit (4 possible values), and a secondary characteristic, denomination (13 ordered values). Sorting means ordering a set of elements by one or more characteristics, taking account of the ordering of values where this is defined.

In this case we find a straightforward isomorphism: Each element in the bridge hand is to be represented by an object having a description list with attributes SUIT and DENOMINATION. A sorted bridge hand is to be represented by a list of such elements, with the ordering of the list to correspond with the ordering of the sort. It now becomes a straightforward (if difficult) compiling job to write a SORT routine that will produce a list with these properties. Moreover, if it is done correctly, it should be possible to write the routine in the generalized form: SORT (0) IN FORMAT (1), where (1) enumerates the attributes, their ordering, and the orderings of the values that define the sorted object.

We shall explore this particular scheme in more detail in Sec. 3. Perhaps enough has been said here to demonstrate that selecting or designing a representation is a problem-solving task that can be attacked with the same general kinds of heuristic techniques as other problem-solving tasks.

SECTION 3
EXPERIMENTS WITH REPRESENTATIONS

In this section, we propose some extensions of the Heuristic Compiler, most of which are motivated by linguistic considerations. In particular, we explore some methods for enabling the compiler to handle input statements in forms that are close to natural language.

There are a number of important respects in which natural languages differ from the usual programming languages. We shall be especially concerned with three of these differences:

1. In natural languages, the *word* is the most important unit of meaning. (For the moment, we do not need to distinguish among "word," "morpheme," and "idiom.") In most computer languages, the *sentence* (usually an imperative sentence, called an "instruction") is the basic unit of meaning. Thus, if a person understands, separately, the verb "sort" and the noun phrase "bridge hand," he can probably obey the instruction, "Sort the bridge hand." In most computer languages, a compiler would not be able to assemble, "Sort a bridge hand," from "sort" and "bridge hand," but would have to be provided with a number of specialized sort routines.

2. In natural languages, most communication makes use of sentences in the indicative or declarative mode. In computer languages, most sentences

are in the imperative mode. Computer languages are primarily languages of command, and not languages of information, description, or advice.

3. In natural languages, many alternative sentences can be phrased that mean about the same thing. The recipient of a natural-language communication is able to decode the communication without too much concern for details of format. In computer languages, there are various harassing constraints on format. Failure to observe these constraints usually causes an error condition.

These differences are, of course, differences of degree and not of kind. Moreover, research on computer languages over the past decade has already made substantial progress toward decreasing or erasing them. Basic processes have become more general and parametrized; various forms of declarative statements have been introduced; compilers have been designed to accept relatively informal input statements. The gap, however, between natural language and computer languages is still large, and is annoying to those who are engaged in man-machine communication.

We are here concerned with extensions of the Heuristic Compiler directed toward reducing these differences. Section 3.1 indicates how generalized processes (verbs) can be introduced into the function description compiler. Section 3.2 describes subroutines for storing and retrieving descriptive information in declarative sentences. Section 3.3 describes an approach toward natural-language flexibility in input statements for the State Description Compiler, making use of the descriptive information provided by the techniques of Sec. 3.2.

.3.1 Generalized Processes

We shall consider two classes of processes: one designated by the verb "find," the other by the verb "sort."

3.1.1 "Find" Processes. The possible interpretations of FIND are numerous to the point of being meaningless. Any routine that takes some symbolic structures as inputs and produces one or more other structures as outputs may be called a process for "finding" the latter. Thus: FIND SINE A, FIND THE STATE DESCRIPTION OF ROUTINE K, FIND THE PROOF OF THEOREM T. From this point of view, a program like the General Problem Solver is simply a fairly general FIND routine.

Hence, any routine flexible enough to interpret correctly the verb "find" wherever it occurs in normal English prose, would have to make considerable use of context. In the present section we shall aim at a lesser degree of flexibility. Consider the two classes of processes typified by:

FIND THE *state description* OF *routine K*

and

FIND A..........ON..........

The first example designates an object associated in a particular way with a specific object, K. In IPL-V there is provided a special format, the description list, for holding such information in memory, and a set of processes for entering and retrieving the information. Section 3.2 examines definite descriptions of this special kind at length. In the present section, then, we shall limit ourselves to the verb "find" as it occurs in instructions like, FIND A ... ON ... , and FIND THE ... ON .... Even this scheme covers a considerable variety of processes:

FIND A symbol, *S10*, ON list *L*.
FIND AN object whose *type* is *A4* ON list structure *L*.
FIND THE *third symbol* ON list *L*.
FIND THE *largest integer data term* ON the lists of list *L*.

In the first two examples, the indefinite article indicates that the object sought is not necessarily unique; in the last two examples it is. In the first two examples the properties that define the object sought are *absolute*—their presence or absence can be ascertained without reference to other objects. In the last two examples, the properties are *relative*; and indeed, in the fourth example, the entire set of objects must be examined before the one sought can be identified. In the first example, the object sought is designated by proper name (and the information is added that it is a symbol). This example can be approximated to the others by rephrasing it: FIND A token *equal to S10* ON list *L*.

With these preliminaries out of the way, we shall describe in detail a rather general FIND process. The object sought will be specified by some sublist of the symbols on the pushdown list of the communication cell, H0. The specification of the place to be searched will be given by other symbols on that pushdown list. Hence, we can symbolize the desired process:

FIND A $F1[(0), (1), \ldots, (k)]$ IN $F2[(k+1), (k+2), \ldots, (n)]$,

where (0), (1), etc. designate, as usual, the symbols on the pushdown list of H0.

We suppose that the compiler is provided with a lexicon that contains, among others, the words "FIND," "F_1[ ]," and "F_2[ ]." The lexical entry for each of these is a description list containing, for "FIND" and "F1," the descriptor IPL ROUTINE, and for "F2," the descriptor TYPE OF OBJECT.

The IPL ROUTINE associated with FIND in the lexicon will contain certain variables, to be replaced by constants derived from an examination of F_1

and F_2. We will first present the routine, roughly as it would appear in the lexicon, and then explain the meaning of certain of the symbols in it. For readability, we depart from IPL-V notation.

```
FIND    FIND ARGUMENTS 0 to K;
        GENERATE [F2] FOR PROCESS [90],
        STOP WHEN SUCCESS OR EXHAUSTED.
  90    FIND ARGUMENTS (K+1) TO N;
        APPLY TEST [F1] TO [ELEMENT],
            IF POSITIVE, REPORT SUCCESS,
            IF NEGATIVE, REPORT FAILURE.
```

As previously indicated, k is the number of arguments in F_1 (n — k) the number of arguments in F_2, and n the number of arguments in the two functions taken together. The first instruction brings into the accumulator the arguments of F2, while 90 brings in the arguments of F1. The numbers k and n — k are to be determined, of course, by examining F1 and F2. The variable, GEN(F2, 90), is to be replaced with a generator obtained from the lexical entry for F2, while TEST(F1) is to be replaced with a test associated with the lexical entry for F1. All the other symbols have obvious meanings.

We can now compile FIND A F1 IN F2 as follows:

1. Get IPL ROUTINE of FIND.

2. Supply values for k, n, and n — k where required.

3. Make list of subroutines required (GEN (F2, 90) TEST(F1)).

4. Get the IPL ROUTINE of TEST, supply it with its arguments, and insert it in the IPL-V code for FIND.

5. Get TYPE OF OBJECT of F2, and get the associated GEN for that type in the dictionary of generators; insert it in the IPL-V code for FIND.

A word may be added to this account to indicate how relative properties are handled in FIND THE THIRD . . . , or FIND THE LARGEST. In these cases, the test needs to be based on a recursive process—in the case of FIND THE THIRD . . . , a counting process; in the case of FIND THE LARGEST . . . , a process that resets LARGEST SO FAR equal to the larger of LARGEST SO FAR and the current integer. The test—the function F1—would, in these cases, make provision for storing in the working memory the intermediate products of calculation.

3.1.2 "Sort" Processes. As our second essay toward generalized processes, we take the verb "sort." Suppose that the objects we wish to sort are description lists. It is easy to construct a general routine, SORT (0) ON (1), where (0) is the list of objects to be sorted and (1) is a specification of the attributes, their ordering, and the orderings of attribute values on which the sorting is to be based. Thus, if (0) were a list of description lists representing the cards in a bridge hand, (1) would specify that the attributes are suit and denomination (in that order), that the suit values are S,H,D,C (in that order) and the denomination values are A,K,Q,J,10,9, etc. (in that order). A further step toward generalization would allow the sort routine to be compiled from a *definition* of the collection of objects to be sorted. Let us see how this can be done when the object to be sorted is a bridge hand. First, we store in memory description lists providing information about the terms LIST, DESCRIPTION LIST, and ATTRIBUTE:

```
LIST
         TYPE:         Class of objects
         ATTRIBUTES:   Type of members
DESCRIPTION LIST
         TYPE:         Class of objects
         ATTRIBUTES:   Attributes
ATTRIBUTE
         TYPE:         Class of symbols
         ATTRIBUTES:   Values.
```

That is to say, a list is a class of objects; the description list for any class of objects of type LIST will have the attribute TYPE OF MEMBERS. A description list is also a class of objects; the description list for any class of objects of type DESCRIPTION LIST will have the attribute ATTRIBUTES. An attribute is a class of symbols; the description list for any class of objects of type ATTRIBUTE will have the attribute VALUES.

Next, we store in memory lists and description lists providing information about the terms BRIDGE HAND, CARD, SUIT, and DENOMINATION.

```
BRIDGE HAND
         TYPE:         List
         MEMBERS:      Cards
CARD
         TYPE:         Description List
         ATTRIBUTES:   Suit, denomination
SUIT
         TYPE:         Attribute
         VALUES:       Spades, hearts, diamonds, clubs
DENOMINATION
         TYPE:         Attribute
         VALUES:       A,K,Q,J,10,9,8,7,6,5,4,3,2
```

Now we can compile SORT THE BRIDGE HAND (0), as follows: From the information just stored, we find that BRIDGE HAND has the type LIST. From LIST, we find that BRIDGE HAND will have the attribute TYPE OF MEMBERS. Finding the value of this attribute, we determine that the members of bridge hands are cards. CARD is a description list, which has the attribute ATTRIBUTES. The attributes of cards are suit and denomination. We would therefore compile the sort routine to sort on suit and denomination, in that order of priority. Examining the values of these two terms, in turn, we find the order in which these values are to be arranged in sorting.

If it were known to the program that a bridge hand is a list of description lists, then the sorting routine could obtain the information about attributes and values by direct examination of one or more examples of a sorted bridge hand, and without being given the information about CARD, SUIT, or DENOMINATION explicitly. If the examples were not too special (e.g., a hand of thirteen spades), the program could determine what attributes a card possessed, which of these was relevant to the sorting, the hierarchy of attributes, and the ordering, if any, of the values of each. This information could then be used to compile the specific sorting routine required.

Thus, we see that the key to providing a generalized routine for a verb like SORT lies in providing syntactically or semantically the information needed to supply the routine with the parameter values it requires. This can be accomplished (syntactically) through a scheme of declarative sentences that describe the objects under consideration; or (semantically) by providing examples that can be analyzed. Moreover, the description itself can be generated inductively from examples.

The description that would allow compilation of the "sort" routine could also be used to compile TEST IF X IS A BRIDGE HAND. Thus, storing descriptions of classes of objects is an important means for factoring sentence meanings of nouns and verbs, respectively. It provides a powerful basis for introducing general processes.

3.1.3 Recursive Functional Languages. Consider an instruction language consisting of a set of functions each admitting as arguments the values of functions of the set. Each of the functions can be regarded as a FIND instruction—i.e., FIND THE VALUE OF F FOR THE GIVEN ARGUMENT VALUES. It may be executed recursively by finding, first, the values of each of its arguments, then using these to compute the value of the function. Hence, the interpreter of such a language may itself be regarded as a generalized FIND instruction.

Next, consider an instruction like SORT OBJECT A, in a recursive functional language. The definition of SORT, if it is a generalized routine like those described in the previous section, may read something like ARRANGE ACCORDING TO THE ATTRIBUTE VALUES OF. The definition has different arguments from SORT itself—it refers to the attribute values of A instead of the object A. The interpreter would need to be general enough to replace SORT A by ARRANGE A BY THE ATTRIBUTE VALUES OF A; then execute FIND THE ATTRIBUTE VALUES OF A, and insert the value of this function as the second argument of the ARRANGE function. We have already indicated how the FIND might be accomplished.

With a little further generalization, the scheme could handle apposition—e.g., SORT THE BRIDGE HAND, A. The phrase in apposition would provide information about the type of the object designated, and as we have seen, this information could be used to find the other argument of the ARRANGE routine. Further light will be cast on apposition in the next section, where we shall discuss modifiers that *identify* an argument, and their relation to modifiers that *describe* the object.

3.2 Definite Descriptions

The meaning of much descriptive and expository prose can be captured in a fairly simple language—a sublanguage of English—that uses only the verb "is" and noun phrases with definite or indefinite articles in subjects and predicates. Consider the following example, which, while it does not fit this restricted form exactly, is not far from it:

> The state description of a routine consists of a list of affected cells. For each affected cell on the list, the state description specifies its input state and its output state.

3.2.1 Syntactic Characterization. We might proceed to formalize this description in either of several ways. I shall call the first of these *syntactical*, since it makes statements about the terms "state description," "affected cells," "input state," and "output state." These statements can then be stored in association with the relevant terms in a lexicon.

> The type of "state description" is "description list";
> The attribute of "state description" is "list of affected cells";
> The type of "list of affected cells" is "list";
> The type of "affected cell" is "description list";
> The attributes of "affected cell" are "input state"
>   and "output state."

We have already seen this kind of description in our discussion of generalized SORT routines in the previous section. Readers who are familiar with Backus normal form will observe that a syntactical description of this kind could be translated into that form (or a slight extension thereof) without much difficulty. Our interest, however, is in staying close to natural English.

3.2.2 Semantic Characterization. An alternative, *semantic*, formalization characterizes a given type of object (STATE DESCRIPTION in this instance) by describing an example:

> X1 is a state description of a routine if
> there are an X0, X2, X3, X4,
> and X5, such that:
> X0 is a routine;
> X1 is the state description of X0;
> X2 is the list of affected cells of X1;
> X3 is a member of X2;
> X4 is the input state of X3;
> X5 is the output state of X3.

Properly interpreted, the example implies the syntactic description we gave previously. Consider, for instance, "X3 is a member of X2." With the convention that only lists have members, this statement implies that X2 is a list. From the previous statement, "X2 is the list of affected cells of X1," we observe that this list is the value of the attribute, LIST OF AFFECTED CELLS, of X1.

We can store the example in memory by storing a description list, X0, with attribute STATE DESCRIPTION having value X1. X1, in turn, is a description list, with attribute LIST OF AFFECTED CELLS having the value X2. X2 is a list whose sole member is X3. X3 is a description list with attribute INPUT STATE having value X4, and attribute OUTPUT STATE having value X5.

3.2.3 Annexing Descriptive Information to an Information Store. Let us use symbols from the X region—e.g., X114, X33—to designate nouns. These nouns will be either proper names (of objects to be represented by lists or list structures) or attributes. Consider now the sentence:

> "X114 is the X33 of the X25 of X105."

In this sentence, which is grammatical if inelegant English, "X114" and "X105" are proper names, while "X33" and "X25" name attributes. The objects referred to in this sentence are X114 (or synonymously, the X33 of the X25 of X105), the X25 of X105, and X105. The problem of annexing the information provided by this sentence to an existing memory store depends on what is already in the store.

Suppose, as a first possibility, that no information has been stored previously about the objects mentioned in this sentence. We store the new information by creating a name, call it X200, and assigning it as the value of attribute X25 of X105. Then we assign X114 as the value of attribute X33 of the newly named object, X200.

Suppose, however, that we had previously stored in memory the information that an object named X130 was the value of attribute X25 of X105. Then, to store the new information, we would first have to find X130, and then assign X114 as the value of attribute X33 of X130.

In the first case, we annexed the new information by two ASSIGN-VALUE processes. In the second case, we annexed the new information by a FIND-VALUE process followed by an ASSIGN-VALUE. We can write a general routine to accomplish this. In processing a sentence like the one we are using as an example, we start at the extreme right and search in memory for the object named. If we find it, we proceed to the left, find the first attribute, and find the value of this attribute of the object. If the value exists, it becomes a new object on which we can repeat the process, moving to the next attribute to the left.

When we fail to find an object meeting the description, we enter a second phase. We now proceed from the left-hand side of the sentence, creating names for new objects as these are needed, and annexing their descriptions to them, until we reach an object that is already mentioned in memory.

Thus, depending on what is already stored in memory, the same piece of information in the input sentence can serve either as a descriptive phrase, providing new information to be annexed to the memory structure, or as an identifying phrase, to be used in locating the place in memory where the new information is to be annexed.

In this scheme ambiguity is entirely possible. It can enter because the scheme allows indefinite, as well as definite description. Again, an example will make the point clear. We consider the following sequence of four input sentences:

> X114 is the X33 of the X25 of X105.
> X115 and X116 are the X99 of the X34 of the X25 of X105.
> X125 is the X41 of a member of the X71 of the X24 of X105.
> X117 is the X75 of the member whose X41 is X125 of the
>   X71 of the X24 of X105.

Suppose we begin with no information about X105 in memory. Then, as we have seen, the first sentence is stored by two ASSIGNs. The first creates a new object, say X200, and assigns X114 as its X33; the second assigns X200 as the X25 of X105.

The second sentence is stored by two ASSIGNs and one FIND. Working from the right, X200 is found to be already in memory as the X25 of X105. But there is no value for attribute X34 of X200. Hence a list, say X201, is created whose members are X115 and X116, and X201 is assigned as the value of X99 of another new object, say X202. Finally, X202 is assigned as the X34 of X200.

Storing the third sentence brings about the creation of X203, whose, X41 is X125; of a list X204, of which X203 is member; and of an object, X205, whose X71 is X204, and which is in turn the X24 of X105.

The fourth sentence introduces a new complication. It refers to "the member of the X71 of the X24 of X105 whose X41 is X125." A series of FINDs will find the X71 of the X24 of X105—that is, X204. The sentence now calls for locating that member of X204 whose X41 is X125. From the previous paragraph, we see that the object in question is none other than X203. Thus X117 would be assigned as the X75 of X203.

Now let us return to the question of ambiguity. Suppose that the fourth sentence read:

> X117 is the X75 of the member whose X76 is X130 of the X71 of the X24 of X105.

Now, when we examine X204, we find, as before, that it has a member, X203. But we have no information to tell us whether or not X203 is "the member of X204 whose X76 is X130." Hence, we do not know whether to assign X117 as the X75 of X203 or to create a new member of the list X204—say X205, and assign X117 as the X75 of X205.

The ambiguity is not a consequence of the particular annexing scheme we have used, but resides more deeply in the nature of things. Let r and s be relations; A, B, C, and X, objects. Suppose we know that ArB and that there exists a Y such that CsY and YrB. Then we can neither affirm nor deny that Y is identical with A. (The same difficulty arises in R. Lindsay's program for annexing genealogical information to a family tree.[9] If we know only that Isaac is a son of Abraham, and Jacob is a son of a son of Abraham, then we do not know whether or not Jacob is a son of Isaac.) Our only recourse is to arrange the annexing routine so that, when it detects such an ambiguity, it outputs an appropriate question.

A program for the annexing process has been written and tested. It will not deal with the ambiguity problem just discussed, but is in all other respects capable of annexing to memory the contents of sets of sentences of the kinds we have been considering.

3.3 Compilation of Routines from Partial Descriptions

One part of the flexibility of natural language depends on the problem-solving capacity of the listener. Information already in his memory allows him to supply details that are omitted from, or only implicit in, the com-

---

[9] See Lindsay's discussion of this problem in [4], pp. 229–230.

munication. Suppose we wish to give a (human) programmer the task of coding a routine in IPL-V for J3. We might tell him:

"Write a routine, J3, that changes the contents of cell H5 from [S1, R0] to [J3, R0]."

The programmer, familiar with IPL-V, knows that H5 is a so-called "pushdown cell," and that what is wanted is to replace the contents of the SYMB field of that cell, whatever they may be, by the symbol "J3."

What instruction would we have to give to the State Description Compiler to induce it to perform the same task? The instructions would read:

"Compile the IPL-V definition of the following routine: The NAME of the routine is J3. The LIST OF AFFECTED CELLS of its STATE DESCRIPTION has a member, whose NAME is H5, whose INPUT STATE is the list, S1, R0, and whose OUTPUT STATE is the list, J3, R0."

Given some such statement, the annexing routine described in the previous section could construct an appropriate description list as input to the State Description Compiler. In Section 1, we showed how the State Description Compiler could then write the desired routine from its state description.

Now the instructions to the compiler have required about three times as many words as the instructions to the human programmer. The reason is easy to see. The essential information to be provided is that the cell to be changed is H5, and that the change is to replace an unknown symbol by the symbol J3. The compiler cannot handle this information without explicit mention that J3 is the first symbol in the list of the output state of affected cell H5 of the list of affected cells of the state description of the routine named J3. The human programmer is capable of supplying this additional information, because he knows what the structure of a state description is like.

The last observation suggests that we might give the compiler the same capability by providing it prior information about the structure of a state description, and allowing it to fill in the implicit detail. Let us employ the language of Sec. 3.2 to see how this might be done.

The complete description list, necessary to the Heuristic Compiler, is equivalent to the following set of sentences:

> Let X100 be a routine whose NAME is J3.
> Let X101 be the STATE DESCRIPTION OF X100.
> Let X102 be a member, whose NAME is H5, of
>   the LIST OF AFFECTED CELLS OF X101.
> Let S1, R0 be the INPUT STATE OF X102.
> Let J3, R0 be the OUTPUT STATE OF X102.

In parallel fashion, we can store in memory a "template" for the description of a routine. We will use symbols from region "Y" to denote variables.

Y1 is the NAME of Y2.
Y3 is the STATE DESCRIPTION of Y2.
Y4 is the LIST OF AFFECTED CELLS of Y3.
Y5 is a typical member of Y4.
Y6 is the NAME of Y5.
Y7 is the INPUT STATE of Y5.
Y8 is the OUTPUT STATE of Y5.
X7 and Y8 are lists.

Now to fit the specific example to the template, we identify J3 with Y1, X100 with Y2, X101 with Y3, X102 with Y5, and so on. Suppose, however, the example were incomplete, as follows:

X100 is a routine whose NAME is J3.
N101 is a cell whose NAME is H5.
S1, R0 is the M1 of X101.
J3, R0 is the M2 of X101.

Here "M1" and "M2" designate attributes whose meanings are not given in the lexicon. It should not be too difficult to devise a process for matching this description with the template. The matching process would discover that X101 has to be identified with Y5, and X100 with Y1. New objects could then be created to correspond with Y3 and Y4, and the appropriate description list stored in memory. The State Description Compiler, taking this description list as its input, could now compile the code for J3.

Our basic proposal, then, for compiling routines from partial descriptions rests on two devices: (1) the use of an annexing routine like that described in Sec. 3.2 as a means for constructing description lists from expository sentences; (2) the use of templates to provide information that is not given explicitly in the input sentences.

A routine for performing this matching process was written about 1965 and tested successfully on examples at the level of complexity of the illustration.

References

[1] NEWELL, A., SHAW, J. C., and SIMON, H. A. Report on a general problem-solving program for a computer. *Information Processing*, Proc. Internat. Conf. Inform. Processing, pp. 256–264. Paris: UNESCO, 1960. [FF]

[2] SIMON, H. A. Experiments with a heuristic compiler. The RAND Corp., Report P-2349, June 30, 1961.
[3] NEWELL, A. (ed.) *Information Processing Language-V Manual.* Englewood Cliffs, N.J.: Prentice-Hall, 1961.
[4] FEIGENBAUM, E. A., and FELDMAN, J. *Computers and Thought.* New York: McGraw-Hill, 1963.

Chapter 2

SOME SEMANTIC METHODS FOR LANGUAGE PROCESSING

LAURENT SIKLÓSSY and H. A. SIMON

Interest in language is not limited to persons who identify themselves as linguists. Experiments in the psychological laboratory, attempts to construct language-processing programs for computers, research in the theory of automata and neighboring portions of mathematics and logic, and investigations of the formal structure of grammars all have contributions to make to our understanding of language and its use by humans. This chapter examines some contributions to semantics that have had their origins during the past decade in the field of computer science, and that have significance for current efforts to push linguistic and psycholinguistic inquiry beyond syntactic into semantic questions.

SECTION 1
INTRODUCTION

Our basic strategy will be to examine some existing computer programs that (1) process strings belonging to some subset of a natural language, and (2) perform tasks involving at least some of the semantic content of the natural language strings. Although they might be interpreted to fit this definition, we will exclude from consideration programs that translate from one natural language to another.

1.1 Semantics

In the programs we shall review, "semantics" has a variety of meanings, as it does also in contemporary linguistics. We will not undertake to make detailed comparisons between the treatment of semantics in these programs and its treatment in linguistic theories which at present have only fragmentary and sometimes conflicting things to say about semantics. When we do refer to linguistic theories, we have in mind something like the views on semantics set forth by Chomsky in *Aspects of the Theory of Syntax* (1965). Very briefly, and incompletely, these may be sketched as follows:

A linguistic theory seeks to explicate the abstract linguistic knowledge—the competence—of a speaker-hearer that allows him to communicate in a language. The theory has three components: syntactic, semantic, and phonological.

The syntactic component consists of a lexicon and two generative grammatical subcomponents. A first grammatical component generates a syntactic structure called the "deep phrase marker" or "underlying phrase marker" which in turn is acted upon by a second grammatical component—the transformations—yielding derived phrase markers and eventually surface (or superficial) phrase markers.

The semantic component operates on the deep structure of a sentence. Besides containing syntactic markers, the lexicon is enriched to contain semantic markers. Semantic markers are interpreted as conceptual notions. The notions may be viewed as sets, and the presence or absence of semantic markers on a lexical item specifically indicates the membership or non-membership of the item in certain of these sets.

With a syntactic rule is associated a projection rule which enforces restrictions (on the basis of semantic markers) on the types of lexical items allowed to fit in the syntactic structure generated by the syntactic rule. Further, the projection rule selects particular readings for a syntactic structure (which may contain substructures for which readings have already been selected).

Most theories in linguistics emphasize competence. Performance, however, is the only available manifestation of linguistic knowledge. Even the usual evidence of competence—the judgment that a string is or is not grammatical in a given language—is a performance, though a performance somewhat different from those common to everyday use of language. Thus, by various indirect means, aspects of performance are used in linguistics to determine competence. On the other hand, in computer programs that process natural language, the difference between competence and performance largely disappears. Since the internal program is itself open to direct inspection, and hence need not be inferred from performance, no curtain obscures the relation between competence and the performance it empowers.

1.2 The Point of View

This section outlines some of the attitudes motivating the lines of work we shall describe. It aims at locating these particular contributions on the general map of linguistic inquiry, and explaining both their similarities with and differences from language research originating outside computer science. These views often are somewhat different from those held by the community of linguists and psycholinguists.

These are not the only attitudes from which language research can start, and perhaps they are not even the most fruitful ones. Until more questions about language have been answered definitively, a prudent strategy is to explore several approaches, allowing the processes of natural selection, rather than a priori argument or polemic, to weed them out and hybridize them. Survival of the fittest is perhaps as potent a mechanism for scientific as for biological evolution.

Four important attitudes are implicit in the work we shall discuss:

1. The concerns usually designated by "syntax" and "semantics," respectively, are not distinct but are mingled along a continuum, with the syntactic component clearly dominating at one end and the semantic component dominating at the other end. This view has been imbedded in much computer science research on language for about a decade and is steadily gaining wider acceptance in formal linguistics today. Little interest attaches to formal definitions that attempt to distinguish sharply between the two components.

2. While it may be useful, for some purposes, to distinguish language "competence" from "performance," the line between is no sharper than the blurry boundary between syntax and semantics. Moreover, most of the characteristics we might be tempted to ascribe to competence are strongly molded by the conditions of language performance and the tasks that performance aims at accomplishing. An important step toward understanding the structure of language is to understand performance systems; and an important route toward understanding performance systems is to write and test computer programs capable of performing.

3. The domain of semantics is language meanings, but the denotatum of "meaning" is neither simple nor homogeneous. A listener, for example, may process language strings under a variety of task instructions (e.g., "remembering," "understanding," "obeying," "answering," "editing," or "inferring"). Each of these tasks requires him to extract certain—but usually not all—aspects of the meanings of the language strings he hears. Given the multiplicity of tasks and the multiplicity of processes a listener may employ under varying circumstances, we must be prepared to find a corresponding

multiplicity of the meanings of "meaning." The programs we shall discuss illustrate this multiplicity.

4. Language-processing systems are complex systems, not simple systems. Simple systems may often be understood by building abstract formal theories about them, deriving logically the consequences of the theories and making simple tests of correspondence between these consequences and the phenomena themselves. Where complex systems are involved, this strategy is usually insufficient. A complementary strategy for understanding complex natural systems involves building artificial systems whose behavior can be compared, in some range of task environments, with the behavior of the natural systems. The technique of investigating complex systems by synthesizing and testing performance models is one of the important contributions of computer science to language study. Applications of this technique form the core of the research we shall describe.

1.3 Hearer, Speaker, and Learner

Research molded by the attitudes just mentioned takes the form of computer programs capable of sophisticated performance in various natural-language processing tasks. These programs often shed light on how human listeners, speakers, and learners might perform similar tasks. Since humans have been the only sophisticated language-using systems, they provide the best source of tasks for testing the capabilities of synthesized systems.

We know, for example, that a human listener, if he hears "John is Jane's father; Bob is John's brother. Who is Jane's uncle?" can often reply: "Bob." If the listener is a computer programmer, and is asked: "Please write an IPL-V program to set the contents of address H5 to equal symbol J3," he can often comply. If a speaker is shown a picture and asked to describe it, he can often produce sentences like: "That is a square above a circle, both inside a triangle."

Humans are capable also of learning languages. The several aspects of human language performance—hearing, speaking, and learning—suggest a corresponding distinction among language-processing programs: hearer programs, speaker programs, and learner programs. We will apply this classification, tentatively, to the systems we will examine though we shall see that some of the programs overlap several categories.

1.4 Ambiguity and Synonymy

A hearer processes natural language strings in order to extract, and possibly store, information from them. A speaker produces such strings from available information in order to transmit information to another. A learner seeks to improve his capability as hearer or speaker, or both. The hearer and speaker processes can be considered, respectively, as processes for decoding meanings from one language form to some other form and processes for encoding meanings into language. In theories of language competence, the analogous processes are the processes for extracting deep structure from surface structure and the processes for generating surface structure from deep structure, respectively.

In the simplest case of transformation from one system of structures to another, the two systems are isomorphic. In this case, the one-to-one relation between them defines a unique transformation from the first to the second and a unique inverse transformation from the second to the first. Then if the two transformations are performed in sequence, the original structure will be recovered.

More generally, we may expect to encounter systems of structures that are connected by many-to-one or by one-to-many transformations. Two of the central phenomena of linguistics—synonymy and ambiguity—are usually interpreted as resulting from incomplete isomorphism between surface structure and semantic reading. Two or more symbol strings that yield the same semantic reading are regarded as synonymous, while a symbol string that is consistent with two or more semantic readings is regarded as ambiguous.

Among the facts that linguistic theory tries to explicate, synonymy and ambiguity have received considerable attention. Syntactic theory has been successful in explaining certain forms of synonymy and ambiguity, namely in the cases where two different sentences yield the same deep structure (synonymy) or two different deep structures yield the same surface sentence (ambiguity). In recent years, the search for the elements of competence that resolve ambiguity has been a major driving force for the extension of linguistics into the realm of semantics.

The transformations from and to language strings that are performed by the language-processing programs we shall consider are a good deal more varied than the extraction of deep structure from surface structure (a preliminary step toward the application of projection rules), and its inverse. We shall be particularly interested to see what new light these general processing capabilities cast on the phenomena of ambiguity and synonymy.

1.5 Syntax and Generality

A prominent feature in several recent attempts to explicate the resolution of syntactic ambiguity by moving toward semantics is the use of a lexicon to imbed various elements of meaning—for example, those useful in accounting for constraints on agreement. The feeling that as grammars become richer they become more "semantic" seems to stem from the fact that, as they exhaust general rules (general in the sense of occurring in virtually every subject-matter context), they incorporate more and more elements that tell what the strings are "about." Thus, a lexical marking on a verb requiring its subject to be an animate noun already tells us that we are dealing with a situation containing animate actors.

On the other hand, generality (independence of subject matter) has been one of the touchstones for distinguishing syntactic from semantic rules. "Semantically unacceptable," applied to a sentence like "The abacus pitched hay," could simply be interpreted as "true in no possible world." Or, to state the matter in reverse, exponents of notional views of universals regard syntax simply as that aspect of language that is so general and basic as to reflect the most universal relational features of the kind of world it is designed to talk about.

The synthetic programs we shall survey exhibit the overlap of syntax with semantics in many ways. For example, in processing input language strings, the hearer programs frequently intermingle semantic transformations, clearly involving the special subject matters the programs are equipped to deal with, with syntactic transformations. The most common deviation of these programs in a semantic direction is that they "know" special word meanings—e.g., that "twice" means "2 times."

We are brought back to the vague word "meaning." Most generally, we test a human's understanding of a word's meaning by his ability to behave differentially and appropriately in response to sentences in which that word occurs. The tests are as varied as the range of response tasks we can set. The programs will illustrate a considerable variety of such tests: translating, determining grammaticality, resolving syntactic ambiguity, determining truth values, answering questions.

In performing these tasks, the various programs will also draw upon a wide variety of mechanisms for instilling meaning into the input strings— mechanisms for storing and getting access to information about the words and the larger structures that occur in these strings. By exhibiting and analyzing these programs, we shall provide concrete and operational referents for a number of the multitudinous meanings of "meaning." I. A. Richards has said that "'meaning' is the centre of obscurantism both in the theory of knowledge and in all discussion." Computer programs that perform natural-language tasks are beginning to direct some beams of light into this dark core of science and epistemology.

1.6 The Programs

Since all but three of the programs we shall use as examples have been described in the literature (Simmons, 1965), we simply provide here a sentence or two of identification and a reference for each. We will refer to each program by the author's name (the first author's name if there are several authors).

Green et al. (1961). Inputs are questions in English about games played by baseball teams. Green's program transforms the sentences to a form that permits search of a systematically organized memory store for the answers.

Lindsay (1961). Inputs are natural language sentences about familial relationships and questions about such relationships. The program transforms sentences to a form that permits it to annex new information to family trees stored in memory and to recover information that is stored, explicitly or implicitly, in the trees.

Simon (1963). Inputs are natural language descriptions of computer programs to be compiled. The program changes the sentences to a form that permits them to be expanded, using information stored in memory, into suitable inputs for a problem-solving compiler. The compiler attempts to construct a computer program fitting the description.

Londe and Simmons (1963). Inputs are simple pictures containing geometric forms. The program learns to classify the forms and their mutual relations, then to generate sentences that describe the pictures.

Darlington (1964).[1] Inputs are natural-language sentences. The program transforms the sentences into statements in one of several logical calculi, then draws logical inferences from sets of statements.

Bobrow (1964). Inputs are natural-language statements of algebra story problems. The program transforms them into algebraic equations, then solves the equations. In doing so, the program may make use of "global information" stored in memory and may request additional information when it is unable to answer.

Raphael (1964). Inputs are natural language statements and questions. The program transforms the sentences into statements of relations, then makes inferences in order to answer questions whose answers are not stored explicitly.

Quillian (1966). Inputs are pairs of words. The program uses a set of definitions in memory to produce natural-language sentences comparing and contrasting the meanings of the input words. The definitions in memory can also be used to choose among alternative phrase markers for natural-language sentences (i.e., to resolve syntactic ambiguity).

Weizenbaum (1966).[2] In conversational mode, the program replies to statements of the person at the console. The conversation is carried on in natural language.

Coles (1967).[3] Inputs are natural-language statements and pictures on a

---

[1] See also Bohnert and Backer, 1967.
[2] See also Colby and Enea, 1966.
[3] See also Kirsch, 1964.

cathode-ray tube. Outputs are phrase markers for the natural-language statements after ambiguities have been resolved by matching to the pictures. The program can also determine whether an input statement is true of a given picture.

Siklóssy (1968). Inputs are pairs, each consisting of a natural language sentence and a "picture" in a functional language. The program learns to produce sentences, in the language used, that express the meanings of pictures.

SECTION 2
HEARER PROGRAMS

By hearer programs, we mean programs that accept input in a natural language—then perform some task on the basis of the input. Although boundaries cannot be drawn neatly, all but three of the programs we have listed are to be viewed primarily as hearer programs. (The three exceptions are Londe, Quillian, and Siklóssy, although each of these, as we shall see, also has certain capabilities for processing natural-language inputs.)

In a typical form of a hearer program (e.g., Green, Raphael), the inputs represent queries that the program interprets and answers. Within certain topical limits (the *topic of understanding*, see Kasher, 1967), the program exhibits "understanding" of the inputs in the precise operational sense that it frequently makes appropriate and correct responses to them. In most of the existing programs, the topic of understanding is relatively narrow, for example, baseball scores (Green), family relationships (Lindsay), computer programs (Simon), algebra word problems (Bobrow), simple pictures (Coles).

A number of the systems (for example, Lindsay, Bobrow, Raphael) are capable of accepting new information as well as queries in natural language. Some of the more recent programs, designed for on-line use in time-sharing systems, are capable of asking for advice—i.e., for additional information to help answer a query. We shall examine the ways in which these programs operate, and the processing mechanisms they employ, attending to the issue of their generality (or lack of it), both with respect to the limits of the topic of understanding and the complexity of syntax they can handle.

2.1 Organization of the Processing

From a linguistic standpoint, we might expect a question-answering program to operate in two stages: in the first stage, the deep structures of the input strings would be discovered; in the second stage, projection rules would be applied to the deep structures and the semantic readings of the input strings would be used to search for the desired information. This linguistic paradigm provides a convenient outline for describing the processes of the hearer programs, although in many cases the analogy holds in only the broadest terms.

Stage I of these programs, then, gives some structure to the input string. In Stage II, the structured input is used to perform certain tasks. Only in two cases (Lindsay, Coles) is the structured input a phrase marker of the kind that is familiar in linguistics. Moreover, in most of the programs there is no sharp separation between the first and second stages—the search for information is mingled with the structuring of the input string. With these reservations and qualifications, it will still be convenient to describe the processing as proceeding in two general stages.

2.2 Structuring the Input

After preliminary processing, usually involving tagging some of the words of the input and using a canonical word representation, the language inputs to the programs are handled in ways that vary along a continuum closely correlated with the severity of the restrictions imposed on the English the program will accept. Speaking roughly, the more explicit, exact, and detailed the "parsing" to which the strings are subjected, the more limited the range of English that will be accepted.

At the end of the continuum, one of the least constricted programs is Weizenbaum's. The program recognizes key words in the input string, ranking them in an order of priority. A string of words, as determined by punctuation (and possibly not a sentence), surrounding the word of highest priority is compared with patterns on a list associated in memory with the key word. If the input matches one of these patterns, the pattern provides structure to the input utterance. For example, suppose the input is "I am not sure I want to go"; that "sure" is the key word of highest priority in this sentence; and that the pattern "*not sure I*," where asterisks designate any (possibly nil) strings, is associated with "sure." The input sentence would match this pattern, "I am" being associated with the first asterisk, and "want to go" with the second.

As the example shows, the patterns are not "tight"—a given pattern can match many utterances, including some incomplete sentences and some nonsense sentences. As a result, a relatively small number of (well chosen) patterns in memory can suffice to match a rich variety of English sentences, including many ungrammatical ones.

Input to Bobrow's and Raphael's programs is processed with the aid of patterns not unlike those used by Weizenbaum. The patterns are "tighter" than those in the latter program, but not so tight as to require every input sentence to be a proper English sentence. Thus, for example, Bobrow's program can accept: "The number of etaoin is five greater than the number of shrdlu. Twice the number of etaoin equals three times the number of shrdlu. How many shrdlu are there?"

At the other end of the spectrum, all input words must exist in the vocabularies of Coles', Darlington's, Green's, and Lindsay's programs. The input sentences are analyzed by a parser according to a specific grammar. The programs at this end of the spectrum are much "brittler" than those at the other end, in that they place very sharp boundaries on the set of input sentences they will accept. In this respect they resemble most artificial languages designed for computer programming, placing strict constraints on the syntax and vocabulary used by the programmer. The programs at the other end of the spectrum have, for the person preparing input, much more the "feel" of flexible natural languages.

From a formal standpoint, the matching patterns in all of these programs can be viewed as the input forms in the rules of standard phrase structure or transformational grammars. As with the analogous forms in grammars, a successful match may initiate a transformation of the input string. However, matching may cause other sorts of actions as well. From a semantic standpoint, it may be more fruitful to regard the Stage I processing as providing an interface between the natural-language strings of the input on the one hand and the symbol structures stored in memory on the other. The Stage I matching facilitates the retrieval of information from the internal store, whose forms of representation may bear no simple relation to the structure of natural language.

Thus, in Green's program, a typical internal memory entry is a set of specifications: e.g., "Month = July; Place = Boston; Day = 7; Game No. = 96; Team = Red Sox; Score = 5; Team = Yankees, Score = 3." An input query might be: "Where did the Red Sox play on July 7?" The Stage I processes transform this query into a specification list also: "Place = ?; Team = Red Sox; Month = July; Day = 7," thus simplifying the processes for retrieving the answer from memory.

Except for the programs of Coles and Lindsay, the State I processing differs in important respects from the processing that would be used to construct the phrase marker of the input. In typical parsing rules, only in the case of function words do the specific properties of specific words play a role. Almost the only lexical information the parser needs about other words is their part-of-speech membership. (This would be less true, of course, of the scheme sketched by Chomsky (1965), which makes broader use of the lexicon.)

In the programs under review, semantic content plays a large role in the Stage I matching processes. Bobrow's program, for example, recognizes such specific synonymies as "twice" = "2 times." Substantive terms that are directly relevant to the topic of understanding have as much significance to such programs as do functional words. Hence, with discourse limited to the topic of understanding, there is no longer a close parallel between the syntactic-semantic distinction on the one hand and the general-specific distinction on the other. While it is correct to say that the matching processes involve special treatment (hence "understanding," in one sense of the term) of *general* terms but not of *specific* terms, it would be incorrect to say that the matching processes are concerned with syntax rather than semantics.

By changing the dictionary of key words, it is rather easy to change the topic of understanding of a program like Weizenbaum's. It would be much harder to change the topic of conversation of Green's program or Bobrow's, where the processing that strings undergo in State I is greatly dependent on certain specific topical terms.

In summary, our analysis shows that we must not take too literally the analogy between the Stage I matching and the extraction of deep structure from surface structure, as the latter extraction process has been viewed by linguists. The programs demonstrate, in a variety of ways, that a hearer program need not possess a complete grammar of the strings it takes as input in order to be able to respond to them, and that, in particular, it need not know the grammar that is used to generate those strings.

The programs we have described also avoid the difficulties that have been encountered in an "analysis by synthesis" approach—that is, discovering deep structure by trial-and-error synthesis of possible structures and testing them against the input strings. All of the programs accomplish their Stage I matching without an inordinate amount of search.

2.3 Using the Structured Input

In Stage II, the structured input obtained from Stage I is manipulated and given operational meaning. In this sense, Stage II is the more specifically task-oriented, although we have already noticed many task-specific elements in the Stage I programs. In Darlington's program, even the particular grammar that is used to structure the input varies with the kind of formal logic (propositional calculus or predicate calculus) that will be used subsequently to draw inferences from the structured inputs. In Bobrow's program, the presence of certain key words in the input (e.g., words identifying the problem as an "age problem") initiates a special Stage I program, distinct from the general one.

Successful pattern matching, during Stage I, triggers a variety of processing mechanisms that make use of the structured input:

1. Information may be added, temporarily or permanently, to memory. Bobrow's system stores new algebraic equations, translated from the natural-language input. The systems of Darlington and Coles store statements in the

predicate or propositional calculus. Lindsay's system stores parts of family trees; Raphael's, relational graph structures. Temporary storage of the structured inputs allows the systems to draw inferences that depend on two or more input sentences. The temporary storage may also be available to the Stage I processes and may alter the processes at subsequent stages. We will provide examples of these phenomena presently.

2. On the basis of the structured input, information may be extracted from permanent or temporary memory for output. Systems that obtain information from permanent memory are usually regarded as "retrieval" systems. Systems that obtain information held implicitly (rather than explicitly) in temporary or permanent memory are usually regarded as "inference" systems. A system may, of course, be both.

2.3.1 Context Across Sentences. Some of the most interesting features of these programs relate to the feedback of temporary and permanent storage to influence the subsequent course of Stage I processing. In general, the Stage I processes operate on one sentence at a time. By making these processes dependent on the temporary storage, accumulated from the processing of prior sentences, context that crosses sentence boundaries is given effect. From these processes we get several cues as to how hearer performance systems can use contextual information to resolve ambiguities. We will cite examples from the programs of Lindsay and Bobrow.

Lindsay's program builds a phrase marker for each input sentence in turn. Then the program extracts from the structured input information that it attaches to a family tree it is building up in memory. Consider two sentences: "A is C's paternal grandfather" and "B is C's father." If the sentences are input in that order, the first one causes the program to build a structure in memory that links A to an unnamed father (call him X) and X to B. When the second sentence is processed, the presence of the structure attached to A is detected and no new structure is built, but the name "B" is attached to the individual, X, previously unnamed. If the sentences were processed in reverse order, the first would create a structure relating B and C; the second would detect the structure attached to C and would create a new structure linking A to B.

Notice that if the first sentence were simply "A is C's grandfather," the program would be unable to determine whether or not A and B's father were the same person. The system will, in fact, process the sentences on the basis of the convention that two persons are distinct unless it is stated or can be inferred that they are the same. Ambiguity here means that there are two or more memory structures that would be consistent with the input sentences —quite analogous to ambiguity when two or more phrase markers are consistent with a sentence.

It was mentioned earlier that Bobrow's program does not ordinarily have to interpret the meanings of the noun phrases it encounters. Since these are simply names for variables that appear in the algebra problems, substitution of different names (provided the substitutions are made consistently throughout any single problem) does not change the equations or affect the subsequent processing. In natural language, however, nonidentical noun phrases often name the same variable. Thus, "the number of newspapers Tom sells" and "the number he sells" may designate the same number. When Bobrow's system finds that it has assigned more variable names than it has equations, it will search for variables that are "nearly" the same, and hence may plausibly be interpreted as identical. The process may, of course, produce incorrect interpretations. This procedure provides a device for handling certain kinds of pronominal reference without incorporating in the grammar specific rules for pronouns. To resolve the ambiguities, semantic knowledge about the structure of algebra problems is substituted for syntactic sophistication. Notice also that the device operates through contexts that extend across sentence boundaries.

Raphael's program employs a similar device. The verb "has" means, in some contexts, "owns"; in others, "has as parts." Suppose the program is presented first with "John owns a chain" and "John is a person and Dick is a person"; later it is presented with "Dick has a chain." Under appropriate circumstances it can (and will) conclude from the first sentence that the relation between a person and a chain is a relation of ownership, hence will translate the last sentence of the example as "Dick owns a chain."

Simon's program provides another example of the use of stored knowledge—in this case both temporary and permanent knowledge—to permit input strings to be structured with a minimum of explicit grammar. The program accepts as input only a very limited range of grammatical constructions, but these create an interesting problem in handling limiting and nonlimiting occurrences of noun phrases and relative clauses.

The initial task of the program—similar to the task of Lindsay's program—is to annex new information to a structure being built up in temporary memory. This structure is a network of binary relations. Suppose we input the sentence:

> K1 is the output state of the cell whose name is H5 on the list of affected cells of the state description of the routine whose name is X100.

Now suppose a structure has already been stored (on the basis of previous input) representing the routine whose name is X100 and its state description. Then the processor, having structured the new input sentence and working essentially from right to left, has to locate in temporary memory (1) first the routine whose name is X100 and then (2) its state description. It has to detect that this state description has no list of affected cells. Now, working on the remainder of the sentence from left to right, it has to assign a symbol for K1; represent the cell (with name H5) whose output state is K1; create a list of affected cells; put the new cell on the list; and attach the list to the state description of routine X100 (located in memory in the previous phase of the processing).

Thus, insofar as the new sentence serves to designate a structure already stored in memory, it is processed from right to left; insofar as it serves to add new relations to that structure, it is processed from left to right. Moreover, the processor does not require prior information as to what part of the sentence is delimiting and what part is not. (It is insensitive, we can say, to the distinction between "that" and "which" in relative clauses of the input sentence.) It does not require the person constructing the input sentences to know exactly what has been stored previously.

2.3.2 Stored Forms to Remove Ambiguities.
The next component of Simon's program takes as input the temporarily stored structures produced by the processes just described. It expands these structures, with the help of information in the permanent store, so that they become suitable inputs to a problem-solving routine that compiles programs. The new processing is required in order to fill in elliptical expressions that occur in the input sentences.

Under appropriate circumstances, a human programmer could respond to an elliptical request like:

"Write a routine, X100, that changes the contents of cell H5 to K1."

The request illustrates both synonymy and ambiguity in natural language —synonymy, because it could be worded in many other ways, yet obtain the same response from the human programmer; ambiguity, because it could have derived (through ellipsis) from more than one sentence and because, out of context, no single meaning can be uniquely recovered.

In Simon's program, the problem-solving processes that actually compile the desired routine need to have their input in a very specific form. In the example before us, the specification would look like this:

Compile a; Name of a = X100; State Description of a = b; List of Affected Cells of b = (c); Name of c = H5; Input State of c = ANY; Output State of c = K1.

The information that Stage I of the program can extract directly from the elliptical request amounts to:

Compile a: Name of a = X100; Name of b = H5; ATT_1 of c = K1.

where "ATT_1" denotes an attribute whose exact nature is not specified, and a, b, and c are (not necessarily distinct) objects.

Stage II of the program resolves the ambiguity by referring to the *canonical form for specifications of routines*, which is stored in permanent memory. The canonical form describes a routine thus:

Compile a: Name of $a = v_1$; State Description of $a = v_2$; List of Affected Cells of $v_2 = v_3$
Affected cell b; Name of $b = v_4$; Input State of $b = v_5$; Output State of $b = v_6$.

where the v's designate variables. The elliptical request is matched to this canonical form. Since the match is not usually unique, the first match obtained is chosen. The unspecified attributes in the request are replaced by the specific names that correspond to them in the match. (For details of the process, see Simon, 1963. The program described in that publication has since been implemented in a computer program.)

The program in its present form suffices only to demonstrate the principle —it is not a practical compiler. It does show that large amounts of flexibility (hence synonymy) and ellipsis (hence lack of specificity, and possibly ambiguity) can be tolerated in the input language, provided information and processes are available in memory for resolving the ambiguities.

2.3.3 **Sensory Information to Resolve Ambiguity.** Coles' program represents still another approach to the resolution of ambiguity. The program interprets input sentences in the presence of sensory information about the outside world to which the sentence is referring. The "outside world" takes the form of a picture on a cathode ray tube (CRT). Stages I and II (which are intermingled) structure the input sentence and transform it into an expression in the predicate calculus. The truth value of the expression is evaluated with respect to the description of the CRT picture. The evaluation yields one of the values: false (F), vacuously true (V), or non-vacuously true (T).

These values can be used in either of several modes. In one mode, if the value is F or V, the program infers that it has found the wrong structure for the input sentence and, backing up, attempts to find an alternative structure that is consistent with its grammar. Consider the sentence:

Each polygon smaller than a triangle which is black is a square.

In this sentence, "which" might be interpreted as referring to "polygon" or "triangle." The program would first try the latter interpretation. If it turned out that there was no black triangle in the picture (hence that the value was V), it would then try the other interpretation.

2.3.4 Summary. The preceding paragraphs illustrate three approaches that permit programs to resolve or reduce ambiguities in input sentences without elaborating the syntactic component of the grammar that is used. The first approach is to annex information from successive sentences to a cumulating temporary memory structure, so that contextual information that reaches across sentence boundaries can be used. Variants of this approach are represented in the Lindsay, Bobrow, Raphael, and Simon programs.

The second approach is to store "forms" in permanent memory containing information that can be used to fill ellipses in incomplete input sentences. This approach is represented in Simon's program.

The third approach is successively to eliminate interpretations of the input that are inconsistent with available information about the outside world. This approach is represented in Coles' program.

Explicating syntactic ambiguity has been a goal in linguistics in recent years. From the programs we have described here, we might draw the tentative conclusion, subject to further experimentation, that the performer's ability to resolve ambiguity is not to be sought in elaborating syntax, but rather in calling on a variety of semantic aids to supplement syntactic rules of interpretation. We will supply yet another example of such an aid when we come to discuss Quillian's program later.

2.4 Types of Stored Knowledge

The amounts and kinds of knowledge available to the hearer programs vary widely from one to another. It is convenient to distinguish between implicit knowledge about the task environment that is built into the patterns used for matching in Stage I and the other types of permanent and temporary knowledge. Explicit knowledge can also be distinguished from knowledge that is encoded into the structure of the stored data and that is therefore available for drawing additional inferences from the explicit knowledge.

2.4.1 Permanent Data Storage. Results of baseball games form the permanent data base used by Green. Bobrow uses a store of useful facts, or "global information," such as: "1 foot equals 12 inches," "Distance equals rate times time," and so on, which can often fill out ellipses in problem statements. Weizenbaum stores a "script," which conists of templates for possible responses to the user.

2.4.2 Temporary Data Storage. The temporary structures are built up anew for each problem presented to the system. Lindsay builds kinship trees; Bobrow constructs algebraic equations; Darlington and Coles construct expressions in the propositional or predicate calculus. Coles also stores a description of a picture on a CRT. Raphael builds a graph in which the nodes designate objects, while the (labeled) edges connecting them represent relations between pairs of objects.

In the linguistic theory used for comparison here, explicit knowledge is stored in the form of semantic markers; implicit knowledge resides in the projection rules (and their selective function). The explicit knowledge only indicates set inclusion or exclusion; the projection rules manipulate these set relationships. It is to be noticed that set inclusion is only one of the relations considered by Raphael, and that the transitivity of set inclusion is the only inferential mechanism used by the semantic theory. The lack of consideration of other relations and inferential mechanisms constitutes a serious weakness in the linguistic semantic theory.

2.5 Inference and Response

Thus far we have discussed mainly the Stage I processing and the annexation of new information to temporary or permanent storage in Stage II. In the hearer programs, the final steps in processing are concerned with providing a response. The structuring of the input and the annexation of information set the stage for the response.

The (implicit) task undertaken by Weizenbaum's program is "Give a reply to the user that will encourage him to say more." It is only in this sense that the program can be regarded as a question-answerer. In the other programs, the nature of the question to be answered, or task performed is much more definite.

Weizenbaum's program proceeds most simply and directly to its response. Associated in memory with the pattern that is matched in Stage I are one or more response templates. A template is converted into a specific response by filling in the values of variables from the corresponding values that have been matched. Consider the pattern "* not sure I *" used in an earlier example. One response template associated with this pattern is "Are you really not sure you 5" where the "5" is a variable to be replaced with the string matched to the second asterisk (the fifth component in the pattern) in the input sentence. Thus, the input string "I am not sure I *want to go*" produces the response "Are you really not sure you *want to go*?"

In Bobrow's program, the first stage having translated the input sentence into algebraic equations in a canonical form, another set of routines uses standard procedures to solve them simultaneously, reporting the answer as the output. Similarly in the Darlington and Coles programs, the output of the first stage is a statement or statements in the notation of formal logic. Darlington uses the formal statements to test the validity of inferences, while

Coles matches them against similar expressions derived from a picture to determine whether the statements are true, false, or vacuous in the universe represented by the picture. All of these programs therefore have inferential capabilities—they obtain information that is contained implicitly, but not explicitly, in the input.

In the Darlington and Coles programs, the inferences take the form of logical deduction; in the Raphael and Lindsay programs, they involve exploiting the transitivity and similar formal properties of the relations stored in memory structures. Thus, Lindsay makes use of the fact that (Father of Father) = Grandfather, while Raphael reasons that if a hand has five fingers and a man has two hands, then a man has ten fingers. In terms of "meanings," we can say that Darlington and Coles use the meanings of logical symbols and the rules of logical inference, while Raphael and Lindsay make use of the meanings of the particular relations that they understand.

Green's program uses counting capabilities to gain some inferential powers. In response to appropriate questions, it can combine the separately stored information about particular games into answers about all the games played by a particular team, during a particular month, or the like. Thus, it can answer the question "How many games did the Yankees win in July?"

SECTION 3
SPEAKER PROGRAMS

Some language-processing programs may best be viewed as speaker programs, although they lack many of the behaviors we usually expect from human speakers. In particular, they lack motivation to initiate speech on subjects "interesting" to them—whether interesting to the listener or not.

Of course, all of the programs make some kind of response, hence they are "speakers" in a limited sense. But even if motivated to initiate messages, only those programs that keep in memory some kind of store of information could behave as speakers—i.e., have something they can talk about. Thus, properly motivated and provided with some additional routines, Green's program could be augmented to give a lecture (probably a very dull one) on the history of a baseball season. If few speaker programs have been written, it may well be due to limits on our present ability both to represent significant aspects of the world inside a computer and to program a computer to explore and discover aspects of the world. Interesting conversations occur among systems that experience, learn from experience, and maintain curiosity toward experience.

In this section, we will comment on the programs that go farthest in their natural language response capabilities. We have already said all that needs to be said about Weizenbaum's program—which is a speaker in the sense that a Rogerian therapist is a speaker, i.e., it keeps the conversation going but makes only a minimal contribution to it. The two other programs that deserve comment in this context are Londe's and Quillian's.

Londe's program is capable of describing aspects of pictures that are presented to it on a CRT. Typically, outputs are of the form "The boy is narrower than, to the right of, and shorter than, the house." Using statistical learning methods, the program learns to recognize classes of bit patterns and to associate them with naming phrases (e.g., "This is a boy"). In the same way, it learns to state in English the relations between pairs of patterns (e.g., "pattern A is to the left of pattern B"). A simple grammar combines the class names of objects and the relations into English sentences that describe the aspects of the pictures it recognizes.

Quillian's program was conceived as a model for human long-term memory. Dictionary definitions of words are stored, in a particular format. Memory is organized so that from any word appearing in a definition the definition of that word can be reached (if it is in memory). Given two words, the program searches the memory network to find paths connecting them. These paths are converted into (crude) English sentences that provide information about the similarities and differences in meaning of the words that have been linked. (Example: Compare: "cry" and "comfort." "Cry is, among other things, to make a sad sound. To comfort can be to make something less sad.")

Quillian has carried out some experiments with a view to showing that the memory structure just described can also be used to resolve logical ambiguities in sentences. His basic idea is that if a word has several definitions, then the intended definition in a given cotext should lead by short paths in the memory to other words that appear in that context. Consider two of the definitions of the noun "whip": (1) a whip is a stick with cord or leather fixed to the end of it, used to give blows in driving animals, etc., or as punishment; (2) a whip is a person responsible for seeing that others of his political group in parliament are present when desired, or do the right things. In the dictionary, a shorter path would presumably join "party" with the second then with the first definition of whip. Hence, the correct meaning of "whip" could be selected in a sentence beginning "The party whip . . .".

Quillian's preliminary experiments with this technique, using a few examples and a very small dictionary, were only marginally successful, but the approach deserves further test. It represents a fourth possible method—to be added to those discussed in connection with the hearer programs—for disambiguating input sentences.

SECTION 4
A LEARNER PROGRAM

Research over the past decade on computer translation of natural language rested heavily on the elaboration of syntax as the principal technique for attaching structure to input sentences and resolving ambiguities in them. The programs we have described in this paper represent a very different emphasis: they call upon several kinds of semantic information, some of it stored in memory, some of it available through sensory channels (e.g., a CRT), to aid relatively simple syntactic capabilities in processing sentences.

The success, however modest, of these efforts suggests that a similar strategy—making extensive use of available semantic knowledge—could be used in a system that could acquire the capability of speaking in a natural language. This is the idea at the core of Siklóssy's program. It leads, as we shall see, to the rather surprising notion that semantic elements may be built integrally into the structure of a speaker's "grammar" from the very beginning.

Siklóssy's program learns to speak a natural language. Its output, like the output of Londe's program, is limited to descriptions of structures representing externally sensed visual scenes. A human, before learning to speak, has already developed a capability to represent in his internal memory relations among objects that are visible to him. It is not known, of course, to what extent it resembles, or differs from, the corresponding capabilities in other mammals.

Siklóssy's program takes this capability as given, and uses it as a basis for acquiring a language capability.[4] We will call the internal representations it uses of visual scenes "pictures." The program is presented with a picture, paired with a sentence in a natural language that describes what is in the picture. The program uses the structure present in the picture to discover the structure of the sentence. It then builds up in memory a pattern that directs a translation from picture to sentence: i.e., if the pattern can be fitted to a picture, it selects elements from the language and forms them into a sentence to express the picture.

In operation, the system first examines the picture and tries to find in memory a pattern that will allow it to generate a corresponding sentence.

---

[4] This has led one commentator to refer to it as a program for "second-language learning"—the "language" of the visual representations stored in memory being, presumably, the first language. If we accept this way of speaking, then, of course, *all* human language learning is learning of a second and subsequent languages.

If it finds an appropriate pattern, it generates the sentence, then matches it to the sentence actually presented. If it fails to find a pattern, or if the sentence generated does not match the sentence presented with the picture, the program uses this information to add to its repertory of patterns and lexical entries.

The set of patterns that cumulate in memory constitutes the "grammar" that the program has learned. The unconventional feature of this grammar is that it does not consist of a system of rules for grammaticality, but of a system of relations that connect possible pictures with possible sentences. Hence, the syntactic component of the patterns is inseparable from the semantic component. While we do not know whether the speaking capabilities of humans are based on a similar intertwining of semantic and syntactic elements, the program suggests a new direction of exploration for speaker performance theories.

We observe that the mechanisms used in the programs are closely allied. A hearer program structures a linear string input in a language for further processing; a speaker program expresses as a language string aspects of structured data; the speaker-learner program builds patterns which are similar to the patterns used by hearer programs. Using a variety of forms of semantic information seems to provide a means for building systems that can have a combined capability for hearing, speaking, and learning language.

SECTION 5
CONCLUSION

It has been the purpose of this chapter to examine a number of computer programs that have capabilities for processing natural language, and that suggest a wide range of mechanisms for bringing semantic elements into the service of language processing. These programs go far beyond even the recent trends in linguistics in crossing the boundary between the conventional, predominately syntactic, domain of linguistic analysis and the general area of cognitive psychology. They treat language behavior as one aspect of man's storing and processing of symbols to deal with the world around him.

Persons who examine these programs may draw many different lessons from them. Some of the principal lessons that we draw are these:

1. Using semantic information in numerous and flexible ways in language processing provides the most promising route to explicating the resolution of ambiguity—a route far more promising than the endless proliferation of a lexicon and of rules of syntax. Liberal use of semantic information is a substitute for sophistication of syntax.

2. Meanings can be extracted by a hearer in many ways besides constructing a phrase marker to represent the deep structure of an input sentence. Only in the most metaphorical sense can the transformation from surface structure to deep structure be taken as the necessary initial step of a paradigm for the extraction of meaning from natural language.

3. Semantic elements can enter language processing through special routines associated with lexical items,[5] through structures built cumulatively from input sentences and stored temporarily in memory, through structures stored in permanent memory, and through information available via sensory channels.

4. A person's knowledge of language, which enables him to perform as hearer and speaker, may not be stored at all in the form of a grammar but instead in the form of a system of translation rules for carrying out transformations between linguistic and semantic forms of representation. While we might formally regard these rules as defining a translation between deep and surface structure, the semantic "deep structure" involved here is quite different from the phrase markers of contemporary linguistic theory.

To understand a body of phenomena we must both open up new lines of possible explanation and eliminate possibilities that don't fit the facts. The research we have described lies largely in the first category—it is a reconnaissance that opens up new possibilities. A next task is to begin to evaluate these possibilities against the facts of human performances that use language.

References

BOBROW, D. C. Natural language input for a computer problem-solving system. Cambridge, Mass.: Project MAC, Report TR-1, 1964. [M]
BOHNERT, H. G. and BACKER, P. O. Automatic English-to-logic translation in a simplified model. IBM Research Report RC-1744, 1967.
CHOMSKY, N. *Aspects of the Theory of Syntax*. Cambridge, Mass.: M. I. T. Press, 1965.
COLBY, K. M. and ENEA, H., Heuristic methods for understanding of natural language in content-restricted on-line dialogue. Department of Computer Science, Stanford University, 1966.
COLES, L. A. Syntax directed interpretation of natural language. Pittsburgh: Carnegie-Mellon University dissertation, 1967. [SS]
DARLINGTON, J. L. Translating ordinary language into symbolic logic. Cambridge, Mass.: Project MAC, Memorandum MAC-M-149, 1964.

[5] In the linguistic semantic theory considered here, processes, namely the projection rules, are associated with structures (phrase markers) but not with lexical terms.

FEIGENBAUM, E. A. and FELDMAN, J. *Computers and Thought.* New York: McGraw-Hill, 1963.

GREEN, B. F., JR., WOLF, A. K., CHOMSKY, C., and LAUGHERY, K. BASEBALL: An automatic question-answer, 1963. [FF]

KASHER, A. Data retrieval by computer: a critical survey. *In* M. Kochen (ed.), *The Growth of Knowledge: Readings on Organization and Retrieval of Information,* pp. 292–324. New York: Wiley & Sons, 1967.

KIRSCH, R. A. Computer interpretations of English text and picture patterns. *IEEE Transactions on Electronic Computers,* Vol. EC-13, No. 4, August 1964, pp. 363–376.

LINDSAY, R. K. Inferential memory as the basis of machines which understand natural language, 1963. [FF]

LONDE, D. L. and SIMMONS, R. F. NAMER: A pattern-recognition system for generating sentences about relations between line drawings. ACM, 20th National Conference, 162–175.

MINSKY, MARVIN (ed.). *Semantic Information Processing.* Cambridge, Mass.: M. I. T. Press, 1969.

QUILLIAN, M. R. *Semantic Memory.* Cambridge, Mass.: Bolt Beranek and Newman Scientific Report No. 2, 1966. [M]

RAPHAEL, B. SIR: A computer program for semantic information retrieval. Cambridge, Mass.: Massachusetts Institute of Technology dissertation, 1964. [M]

SIKLÓSSY, L. Natural language learning by computer. Pittsburgh: Carnegie-Mellon University dissertation, 1968. [SS]

SIMMONS, R. F. Answering English questions by computer, a survey. *Communications of the ACM,* **8**, No. 1, 53–70, 1965.

SIMON, H. A. Experiments with a heuristic compiler. *Journal of the ACM,* **10**, 493–506, 1963. [SS]

WEIZENBAUM, J. Contextual understanding by computer. *Communications of the ACM,* **10**, No. 8, 474–480, 1967.

———. ELIZA: A computer program for the study of natural language communication between man and machine. *Communications of the ACM,* **9**, No. 1, 36–45, 1967.

Part II

GENERATING INTERNAL REPRESENTATIONS

The two chapters of Part II, by Thomas Williams and Donald Williams, respectively, are concerned with how an information processing system moves from a condition of innocence about a particular task domain to a state in which it possesses a program for tackling problems from that domain. In computers, that step usually involves reading into memory an appropriate problem-solving program. In humans, it is taken by processes usually labeled "instruction," "training," "experience," and the like.

The work of T. Williams is concerned with reducing the amount of new instruction an information processing system must be given in order to tackle a new task from a broad domain (card and board games in Hoyle's *Book of Games*). Williams shows that if the system already has available general information about the kinds of objects (e.g., cards, men) and processes (e.g., move, draw) it will encounter, the additional information it needs is roughly equivalent to the rules of the game as they are found in Hoyle.

Williams' work takes the form of a computer language in which it is easy to write programs for a large variety of card and board games and an interpreter that is capable of translating these programs, in turn, into machine language programs capable of playing the games. Though the programs are not written in English, but in a formal language, they come close to being sentence-by-sentence translations of the rules of the game as stated in Hoyle.

The programming language includes a number of modular primitives that perform certain elementary tasks, common to many games. For example, certain modules help to make legal moves in a game; other modules look for the repetition of patterns in the data structures that represent the game board or hand of cards. Game-playing programs are constructed by linking the modules together. The modules are analogous to—and probably similar to—the building blocks that a human draws from memory (his previous knowledge of the language and actions of card and board games) and arranges into a program when he reads Hoyle in order to learn a new game.

The program that Williams writes for a game goes beyond a description of the game and a definition of legal move, and includes an elementary strategy for selecting among legal moves. It would be possible to extend his system (though he does not do so) to separate the legalities from the strategies. By introducing disjunctive nodes into the program (a notion related to R. Floyd's concept of *non-deterministic algorithm*), it could be expanded to describe the alternative moves available at each choice point. Then strategic subroutines could be added to make the actual choices among alternatives at these points. If the system were modified in this way, the similarities between it and a human player would increase, and the resemblance of the program with disjunctive nodes to the game descriptions in Hoyle would become closer. Separating legalities from strategies would also facilitate the introduction of learning processes.

D. Williams' research also has the goal of reducing the information required by a program to enable it to do new tasks. His approach to the problem stems from the observation that humans frequently learn what is required of them in a task not by interpreting instructions but by examining worked-out examples. (Commonly, they make use of both instructions and examples.) He takes as his task domain a range of items that commonly appear on standard intelligence tests, including series completion, symbol analogy, and other items that do not involve word meanings. His program is also organized in modular fashion, some modules being capable of detecting the presence of certain relations ("same," "next") between elements of a test item; others of extrapolating from given symbols, using such relations; others of replacing blanks with appropriate answers, and so on.

His program operates in two phases. In the first phase, it analyzes the examples to determine the nature of the test, and what is required by way of an answer. This information is used to build from the modules a "test taker" program. The latter program then proceeds to take the test. Thus, D. Williams has carried matters one step farther than T. Williams did: his system contains not only a language of tasks and an interpreter for that language, but also means for automatically generating appropriate task-performing programs from the language.

Taken together, these two studies substantially advance our knowledge of where the program and the internal representation come from when a human confronts a new (to him) task domain. Since the learning tasks they deal with are non-trivial ones for adult humans, these programs provide calibrating data that indicate how much information must be provided (and in what forms) to enable an information processing system to respond intelligently to new tasks.

Chapter 3

SOME STUDIES IN GAME PLAYING WITH A DIGITAL COMPUTER

Thomas G. Williams

SECTION 1
INTRODUCTION

Many tasks that people do easily are actually quite complex. This point has become increasingly clear with the development of the digital computer. Simple tasks such as recognizing printed characters, interpreting the English language, or playing simple games are very difficult to program on a computer, yet we regularly teach children how to do them. Achievement of any well developed learning or generalizing behavior has been, so far, almost impossible. The studies reported here concern an effort to program the computer to play all games, giving it only some form of the rules of a game and some descriptions of the objects used in playing the game. The intent is to use such a program to investigate generalization and learning behavior.

1.1   A Brief Survey of Game Playing Programs

Game playing has always been a popular activity in artificial intelligence. This is partly because game playing gives the programmer the opportunity to match wits with his creation, and partly because game playing affords a well-defined problem-solving environment with rules of procedure and performance goals. This latter condition simplifies the environment in which the program must work and allows easy evaluation of performance, but, because game playing is certainly non-trivial, still leaves the programmer with a situation complex enough to make the problem interesting.

The usual goal in writing a game playing program is to make as clever a program as possible, using lookahead methods to see what would happen if a particular move were made, and sometimes building in some learning procedures. Probably the best game player yet written is Samuel's program to play Checkers [9]. Not only does this program play championship Checkers, but it achieves this level of performance by use of various learning heuristics. Furthermore, it learns at a much higher rate, in terms of games played, than a human does. This program is a landmark in artificial intelligence.

Most other game playing research uses the game of Chess. There have been many Chess programs written, none of them very good. Reference [7] by Newell, Shaw, and Simon discusses most of the earlier Chess playing programs, as well as the problems involved in writing a good Chess program.

1.2 Definition of the Problem

The problem studied here is the duplication, by a digital computer program, of human behavior in a game playing environment. The environment is chosen because games have well-defined rules of procedure and well-defined performance criteria. The situation is one where we have a human subject, a set of rules for a particular game, a set of the objects used in playing this game, and an opponent. If the information about the game is complete enough, the subject will, if motivated, play the game against the opponent. His play will be poor if he is not familiar with the game, but will improve with practice.

This situation is interesting because it shows three distinct aspects of human behavior that we would like to be able to produce on a digital computer. First, it demonstrates the ability of humans to apply statements about general conditions to specific instances. The rules of a game do not specify the action required in all of the possible situations, but state more generally the situations that can occur and the actions required. Second, this behavior demonstrates human ability to adapt previous experience in unrelated situations to a new situation. The rules of the game do not cover everything. They do not describe the searching and recognizing operations required for a game, just the conditions to be searched for. Third, this situation shows the ability of humans to use previous experience in this and other similar situations to improve upon their performance.

The goals of this study are not necessarily to simulate exactly this human behavior. They are to study ways of implementing this learning and generalizing ability on the computer.

The approach to this problem taken here is the development of a computer program (called the *General Game Playing Program*, GGPP) capable of using some form of the rules of a game and descriptions of the objects used in a game to find legal moves, and sometimes good moves.

The remainder of this paper is a discussion of the GGPP program, its uses and implications. Section 2 discusses the general abilities of the program and compares them with those of the human. Section 3 is a detailed description of the program and how it is used to play games. Section 4 gives examples of games played with GGPP. Section 5 discusses the internal representations for games that are used in GGPP. Section 6 shows how GGPP could be used for learning and generalization. Finally, Section 7 analyzes the classes of games that can be played with GGPP and Section 8 presents some conclusions about the system. The Appendix provides some definitions of the primitive routines, system cells, reserved identifiers, and error codes.

SECTION 2
GGPP AND HUMAN BEHAVIOR

The object of this section is to compare the abilities of GGPP with those of a human. Human behavior is used because humans are good at the things that we would like GGPP to be good at, and because the ease with which GGPP can be used to play games depends upon how well the abilities of GGPP correspond to those of a human.

First, GGPP is general to the extent that it can play most common board and card games. Further discussion of the generality is, however, postponed until Section 5 to allow complete specification of the program.

In order that GGPP be simple to use, the amount of information needed by GGPP to play a game should be roughly equivalent to the amount of information needed by man. Here "information" is used loosely and not in its information theory sense. Since the form of the information supplied to GGPP differs from that supplied to a human, there is no good way of making a quantitative comparison. However, since the amount of adaptation that must be performed on rules of games as written to make them usable by GGPP is small, the information difference is also small.

The best indication of the differences in information requirements is obtained by a comparison of the various types of information needed to play games. The Control Data G-21 is not equipped with scanning and manipulating equipment, hence cannot interact directly with the real world. In particular, all input to this program is by punched card or teletype, and all output is printed by a line printer or teletype.

The information and abilities needed by a human to play a game can be roughly divided into three categories:

1. General information and experience acquired in other environments and other game playing situations;

2. Information about the form and interrelations among the various objects used in playing the game; and

3. Information acquired from the rules of the game.

2.1 General Information and Experience

Two kinds of previous experience may be relevant to a game playing situation. One is experience involving physical interaction with the real world. Most humans would enter a game playing situation with full knowledge of the motor actions needed to move a piece on a board or move a card. The other relevant experience is in pattern recognition. All game playing requires that various symbols, objects, and combinations of these be recognized or compared; in fact, pattern recognition is probably the most important ability needed for game playing. Other abilities needed include counting, memory, and arithmetic.

These abilities are supplied in GGPP in the form of primitive routines. There are primitive routines that move pieces, move cards, count, and search for patterns. As mentioned earlier, however, physical operations are indicated on a printer.

2.2 Form and Interrelations of Objects

The information needed by humans about the objects used in playing a game is usually obtained visually by looking at the objects, looking at pictures of the objects, or reading about them. For example, inspection of a deck of cards will show that many of them have integers printed on them; those that don't, have an A, J, Q, or K, along with a picture. From this, it may be induced that there is some ordering of the cards. There are also funny markings that look something like ♡, ♣, ♦, or ♠. From this, one might induce that there exist four sets of cards in a deck.

These various relations and orderings must be supplied to GGPP if they are significant in the game. This is done by giving descriptions of each of the objects used in the game. Although routines are provided for generating some of the descriptions for cards and boards, data specification is one of the more difficult things about using GGPP to play a game.

For example, to play Tic-Tac-Toe, we would have to supply the following kinds of information:

1. The game is played on a square board, three cells on a side.

2. The cells are initially empty.

3. The symbols X and 0 are used in the game and are placed on the board cells.

The complete data specification for Tic-Tac-Toe is given in Section 4.

2.3 The Rules of the Game

Information about the rules and goals of a game is acquired by the human player by scanning and interpreting alphanumeric text. This form must be adapted for use with GGPP. The changes involve making the rules more precise and expressing them in terms of the GGPP primitive operations.

The input form of a rule or a goal is an "if-then" clause. The idea is that the "if" portion describes a situation or a relation among objects. The "then" portion describes the action that should be taken if that situation exists. For example, a rule for Tic-Tac-Toe could be expressed as:

"If an empty square exists then put an X on it."

In the actual input form, such concepts as "empty square" and "put" would be expressed in terms of the GGPP primitives.

Often, strategies can be expressed in the "if-than" structure. When this is possible, the strategies can also be given to GGPP allowing it to play well as well as legally.

The foregoing discussion serves to show the connection between the program and human behavior. It shows that GGPP does require some adaptation of rules before it can be used to play a game. Nevertheless, GGPP does possess distinct advantages over other programming systems in dealing with a game playing environment.

SECTION 3
USE OF THE SYSTEM

This section describes how the system is used to play games. To do this, it is convenient to look on GGPP as an interpreter for a programming language. This programming language will be called the Game Playing Language, GPL, and will be used to express the rules of the games being played. This section describes, in general, the use of the system. The Appendix describes in detail the primitive routines and the system calls.

3.1 The Programming System

The GGPP and its primitive routines are written in the list processing language IPL-V. Therefore, the data and programs which the primitives and interpreter operate on respectively must be in a form compatible with the IPL-V system.

The basic data form in the IPL-V system is the list. A list is a sequence of words in memory tied together by having each word in the list contain the address of its successor. This linked structure is a single unit of data. The structure is referred to by its name which is the name of the first cell in the list.

In the simple list, the information contained in the cell represents a symbol or other basic unit of information. When a more complicated structure is required, the list structure is used. In the list structure, the information contained in the cell may be a symbol or may be the name of some other list structure. This provides added flexibility in data structures.

To communicate with the outside world, the IPL-V system is designed to use both numbers and symbols of the form:

$$\langle \text{character} \rangle \langle \text{dddd} \rangle$$

where a $\langle \text{character} \rangle$ is one of the following:

A B C D E F G H I J K L M N O P Q R S T
U V W X Y Z + − * = $ (/) . ,

and $\langle \text{dddd} \rangle$ is an integer. This kind of symbol will be called an IPL-V symbol.

To allow less restricted communication with the outside world, the GPL system contains an assembler which takes program and data cards punched in the format to be described and converts these to IPL-V data forms. The system also contains output routines to convert from the IPL-V data form to a more readable one when output is required.

3.2 Basic Forms of GPL Data

This section discusses the basic data forms used in the GPL language. The syntax for these forms is given in Figure 1. The discussion will consider how some of these forms are represented in the IPL-V system and how the problems of playing games can be expressed in these forms.

3.2.1 *Identifiers or Symbols.* Identifiers or symbols are used to name things. They can be used for names of discrete objects, such as cards, or for names of lists and list structures of objects, such as decks of cards.

An identifier is a string of characters which are not delimiters, starting with a character which is neither an integer nor a delimiter. The symbols allowed in the GPL system are shown in Figure 1, as are the delimiters.

Identifiers may, in general, be freely invented; the following restrictions pertain:

⟨empty⟩ ::=
⟨digit⟩ ::= 0 | 1 | 2 | 3 | 4 | 5 | 6 | 7 | 8 | 9
⟨delimiter⟩ ::= : | (|) | , | / | ; | → | ∧
⟨legal character⟩ ::= ⟨digit⟩ | ⟨delimiter⟩ | ⟨letter⟩ | + | − | = | . | $ | * | ' | ← | → | ¬ | ₁₀ | ∨ |
              ∧ | ≠ | > | < | [| [ ]] | ↑ | ↓
⟨letter⟩ ::= A | B | C | D | E | F | G | H | I | J | K | L | M | N | O | P | Q | R | S | T | U | V | W | X | Y | Z
⟨initial character⟩ ::= ⟨letter⟩ | + | − | ˙ | = | . | $ | * | ' | ← | ¬ | ₁₀ | ∨ | ≠ | > | > | [[ ]] | ↑ | ↓
⟨identifier⟩ ::= ⟨initial character⟩ | ⟨identifier⟩⟨initial character⟩ |
              ⟨identifier⟩⟨digit⟩
⟨integer⟩ ::= ⟨digit⟩ | ⟨integer⟩⟨digit⟩
⟨symbol⟩ ::= ⟨identifier⟩ | ⟨integer⟩
⟨unnamed list⟩ ::= ⟨symbol⟩ | ⟨unnamed list⟩, ⟨symbol⟩
⟨list⟩ ::= ⟨identifier⟩ | : ⟨unnamed list⟩
⟨list structure symbol⟩ ::= ⟨symbol⟩ | (⟨unnamed list structure⟩) |
              ⟨function designator⟩
⟨unnamed list structure⟩ ::= ⟨list structure symbol⟩ |
              ⟨unnamed list structure⟩, ⟨list structure symbol⟩
⟨list structure⟩ ::= ⟨identifier⟩ : ⟨unnamed list structure⟩
⟨function designator⟩ ::= ⟨identifier⟩(⟨unnamed list structure⟩) |
              ⟨identifier⟩ | ⟨empty⟩
⟨conditional segment part⟩ ::= ⟨function designator⟩ |
              ⟨conditional segment part⟩ ∧ ⟨function designator⟩
⟨conditional segment⟩ ::= ⟨conditional segment part⟩ →
⟨operational segment⟩ ::= ⟨function designator⟩ ;
⟨linking segment⟩ ::= ⟨identifier⟩
⟨statement⟩ ::= ⟨conditional segment⟩⟨operational segment⟩⟨linking segment⟩

Figure 1 *GPL syntax*

1. Certain identifiers are reserved identifiers, that is, they already mean sómething to the system.

2. Although identifiers may be any length, storage considerations and the operation of the IPL-V system necessitate the inspection and retention of the rightmost five characters. [If an identifier is longer than 5 characters, only the last 5 (reading from left to right) non-blank characters will be inspected and retained for output. Thus, 2 distinct identifiers having the same 5 last characters will be considered by the assembler to be the same identifier.]

3. Certain symbols will be taken as IPL-V symbols without translation. These are symbols of the form:

⟨R⟩ ⟨digit⟩ ⟨anything⟩
⟨I⟩ ⟨digit⟩ ⟨anything⟩
⟨J⟩ ⟨digit⟩ ⟨anything⟩

These will be read as being-the IPL-V symbols Rdddd, Idddd, or Jdddd respectively, where dddd represents the integer formed by deleting all non-digit characters from the rest of the identifier.

4. Symbols of the form:

$$\langle L \rangle \langle digit \rangle \langle anything \rangle$$

are called local symbols and are used in routines. Their use is explained in the section on routines. Their use anywhere else can cause chaos, but such use will not be detected by the assembler.

It is important to realize that only the reserved identifiers have any meaning to the system. No matter what the meaning of the identifier to the programmer, it is just a string of binary bits to the computer. Any properties that the programmer needs to associate with a particular identifier must be on a description list. See the section on described data for this.

3.2.2 Lists. A list is a sequence of identifiers. The name of the list occurs first on the card, followed by a colon. The identifiers on the list follow, separated by commas. Spaces are ignored.

Example. Legal lists.

BOARD: BA, BB, BC, BD, BE, BG, BH
HAND: S1, H8, C6

Lists are assembled by the assembler into IPL-V form.

Lists are useful for describing such things as decks of cards and hands of cards. Here the symbols on the lists are the cards that comprise that deck or hand. A list is also useful in describing a board. In this case, the symbols on the list represent the individual cells of the board. The user is, of course, free to invent any use for a list that he desires.

3.2.3 List Structures. List structures are lists that may contain the names of other list structures as symbols. List structures are more general data forms capable of representing more complicated structures. The ability to use list structures gives added flexibility to programs.

The programmer has several choices in writing a list structure in the GPL language. He may, if he wishes, name every list used in the list structure.

Example. List structure with explicitly named sublists.

LSTR: LST1, LST2, LIST3
LST1: A, B, C
LST2: E, F, G
LIST3: H, I, J

The programmer may also write lists in the list structure in parentheses without explicitly naming them. In assembling a list structure written this way, names would be assigned by the system to the sublists in parentheses.

Example. List structure with parenthesized sublists and an equivalent structure.

```
LISTR: A, B, (C, D), (((X, Y), Z), W), F
LISTR: A, B, *1, *2, F
*1: C, D
*2: *3, W
*3: *4, Z
*4: X, Y
```

If necessary, function designators may appear in list structures, either alone or in sublists. The section on programs discusses function designators.

3.2.4 Described Data. It is often necessary to be able to associate properties with symbols or list structures. For example, in playing cards, one would want to be able to associate a rank and suit with each card. Or, in playing a board game, one would want to be able to find out what kind of piece, if any, was on a particular square. In GPL, this is done by means of a description or property list. A description list for a symbol or a list structure contains the attributes we wish to use and the values of these attributes associated with that symbol or list structure. The first symbol on the description list is an attribute. The second symbol is the particular value of that attribute for the data being described. The third symbol, if any, is another attribute; the fourth symbol is its value, and so on. Description lists are written following a /.

Example. Description list.

```
QHT:/ SUIT, HEART, RANK, QUEEN
```

QHT has the value HEART for the attribute SUIT and the value QUEEN for the attribute RANK.

3.2.5 Programs. Programs are list structures. In writing programs, however, the relative locations of symbols in the structure are quite important. Therefore, additional punctuators are used so that the assembler will know where to put things. This section discusses the formation of programs; a later section explains what a program does.

The basic unit of the GPL program is the statement. There are three types of statements: statements with external names, statements with local names, and statements with no name. The type of name determines the statement sequencing.

Each statement can have three segments in this order: a conditional segment, an operational segment, and a linking segment. The conditional segment is terminated by a "→"; the operational segment is terminated by a ";"; and the linking segment is terminated by the end of the card or a "|." The name, if any, is first on the card and is followed by a ":" as for lists. The syntax is given in Figure 1.

Example. Statement with external name.

PLAY1 : SEARCH(BOARD,X3,ROW)→MOVE(BOARD,OUTF,XMOVE) ;WIN

PLAY1 is the external name of the statement. SEARCH(BOARD,X3,ROW) → is the conditional segment; MOVE(BOARD,OUTF,XMOVE); is the operational segment; and WIN is the linking segment.

Example. Statement with no name.

SEARCH(BOARD,X2,ROW)→MOVE(BOARD,OUTF,XMOVE) ;WIN

SEARCH(BOARD,X2,ROW) → is the conditional segment; MOVE(BOARD, OUTF,XMOVE); is the operational segment; and WIN is the linking segment.

Any of the segments may be empty. The punctuator may or may not be used. If the punctuator is used, a SET+ instruction will be assembled for a conditional or operational segment, nothing is assembled for a linking segment. If the punctuator is not used, the function designator will be taken to be the first segment of the statement which has not yet been defined. Any statement will have SET+ instructions added to it until there are at least two segments.

Example. Empty operational segment.

QUIT: DRAW;

The conditional segment is DRAW because the conditional segment had not been defined when the ; was found on the card. The operational segment will be a SET+ instruction. There will be no linking instruction.

Example. Empty conditional segment.

QUIT:→DRAW;

Because the → punctuator was used, the conditional segment is empty and will be a SET+ instruction after assembly. DRAW will be the operational segment. There will be no linking segment.

Conditional segments may be compound, that is, they may consist of many function designators separated by the character ∧.

Example. Statement with a compound conditional segment.

PBA: TSTA∧TSTB∧TSTC→MOVE(BOARD,OUTF,XMOVE);

TSTA ∧ TSTB ∧ TSTC ∧ is a compound conditional segment.

The normal sequencing of the GPL interpreter is to execute the conditional segment and then execute the operational and linking segments or the conditional segment of the next statement depending on whether a test cell has been set to be $+$ or $-$. The use of external and local names controls which statements have successors.

A statement with an external name starts a new program list and clears the local symbol table. The statement preceding a statement with an external name has no successor. The name of the statement is the name of the program list.

A statement with a local name is placed at the end of the program list and the local name is entered into a symbol table. The statement with the local name may be referred to by that name until the occurrence of the next statement with an external name.

A statement with no name is placed at the end of the program list. The symbol table is not affected.

Placing a statement in the program list consists of the following operations. First, a mark, PMARK, is put at the end of the list. Then the conditional, operational, and linking segments are each placed at the end of the program list. If the conditional segment is compound, each function designator is placed at the end of the program list and followed by a mark, AMARK.

Example. Statements and equivalent program list.

```
        PLAY1: SEARCH(BOARD,X3,ROW)→WIN;
               SEARCH(BOARD,X2,ROW)→SET(GD,YES);WIN
 PLAY1: SEARCH(BOARD,X3,ROW),WIN,PMARK,SEARCH(BOARD,X2,ROW),
        SET(GD,YES),WIN
```

3.3 Interpretation of Statements and Programs

This section defines what happens when GGPP runs. It describes in detail the execution of segments and how inputs and outputs to the routines are handled.

3.3.1 Flow of Control Through Statements. Each statement in a program list is interpreted by GGPP. Interpretation starts with the first statement in the program list, that is, the statement with the external name. Interpretation of the program list stops when the end of the list is reached. If the program was called as a subroutine by another, control returns to the calling program when the subroutine is completed. Otherwise, the program is finished.

The first step in the interpretation cycle is the execution of the routine named in the conditional segment with the indicated inputs. This routine will set the test cell $+$ or $-$. The interpreter will then inspect the test cell. If the test cell is positive, the routine named in the operational segment will be executed. After this, control is transferred to the routine named in the linking segment. If there is no linking segment, control will pass to the next statement.

If the test call is negative, control is transferred to the next statement. If there is no next statement, the interpreter will stop as described above. If the conditional segment is compound, parts will be executed sequentially in left to right order. After each execution, the test cell is inspected. If at any time it is negative, control passes to the next statement without further execution of the rest of the statement. If the test cell is always positive, the operational and linking segments will be executed as described above.

3.3.2 Execution of Segments.
Conditional and operational segments specify routines to be executed. The inputs to these routines are specified in normal functional notation.

Example. Segment and inputs.

SEARCH(BOARD,XA,ROW)

The routine SEARCH is to be executed with the inputs BOARD, XA, and ROW.

When execution of a routine is called for, the inputs are placed in a pushdown stack. A pushdown stack is a special type of storage location which is constructed like a cafeteria well for holding trays. When a tray is put into the well, all trays below it are pushed down one level. When a tray is removed, all other trays pop up one level. A pushdown storage stack works on the same principle. Putting a symbol into the cell pushes the other symbols in the cell down one level. Removing a symbol from a cell pops up all other symbols. In GPL, the inputs are placed in the input stack in the reverse of the order in which they are listed so that after all inputs are in the pushdown stack, the first input named is at the top of the stack.

Only one pushdown stack is used. At times, when executing a routine as a subroutine of another, it is necessary to separate the inputs of the subroutine from those of the calling routine. For this purpose, a marker, SMARK, is put into the stack before the subroutine inputs.

When all the inputs to a routine have been placed in the stack, the routine is executed, taking its inputs from the stack and leaving its outputs there.

All symbols originally in the stack that are not used by the routine remain there.

After execution, the symbols in the stack (up to the first SMARK) are all removed and placed, in the same order, on an empty list called the output list. This is done to remove all unnecessary symbols from the stack. Inputs to routines may refer to the symbols on this list. Since the output list is empty before the contents of the stack are placed in it, it follows that the only symbols that can be accessed by inputs to a routine are the outputs of the previously executed routine. Symbols needed for later use may be called from the output list and placed in storage.

Each input to a routine is inspected before it is placed in the input stack. If the symbol is not: (a) the name of a GPL routine, (b) the name of a GPL primitive, or (c) the name of a function designator, it is put into the stack.

If the input is the name of a GPL routine, the routine is executed immediately. It will take its inputs from the stack and leave its outputs there. After execution, the next input symbol is processed.

If the input is the name of a GPL primitive, the name of the output list is put into the stack. The routine is then executed. After execution, the next symbol is processed.

If the input is the name of a function designator, SMARK is put into the stack. The designated function is then executed in the same manner as conditional or operational segments (which are themselves function designators). After execution, the routine stored in the cell SELECT.IN is executed. The purpose of this routine is to select one of the outputs left by the function, and leave it in the stack. All other outputs and the SMARK are to be removed. The system initializes the contents of SELECT.IN to a routine which will take the first output in the stack. After execution of this routine, the next input in the stack is processed.

After all the inputs have been processed and stored in the stack, the routine named by the function designator is executed.

3.4 Input Card Format

GPL programs and data lists are punched one on a card, starting in column 4. Punching may extend to the end of the card (column 80). Data and programs may be intermixed in any way desired. Spaces may be used freely; they are ignored.

If a statement or list is too long to fit on a single card, it may be continued on a continuation card. Continuation cards are indicated by punching a C in column 3.

Everything on a card after a "|" is ignored. This convention can be used for comments.

The last card in the deck must have the word START: as the first word on the card beginning in column 4. The name of the routine where execution is to be started should follow. The assembler will be erased and execution of the GPL program will start at the specified routine.

3.5 Special Facilities of GPL

This section discusses the use of some of the more complicated primitive routines of the GPL system. All primitives are defined in the Appendix. The reader may wish to skim this section and return to it later for reference.

3.5.1 The SEARCH Routine and Patterns. The GGPP system is equipped with a fairly general, fairly efficient routine for performing searches on boards and among lists of cards. This routine is named SEARCH. This section describes the operation and use of this routine.

The central problem that this routine is designed to handle may be expressed as follows. There exists some universe of symbols. Each symbol has properties associated with it. There are two functions, one which operates upon the universe to produce a sequence of subsets of the universe, and the other which operates upon subsets and produces a $+$ or a $-$ output. The first function will be called the set generating function; the second, the set testing function because it has a binary output. The combination of a set generating function and a set testing function defines some criterion for members of the universe.

We would like to search the universe to see what members satisfy this criterion. There are two problems associated with these searches. One is to specify the nature of the set to be generated and the criterion to be used in some general but simple manner. The other is to perform these searches efficiently.

In GGPP, both the generating and testing problems are handled in the one routine SEARCH. The inputs to this routine are the universe to be searched (such as a board), the characteristics of the sets to be generated, and the criterion for testing the set once it has been generated.

3.5.1.1 THE SET TESTING FUNCTION. The criteria for testing the set of symbols are specified by a list structure called a pattern. Testing the set of symbols is done by testing each symbol in the set sequentially. The properties that each symbol should have are specified by the symbols on the pattern, which are called cell test units (CTU). Symbols in the set to be tested are tested against the CTU in the order of the CTU's on the pattern.

Properties of symbols in PGL are specified in description lists. Therefore, the CTU specifies what the description list of the symbol should have on it if there is to be a match. In its simplest form, the CTU is just a list of attributes and values. The values of the attributes on the CTU are compared with the values of the same attributes on the symbol being tested. If all the values are the same, the symbol matches the CTU. If not, the symbol does not match the CTU.

Example. CTU and symbols.

>CTUA: OCCUPIED, BLACK, LOCATION, CORNER
>SYMBA:/ OCCUPIED, WHITE, LOCATION, CORNER
>SYMBB:/ OCCUPIED, BLACK, LOCATION, CORNER

CTUA matches SYMBB and does not match SYMBA.

To reduce the number of CTU's that might have to be written and to increase the flexibility of the CTU in specifying the conditions to be met, a large number of special properties have been provided for CTU's.

1. Indirectness. Each attribute and value on a CTU is taken to be an address in the computer. The contents of this address are inspected to see if it is a GPL external symbol. If so, the attribute or value is replaced by the contents of the address (symbol) on the CTU. The test is then repeated. The contents of symbols may be set by the SET primitive. This test and replacement occur every time the SEARCH routine is executed, so a single CTU may have many different values.

Example. Indirectness.

>CTUA: LOCATION, PLACE

If the primitive SET(PLACE,CORNER) is executed before the CTU is used in a pattern, CTUA is effectively:

>CTUA: LOCATION, CORNER

If later on in the program, the primitive SET(PLACE, CENTER) is executed, CTUA is effectively:

>CTUA: LOCATION, CENTER

2. Function Designators and Routines. Each value in the CTU is tested to see if it is the name of a GPL function designator, GPL primitive, or GPL routine. If the value is one of these, the routine so named is executed (after a SMARK is put into the stack). After execution, the routine in location SELECT.PAT is executed. This routine is supposed to select one of the outputs in the stack. The selected output is left in the stack after all the

outputs and the SMARK have been removed. After execution of this routine, the output in the stack replaces the value on the CTU. If there is no output from the routine, the symbol NOTNG is used. The cell SELECT.PAT is initialized to a routine which selects the first of the outputs in the stack, but the user may store the name of any routine with the above characteristics in the cell.

3. Equality. When the values of the attribute on the symbol and on the CTU are found, a special equality test, EQUAL, is used. This test will indicate equality in the following cases:
 (a) the two values are identical symbols,
 (b) the two values are equal integers,
 (c) either or both of the values is EVERY,
 (d) the value of the attribute is a list and the value on the CTU is on this list.

4. Nothing. A special value, NOTNG, is used when the attribute on the CTU is not to be on the description list of the symbol being tested. This value will also indicate a match if the value on the description list of the symbol is NOTNG.

5. Negation. At times, it is useful to specify that the attribute value on the symbol be anything but the attribute value on the CTU. To indicate this, the symbol NOT is used before the attribute-value pair on the CTU. A CTU containing NOT will also match if the attribute specified is not on the description list of the symbol under test.

Example. Negation.

```
CTUA: NOT, OCCUPIED, BLACK
SYMBA:/OCCUPIED, BLACK
SYMBB:/ OCCUPIED, WHITE
SYMBC:/ OCCUPIED, RED
SYMBD:/
```

CTUA will match SYMBB, SYMBC, and SYMBD, but will not match SYMBA.

6. Lists. The CTU can specify that a symbol be on a list. To do this, use the symbol LIST followed by the name of the list on which the symbol should be.

Example. List.

```
CTUA: LIST, C.CELL
C.CELL: CELL.A, CELL.B, CELL.C
CELL.A:/
CELL.D:/
```

CTUA will match CELL.A, but will not match CELL.D.

6. Value Count. When an attribute can have multiple values, it is sometimes necessary to count the number of occurrences of a particular value on a value list. This is done in a CTU with the following sequence: first the symbol CNTVAL, next the attribute-value pair, and finally the number which the count should be tested against on the CTU. The test used is EQUAL.

Example. Value Count.

```
CTUA: CNTVAL, OCC, BLACK, 2
SYMB:/ OCC, (BLACK, WHITE, WHITE)
SYMC:/OCC, (BLACK, WHITE, BLACK)
```

CTUA will match SYMC, but will not match SYMB.

CTU's can have more than one attribute-value pair. A CTU will match a symbol if all of the attribute-value pairs on the CTU match those on the symbol. Only the attributes and values that occur on the CTU will be tested. The symbol may have other attribute-value pairs not mentioned in the CTU. These will have no effect on the results of the test.

3.5.1.2 SET GENERATION. Two methods of generating sets to be tested are provided in GPL. The first method is the use of a routine that generates the symbols of the set sequentially, outputting one cell of the set each time it is executed.

The second method is built into the SEARCH routine and uses the concept of adjacent cells. Suppose each symbol or cell in the universe being searched had the symbols that are adjacent to it on its description list. The attributes on the description list would be the directions in which one would go to get a particular adjacent symbol. Then, if a starting cell were specified, the rest of the set could be specified by giving a list of directions which could be used to get the next cells.

This is precisely the method used. The inputs to the SEARCH routine, besides the pattern, are the list of starting cells, usually the entire universe to be searched (but see also Section 3.5.1.5), and the list of directions to use in getting the next symbols in the set to be tested. Since the set of symbols generated by the list of directions depends upon the starting symbol used, one direction list can specify many different sets of cells.

It should be obvious that the use of the words "adjacent" and "direction" is only to give a physical description for the method. Any symbols can be put on any description list as the value of any attribute desired, and the resulting data structure can be used with the direction-list method.

Various list structures are allowed in direction lists. The following rules apply:

1. If the direction list contains a sublist of directions, all sets of directions generated by taking each direction on the sublist one at a time will be used. Many sublists can appear on a direction list. Sublists cannot appear on lists that are already sublists, however.

Example. Direction sublists.

DIREC: A,B,(C,D),(F,G),E

This single direction list is equivalent to using the following four lists, in the order given.

*1: A,B,C,F,E
*2: A,B,C,G,E
*3: A,B,D,F,E
*4: A,B,D,G,E

2. If the direction list contains the name of a GPL routine or a GPL primitive, the routine or primitive will be executed with the direction used to get the current cell in the input stack. Function designators are not allowed in direction lists. Three primitives are provided explicitly for use in direction lists: SAME, EXCP, and PERP. These are defined in the Appendix.

Example. Routines in direction lists.

DIREC: (A,B,C),SAME,SAME

DIREC is equivalent to using the following lists in the order given.

*1: A,A,A
*2: B,B,B
*3: C,C,C

It is important that the direction list be long enough for the pattern. The number of symbols tested is determined by the length of the pattern, not the length of the direction lists. Since the first cell of the set is provided, the direction list should be no shorter than $(n-1)$ if the pattern has (n) CTU's on it.

Example. Pattern and direction list.
Suppose a Tic-Tac-Toe board is set up with description lists giving adjacent cells in directions D1–D8 as shown here:

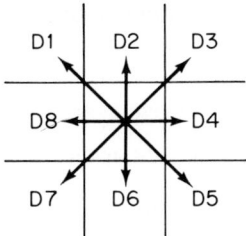

Let the board cells be B1–B9, as shown here:

Let occupation of a square by X be denoted by the attribute-value pair OCCUPIED, X. The pattern X3 with the direction list ROW will match on all instances of 3 X's in a row.

```
BOARD: B1,B2,B3,B4,B5,B6,B7,B8,B9
OCCX: OCCUPIED, X
X3: OCCX,OCCX,OCCX
ROW: (D1,D2,D3,D4), SAME
```

We can reduce the number of cells looked at and still find all occurrences of 3 X's in a row. Using the list LESS.CELLS in place of BOARD will do this.

```
LESS.CELLS: B1,B4,B7,B8,B9
```

3.5.1.3 OTHER TYPES OF PATTERNS. The patterns just described are called simple patterns. There are two other types of patterns. These are repeatable patterns and expandable patterns. These are useful for, among other things, searching for legal moves in games where the number of cells involved in a move may not be known.

3.5.1.3.1 *Repeatable Patterns.* Repeatable patterns are used where a part of a pattern may be repeated an indeterminate number of times. They are useful for searching for such things as capture moves in checkers and non-capture queen, rook, or bishop moves in chess.

A repeatable pattern is indicated by putting a REP symbol before the section of the pattern which is to be repeated. This section of the pattern will be repeated on an extended number of symbols in the set being tested until a match fails to occur.

Example. The pattern JUMP

JUMP: BLACK,REP,RED,EMPTY

is equivalent to the sequence of patterns

*1: BLACK, RED, EMPTY
*2: BLACK, RED, EMPTY, RED, EMPTY
*3: BLACK, RED, EMPTY, RED, EMPTY, RED, EMPTY
.
.
.

It will be tried on sets starting with the same symbol until one of the patterns fails to match.

The operation of SEARCH on a repeatable pattern starts by testing the shortest pattern: the one with no repeats. If this particular set matches the pattern with no repeat, the pattern is extended by adding the part after the repeat bracket REP. The set of cells on which the non-repeated part passed is also extended. The extended parts of the pattern are matched with the extended part of the symbol set. If a match occurs, the pattern and set are extended again. Any time a match fails, testing on the particular symbol set stops.

Repeatable patterns are designed to be used with symbol sets generated by the direction list method. For use with repeatable patterns, direction lists also contain the REP symbol. The REP symbol is placed before the direction used to get the first symbol of the extended set from the last tested symbol of the set.

Example. The action of SEARCH on a repeatable pattern.
Let DIR be a direction list used with the pattern JUMP of the previous example.

DIR: REP, D1, D2

When SEARCH is executed using JUMP and DIR, the first symbol is obtained from the list of starting symbols given to the routine. It is tested with the CTU BLACK. If the symbol does not match the CTU, testing stops on that starting symbol. If the symbol matches the CTU, the second symbol is obtained from the first by using D1 (the REP is ignored) and tested with the CTU RED. Again, testing stops if the symbol does not match the CTU. If the second symbol matches the CTU RED, the third symbol is obtained from the second by using D2 and is tested with EMPTY. If the third symbol matches the CTU, an instance of the pattern has been found. Testing will proceed on the repeated portion of the pattern. If the third symbol does not match the CTU, testing stops on that set.

To repeat the pattern, the REP symbol is found on the pattern and direction list, and testing starts at the symbols following it. A fourth symbol is found from the third by using D1, since D1 follows the REP. This fourth symbol is tested with the CTU RED, since RED follows REP on the pattern. Testing continues in the same manner as described above.

3.5.1.3.2 *Expandable Patterns.* Expandable patterns are designed for searching for situations where the first and last symbols are separated by an undetermined number of other symbols. These situations can arise in searching for capture moves of queens, rooks, and bishops in Chess.

An expandable pattern is indicated by placing the brackets EXP.O (expand open) and EXP.C (expand close) around the part to be expanded. The expanded part will be repeated as many times as necessary to find a match.

Example. The pattern CAPT

    CAPT: WHITE, EXP.0, EMPTY, EXP.C, BLACK

is equivalent to the sequence of patterns

    *1: WHITE, BLACK
    *2: WHITE, EMPTY, BLACK
    *3: WHITE, EMPTY, EMPTY, BLACK
        .
        .
        .

In effect, each pattern in the sequence will be tried until a match is found.

The operation of SEARCH with an expandable pattern starts with a test of the pattern without using any of the CTU's indicated in the expand brackets. If this test passes, no further testing of the set is done. If this test does not pass, but all symbols except the last one in the set did pass, the last symbol in the set is retested with the first CTU in the expand brackets. If this test also fails, no further testing is done on that set. If this test passes, all other CTU's in the expand brackets and the last CTU in the pattern are tested on extensions of the symbol set. Depending on which CTU's did or did not pass, testing is terminated with a found pattern, testing is terminated with no pattern found, or the pattern is expanded again.

If any CTU in the expand brackets fails to match, the testing is terminated without finding a match. If all CTU's in the expand brackets and the last CTU of the pattern match, a pattern has been found. If the last CTU on the pattern fails to match, but all other tests have passed, the pattern is expanded again.

Expandable patterns are designed for use with sets generated by the direction list method. For use with expandable patterns, direction lists must have an EXP.0 bracket before the direction used to get the second symbol of the expanded part from the first symbol of the expanded part. The first symbol in the expanded part is the symbol on which the last CTU of the pattern failed. This bracket may go anywhere in the direction list.

Example. The action of SEARCH on an expandable pattern.
Let DIRM be a direction list used with the pattern CAPT of the previous example.

DIRM: D1, EXP.0, D2

When SEARCH is executed on CAPT and DIRM, the first symbol is tested with WHITE. If the test fails, no further testing is done. If the first symbol matches the CTU, the second symbol is generated using D1. The second symbol is tested with BLACK. If it passes, the pattern has been found. If it fails, the second symbol is tested with EMPTY, because EMPTY follows the EXP.0 bracket. If this fails, no further testing is done. If this matches, the third symbol is generated using D2, because D2 follows the EXP.0 bracket in the direction list. Depending on the results of testing this third symbol, the SEARCH routine either stops with the pattern found or expands the pattern again.

3.5.1.4 PATTERN OUTPUTS. Discovering that an instance of a pattern exists may not be particularly useful unless information about the particular instance of the pattern that matched is available. Therefore, the SEARCH routine has provisions for providing information about the pattern matches found.

The outputs of the pattern recognizer are description lists. The number of symbols in the set on which the pattern matched is automatically on the output list as the value of the attribute NUMBER. The symbols on which the pattern matched may be placed on the output description list by the user.

Every CTU in a pattern is tested to see if it has the attribute OUTPT on it. If the CTU has OUTPT on it, then the symbol that matched the CTU is placed on the output description list as a value. The attributes for this value are the symbols that are the values of OUTPT on the CTU.

The output system is the same for expandable patterns as for simple patterns. There is a small difference in the way repeatable patterns are handled. When a match on a repeatable pattern is found, an output description list is generated as described. Before the repeat is executed, however, a copy of the output list, an internal list used by SEARCH from which the output description lists are generated, is made and all information about the last cell in the pattern is deleted from this copy. Then the repeat is executed. This is done for the following reason: if the repeated part matches, the last cell in the pattern before the repeat is usually not changed.

Every time a pattern match is found, one of these output description lists is generated. The SEARCH routine tries to match the pattern on all possible symbols before stopping. After all possible matches have been found, the outputs are all left in the stack. The order of the outputs will be the order in which the matches were found. Starting cells for sets are selected in the order that they appear on the list which is input to the routine.

3.5.1.5 EFFICIENCY. One of the problems of searching a very large universe of symbols is that it may take a long time. Fortunately, the results of past searches can often be used to reduce the number of starting symbols looked at. By not searching symbols that cannot match the pattern, as determined by past searches, a significant amount of work can be eliminated.

The SEARCH routine contains a method for reducing the number of initial symbols examined. The programmer can specify whether this subprogram is to be used on all patterns, on some patterns, or not at all. If desired for all patterns, the symbol YES should be stored in the cell GLOBL. If desired for some patterns, the symbol YES should be stored in GLOBL and the attribute-value pair LCL, NO should be stored on the description list of all patterns on which the method is not to be used. If the method is not to be used at all, the symbol NO should be stored in the cell GLOBL. The system will initialize GLOBL at YES, so that, if nothing is specified, the method will be used.

The method works by remembering all starting cells on which the first CTU of a pattern matched. In addition, every time the description list of a symbol is changed, or every time a symbol is moved from one list to another, the symbol involved is placed on all lists of remembered starting cells. Thus, the list of starting symbols for a particular pattern contains the symbols where the first CTU of the pattern has matched plus all symbols that have changed since the last time that the pattern was used in the SEARCH primitive. Every time SEARCH is executed and the initial symbol reduction method is being used, the list of starting symbols associated with the particular pattern is used instead of the entire universe. Symbols on which the first CTU does not match are automatically deleted from this list.

The list of starting symbols for a particular pattern is associated with the board and the name of the pattern. The name of the pattern is an attribute of the board. The value of the pattern is the name of a list of the first CTU's which the pattern has had, followed by the lists of initial symbols on which that CTU has matched. This list is in description list form. To find the list of starting symbols, the CTU is assembled into its final form by evaluation of all references that need evaluation. This assembled CTU is compared with the stored CTU's. When a match is found, the next symbol on the list is the list of starting cells. The system does all of this automatically.

One can also have lists of starting cells associated with a list of directions. There may be starting symbols from which the necessary number of additional symbols cannot be generated because of "running off the board" or similar difficulty. A list of the cells from which the necessary number of additional symbols can be generated can be stored on the description list of the board as the value of the name of the list of directions. When the direction list is used, these starting symbols are compared with the list of starting symbols associated with the pattern. Only the symbols on both lists are used. The use of starting symbols associated with the direction list occurs whether or not the other method of finding starting symbols is used.

Example. Suppose for a particular instance of a pattern P1, *1 is a list of cells where the first CTU of the pattern matched; and B4 and B5 have been changed since the last time that that instance of the pattern was used. Suppose also that the list *2 of starting symbols is associated with the direction DIRC.

*1 : B1,B5,B8,B22
*2 : B1,B2,B3,B4,B5

Then if SEARCH is executed with the particular instance of P1 with which *1 is associated and the direction DIRC, *3 is the list of starting cells that will be used.

*3 : B1,B4,B5

A few other comments should be made on the subject of efficiency. The first is that, although the special properties of the CTU's can be quite useful, evaluating them takes time. If the programmer is using CTU's which do not require evaluation, he can indicate this by putting the attribute-value pair EVAL, NO on the description list of the CTU. If the pattern is made up entirely of CTU's that do not need evaluation, this pair should be placed on the description list of the pattern. If the attribute EVAL is not present, the system assumes that the CTU's of the pattern will need to be evaluated.

Second, if the method for finding initial symbols is being used, the amount of time saved by this depends upon the time required to find the list of initial symbols and the number of starting symbols eliminated. The time required to find the list of initial symbols depends upon the number of different instances of the first CTU on the pattern. The more different instances used, the longer it will take to find the list of starting cells. Also, the longer the CTU itself, the longer it will take to find this list. It is obvious that there are some situations where use of the method will take longer than a simple search of the entire universe.

3.5.2 Moves. A move on a board is usually performed by altering description lists of various symbols. There are four basic changes one can make, and there are four primitive routines for making these changes:

1. ADD1. Add a symbol to the value list of an attribute.
2. DELA. Delete all occurrences of a symbol from the value list of an attribute.
3. DEL1. Delete one symbol from the value list of an attribute.
4. CHNG. Change the value of an attribute of a symbol.

The inputs to these routines are the attributes and values affected and the symbols to be changed. There is also one special attribute value, PVAL (Present Value), that can be specified. If PVAL is used as an attribute value in DELA or DEL1, the value of the attribute that is specified in the input is removed from the description list of the symbol and placed at the end of a special list. If PVAL is used as an attribute value in ADD1 or CHNG, the first symbol on this special list is removed and is used in place of PVAL. If used in board games, for instance, PVAL allows the user to remove a piece from one square and place it on another without actually specifying what the piece was.

In addition to these four routines, there is also one other routine, MOVE, which incorporates all of these routines and is designed to work with the output of the SEARCH routine.

The basic input to this routine is a "move list." The components of the move list are an output type and a change list. The output type is the attribute on the output list from the SEARCH primitive which has the board symbols as values. The change list gives the type of change to be made on the symbols of that output type, and the attribute-value pair information needed to make the change. The output type and change list name occur sequentially on the move list. There may be as many output type-change list pairs as necessary.

Example. Move list

MOVEL: OUT1,CHANGE1,OUT2,CHANGE2

The information in the change list is, first, the type of change desired. This is the name of one of the four primitive routines for making changes. The second piece of information on the change list is the name of a list, in description list form, which gives the attributes which are to be changed and the values affected. PVAL may be used as an attribute value on this list.

Example. Move list.

XMOVE: MINE, ((DEL1, (OCCUPIED, BLACK))

The move list XMOVE specifies that symbols on an output list which are the values of attribute MINE are to be changed. The change list specifies that the change is to be a deletion of one of the symbols BLACK from the value list of attribute OCCUPIED.

3.5.3 Board Generation Routine.

To use the primitive SEARCH on boards, it is necessary to have a board set up with description lists giving adjacent symbols in all necessary directions. These data can be put in on cards, or they can be generated by use of the routine BDGEN.

There are two basic routines in BDGEN. The first assembles board symbols linked together in perpendicular directions. The second takes this structure and adds links in directions which are composed of moves in one or more of the basic perpendicular directions, such as diagonals.

The basic unit of data for a board description is a list of five symbols:

BD: CELL.TYPE, DIRECTION, PA, PB, NUMBER

The first symbol identifies the type of symbol to be assembled. This may be a described identifier, an identifier, a name of a list of cells, or another board generator input (in parentheses). The second symbol is the direction in which cells of the type of the first symbol are to be linked. If two symbols are to be linked together in direction D, with A the first instance generated and B the second instance generated, then A is the value of D on the description list of B. If a description list of opposite directions is provided, then links in the opposite direction will also be assigned.

The third and fourth symbols are relevant when two lists of symbols are to be linked. Linking two lists of symbols together means that each symbol from the first list is linked to the corresponding symbol in the second list. The correspondence is established by the PA and PB in the input. PA is the number of the symbol on the first list at which linking is to start; PB is the number of the symbol in the second list. Usually, either PA or PB or both are 1.

The fifth symbol on the input list is the number of things of the type of the first symbol that are to be linked together.

Some of the symbols can be eliminated. If the input list is three symbols long, the symbols will be CELL.TYPE, DIRECTION, and NUMBER. PA and PB are assumed to be 1. If the list is four symbols long, the symbols will be CELL.TYPE, DIRECTION, PA, and PB. NUMBER will be taken to be 1.

The input to the BDGEN routine is either a single basic form or a list of basic forms. The output of the routine is a list of the symbols that were generated, in order of generation. The following rules govern what the output is and which symbols are linked to which other symbols.

1. If the board description is a single list with CELL.TYPE a described identifier, the output is a list with the number of symbols NUMBER on it.

Each symbol has a copy of the description list of the described identifier as its description list initially. Each symbol is then linked with the next in the direction DIRECTION and the opposite of that direction.

2. If the board description is a single list structure containing another board description in CELL.TYPE, this board description is used to generate lists of cells as described in 1 above. The NUMBER indicates the number of lists generated. The generated lists are linked together in the direction specified. Each list is linked only to the list generated next. The output of the entire list structure is a list of all symbols generated.

3. If the board description is a list of board descriptions, they are processed sequentially. If the CELL.TYPE of the description is a list, this list is linked to the output list of the board list generated by the preceding board list and only that board list. Although each description links only with the output list of the previous description, the output for the entire list input is a list of all the symbols generated.

Example. Board Descriptions.

>BOARD: A, D2, 3
>A:/

Three symbols will be linked together in direction D2. If a description list of opposite directions is available, the opposite direction links will also be assigned. No symbol will have a description list containing anything but the linking information.

>BOARD: B, D2, 3
>B:/ OCCUPIED, BLACK

Three symbols will be generated and linked as outlined above. Each symbol will have the attribute-value pair OCCUPIED, BLACK on it, as well as the linking information.

>BOARD: (A, D2, 3), D1, 3

One list will be generated as in the first example. Then a second list will be generated and linked to the first in direction D1. A third list will be generated and linked to the second in direction D1. The output will be a list of the nine symbols generated, in the order that they were generated. To make an 8 × 8 Chess board, replace the 3's by 8's.

>BOARD: ((A,D2,3),D1,1),((A,D2,3),D1,1),((A,D2,3),D1,1)

This is equivalent to the structure immediately above.

>BOARD: ((A,D2,3),D1,1),((A,D2,3),D1,1,1,2),((A,D2,3),D1,1,1,2)

This is the same as the previous example except that list linking starts with the first symbol in the first of the two lists to be linked and the second symbol in the second of the two lists.

3.5.4 Card Ordering Routine. The principal means of checking relative card rank in GPL is the use of a list having the cards in descending or ascending order. This list may be supplied to the system on cards or may be generated by the primitive CDRANK.

The inputs to CDRANK are the lists describing card ranks and the names of the lists upon which the card symbols are to be placed. A list of cards in ascending order and a list of cards in descending order are generated.

The rank description input is a list with one or two symbols. The first symbol is the name of the "card rank list"; the second symbol is the name of a list on which the suits are ordered in descending order. The second symbol may be missing, in which case a standard ranking SPADE, HRT, DIAMD, CLUB will be used.

The form of the card rank list is either a list of numbers and symbols denoting individual card ranks (if card rank is independent of suit) or a list of such lists. Description lists are used to indicate which suits are to be used with which lists and whether the ranking is for trump or no-trump. TNT is the attribute for the values TRUMP (trump) or NTRMP (non-trump). Specific cards as well as ranks may appear on these lists.

Example. Input to CDRANK

        CDS: RNK, (SPADE, CLUB, DIAMD, HRT)
        RNK: K, Q, J, A, 2, 3, 4, 5, 6, 7, 8, 9, 10

3.5.5 Sequencer. All games except Solitaire require different players to make their plays in sequence. To make this easier to program, the primitive SEQCR is available to execute programs in sequence. SEQCR uses two system cells. The first cell PSEQ contains the name of a "sequence list," which describes the sequence of routines to be executed. The other cell, PNUM, contains an integer which specifies the number of routines in sequence to be executed.

The sequence list contains the names of sublists called "player lists." There is one player list for each player in the sequence. The symbols on the player list are the routines to be executed for the particular player. These routines will be executed in the order that they appear on the player list. The description list of the player list contains information for setting certain cells. The attributes on this description list are the names of the cells and the values are the symbols to be stored in those cells. The primitive SET is used to store the information in the cells before the routines are executed. The phrase "execute the player list" means to set the information into the cells as specified by the description list of the player list and then to execute the routines named on the player list.

The only input to SEQCR is the name of the first player list to be executed. SEQCR will execute player lists in the order in which they appear on the sequence list. PNUM specifies the number of player lists to be executed. If the end of the sequence list is reached before the specified number of player lists has been executed, the sequence is restarted at the first player list on the sequence list.

Example. SEQCR.

```
SEQ:  PLR1,PLR2,PLR3
PLR1: PLAY/HAND,HAND1
PLR2: PLAY/HAND,HAND2
PLR3: PLAY/HAND,HAND3
```

SEQ is a sequence list; PLR1, PLR2, PLR3 are player lists. PLR1, for example, specifies that the symbol HAND1 is stored in cell HAND, and then the routine PLAY is executed.

If PSEQ contains the symbol SEQ and PNUM contains the integer 3, then execution of the statement

```
SEQCR(PLR3);
```

will cause the player lists PLR3, PLR1, PLR2 to be executed in that order. SEQCR then quits.

SECTION 4
EXAMPLES OF GAMES

This section gives examples of games and how they are programmed for GGPP. Four games are used: Tic-Tac-Toe, Checkers, Eights, and Hearts. The rules for these games are taken from reference [5]. The primary purpose of these examples is to show how the games are programmed. Therefore, efficiency is sacrificed for clarity. Also, BDGEN and CDRANK are not used so the form of the data can be illustrated. The figures give annotated copies of the data, programs, and outputs for the games.

4.1 Tic-Tac-Toe

Tic-Tac-Toe is used because it is a simple game, yet it demonstrates the use of the routine SEARCH. The program is designed to play both sides of the game. The same strategy is used for both sides.

```
BOARD:  B5,B1,B3,B7,B9,B2,B4,B6,B8
DIRC:   D1,D2,D3,D4,D5,D6,D7,D8
B1:   /  D4,B2,D5,B5,D6,B4
B2:   /  D4,B3,D5,B6,D6,B5,D7,B4,D8,B1
B3:   /  D6,B6,D7,B5,D8,B2
B4:/  D2,B1,D3,B2,D4,B5,D5,B8,D6,B7
B5:/  D1,B1,D2,B2,D3,B3,D4,B6,D5,B9,D6,B8,D7,B7,D8,B4
B6:/  D1,B2,D2,B3,D6,B9,D7,B8,D8,B5
B7:/  D2,B4,D3,B5,D4,B8
B8;/  D1,B4,D2,B5,D3,B6,D4,B9,D8,B7
B9:/  D1,B5,D2,B6,D8,B8
OCC:    OCCUP, TYPE
OPOCC:  OCCUP, OTYPE
EMP:    OCCUP,NOTNG/OUTPT, PLACE  |EMPTY SQUARE
ROW3:   OCC,OCC,OCC
ROW2,1: OCC, EMP, OCC
ROW2.2: OCC,OCC,EMP
BLCK1:  OPOCC,OPOCC,EMP
BLCK2:  OPOCC,EMP,OPOCC
EMPT:   EMP
ROW:    DIRC,SAME, SAME
PMOVE:  PLACE, (CHNG, (OCCUP.TYPE)).
```

Figure 2a *TTT data description*

4.1.1 Data Description. The data used in Tic-Tac-Toe (hereafter abbreviated TTT) are shown in Figure 2a. These data are in two parts: the information about the board, and the patterns and directions needed to describe the moves and goals of the game.

Identifier BOARD is the name of the list of the cells on the board. These cells (B1–B9) have the description lists indicated. These description lists give the adjacent cell information needed by SEARCH. For comparison, the board cell identification and direction meanings are indicated in the drawings below. The list DIRC is the list of all directions used. It is used in the input to SEARCH.

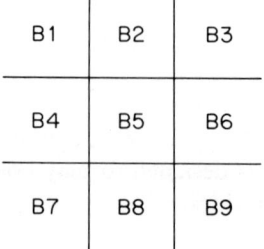
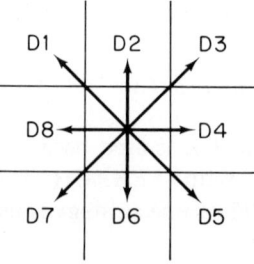

Other data supplied to the program are the CTU's, patterns, and the direction lists needed for the searching operations. OCC, OPOCC, EMP are CTU's; ROW3, ROW2.1, ROW2.2, BLCK1, BLCK2, and EMPT are patterns; ROW is a direction list; and PMOVE is a move list.

The CTU OCC is used to test whether the cell is occupied. The attribute for occupation is OCCUP. The value of OCCUP on the CTU is TYPE. When the CTU is actually used, the cell TYPE will contain either an X or an O, and hence X or O will be the value that the CTU will test for. Thus, this CTU can be used for either side in the game. The CTU OPOCC is used to test whether a cell is occupied by the opponent. The cell OTYPE will contain an X if TYPE contains an O or vice versa. The CTU EMP is used to test whether a cell is not occupied. Notice that none of the board cells B1–B9, as loaded, are occupied (that is, none of them have the attribute OCCUP on them). This means that the CTU EMP will match any of these cells until they are changed.

Notice that the CTU EMP has a description list. The attribute OUTPT appears on this list with the value PLACE. This means that, whenever a pattern match is found, the name of the cell that matched EMP will be on the output description list of the pattern recognizer routine. The cell name will appear as the value of the attribute PLACE.

These CTU's are used in the patterns. The direction list ROW is used for all of these patterns except EMPT, where no direction list is needed because the pattern is only one CTU long.

Pattern ROW3 checks for three of the same symbols in a row. This is the goal of the game. Pattern ROW3 will have no output except that the number of cells in the match was three, but since it tests for the presence of the goal of the game, no changes on the board are required if the pattern is found.

Patterns ROW2.1 and ROW2.2 test for the conditions of two symbols of the same kind and a blank in a row. Two patterns are necessary because the pattern may occur in two forms: (X,X,blank) or (X,blank,X). It is not necessary to have a pattern for (blank,X,X) because, since all directions are used, this pattern will be picked up as a backwards occurrence of (X, X,blank). The output from either of these patterns, if a match is found, is a description list containing the name of the empty cell as the value of the attribute PLACE. This is used by the program to play the appropriate symbol on the empty cell.

Patterns BLCK1 and BLCK2 test for the same conditions as ROW2.1 and ROW2.2 except that they look for the pattern in the opponent's pieces. Again, the output description list contains the empty cell so that it can be played on to block the opponent.

The pattern EMPT is used to find any empty cell. The output description list will contain the name of the empty cell found. There will be one output description list for each empty cell found.

```
INITIAL:  SET(GLOBL,NO); XPLAY
XPLAY:    SET(TYPE,X,OTYPE,O);
          PLAY → TWIN ;OPLAY
          DRAW;
OPLAY:    SET(TYPE,O,OTYPE,X);
          PLAY → TWIN ;XPLAY
          DRAW;
PLAY:     SEARCH(BOARD,ROW2.1,ROW,ROW2.2,ROW) →
              MOVE(BOARD,OUTF,PMOVE); DONE
          SEARCH(BOARD,BLCK1,ROW,BLCK2,ROW) →
              MOVE(BOARD,OUTF,PMOVE) ;DONE
          SEARCH(BOARD,EMPT) → MOVE(BOARD,OUTF,PMOVE); DONE
TWIN:     SEARCH(BOARD,ROW3,ROW) → PRTSYM(CONT(TYPE)))WIN
START: INITIAL
```

Figure 2b TTT program

4.1.2 Program. The program for playing TTT is shown in Figure 2b. The program that does the actual playing is PLAY. XPLAY and OPLAY set up the conditions for the different sides. TWIN is used to test to see if the game is over. INITIAL is used to turn off the initial cell reduction method in SEARCH and start the program going.

The sequence of operations in PLAY is as follows. The routine first looks for an opportunity to win by searching for an instance of pattern ROW2.1 or ROW2.2. If this exists, it plays in the empty cell, and exits. The test cell is $+$ upon exit because the MOVE primitive set it $+$. If the patterns for a win do not exist, the program then looks for an opportunity to block the opponent. If this exists, the play is made and the routine again exits with the test cell $+$. If this opportunity to block does not exist, the routine looks for an empty cell. If there are any, a play is made in the first such empty cell, and the routine exits with the test cell $+$. If there are no empty cells, the routine exits with the test cell $-$, because SEARCH set it $-$.

The routine PLAY is used by both XPLAY and OPLAY. The operation of these two routines is the same except that one plays X and one plays O, so only XPLAY will be described. The first operation of XPLAY is to set TYPE to X and OTYPE to O. It then executes PLAY. PLAY is the routine in a conditional segment, so the next step depends upon how PLAY set the test cell. If the test cell is $+$, TWIN is executed. TWIN tests to see if a winning pattern exists. If it does, TWIN will stop the program by executing the routine WIN. If the winning pattern does not exist, control will return to XPLAY. At this point, XPLAY specifies that control is to go to OPLAY, because, although a move was made, X has not yet won.

If PLAY has set the test cell $-$, the routine DRAW is executed. This routine stops the program. The program is stopped because PLAY was unable to find any place to play.

4.1.3 Strategy in TTT. The TTT program described here contains a fair amount of strategy. The rules of the game actually only specify that a marker must be placed on an empty square. This is expressed by the third line of the PLAY subroutine. The rest of the PLAY program is strategy.

Strategy is also contained in the ordering of the cells on the list BOARD. The SEARCH primitive outputs are in the order that the matches were found. The PLAY routine specifies that the first empty cell found by SEARCH is to be used when none of the other patterns match. The ordering of the cells on the BOARD list means that, in the absence of forced moves, the center cell will be played on first, then the corner cells. This is good defensive TTT strategy.

4.1.4 Results of the TTT Program. Figure 2c shows the output from a run of the TTT program. Each list printed shows the result of a move. As can be seen, the outcome was a draw, as would be expected with both players using the same defensive strategy.

4.2 Checkers

In form, Checkers is much like TTT. The real difference is that there are more board squares, more possible moves, and a different goal structure.

4.2.1 Data Structure. Figure 3a shows the data for Checkers, and shows the numbering of the board squares and the directions. The form of the data is like that of TTT, only there are more of them. They will therefore be described briefly.

List BOARD is again the list of board squares. The occupation of squares is described by two attribute-value pairs representing the type of the piece (MAN or KING) and the color of the piece (RED or BLACK). The initial position is specified in the input. This board structure could have been generated by BDGEN.

The CTU's are OPCE, EMPT, MYMAN, MYKNG, RDKNG and BLKNG. All of these except RDKNG and BLKNG are used in searching for moves. RDKNG and BLKNG are used when looking for the situation where a MAN becomes a KING.

The patterns MCAP and KCAP test for situations where a capture by a MAN or a KING is possible, respectively. Patterns MMVE and KMVE search for situations where a move by a MAN or a KING, respectively, is possible. KRED and KBLK are the patterns for making a MAN into a KING.

	B5		B7		B9
	OCCUP		OCCUP		OCCUP
	X		O		X
	D1		D2		D1
	B1		B4		B5
	D2		D3		D2
	B2		B5		B6
	D3		D4		D8
	B3		B8		B8
	D4		B4		B2
	B6		OCCUP		OCCUP
	D5		X		O
	B9		D2		D4
	D6		B1		B3
	B8		D3		D5
	D7		B2		B6
	B7		D4		D6
	D8		B5		B5
	B4		D5		D7
B1			B8		B4
	OCCUP		D6		D8
	O		B7		B1
	D4		B6		B8
	B2		OCCUP		OCCUP
	D5		O		X
	B5		D1		D1
	D6		B2		B4
	B4		D2		D2
B3			B3		B5
	OCCUP		D6		D3
	X		B9		B6
	D6		D7		D4
	B6		B8		B9
	D7		D8		D8
	B5		B5		B7
	D8				DRAW
	B2				

Figure 2c Output from the TTT program

DRED and DBLK are direction lists used for moves by pieces of type MAN. ALDIR is used for KING moves.

REMVE is a change list calling for the deletion of whatever is on the board square. This change list is used in the move lists MVMAN and MVKNG which are used for MAN moves and KING moves respectively. The other move list is MKKNG which is used to make a KING.

4.2.2 Program. Figure 3b shows the program used to play Checkers. PLAY is the program that uses the rules of the game. Possible moves are searched for in the following sequence: (a) capture of an opponent piece (or many of them) by a MAN; (b) capture of an opponent piece (or many of them) by a KING; (c) any move by a MAN; and (d) any move by a KING. Since capture moves are found first, this sequence satisfies the rule that captures be made whenever possible.

```
  BOARD:   B1,B2,B3,B4,B6,B5,B7,B8,B9,B10,B11,B12,B13,B14,B15,B16,B17,
C B18,B19,B20,B21,B22,B23,B24,B25,B26,B27,B28,B29,B30,B31,B32
  B1 :/    D4,B6,D6,B5,D15,D15,COLOR,BLACK,TYPE,MAN
  B2 :/    D4,B7,D6,B6,D15,D15,COLOR,BLACK,TYPE,MAN
  B3 :/    D4,B8,D6,B7,D15,D15,COLOR,BLACK,TYPE,MAN
  B4 :/    D6,B8,D15,D15,COLOR,BLACK,TYPE,MAN
  B5 :/    D2,B1,D4,B9,COLOR,BLACK,TYPE,MAN
  B6 :/    D2,B2,D4,B10,D6,B9,D8,B1,COLOR,BLACK,TYPE,MAN
  B7 :/    D2,B3,D4,B11,D6,B10,D8,B2,COLOR,BLACK,TYPE,MAN
  B8 :/    D2,B4,D4,B12,D6,B11,D8,B3,COLOR,BLACK,TYPE,MAN
  B9 :/    D2,B6,D4,B14,D6,B13,D8,B5,COLOR,BLACK,TYPE,MAN
  B10:/    D2,B7,D4,B15,D6,B14,D8,B6,COLOR,BLACK,TYPE,MAN
  B11:/    D2,B8,D4,B16,D6,B15,D8,B7,COLOR,BLACK,TYPE,MAN
  B12:/    D6,B16,D8,B8,COLOR,BLACK,TYPE,MAN
  B13:/    D2,B9,D4,B17
  B14:/    D2,B16,D4,B18,D6,B17,D8,B9
  B15:/    D2,B11,D4,B19,D6,B18,D8,B10
  B16:/    D2,B12,D4,B20,D6,B19,D8,B11
  B17:/    D2,B14,D4,B22,D6,B21,D8,B13
  B18:/    D2,B15,D4,B23,D6,B22,D8,B14
  B19:/    D2,B16,D4,B24,D6,B23,D8,B15
  B20:/    D6,B24,D8,B16
  B21:/    D2,B17,D4,B25,COLOR,RED,TYPE,MAN
  B22:/    D2,B18,D4,B26,D6,B25,D8,B17,COLOR,RED,TYPE,MAN
  B23:/    D2,B19,D4,B27,D6,B26,D8,B18,COLOR,RED,TYPE,MAN
  B24:/    D2,B20,D4,B28,D6,B27,D8,B19,COLOR,RED,TYPE,MAN
  B25:/    D2,B22,D4,B30,D6,B29,D8,B21,COLOR,RED,TYPE,MAN
```

Figure 3a Checkers data

```
B26:/   D2,B23,D4,B31,D6,B30,D8,B22,COLOR,RED, TYPE,MAN
B27:/   D2,B24,D4,B32,D6,B31,D8,B23,COLOR,RED,TYPE,MAN
B28:/   D6,B32,D8,B24,COLOR,RED,TYPE,MAN
B29:/   D2,B25,D16,D16,COLOR,RED,TYPE,MAN
B30:/   D2,B26,D8,B25,D16,D16,COLOR,RED,TYPE,MAN
B31:/   D2,B27,D8,B26,D16,D16,COLOR,RED,TYPE,MAN
B32:/   D2,B28,D8,B27,D16,D16,COLOR,RED,TYPE,MAN
OPCE:   COLOR,OSIDE  /  OUTPT,CAPT
EMPT:   COLOR,NOTNG,TYPE,NOTNG/  OUTPT,FINAL
MYMAN:  COLOR,MSIDE,TYPE,MAN/  OUTPT,INIT
MYKNG:  COLOR,MSIDE,TYPE,KING/  OUTPT,INIT
RDKNG:  COLOR,RED,TYPE,MAN,D15,D15,/  OUTPT,KSQR
BLKNG:  COLOR,BLACK,TYPE,MAN,D16,D16/  OUTPT,KSQR
ALDIR:  D2,D4,D6,D8
OPDIR:  /D2,D6,D4,D8,D6,D2,D8,D2
DRED:   REP,(D2,D8),SAME
DBLK:   REP,(D4,D6),SAME
DKNG:   ALDIR,SAME,REP,EXCP,SAME
REMVE:  CHNG,(COLOR,NOTNG,TYPE,NOTNG)
MVMAN:  INIT,REMVE,CAPT,REMVE,FINAL(CHNG,(COLOR,MSIDE,TYPE,MAN))
MVKNG:  INIT,REMVE,CAPT,REMVE,FINAL,(CHNG,(COLOR,MSIDE,TYPE,KING))
MKKNG:  KSQR,(CHNG,(TYPE,KING))
MCAP:   MYMAN,REP,OPCE,EMPT
KCAP:   MYKNG,REP,OPCE,EMPT
KRED:   RDKNG
KBLK:   BLKNG
MMVE:   MYMAN,EMPT
KMVE:   MYKNG,EMPT
```

Figure 3a (*cont.*)

To find all legal moves from a given position, it is only necessary to input both capture patterns to SEARCH in one statement and both non-capture patterns in the next statement. The operational segments of each statement could specify the routine to operate on these legal moves. In this way, all capture moves would be found. If there were no capture moves, all non-capture moves would be found.

Other routines do the following: REDPL and BLKPL play the two different sides of the game. They use PLAY and RDK or BK. The game terminates if PLAY cannot find a move. RDK and BK take care of making kings when possible.

4.2.3 *Results of the Checker Program.* Figure 3c shows the output, up to the first capture move, of the Checker program. Each move requires two attribute-value changes for each board cell and these are shown separately.

```
PLAY:   SEARCH(BOARD,MCAP,CONT(DIR)) → MOVE(BOARD,LONG1,MVMAN);DONE
        SEARCH(BOARD,KCAP,DKNG) → MOVE(BOARD,LONG1,MVKNG);  DONE
        SEARCH(BOARD,MMVE,CONT(DIR)) → MOVE(BOARD,OUTF,MVMAN); DONE
        SEARCH(BOARD,KMVE,DKNG) → MOVE(BOARD,OUTF,MVKNG);  DONE
REDPL:  SET(MSIDE,RED,OSIDE,BLACK,DIR,DRED,GLOBL,NO);
        PLAY → PAGE;  RDK
        PRTSYM(CONT(MSIDE));LOSE
RDK:    SEARCH(BOARD,KRED) → MOVE(BOARD,OUTF,MKNG);BLKPL
        ;BLKPL
BLKPL:  SET(MSIDE,BLACK,OSIDE,RED,DIR,DBLK);
        PLAY → PAGE;  BK
        PRTSYM(CONT(MSIDE));  LOSE
BK:     SEARCH(BOARD,KBLK)→MOVE(BOARD,OUTF,MKNG);REDPL
        ;REDPL
START:  REDPL
```

Figure 3b Checkers program

The program is written to take the first legal move it finds. This makes it very sensitive to the order of the cells on the list BOARD. As presently written, the program when playing RED tends to move a piece forward until it is captured. When playing BLACK, the program tends to try to move rear pieces forward.

4.3 Eights

Eights is a card game. The rules for the game are shown in Figure 4a. These rules have been divided into sections but otherwise have been copied directly from reference [5]. The program and data for playing Eights are shown in Figure 4b. These too have been divided into sections but otherwise have been taken from the assembly listing. Each section of Figure 4b is roughly the GGPP form of the statements of the same numbered section of Figure 4a. The numbered paragraphs below also refer to these sections.

1. The number of players is not explicitly given to the program. The information is contained in the sequence list SEQ which has only two player lists.

2. In Hoyle, only a brief description of the cards is needed because these are standard items. For GGPP, a complete description is needed, as shown. This description can be assembled into the system and need not be supplied in the program. It is shown here to demonstrate what it looks like.

3. This program is given the cards already dealt out. HAND1 is one hand, HAND2 is the other. STOCK is the stock and DISCRD is the starter.

[1]	[2]	[2] (cont.)
B21	B9	COLOR
D2	D2	BLACK
B17	B6	D2
D4	D4	B10
B25	B14	D4
COLOR	D6	B18
NOTNG	B13	D6
TYPE	B5	B17
MAN	D8	D8
B21	COLOR	B9
D2	NOTNG	
B17	TYPE	
D4	MAN	
B25	B9	
COLOR	D2	
NOTNG	B6	
TYPE	D4	
NOTNG	B14	
B17	D6	
COLOR	B13	
RED	D8	
D2	B5	
B14	COLOR	
D4	NOTNG	
B22	TYPE	
D6	NOTNG	
B21	B14	
D8	COLOR	
B13	BLACK	
B17	D2	
TYPE	B10	
MAN	D4	
COLOR	B18	
RED	D6	
D2	B17	
B14	D8	
D4	B9	
B22	B14	
D6	TYPE	
B21	MAN	
D8	(cont.)	
B13		

Figure 3c Trace of Checkers program: [1] first move by RED; [2] first move by BLACK; [3] second move by RED; [4] second move by BLACK; [5] capture move by RED

[3]	[4]	[4] (cont.)
B17	B6	D4
TYPE	D2	B14
MAN	B2	D6
COLOR	D4	B13
NOTNG	B10	D8
D2	D6	B5
B14	B9	COLOR
D4	D8	BLACK
B22	B1	TYPE
D6	COLOR	MAN
B21	NOTNG	
D8	TYPE	
B13	MAN	
B17	B6	
TYPE	D2	
NOTNG	B2	
COLOR	D4	
NOTNG	B10	
D2	D6	
B14	B9	
D4	D8	
B22	B1	
D6	COLOR	
B21	NOTNG	
D8	TYPE	
B13	NOTNG	
B13	B9	
COLOR	D2	
RED	B6	
D2	D4	
B9	B14	
D4	D6	
B17	B13	
B13	D8	
TYPE	B5	
MAN	COLOR	
COLOR	BLACK	
RED	TYPE	
D2	NOTNG	
B9	B9	
D4	D2	
B17	B6	
	(cont.)	

Figure 3c (cont.)

[5]	[5] (cont.)	[5] (cont.)
B13		
TYPE	D6	D4
MAN	B13	B10
COLOR	D8	D6
NOTNG	B5	B9
D2	COLOR	D8
B9	NOTNG	B1
D4	TYPE	COLOR
B17	MAN	RED
B13	B9	TYPE
TYPE	D2	NOTNG
NOTNG	B6	B6
COLOR	D4	D2
NOTNG	B14	B2
D2	D6	D4
B9	B13	B10
D4	D8	D6
B17	B5	B9
B9	COLOR	D8
D2	NOTNG	B1
B6	TYPE	COLOR
D4	NOTNG	RED
B14	B6	TYPE
(cont.)	D2	MAN
	B2	
	(cont.)	

Figure 3c *(cont.)*

4. The play sequence is described by the sequence list SEQ.

5. PLAY is the routine which actually plays the game. AVMTCH is a primitive that finds all symbols on a list that have the same values for an attribute as on a test symbol. This routine is used to find cards of the same rank or suit as the top of the starter pile. Finally, the function designator FIND(DISCRD, 1) is used to get the top of the starter pile.

6. TWIN is used to test for completion of the game. As played here, the game is won by the player that plays his last card. TWIN counts the number of symbol 5 on the hand list. If this count is equal to zero, the game is over.

7. Section 7 does not appear in Figure 4a. It essentially tells the computer to go play the game. This instruction is not usually needed when dealing with people. It should be noted here that PNUM is not set. PNUM is ini-

tialized by the system to zero. This means that play will cycle indefinitely. TWIN stops the program when one player has won.

4.3.1 *Results of the Program.* Figure 4c shows some of the first moves of the program. It obviously plays legally.

4.4 Hearts

This section describes a program to play one hand of Hearts. This game differs from Eights in that it is a "trick winning" or more exactly "trick losing" game. The object of the game is to avoid taking any tricks with hearts in them or with the Queen of Spades. A player must follow suit when able to.

The strategy used in the program is to take no tricks if possible. If

---

EIGHTS

This game is also called CRAZY EIGHTS or SWEDISH RUMMY. It is identical with a game called CRAZY JACKS except that in the latter jacks are the wild cards. Whereas most of the Stops games are best for five or more players Eights is best for two.
(1) PLAYERS. From two to seven.
(2) CARDS. A regular pack of 52, with five or fewer players. With more, use two packs shuffled together.
(3) THE DEAL. With two players, each receives seven cards, dealt one at a time. With more than two, each receives five cards. The rest of the pack is placed face down in the center of the table to form the *stock*. Its top card is turned face up beside it as the *starter*.
(4) THE PLAY. The turn to play rotates to the left (clockwise), beginning with the opponent at left of the dealer.
(5) A play consists of placing one card face up on the pile begun by the starter. Each card played must match the previous play in either suit or rank: on the ♡6 any heart or any six may be played. If unable to play in turn, a player must draw cards from the top of the stock and add them to his hand until able to play. After the stock is exhausted, a player unable to play must pass. A player may draw from the stock even when he has a playable card.
EIGHTS. The eights are wild. An eight may be played upon any preceding card, regardless of its suit or rank. The owner of the eight must specify a suit (not necessarily its own) which the eight calls for, and the next player must follow with that suit or with another eight.
(6) SCORING. Play ends when any player gets rid of the last card in his hand. He scores the total of the cards remaining in all other hands: 50 for each eight, 1 for each ace, 10 for each face card, the index value for each other card. Score is kept on paper. Each deal may be settled as a separate game, but when two play, it is usual to award the game to the one who first reaches 100 points or more.

Figure 4a Rules for Eights

(2)   DECK: S1,S2,S3,S4,S5,S6,S7,S8,S9,S10,SJ,SQ,SK,
         C H1,H2,H3,H4,H5,H6,H7,H8,H9,H10,HJ,HQ,HK,
         C D1,D2,D3,D4,D5,D6,D7,D8,D9,D10,DJ,DQ,DK,
         C C1,C2,C3,C4,C5,C6,C7,C8,C9,C10,CJ,CQ,CK
           S1:/   SUIT,SPADE,RANK,1
           S2:/   SUIT,SPADE,RANK,2
           S3:/   SUIT,SPADE,RANK,3
           S4:/   SUIT,SPADE,RANK,4
           S5:/   SUIT,SPADE,RANK,5
           S6:/   SUIT,SPADE,RANK,6
           S7:/   SUIT,SPADE,RANK,7
           S8:/   SUIT,SPADE,RANK,8
           S9:/   SUIT,SPADE,RANK,9
           S10:/   SUIT,SPADE,RANK,10
           SJ:/   SUIT,SPADE,RANK,J
           SQ:/   SUIT,SPADE,RANK,Q
           SK:/   SUIT,SPADE,RANK,K
           H1:/   SUIT,HRT,RANK,1
           H2:/   SUIT,HRT,RANK,2
           H3:/   SUIT,HRT,RANK,3
           H4:/   SUIT,HRT,RANK,4
           H5:/   SUIT,HRT,RANK,5
           H6:/   SUIT,HRT,RANK,6
           H7:/   SUIT,HRT,RANK,7
           H8:/   SUIT,HRT,RANK,8
           H9:/   SUIT,HRT,RANK,9
           H10:/   SUIT,HRT,RANK,10
           HJ:/   SUIT,HRT,RANK,J
           HQ:/   SUIT,HRT,RANK,Q
           HK:/   SUIT,HRT,RANK,K
           D1:/   SUIT,DIAMD,RANK,1
           D2:/   SUIT,DIAMD,RANK,2
           D3:/   SUIT,DIAMD,RANK,3
           D4:/   SUIT,DIAMD,RANK,4
           D5:/   SUIT,DIAMD,RANK,5
           D6:/   SUIT,DIAMD,RANK,6
           D7:/   SUIT,DIAMD,RANK,7
           D8:/   SUIT,DIAMD,RANK,8
           D9:/   SUIT,DIAMD,RANK,9
           D10:/   SUIT,DIAMD,RANK,10
           DJ:/   SUIT,DIAMD,RANK,J
           DQ:/   SUIT,DIAMD,RANK,Q
           DK:/   SUIT,DIAMD,RANK,K

Figure 4b Program and data for Eights

```
          C1 :/    SUIT,CLUB,RANK,1
          C2 :/    SUIT,CLUB,RANK,2
          C3 :/    SUIT,CLUB,RANK,3
          C4 :/    SUIT,CLUB,RANK,4
          C5 :/    SUIT,CLUB,RANK,5
          C6 :/    SUIT,CLUB,RANK,6
          C7 :/    SUIT,CLUB,RANK,7
          C8 :/    SUIT,CLUB,RANK,8
          C9 :/    SUIT,CLUB,RANK,9
          C10 :/   SUIT,CLUB,RANK,10
          CJ :/    SUIT,CLUB,RANK,J
          CQ :/    SUIT,CLUB,RANK,Q
          CK :/    SUIT,CLUB,RANK,K
(3)       HAND1 :C6,H7,C4,D4,D7,S7,C9
          HAND2 :S6,H5,SK,H3,S10,C10,CJ
          DISCRD:  S1
          STOCK:   H4,C8,H10,SJ,HK,S2,D9,H6,S4,DK,H8,S5,S8,D6,C1,DQ,D1,C3,D10,
       C  C7,D3,CK,D5,SQ,CQ,HQ,HJ,H9,S3,DJ,D2,S9,H1,C5,H2,C2,D8
(5)       PLAY:  AVMTCH(CONT(HAND),FIND(DISCRD,1),SUIT) →
       C              LSTCHG(CONT(HAND),DISCRD,OUTF) ;TWIN
                 AVMTCH(CONT(HAND),FIND(DISCRD,1),RANK) →
       C              LSTCHG(CONT(HAND),DISCRD,OUTF) ;TWIN
                 AVMTCH(CONT(HAND),S8,RANK) →
       C              LSTCHG(CONT(HAND),DISCRD,OUTF) ;TWIN
                 TGTR(CNTMS(CONT(HAND)),0) →
                      LSTCHG(STOCK,CONT(HAND)) ; PLAY
(6)       TWIN :TEQU(0,CNTMS(CONT(HAND)))→PRTOUT;  DONE
                 PAGE;  DONE
          PRTOUT:PRTSYM(CONT(HAND));
                 WIN;
(4)       SEQ:  PLR1,PLR2
          PLR1:  PLAY/HAND,HAND1
          PLR2:  PLAY/HAND,HAND2
(7)       EIGHTS: SET(PSEQ,SEQ);
                  SEQCR(PLR1);
          START:  EIGHTS
```

Figure 4b (*cont.*)

HAND1			HAND2	
C6			H5	
	SUIT			SUIT
	CLUB			HRT
	RANK			RANK
	6			5
H7			SK	
	SUIT			SUIT
	HRT			SPADE
	RANK			RANK
	7			K
C4			H3	
	SUIT			SUIT
	CLUB			HRT
	RANK			RANK
	4			3
D4			S10	
	SUIT			SUIT
	DIAMD			SPADE
	RANK			RANK
	4			10
D7			C10	
	SUIT			SUIT
	DIAMD			CLUB
	RANK			RANK
	7			10
C9			CJ	
				SUIT
	CLUB			CLUB
	RANK			RANK
	9			J
ISCRD			ISCRD	
S7			S6	
	SUIT			SUIT
	SPADE			SPADE
	RANK			RANK
	7			6
S1			S7	
	SUIT			SUIT
	SPADE			SPADE
	RANK			RANK
	1			7
	(A)		S1	
				SUIT
				SPADE
				RANK
				1
				(B)

Figure 4c Traces of Eights program: (A) play from HAND1; (B) play from HAND2.

DLIST:	TOP,S1,H1,D1,C1,SK,HK,DK,CK,SQ,HQ,DQ,CQ,SJ,HJ,DJ,CJ,S10,
C	H10,D10,C10,S9,H9,D9,C9,S8,H8,D8,C8,S7,H7,D7,C7,S6,H6,D6,C6,
C	S5,H5,D5,C5,S4,H4,D4,C4,S3,H3,D3,C3,S2,H2,D2,C2

[Remainder of data lists same as in Figure 4b.]

Figure 5a Data for Hearts

it is necessary to play a card higher than the highest one currently in the trick, the program will play the lowest card possible. If void in the suit led, the program plays the highest card in its hand.

4.4.1 Data. The data, shown in Figure 5a, are the same as for Eights except for the list DLIST. This list has the cards ranked in descending order. The method used in GGPP to determine relative ranks of cards is to see if one card follows another on a list such as DLIST. In this case, we are interested in finding cards that do not outrank a given card, so a list of cards in descending order is used.

Another input datum is the hand used by the program. All the cards in this game are dealt out, so there is no stock.

4.4.2 Program. Figure 5b shows the program used in playing the hand of Hearts. The program executed to play the hand is PLAY. The first thing that PLAY does is to check to see if a lead is called for. It does this by checking the contents of cell TLD, which will have been set YES if the program is

```
     PLAY:  EQUAL(CONT(TLD),YES);  LEAD
            AVMTCH(HAND,CONT(HIGH),SUIT) →
  C            STORB(SSUIT,OUTA);  SS
            FOLLOW(TOP,DLIST,HAND) →
  C            LSTCHG(HAND,TRICK,OUTF);DONE
     SS:    FOLLOW(CONT(HIGH),DLIST,SSUIT) →
  C            LSTCHG(HAND,TRICK,OUTF);  OUT
            FOLLOW(TOP,DLIST,SSUIT) →
  C            SET(HIGH,OUTL);
            LSTCHG(HAND,TRICK,CONT(HIGH));  OUT
     OUT:   INALL(SSUIT);  DONE
     LEAD:  FOLLOW(TOP,DLIST,HAND) →
  C            SET(LED,OUTL);
            LSTCHG(HAND,TRICK,CONT(LED));
            SET(HIGH,CONT(LED));
            SET(TLD,NO);
```

Figure 5b Program for Hearts

to lead. If a lead is called for, the lowest card in the hand is led by the routine LEAD. This card is stored in cell LED, the card led; cell HIGH, the highest card of the same suit currently in the trick; and is also placed on the list TRICK, which is the list of cards played to the current trick. Then the cell TLD is set to NO, indicating that a card has been led.

If the program is not supposed to lead, it finds all cards of the same suit as the lead in its hand. If none, it plays the highest card it has, regardless of suit.

If the program has cards of the same suit as that led, these are stored on list SSUIT. The program then checks to see if any of these cards are lower than the highest card of the trick that is of the same suit as the card led. If it has one or more "losers", it plays the highest of them. If not, it plays the lowest of the cards on the list SSUIT. If forced to play a card that could capture the trick, this card is also stored in the cell HIGH. This relieves the executive, which executed the program for this hand, from having to determine which card is the highest. The program exits through the routine OUT which simply clears the list SSUIT to get ready for the next trick.

4.4.3 Results of the Program. Figure 5c shows some of the cases on which the program has been run. It plays by the strategy described, which is a fair strategy, but not an excellent one. In particular, it does not get rid of the Queen of Spades as soon as possible.

Hand 1: SK,S1,C2,C4,CJ,H5,D4,D5,D8,D7
Card Led: C8
Play: C4

Hand 2: SK,S1,C2,C4,CJ,H5,D4,D5,D8,D7
Program to Lead
Play: C2

Hand 3: SK,S1,S2,S4,SJ,H5,D4,D5,D8,D7
Card Led: C8
Play: S1

Hand 4: S5,S1,C10,CQ,CJ,H5,D4,D5,D8,D7
Card Led: C8
Play: C10

Figure 5c Hearts play

4.5 Conclusions

This section has given examples of some of the games that can be played with GGPP. By selecting games of different natures, we have tried to give an indication of the generality of GGPP. These examples also show some of the things that are wrong with GGPP. Consideration of the deficiencies of GGPP is taken up in Section 5.

SECTION 5
INTERNAL REPRESENTATION

The previous sections have discussed and demonstrated the various forms in which the objects, rules, and goals of a game are represented in GGPP. These forms constitute the internal representation of the game on the computer. This internal representation is generated from the external representation, which is given in Hoyle. The purpose of this section is to compare the external and internal representations and show that the internal representation used is a good one.

5.1 Specifications for an Internal Representation

In order to solve the problems of generality and learning in game playing, GGPP must have certain characteristics inherent in its internal representation. These characteristics form a framework into which the internal representation must fit.

5.1.1 Generality. The representation must allow the specification of a large number of games. The external representation does this quite well.

5.1.2 Human Usability. The internal representation must be similar to the external representation. In GGPP, the user must translate from the external representation to the internal representation. The closer the two representations, the easier it is to perform the translation. If a translator program were provided, the job is still easier if the two representations are similar.

5.1.3 Microscopic Machine Usability. The elements of the internal representation should be in a form that is easily used and manipulated by the computer. If the elements of the internal representation are close to the data forms the machine was designed to manipulate, the action routines needed by the system will be easier to write and will be more efficient.

5.1.4 Similarities. The internal representation should reflect the various similarities that occur among games as presented in the external representation. This is especially important for learning and generalizing, although it also simplifies writing primitive routines.

5.1.5 Macroscopic Machine Usability. The internal representation should be organized so that information needed by other routines such as learning and generalizing routines is easily available.

In general, the microscopic machine usability requirement is incompatible with the others. Representations that are general and readable are not usually ones that are easily processed by the commands that are in the repertoire of the average computer. Therefore, some compromise must usually be made between machine efficiency and the other requirements.

5.2 Evaluation of the Internal Representation

This section discusses the organization of the internal representation and its implementation. In general, the organization and implementation of the internal representation reflect all conditions except microscopic machine usability. To compensate for this, certain of the primitive routines have methods built into them to make some operations more efficient.

5.2.1 Organization. The internal representation of a game is a model of the situation. All of the objects, such as pieces, boards, cards, etc. are represented in the computer by name. The representation of an object contains a description of all of the necessary features of that object. The rules simply define the allowed operations on these objects.

This is a good general organization for game playing simply because game playing situations are presented in these terms. This makes translation easy, allows many games to be represented, reflects the similarities of games, and makes it easy to get necessary information about the progress of a game from the representation.

5.2.2 Implementation. The implementation of this organization must allow the largest possible number of different situations to be modeled. This requires (a) a general ability to describe objects and properties of objects, and (b) a general ability to describe operations on objects. The various phases of the implementation are discussed below.

5.2.2.1 LIST STRUCTURES. The list structure method of organizing data is used for the following reasons.

1. List structures allow primitive routines to operate without explicit knowledge of the number of objects used in a game. For instance, it is not necessary to specify the number of cards in a hand or the size of a board. This simplifies the primitive routines.

2. List structures allow generalization from other games to be made without knowledge of the number of objects involved in the game (see Section 6).

3. List structures make it easy to change various parts of the internal representation in the course of playing a game without reorganizing the memory or wasting space.

4. List structures allow special conditions that apply to only a few of the objects to be specified without requiring a specification on all objects. It is not necessary to specify that a particular cell does not have a property, nor is it necessary to leave space for conditions that may be needed later.

5. List structures make tree searching easier (see Section 6).

Once the decision to use list structures is made, it is then important to decide how to use them. There are two choices: (a) use a language designed to use list structures such as LISP or IPL-V; or (b) imbed list-structure-processing subroutines in another language such as ALGOL. Since IPL-V was available, it was used. This affects many of the other choices available in designing the internal representation.

5.2.2.2 DESCRIPTION LISTS. Description lists are used to assign properties to symbols because primitive operations for working with description lists are available in IPL-V. Since the search operations needed for description lists are in IPL-V primitives, they operate faster than equivalent operations written in IPL-V.

5.2.2.3 REPRESENTATION OF RULES. Rules specify actions to be performed. Therefore, the internal representation of a rule must contain descriptions of operations on data. There is a small number of primitive operations that are common to all games. Thus the rules of a game may be represented as a sequence of these primitive operations with the appropriate inputs. An interpreter is used to convert this statement of a rule to the actions it specifies.

The form of a rule is the "if-then" statement. This is used because it is a convenient way to describe a rule and because it eliminates the need for explicit statements of sequences.

5.2.2.4 THE IMPLEMENTATION OF THE GGPP INTERPRETER. There are a number of facets of the implementation of the GGPP interpreter that deserve consideration. First, the interpreter is written in IPL-V because this language is used for the list structures. This means that the internal form of a statement is a list structure because list structures and symbols are the only data forms that IPL-V will handle. Other features of the interpreter are also conditioned by the use of IPL-V. Consideration of some of the other features of the interpreter follows.

5.2.2.4.1 *Handling of Inputs*. Inputs to routines are assembled in a pushdown stack for three reasons. First, the use of a pushdown stack permits the use of an unspecified number of inputs to the routines. Second, inputs to the IPL-V primitive routines are handled this way. Since the interpreter assembles the inputs into the same pushdown stack that the IPL-V primitives use, IPL-V primitives can and are used as GPL primitives.

Third, it is common when writing routines in IPL-V to use this pushdown stack for communication of inputs and outputs. Therefore, no new conventions are used in writing primitive routines for GPL.

5.2.2.4.2 *Handling of Outputs.* Outputs of a routine are available for use by the next routine. This is done so that the action of the routine executed in the operational segment can depend upon what was found by the conditional segment. These outputs are available only to the next routine so that useless symbols and list structures do not accumulate in memory.

5.2.2.4.3 *Use of the Stack Marker.* The stack marker is used in the pushdown stack to isolate inputs to routines and to allow a routine to know when it has processed all inputs. The ability to keep processing until there are no more inputs is quite useful.

5.2.2.5 THE PATTERN LANGUAGE. One of the fundamental abilities needed in a game playing system is the ability to search for something. In GGPP, searching is done mainly by the SEARCH primitive, although others are available. The conditions to be searched for are described by patterns and CTU's.

5.2.2.5.1 *The CTU.* A CTU is essentially a list of attribute-value pairs. This form is used because the properties of an object are also described by attribute-value pairs. The test for a match of a CTU and a symbol is a logical "and" of the tests on the individual attribute-value pairs because multiple conditions are common in game playing. For instance, in playing a board game, we might want to test the contents of a board cell and its location on the board.

The special properties of the CTU are available for convenience or generality or both. For example, the indirectness property is primarily a convenient one; it reduces the number of CTU's that must be written. The equality and negation properties, however, increase the flexibility of the CTU and allow it to describe more situations.

5.2.2.5.2 *The Pattern.* The pattern is used to allow specification of tests on a set of symbols. Since the number of symbols in the set is usually finite, a list of the tests for the symbols in the set is the easiest way to specify the test.

The CTU's in the pattern are tested against symbols in sequence because this saves symbol generation time. The full set of symbols is generated only if all symbols in the set match, or if all but the last symbol in the set match. Also, for many patterns used, the ordered nature of the test is important. It may be useless or wrong to test the second symbol in the set as generated with the first CTU on the pattern. The cost of testing in sequence is that all possible sequences must be represented with patterns when ordering is irrelevant. For instance, in Tic-Tac-Toe, it is necessary to have one pattern for X,X,EMPTY; and another for X,EMPTY,X.

The repeatable and expandable patterns are included because they are useful for finding moves in chess and checkers. They are, however, useful for other purposes in other games, particularly in evaluating what must be done to reach certain desired positions.

5.2.2.5.3 *The Direction List.* In SEARCH, directions are used to specify the characteristic of a set from which many instances of that set can be generated. This is convenient in board games because we often test cells adjacent to other cells. The description lists can be set up so that other, non-adjacent cells can also be obtained from a particular cell. Thus, we search all over the board. The method can also be used in card games, and is particularly useful for games in the Rummy family.

The method is not particularly useful, however, when it is necessary to search a closed loop. There is no way to orient the search toward closing the loop. Nor is there a fast way to return to the cell you started from and test in a different direction. The only way to do this is to use one of the direction list routines to find the direction which will return you to the starting cell, and use an empty CTU in the pattern to retest this cell. In short, the direction list method is a very useful, but not perfect, method for generating sets.

5.2.2.5.4 *Pattern Recognizer Output.* The form of the SEARCH routine output was selected because it can represent a large number of different situations and because the user can select just what he wants on the output. This allows the user to tailor the output description list to the needs of the program which is to use the output.

5.2.2.6 REPRESENTATION OF BOARD GAMES. Given the list structure representation for objects, there is still a large number of ways that a board game can be represented. However, it is necessary to select some uniform representation for board games so that the primitive routines can operate efficiently. This representation must be general enough to encompass all board games.

The difference in representations of board games is one of emphasis, as long as a modeling representation is used. In the representation used, the emphasis is on the board. Search and moves start on the board and its cells; pieces need not be represented directly but can be attribute values. Other representations are possible. In particular, a piece-oriented representation could be used in which lists of pieces are used with the board cell occupied by a piece on the description list of that piece.

The main reason for using a board-oriented representation is the importance of the board, In most games, the geometry of the board is very important. To move a piece, it is necessary to look at the squares of the board in the vicinity of the piece and to test the pieces on them. Finding squares in the vicinity of another requires that a structure similar to the ones used in Section 4 be available. Since it is necessary to be able to find adjacent cells and to find out what piece, if any, is on them, the easiest thing to do is to make the entire search board-oriented. Note that the search reduction method essentially keeps track of the board cells that contain pieces so that the sacrifice in efficiency is not too great.

5.2.2.7 REPRESENTATION OF CARD GAMES. Card games are represented by having lists of cards represent the various hands and stacks of cards that are used in the game. This representation is used for two reasons. First, card games are described in terms of aggregates of cards. The words "hand," "deck," "stock," "discard pile," and others all refer to a set of cards. In the list structure framework, the natural thing to use to represent these sets is the list.

Second, except for the action routines, this representation is compatible with that used for board games. In board games, we search for symbols (board cells) with certain properties. In card games, we also search for symbols (cards) with certain properties. For example, in playing Rummy games, we search the cards of the hand for a card with a certain rank or suit. Thus, the two search problems arc similar. Therefore, the list representation is a good one to use in a general game playing program.

The cost of this representation is a difference in the way moves are made in board and card games. Moves in board games are made by changing description lists; moves in card games are made by changing lists. Two different routines are needed. This cost, however, does not outweigh the advantages of this representation.

5.3 Some Conclusions about the Representation

The greatest deficiency in the representation is efficiency. The system is simply not very efficient. The system uses an interpreter to operate upon the representation of the rules, and interpreters are inefficient. To make matters worse, the system is written in IPL-V, which is an interpreted language. The average IPL-V instruction on the G-21 takes 1 millisecond, compared with a memory cycle time of 6 microseconds. The GGPP interpreter takes a minimum of 120 ILP-V instructions to interpret an entire statement.

It is important, however, to consider the reasons for the inefficiencies of the system. Not all of the slow running speed of the system (it is very slow, taking about 12 seconds to make a Tic-Tac-Toe move) should be attributed to the representation; nor are all of the 120 IPL-V instructions required to interpret a statement directly related to the representation. There are many things that the interpreter must do that are difficult to do in IPL-V. In these cases, many interpretation cycles of IPL-V are needed to get around the shortcomings of the system. The system cannot be judged on the basis of its implementation in IPL-V.

5.4 Some Other Representations

There are other representations that have been used or proposed in general problem solving programs. Although it is not possible to discuss all possible representations, two of them should be mentioned. Details of these systems may be found in the references cited.

One representation being developed by McCarthy [3] uses the first order predicate calculus as a formal system in which all problems can be reduced to problems of proving theorems in that system. The problem with this is that it is not obvious how to represent games in this system, and that the theorem provers are not good enough to handle a large problem like a game.

The other representation is the one used by Newell, et al. [7] in GPS. This represents a problem as an initial state, a final state, and a set of operators which operate on the states to produce new states. The problem is solved when a sequence of operators is found which transforms the intial state into the desired state. At the present time, there are two defects in this approach. The first is that GPS, as presently written, is a very large program, but the problems that it handles do not yet have anything like the complexity of a game playing problem. It is not feasible yet to play games with GPS. The second is that this formulation is not as natural for game playing as the one used.

The representation used in GGPP really seems to be the best for the problem. The model is fairly close to the external representation, and is, in general, easy to use. The representation is certainly general enough for use in learning and generalizing. Other existing representations of general problems, in their current state of development, offer no advantage over the one used and are harder to use.

SECTION 6
PROBLEMS IN LEARNING AND GENERALIZATION

This section discusses the problems of learning and generalization. Several methods of achieving learning and generalization using GGPP are proposed and discussed.

6.1 Move Selection

The basic problem in game playing is the selection of the proper move. The rules of the game define a set of moves which are legal. Of this set, some of the moves are "better" then others in that they are more likely to lead to the winning of the game. Strategies for a game are usually statements of principles that can often be used to select some of the better moves. It is rare, however, that rules and strategies, as known by humans, will define a unique move in each particular situation.

The usual approach to move selection is to generate a tree of possible moves from the given position. In other words, starting from the given position, some or all of the legal moves are made. Then, from each of the resulting positions, some or all of the legal moves are again made. This process is continued until the end of the game is reached, or until a time or storage limit has been exceeded. If the move generation reaches the end of the game, it is possible to work backward in the tree to the original position and identify the best move. It is rarely possible, however, to apply this strategy, because the tree is simply too large. Therefore, in practice, a small portion of the tree is generated and the end positions in this tree are evaluated by some kind of function. Also, at each level of generation, moves may be generated or evaluated, and only the best or most plausible ones selected. Using the results of the evaluation, the program works backward in the tree to the original position and selects the best move.

The reason that tree searching is needed at all is that the evaluation functions are not selective enough to find the best move immediately. Tree searching is a way of improving the selectivity of the evaluation function. For example, a poor move should be reflected in a situation that becomes progressively disastrous as the searching continues forward.

The better and more selective the evaluation function, the better the program will play with the same amount of searching; or the amount of searching may be reduced without affecting the quality of play. If the evaluation function is good enough, it may be possible to eliminate all tree searching. Since time and storage limit the amount of tree searching that can be done, improving the evaluation function is also a good way to improve the playing ability of the program.

Evaluation functions are usually composed of a number of different terms. These try to measure how well the situation being evaluated achieves certain subgoals known, or at least suspected, to be useful in the game. This is usually done more or less numerically. After each term is evaluated, they all are weighted in some fashion to obtain the evaluation of the position.

One way of programming learning is to allow the computer to assign the relative importance of each subgoal. The weights of the subgoals are varied as games are played. The subgoals that are prominent in winning games are consistently weighted more heavily than those that appear in losing games. In time, the good subgoals will be present with the proper weights in the evaluation function.

The nature of game playing makes it quite important to develop good subgoals. Each game involves many decisions. Some of these decisions will be better than others. Assigning credit to all subgoals used in the entire game on the basis of whether the game was won, lost, or tied is simply not realistic. Furthermore, in complicated games, it will take a long time to play the game, and thus playing the number of games required to learn subgoals could take too much computer time. Therefore, it is necessary to have a set of good subgoals and reinforce experimental subgoals on the basis of how well they generate situations known to be good on the basis of old subgoals known to be good.

6.2 Subgoal Generation

Because of the importance of subgoals, it would be very interesting to have a program that could discover some of its own subgoals. There are at least three possible ways to do this. They are (a) modification of the goal structure of the particular game, (b) generalization of subgoals used in other games, and (c) recognition of new subgoals by processing positions from which good moves are made.

6.2.1 Goal Structure Modification. The object of modifying the goal structure of a game is to try to develop a description of the situations from which the actual goal should be easy to attain. When these descriptions can be developed, they make very good subgoals. There are two different structures that are commonly used in playing games. One is arithmetic in nature; the other is associated with patterns. Arithmetic goals are such things as scores and counts of objects. Pattern goals occur in games such as Tic-Tac-Toe, Hex, and Chess.

When the goal is a pattern, it can be easily modified by putting other

CTU's in it while retaining the structure and the symbol generating routine. This results in patterns that are close to the goal but, because of the changes, may be more widely applicable. A simple example of this is the modification of the goal structure in Tic-Tac-Toe. If the goal is three X's in a row, one modification of this is two X's and a blank in a row. This is obviously a good subgoal. Of course, straight replacement of CTU's in the pattern will lead to a large number of other subgoals less useful than this one. However, learning could be used to eliminate the poor ones.

An example of modification of arithmetic goals can be found in Checkers. The goal of Checkers is to deny the opponent any possible move. This goal is expressed in GGPP by a pattern search on the board, followed by a count of the number of matches found. Modification of this goal consists of replacing a test zero on the number of output found by a test less than the ones counted previously. The subgoal is thus to reduce the number of available moves of the opponent. Another example is in a game where some score is to be obtained. The subgoal here is to raise (if the goal is to obtain a higher score than the opponent) or lower (if the goal is to score less than the opponent) the score. Again, learning must be used to see if the subgoals are useful.

After the subgoals are found, other things can be done. One of them is to apply the concept that "if one occurrence of a subgoal is good, then more are better." Thus, multiple subgoals will be tested for. Another is the concept that "if it is good for me to have it, it is bad for my opponent to have it."

There is a limit to the ability that can be acquired by a program using these methods. This is because there are certain concepts that are useful in a game that do not show up in the rules and goals of the game. As an example of this, consider how a Tic-Tac-Toe program would function using these methods. As mentioned earlier, the subgoal that would be generated and found useful would be 2 X's and a blank in a row. The program would not find the following excellent strategies:

1. If the center cell is empty, place an X on it.

2. If a corner cell is empty, then place an X on it.

The reason for this is that the concept of center and corner is not in the rules or goal of the game, and hence it cannot be developed by these methods.

6.2.2 Generalization. The above leads to consideration of how goals and subgoals developed for other games might be used. We notice that often goals of one game are useful subgoals in other games. For instance, the goal of Checkers involves the mobility of the opponent's pieces. This concept is known to be useful in Chess and many card games. The goal in Chess is to capture the king. This can lead to the concept of piece capture which is a useful concept in Checkers, Backgammon, and other games. Thus, the ability to generalize from one game to another would be a very powerful ability in a game learning program.

A simple copy of rules and goals of one game is not going to provide subgoals for another. We need to transfer the concept of what is being done in one game to another. This can be done if the form of the program has some relation to the task the program is doing. In this case, it should be possible to transfer a concept by taking the program used in one game and replacing the data used in it by the data of the new game, since these data will simply be information about the objects and rules of the game.

As an example of how this might be done, consider the development of a mobility subgoal for Chess by using that of Checkers. The program for mobility in Checkers consists of searches for various patterns on a board, followed by a count of the number of patterns found. Looking at the Checker program, it would be possible to discover that the patterns involved in the subgoal are similar to those involved in generating moves. Thus, conversion to Chess involves taking the mobility program, substituting the board for Chess, and replacing the legal move patterns of Checkers by those for Chess. We then have a mobility subgoal for Chess.

6.2.3 Recognition of New Subgoals. A third method of generating new subgoals involves looking back at a position from which a good move has been made and trying to abstract the characteristics of the position that allowed the good move to be made. For example, consider a position in Chess where a knight is attacking both a queen and a rook. If there is no "forking" subgoal, this position might not be recognized as a good one. But, after the opponent has played, the program might capture one of the pieces. This can be recognized as a good move. The problem is to go back to the original position and determine what there was about the position that allowed the program to capture the piece.

This is a difficult problem in pattern recognition. The only aid to the solution of the problem is that the pattern desired has something to do with the legal moves of the game.

SECTION 7
GENERALITY

The purpose of this section is to show how many of the games in a particular Hoyle can be played by the GGPP system. This is done by classifying the games into various groups according to the concepts needed to play the games and showing, by reference to the examples in Section 4, which of these concepts are in the system. The Hoyle used is reference 5. Table 1 shows the various groupings to be used and the number of games and significant variations that are in each group.

Table 1

Type of game	Number of games
Trick-winning card games	48
Poker	11
Stops	6
Rummy and similar children's games	29
Other card games	25
Board games	9
Total	128

The rest of this chapter will discuss each group.

7.1 Trick-Winning Card Games

Two basic concepts are needed in trick-winning games. One is the concept of relative card rank; the other is the concept of "same suit." The game of Hearts given in Section 4 illustrates how these concepts are expressed in GGPP.

To complete the analysis of trick-winning games, it is necessary to examine all of the features that distinguish one trick-winning game from another. By doing this, we can identify all concepts needed to play any of these games. The features of various trick-winning games fall into one or more of the following categories:

(a) Selection of the trump suit
(b) Relative rank of cards
(c) Rules for playing cards to a trick
(d) Scoring
(e) Number of cards in play
(f) Deck used
(g) Method of dealing cards

Of these categories, only (a), (c), and (d) can possibly cause trouble. Relative rank of cards, (b), is determined by a list which can represent all possible rankings of the cards. The system does not care how many cards are in play or how many cards are in the deck. Any method of dealing cards can be programmed by using the primitives that move cards from one list to another, as long as a shuffled deck is provided. There is no primitive for shuffling a deck in the system currently, but it is not difficult to add one.

7.1.1 Trump Suit Selection. There are two ways in which the trump suit is selected. One is by auction or bidding; the other is by turning up one of the cards that have not been dealt.

It is easy to write a program in GGPP to bid legally. It is only necessary to output a symbol that is of higher rank than the previous symbol, or to output a symbol which is the equivalent of "Pass." Good bidding is, however, difficult. This is because bidding strategy may involve concepts not in the system. GGPP is not, in general, capable of expressing strategy for games.

The other method of selecting the trump suit is to turn up the first undealt card. The suit of this card is either the trump suit for that hand, or is a proposed suit which various players have the option of selecting or rejecting. Since the suit of a card is carried on the description list of a card, it can always be found. Acceptance or rejection of the suit as trump is a matter of strategy.

7.1.2 Rules for Playing Cards to a Trick. There are two different rules governing what cards may be played to a trick. One rule requires a player to follow suit if possible. This rule is illustrated in the Hearts program. The other rule allows a player to trump even if able to play a card of the suit led. This poses no problem because trump cards can always be identified. In particular, if the trump cards are not all of the same suit, a list of trump cards can always be provided and a CTU can be used to test for them.

One minor variation in playing rules allows a player to keep certain cards in his hand when they might otherwise be played to meet the requirement of following suit. This variation is handled with a list of such cards.

7.1.3 Method of Scoring. There are three common methods of scoring. The first method is to base the score on the number of tricks won. This is easy to program since the number of tricks won can easily be counted. Scoring is simply a matter of addition or subtraction.

The second method of scoring is based upon winning or holding certain cards. For example, in Seven Up, points are scored for winning: face cards, the highest card of the trump suit, and the jack of the trump suit. A point is also scored for holding the low card of the trump suit initially. This scoring system presents no problems because the high and low cards of the trump suit may be identified with the FOLLOW primitive, while the Jack of trumps and the face cards may be identified by their description lists.

The third method of scoring is based upon holding certain sets of cards in the hand. In trick-winning games, these sets are always similar to the sets that are used in Rummy. These sets will be discussed in the section on

Rummy, since the only problem in programming this scoring method is testing whether the sets exist.

7.1.4 Conclusions. This section has shown that there is no difficulty in playing any trick-winning game legally. Since trick-winning games constitute over one-third of the games listed in reference 5, this shows that GGPP is fairly general even if it could not play any other games.

7.2 Stops

There is a large family of games called "Stops." In these games, the object is to get rid of all of one's cards by playing them upon piles on the table. There are two rules used in the various games to determine the cards that can be played. Cards to be played must be of the same rank or suit as cards on the table, or cards to be played must be in sequence with cards on the table. Differences in the games are in the particular rules used and in the number of piles used.

These games can all be played in GGPP. Eights, which is shown in Section 4, is a member of this family. It shows how the rules of same rank and suit are handled. Finding cards in sequence with another card, the other basic rule of the Stops family, is done with the SEARCH routine. Each card has on its description list the name of the next card in the sequence. With this data description, the SEARCH routine with the direction list method may be used to find sequences of cards. Although there are only 6 Stops games listed in Table 1, there are many other Stops games which are considered to be obsolete in the United States.

7.3 Poker and Rummy

Games in the Poker and Rummy families are treated together here because, although the object and methods of play in the two games are different, the things to be searched for in hands are the same. In fact, Rummy got its current name from the British who called it Rum (queer) Poker.

The object of both games is to form sets of cards. A set may, in general, be of two types: a group of three or more cards of the same rank, or a sequence of cards (in Rummy, the sequence must be of cards of the same suit). The problem in programming these games is to find these various sets.

A group of cards may be found by counting the number of cards of a particular rank. This is most easily done by counting the number of cards that match CTU's that specify a certain rank. Patterns can also be used to test for groups (by putting cards of the same rank on description lists).

Sequences of cards may be found by using the direction list method in the SEARCH primitive. Each card has the name of the card that is next to it in ascending or descending (or both) sequence on its description list. Patterns can then be written that will find various ascending or descending sequences of cards.

Therefore, it is possible in GGPP to express the basic forms needed for these games. As for trick-winning games, the variations in the games are analyzed below to find concepts that might not be in GGPP.

7.3.1   Poker. Variations in Poker games fall into the following categories:

(a) Wild cards
(b) Betting rules
(c) Number of cards dealt
(d) Number of betting intervals and opportunities to draw more cards
(e) Special combinations of cards

Betting, like bidding, is easy to do legally in GGPP. None of the variations in betting rules, such as minimum requirements for opening, are at all difficult to program. Like bidding, however, betting is difficult to do well. At best, a Poker program will be fairly long because of the large number of alternatives available in a Poker game.

Wild cards cause no trouble in GGPP. Wild cards can have the value EVERY for rank and suit values, in which case they will match everywhere. Or, the cards that are wild may be searched for by special CTU's. The same is true of any special combinations of cards—special patterns can be provided to search for these.

The system does not care how many cards are dealt. Nor does the number of betting intervals or number of draws make any difference to the system. Each draw can be handled the same way as any other, or less restrictive patterns can be used to indicate situations that might be improved by the next round of cards.

Thus, the only problem in playing Poker games is betting. Everything else is well within the capability of the system.

7.3.2   Rummy. As shown in Table 1, there are a large number of Rummy games. Most of the games differ in that various requirements must be met before one of the basic plays is made. The peculiarities of the Rummy games fall into the following categories:

(a) Wild cards
(b) Object of game
(c) Scoring
(d) Number of cards in deck and number of cards dealt
(e) Removal of cards from the discard pils
(f) Types of sets allowed

(g) Melding requirements

Despite the number of categories, Rummy games are easy to program. This is because none of the peculiarities causes much difficulty. The worst that can happen is that a large number of possibilities may have to be accounted for. The analysis by category follows:

As mentioned in previous sections, the following peculiarities will cause no trouble: (a) wild cards and (d) number of cards in deck and number of cards dealt.

There are two distinct goals used in Rummy games. One is to score points by melding cards, the other is to get rid of all of the cards in the hand. It is easy to check to see if the game is over in either case.

Scoring variations involve the point values of cards and melds. Since these have to be specified for any game in the Rummy family, the different values in different games do not cause any extra difficulty.

The Rummy games allow a player to take the top card of the discard pile, take any card in the discard pile, or take the entire pile. As far as the system is concerned, it is just as easy to do any one of these.

Restrictions on the types of sets allowed simply limit the kinds of sets which can be used. No new sets are ever involved.

Melding requirements specify that a certain score must be achieved before a meld can be made. Since all variations of scoring can be programmed, all of these melding requirements can also be programmed.

In conclusion, then, this section has demonstrated that all Rummy games can be programmed with the concepts that are in the system. Rummy games may not be easy to program because of the very large number of rules and exceptions, but no system can make this easy.

7.4 Other Card Games

GGPP can play the games in all of the families mentioned above. It is the games that do not fit into any of these families that the system is not likely to be able to play. This is simply because these games do not necessarily use concepts of wide applicability. Therefore, these concepts are not in the system. Two examples of games that the system cannot play easily are Casino and Cribbage. These games both involve finding sets of cards in the hand or on the table whose face values add up to a certain number. This requires the generation of all combinations of a certain number of the symbols on certain lists; e.g., all combinations of the symbols of a hand taken two at a time. The system has no primitive routine for doing this and it is not easy to program it in the system.

There is also one class of games that cannot be played because of the sequential nature of the system. The system is designed to make one complete play before proceeding to the next player. However, certain games, such as double solitaire and some children's games, are not played this way. In these games, a player can make a play at any time whether or not some other player is doing something. The system, as presently written, cannot play these games.

7.5 Board Games

Unfortunately, board games cannot be divided into families as easily as can card games. There are, however, two families that can be discussed.

One family of board games are those games that require recognition of patterns of objects on a board to find a move. Examples of this type of game are Chess and Checkers. Games in this family can be played by the system if the patterns can be expressed in the pattern language. Chess and Checkers are examples of games whose patterns can be expressed in the pattern language. A concept that cannot be expressed in the pattern language is that of the encirclement of one piece by opponent pieces. The patterns of each game in the family must be tested, however, because it is not possible to make a general statement.

The other family of board games consists of games in which pieces must be moved a specified number of squares in a given direction. Examples of games in this family are Backgammon, Kalah, and Monopoly. These games can be played using the ADVANCE primitive if the program can determine the number of squares that are to be moved. This is usually determined by dice or cards. Thus, with the addition of a dice-throwing subroutine to the system (a trivial matter), these games can be played.

7.6 Conclusions

This section has shown the wide range of games that the system can play. It has shown what concepts are needed to play classes of games and their variations and how these concepts are available in GGPP. It has also indicated what games the system cannot play. The number of games that the system can play far outnumbers the number of games that it cannot.

SECTION 8
CONCLUSIONS

Sections 4, 5, and 6 have discussed and evaluated GGPP as an attack on the problem defined in Section 1. This section will, therefore, summarize the two main features of the system.

First, as shown in Section 4 and discussed in Section 7, the system will play a large number of card and board games. Much of this ability comes from the internal representation and a small number of the primitive routines. In particular, the primitive routines that use patterns and CTU's can be used for finding situations in most games. The general descriptive ability of CTU's and patterns comes from the list structure representation of data. Thus, at least for searching, a general method is available.

Second, GGPP can be used for further investigation of generalization and learning. Section 6 suggests some methods for doing this, and there are undoubtedly others. Part of this ability stems from the capability of GGPP to play many games; part from the flexibility of the interpreter, which allows new abilities to be added if necessary. This ability is the best reason for the existence of GGPP.

APPENDIX
PRIMITIVE ROUTINES

This Appendix documents the primitive routines mentioned in the text and in problems. Each routine is listed, in alphabetical order, with its inputs and outputs and with a brief description of its operation. The more complex primitives have been described in Section 3.

The inputs to a routine are numbered in the order in which they appear in the stack. Often, an input type, or a set of input types, can be repeated an unlimited number of times. These are indicated by the word "repeatable" after the description of the inputs. Inputs appearing on the same line are repeatable as a set. The operation of the primitive on the repeated inputs is the same as its operation on the first such input.

Some primitives may have an unspecified number of outputs. These are left in the stack after execution of the primitive.

Unless otherwise indicated, all inputs that search for something will set the test cell + if it is found and − if it is not. Many primitives that are not conditional will set the test cell +. Others do not affect the test cell. The description will indicate which is the case.

Certain IPL-V routines are used for several primitive operations. Therefore, when program lists are printed, the printed form may not coincide with the input form. The descriptions will indicate to which routines this will happen.

ADD1

Inputs: (1) attribute
          (2) value

(3) symbol or list of symbols

Outputs: none

ADD1 adds input (2) as a value of input (1) to all symbols specified by input (3). If (2) is PVAL, the value is taken from a special list; see Section 3.5.2. The test cell is set $+$. The changed symbols are printed.

ADVANCE

Inputs: (1) integer
           (2) direction
           (3) board symbol or other symbol with a description list

Outputs: (1) board symbol

ADVANCE will start from the symbol specified in input (3) and using input (2) the number of times specified by integer (1) will find another symbol. Each time input (2) is used, it is used on the output left by the last execution. The operation is to find the value of input (2) on input (3). The symbol found is left as output. If a symbol cannot be found, there is no output and the test cell is set $-$.

AVMTCH

Inputs: (1) list of symbols
           (2) symbol
           (3) attribute

Outputs: symbols

The value of input (3) is found on the description list of symbol (2). This value is compared with the value of the attribute on each of the symbols in list (1). All symbols where a match occurs are left in the stack. If no matches occur, there will be no output and the test cell will be set $-$.

BDGEN

Inputs: (1) board description list
           (2) name of list where generated symbols are to be placed

Outputs: none

BDGEN generates a board as described in Section 3. The routine uses the following system cells:

OPDIR. Description list of perpendicular directions. Each direction is an attribute, its value is the opposite direction.

CMPDIR. Description list of composite directions. Each composite direction is an attribute on this list. The value is the sequence of directions equivalent to the single direction.

BDGEN will set the test cell +.

CDRANK

Input:　　(1) card rank description lists
　　　　　(2) name of trump suit; NOTNG if none
　　　　　(3) name of list of all cards
　　　　　(4) name of list where cards are to be placed in ascending order
　　　　　(5) name of list where cards are to be placed in descending order

Outputs:　none

CDRANK provides ordered lists of cards. It has been described in Section 3. CDRANK will set the test cell +.

CHNG

Inputs:　　(1) attribute
　　　　　(2) value
　　　　　(3) symbol or list of symbols

Outputs:　none

CHNG changes the value of input (1) to the symbol specified by input (2) on all symbols specified by input (3). If (2) is PVAL, the value is taken from a special list; see Section 3.5.2. All changed symbols are printed. The test cell is set +.

CNTMS

Inputs:　　(1) list
　　　　　(2) CTU

Outputs:　(1) integer

CNTMS will count the number of symbols on the list named by input (1) that match the CTU (2). If input (2) is empty, CNTMS will count the number of cells on list (1). The test cell is set +.

CONT

Inputs:　　(1) name of a cell

Outputs:　(1) contents of the cell

CONT will leave the contents of the input symbol in the stack and set the test cell +. If the input symbol is empty, there will be no output and the test cell will be set —.

DELA

Inputs:	(1) attribute
	(2) value
	(3) symbol or list of symbols
Outputs:	none

DELA will remove all occurrences of the value (2) from the value list of the attribute (1) on all symbols specified by (3). If the value is not on the description list, the test cell will be set —. Otherwise, the test cell will be set +, and the changed symbols printed. If PVAL is input (2), the attribute and value will be removed from the description list and placed at the end of a special list. See Section 3.5.2. The test cell is set +, and the changed symbols printed.

DEL1

Inputs:	(1) attribute
	(2) value
	(3) symbol or list of symbols
Outputs:	none

DEL1 is the same as DELA except that only one occurrence of the value is removed.

DONE, DONTG

Inputs:	none
Outputs:	none

Neither of these routines does anything. The test cell is not changed. If printed, DONE will print as DONTG.

DRAW

Inputs:	none
Outputs:	none

DRAW prints the word DRAW and terminates the running program.

EQUAL

Inputs:	(1) first symbol

(2) second symbol

Outputs: none

EQUAL tests the two input symbols for equality. The equality test is the same as that used in SEARCH; see Section 3.5.1. The test cell is set + if the symbols are equal, — if the symbols are not. If the two symbols are known to be integers, TEQU will have the same effect and will run faster.

EXCP

Inputs: (1) direction

Outputs: (1) list of directions

EXCP is usually used in direction lists used by SEARCH, which supplies it with the appropriate input. First, EXCP will find the value of the input on the list OPDIR, the description list of opposite directions. It will then copy the list ALDIR and delete the symbol found from the description list. The name of this copy is the output. The result is a list of all directions except the direction opposite to the input direction. If no list can be found, the test cell is set —. This routine can be used for other purposes by putting the appropriate lists into the system cells.

FIND

Inputs: (1) symbol or name of a list
(2) integer or symbol, repeatable

Outputs: (1) symbol or list name

FIND is suppose to find something. The input (1) is taken to be the starting point. Input (2) is then tested. If it is an integer (n), the nth symbol on the list (1) is found. If (2) is a symbol, this symbol is used as an attribute and the value of this attribute on the input (1) is found. The symbol found serves as the starting point for the next input (3), if any. If the symbol is found, it is left in the stack, and the test cell is set +. Otherwise, there is no output and the test cell is set —.

FOLLOW

Inputs: (1) symbol
(2) list structure
(3) list
(4) CTU or empty, repeatable

Outputs: symbols from the list named in input (3)

FOLLOW first finds all symbols on the list (3) that match any of the CTU's given in the inputs. If no CTU's are supplied, all symbols on input (3) are used. It then finds input (1) on list structure (2). The output consists of all symbols found in the first step that are below input (1) on list structure (2). If there are no symbols, the test cell is set —. The symbols will be in the order in which they appear on list structure (2). If symbol (1) cannot be found on (2), an error is indicated.

INALL

Inputs: (1) list of symbols

Outputs: symbols

INALL takes all symbols from the list named in input (1) and leaves them in the stack. The order is preserved. The test cell is set +. If there are no symbols on the list, an error is indicated. The list is cleared.

LOSE

Inputs: none

Outputs: none

LOSE prints the symbol LOSE and terminates the running program.

LSTCHG

Inputs:
(1) name of a list from which symbols are to be removed
(2) name of a list to which symbols are to be added
(3) symbols or empty, repeatable

Outputs: none

LSTCHG removes all symbols specified by inputs (3), (4), ... from list (1) and adds them at the front of list (2). The test cell is set + unless a symbol is not on list (1). If there are no inputs (3), ..., the first symbol on list (1) is removed and added to list (2).

MOVE

Inputs:
(1) name of list whose symbols are to be changed
(2) pattern recognizer output
(3) move list

Outputs: none

MOVE has been described in Section 3.5.2. It makes moves indicated by the move list on the symbols indicated by the SEARCH output. All cells changed are added to the lists of starting cells used by SEARCH if this feature of

SEARCH is being used. All cells changed are printed when the change is completed.

OUTF

Inputs: none

Outputs: (1) the first symbol left by the previous routine

OUTF leaves the first symbol left in the stack by the previous routine in the stack. The test cell is set $+$. If there were no symbols left by the previous routine, the test cell is set $-$.

PAGE

Inputs: none

Outputs: none

PAGE moves the paper in the line printer to the top of the next page. It does not affect the test call.

PERP

Inputs: (1) direction

Outputs: (1) list of directions

PERP is designed for use in direction lists. PERP finds the value of input (1) on the description list of the cell named PPDIR. This value is left in the stack. For direction lists, the value can be a list of directions perpendicular to the input direction. The routine can be used for any purpose needed, however. The test cell is set $+$ unless there is no value of the attribute.

PRTSYM

Inputs: (1) symbol

Outputs: none

PRTSYM prints the symbol named by input (1). After the symbol is printed, its description list, if any, is printed. The test cell is set $+$.

SAME

Inputs: (1) direction

Outputs: (1) same direction

SAME leaves the input as the output and sets the test cell $+$. It is designed for use in direction lists. SAME will be printed SET$+$.

SEARCH

Inputs: (1) board or other universe to be searched
(2), (3) pattern, direction list or name of symbol producing routine, repeatable

Outputs: description lists for patterns matched

SEARCH is the pattern recognizer routine. It is described in detail in Section 3.5.1.

SEQCR

Inputs: (1) name of first player list to be executed

Outputs: none

SEQCR will execute player lists in the sequence specified by the list in cell PSEQ, starting with the player list named in (1). The number of player lists executed is specified by the integer in PNUM. PNUM is initially 0. If PNUM is not set to an integer greater than zero, SEQCR will never terminate. When SEQCR exits, the test cell is set +.

SET

Inputs: (1), (2) cell name, symbol; repeatable

Outputs: none

SET stores the input (2) into the cell named by input (1). Each additional pair of inputs is treated the same way. The test cell is set +.

STORB

Inputs: (1) name of a list
(2) symbol, repeatable

Outputs: none

STORB puts the symbols in the stack at the beginning of the list named by (1). The symbols are in the same order on the list that they were on the stack. Any symbols originally on the list appear below the new symbols. The test cell is set +.

TEQU, TGTR, TLSS

Inputs: (1) integer
(2) integer

Outputs: none

These routines test for a relation between the integer inputs.
TEQU sets the test cell + if (1) equals (2), — otherwise.
TGTR sets the test cell + if (1) is greater than (2), — otherwise.
TLSS sets the test cell + if (1) is less than (2), — otherwise.

WIN

Inputs: none

Outputs: none

WIN prints the symbol WIN and terminates the running program.

References

[1] FEIGENBAUM, E. A. and FELDMAN, J. (eds.). *Computers and Thought.* New York: McGraw-Hill, 1963.
[2] GARBER, M. Clink, clank, think. *Chess Life*, February, 1964.
[3] MCCARTHY, J. Programs with common sense. *In* D. V. Blake and A. M. Uttley (eds.), *Symposium on the Mechanization of Thought Processes.* London: H.M.S.O., 1959. [M]
[4] MINSKY, M. Steps toward artificial intelligence. *Proceedings of the Institute of Radio Engineers*, **49:** 8–30, January, 1961. [FF]
[5] MOREHEAD, A. H. and MOTT-SMITH G. *Hoyle's Rules of Games.* New York: New American Library of World Literature, 1963.
[6] NEWELL, A. (ed.) *Information Processing Language-V Manual*, 2d Ed. Englewood Cliffs, N. J.: Prentice-Hall, 1964.
[7] NEWELL, A., SHAW, J., and SIMON, H. Chess playing programs and the problems of complexity. *IBM Journal of Research and Development* **2:** 320–335, October, 1958. [FF]
[8] NEWELL, A., SHAW, J., and SIMON, H. Report on a General Problem Solver. *Information Processing.* Paris: UNESCO, 1959. [FF]
[9] SAMUEL, A. L. Some studies in machine learning using the game of checkers. *IBM Journal of Research and Development* **3:** 211–229 July, 1959. [FF]

Chapter 4

COMPUTER PROGRAM ORGANIZATION INDUCED FROM PROBLEM EXAMPLES

Donald S. Williams

SECTION 1
THE APTITUDE TEST TAKER

A potentially useful artificial intelligence problem is to design a computer program that can induce its own performance strategy. A specific example would be the automatic organization of a computer program to perform a task on the basis of worked examples of the task.

Aptitude tests are a promising candidate for such an induction program, for they have served as a basis for computer models of human performance and as a yardstick of achievement for intelligent machines. In taking aptitude tests, students must organize their problem-solving methods before dealing with the specific test items that are presented.

Interests in induction and problem solving are combined here in a program called the Aptitude Test Taker (ATT), which uses worked examples of items from an inductive reasoning task to organize a computer program to perform the task. The program, while influenced by human performance, does not try to simulate exactly the processes used by human beings; its development has been based both on computer models of human performance and on artificial intelligence research.

ATT, using its Test Form Analyzer, constructs a representation of the task (the Task Form Specification) from a small set of worked examples. Suppose the Test Form Analyzer is presented with the following array of symbols:

    Problem: AABC   ACAD   ACFG   AACG

    Answer: ACFG

From this information alone, the Analyzer assembles a program (the Test Item Taker) that is now prepared to take a test consisting of a battery of similar items, for example:

    1. XURM   ABCD   MNOP   EFGH

    2. KABC   KEFG   LOPQ   KUVH

Although the task was only vaguely defined by the example given previously, humans normally respond to these two items with the answers "XURM" and "LOPQ," respectively, and we would expect ATT to do the same—to perform at the human level. Thus, the conditions of performance and the limits of our expectations are set by the known performances of human beings.

1.1 Antecedents

The forms of concepts used by ATT and the order in which they are considered were influenced by the work of Hunt on concept formation (Hunt, 16; Hunt and Hovland, 17; Hunt, Marin, and Stone, 18). To avoid the complications of short-term memory, which is important to human performance when test items cannot be viewed as wholes (Cahill and Hovland, 4), the tasks for ATT are always considered to be presented as paper-and-pencil tests.

The task of going from worked examples to a computer program for taking a test has also been considered by others. Kilburn, Grimsdale, and Sumner (19) developed a system to assemble programs that could handle number series tests. In their system, the component subroutines and the final program were assembled randomly and tested on subparts of the series to be extrapolated. With the proper training sequences, programs were assembled that solved some number series test items. Solomonoff (25, 26) has also proposed a program that develops transformation rules to deal with number series tasks. However, his program, like the others mentioned here, would require a long training sequence compared to the one used by ATT.

Amarel (2) has described a system that forms transformation programs to process two-argument functions in a first-order axiom system. Uhr (27, 28) has developed a series of programs that translate natural language strings from one language to another. While he indicates that his programs could be adapted to the type of input strings ATT considers, he does not specify the precise modifications that would be required. The programs of Solomonoff, Amarel, and Uhr are discussed further in Section 5.

Other computer programs require an exact specification of a task in order to tackle it. Simon and Kotovsky (24) have written a program of this sort to model human behavior in the letter series task. Ernst and Newell (5) have studied the behavior of a system (the General Problem Solver) designed to handle a whole range of tasks, including letter analogies; Abrahams, Hansen, and Pivar (1), building on the Simon and Kotovsky approach, have developed algorithms to solve series tests. These problem solvers are discussed in Section 6.

1.2 Procedure

ATT's task is one that humans perform regularly, so that some standards for ATT's performance can be derived from the studies of human performance by Hunt (16, 17, 18), Jenkins (reported by Amarel, 2), Guilford (10, 11, 12, 13, 15), and others. Simon and Kotovsky's Concept Former (24) indicates what can be expected from a heuristic computer program taking an aptitude test.

However, additional data to provide norms for ATT were gathered from 24 college students, each of whom took two aptitude tests; and from two other students, whose eye movements were filmed with the help of A. Winikoff (30). The latter data are valuable for gaining insight into component processes.

Guilford's (8, 9, 10, 11, 14) "Structure of Intellect" model was used to select tests from the batteries he developed for studies of high-level personnel. The selection of tests is discussed in Section 4.

1.3 Structure

The Aptitude Test Taker, as shown in Figure 1, consists of (a) the Test Form Analyzer, (b) the Test Item Taker Executive, and (c) a number of routines that are assembled by the Executive into the Test Item Takers.

The *Test Form Analyzer* accepts as input sample aptitude test items and their answers, taken from the instructions for the original aptitude tests, and, using a feature extraction technique, builds the *feature list* in the following way:

After it has abstracted features classifying an example as to (a) the form of the answer, (b) the type of symbols used, and (c) the format, the Test Form Analyzer builds a few trial Test Item Takers and executes them,

146 Computer Program Organization Induced from Problem Examples

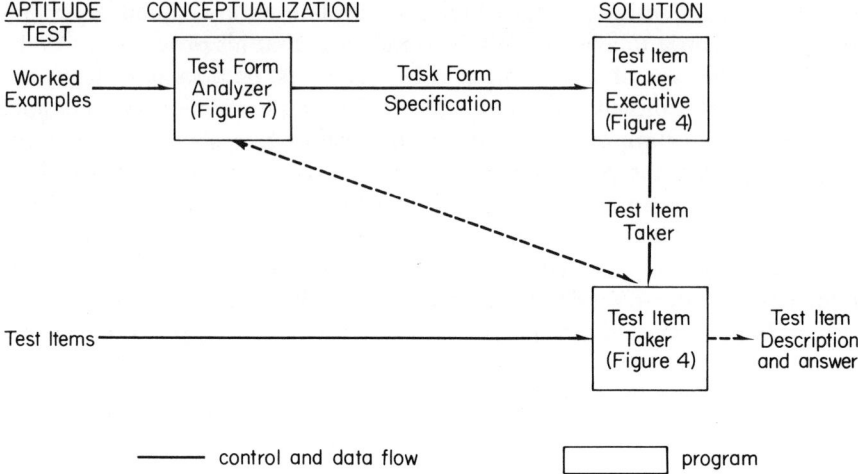

Figure 1 Aptitude Test Taker. Major sections of ATT showing principal function, data flow, control, and references to figures giving additional detail. See the text for explanation of the broken-line relation between Test Form Analyzer and Test Item Taker.

using the sample test as input. The performance of a Test Item Taker is evaluated by examining the Test Description, if any, it produces; and the evaluation, abstracted by the Test Form Analyzer, is entered in the feature list. The Test Form Analyzer then abstracts the feature list to construct the task form specification.

The *Test Item Taker Executive*, using the task form specification, assembles a Test Item Taker appropriate to the aptitude test represented by the examples.

The *Test Item Taker* accepts as input the test items taken from the same aptitude test that furnished the instructions to the Test Form Analyzer. The Test Item Taker attempts to construct a test item description for each item, and then use that description to find an answer.

The Test Item Taker, when it is operating as a part of the Test Form Analyzer, has the abilities to modify itself, to create a new Test Item Taker, and to create new plans. It lacks the ability to recall things it has learned on previous tests, to create new Test Item Taker Executives and Test Form Analyzers, or to function without a programmer. Hence, it is still lacking in some of the attributes that Baker (3) suggests are essential to solving problems by understanding (Newell, 20).

1.4 Organization of this Study

The Aptitude Test Taker operates on structures and keeps its records in structures. Its important data structures (the test item representation the task form specification, the Test Item Taker, and the test item description) are discussed in Section 2. Section 3 describes how ATT builds the structures. Section 4 discusses the human performance data used to evaluate ATT and how well ATT meets the expectations set for it. Section 5 compares ATT with other programs and proposals for programs that induce a performance strategy from worked examples. Section 6 compares ATT with programs that solve inductive reasoning tasks. Since ATT is coded in IPL-V, which is typically unreadable, the routines are described informally.

The Aptitude Test Taker has served as a vehicle for investigating the computer conceptualization of several inexactly defined tasks (listed in the Appendix) and the solution of these tasks with a parsimonious set of operators.

SECTION 2
DATA REPRESENTATION

Data representation affects not only the performance and generality of a computer program but our view of the task. To generalize beyond ATT, this section both describes data representations and examines their consequences.

The Test Form Analyzer and the Test Item Taker routines are encoded in the list processing language, IPL-V (Newell and Kelley, 21), the internal representation consisting of IPL symbols, lists, list structures, and print lines that can be accessed and modified by any part of ATT. The structure of the representation cannot be altered.

The major data representations used in ATT are the test items, alphabets, task form specifications, test item takers, and test item descriptions, each of which (except "alphabets") is discussed under its own heading. Alphabets have the same form as the test items (linear strings) and are a permanent part of the program. Their use is covered in Section 3. All of the data representations except for the test items, alphabets, and descriptor directories are generated by the program itself.

Section 3 describes the use and construction of the data representations and defines the Test Item Taker as a routine.

2.1 Test Item Representation

The test items, including examples, are stored as linear strings, preserving the original spacing. A string is limited to 77 characters and spaces, acceptable to the input/output routines of the computer being used.

By using serial test items and retaining the original test format one avoids the need for an input conversion routine and maintains a close correlation between the eye-movement data of students solving the items and the type of move routines that can be implemented in the program. The format does not admit as wide a range of tasks as the General Problem Solver (Ernst and Newell, 5, 6) considers, but makes the Test Form Analyzer more manageable by removing from consideration (a) the external representation of other classes of tasks, (b) the recognition of a large number of input types and (c) the conversion program to take the test item into the internal representation.

To understand better the importance of test item representation, consider what would be involved in including geometry-analogy problems (Evans, 7) in ATT along with the letter analogies and number relations tests. Each of these three tasks requires finding a relation between A and B, and between C and D, and then finding the symbol that bears the same relation to E. The geometry-analogy test items could be handled internally by representing the connectivity relations symbolically, rather than expressing them implicitly by position. This recoding would greatly complicate the required move routines and would call for additional operators and expansion of the Test Form Analyzer. These additions would be peripheral to the task of organizing a system to solve tasks by recognizing test item features.

2.2 Task Form Specification

The Task Form Specification (TFS) is the means for passing information between the Test Form Analyzer and the Test Item Taker Executive. The division point between them determines the requirements placed on the Test Form Analyzer and the efficiency and performance of the Test Item Taker. The TFS sets the starting form of the Test Item Taker for each test item, since adaptive changes in the Test Item Taker are not retained between test items. If the TFS is too vague or too specific, the Test Item Taker cannot solve the tests presented to it.

To see the general character of the TFS, consider the following problems and their specifications.

(1) The L. L. Thurstone letter series test,

$$C D C D C D C \_ ,$$

would be specified as: "find *relations* in a *string* of *letters*, *replace* the _."

(2) *Letters* can be exchanged for *numbers* giving a number series test item ("find *relations* in a *string* of *numbers*, *replace* the _ _") such as:

$$1\ 2\ 3\ 4\ \_\ \_ .$$

(3) Changing the answer form ("replace the _") to "state the *exceptional*

element," the new form is illustrated by:

$$1\ 2\ 3\ 3\ 5\ 6,$$

where the correct answer is 3.

(4) Returning to the letter series description and changing *string* to *groups*, the TFS becomes "find *relations* in a *group* of *letters*, *replace* the _," which describes the letter analogies test:

$$A\ B\quad M\ N\quad G\ \_\ .$$

(5) Changing *relations* to *properties* in the Task Form Specification and the answer form to "state the *exceptional element*," the specification becomes "find *properties* in a *group* of *letters*, state the *exceptional element*," which describes:

$$A\ A\ B\ C\quad A\ B\ C\ D\quad A\ A\ G\ H\quad A\ A\ Y\ Z,$$

where the exceptional element is ABCD.

In the preceding examples, the *problem form* and *answer form* have been demonstrated. The third component of the TFS is the *feature list*, containing the features that the Test Form Analyzer has tested against the examples and the results of these tests. In addition to keeping track of the actions of the Test Form Analyzer, the feature list governs the selection of features to be tested, and determines what elements are to be added to the problem form and answer form lists. The Test Form Analyzer currently uses as many as twelve features to describe examples.

The general structure of the TFS shown in Figure 2 depicts the three components that have been discussed. The feature list is created first. As each new item of information is added to it, the list is checked to see if it now has sufficient information to select an element for the answer form or problem form lists. The *symbol* element on the answer form list is used only in replacement tasks (to specify what symbol is to be replaced with the correct answer). The answer form is usually the first element to be completed, followed by the symbol type, format, and descriptor type of the problem form.

The complete list of elements for the TFS is presented in Figure 3. Only two elements, value and property, need be mentioned. *Value* as the answer form means a verbal description of the test item. *Property* as a descriptor type means a characteristic possessed by each unit in the test item, e.g., "each group has two identical elements."

The *answer form* determines which test item descriptions and answers are acceptable for the Test Item Taker Executive. The *problem form* is used by the Test Item Taker Executive to assemble a Test Item Taker best suited

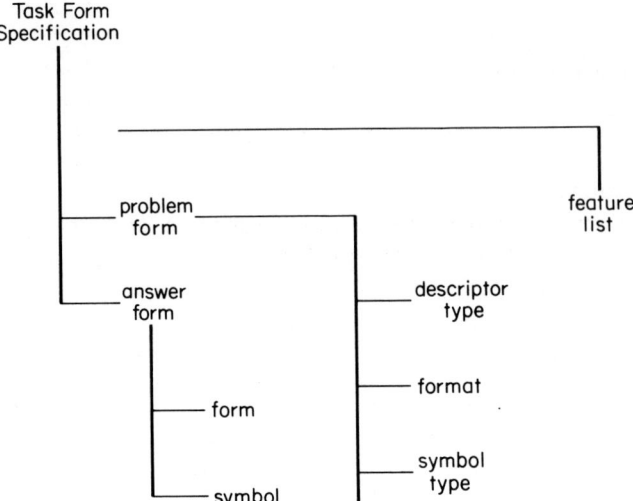

Figure 2 The Test Form Analyzer.

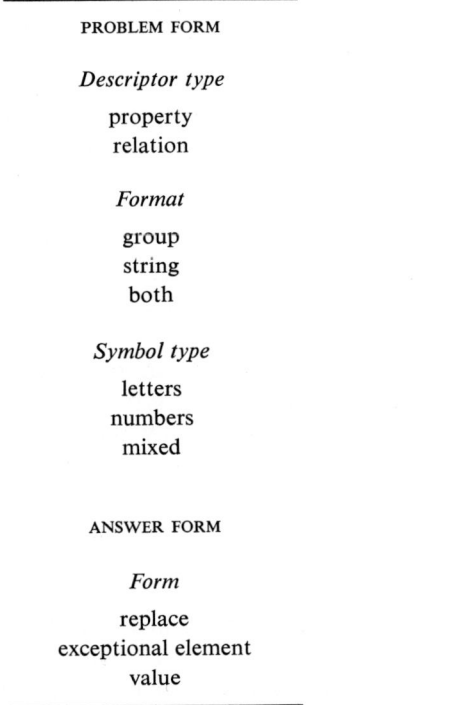

Figure 3 Elements of the Task Form Specification.

to the examples presented to the Test Form Analyzer. If the problem form turns out not to be correctly specified, the Test Item Taker can adapt, but only within limits, to the test item actually presented. Experience with ATT indicates that the proper function of the problem form is to minimize the adaptation required of the Test Item Taker but not to eliminate it. In any improved form of the system, we would want the Task Form Specification to provide advice or guidance to the Test Item Taker Executive.

2.3 Test Item Taker

A Test Item Taker (TIT) includes an executive routine, and context, move, descriptor, operator, and action routines (see Figure 4). A TIT is both a data structure and a computer program. As a data structure, it can be accessed and modified by ATT routines, including the routines in the TIT itself. The self-modification permits planning and adapting, while its explicit format permits monitoring and facilitates understanding the operation of the TIT.

Experience with the TIT indicates that its structure, shown in Figure 4, is adequate for the task and that its further evolution should focus on the development of the descriptor and move routines.

The TIT executive selects a *context routine* and the first *descriptor routine*. In turn, the context routine selects a *move routine* and *action routine* while the descriptor routine fills in the matching *operator routine*. These routines will be explained shortly, but some notion of their meaning can be gained from the labels in Figure 5. The Test Item Taker structure is inter-

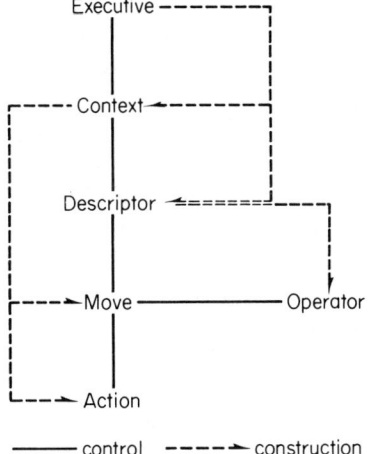

Figure 4 Test Item Taker structure. The hierarchy of routine sets that form an Aptitude Test Taker.

Context	Move
group	group
string	string
both	

Descriptors	Operators
same	same
next*	next
addition*	mathematical
subtraction*	
multiplication*	
division*	
replace	replace
remove	remove
double element	double element
identical elements*	identical elements

Actions

replace
value
exceptional element

* Based on generalized *next*.

Figure 5 Routines presently defined for the Test Item Taker.

rogated before passing control to a lower routine (descent) to allow modification of the TIT at the time information is discovered without interfering with the later return of control to the correct higher level routine (ascent). In Figure 4 the solid lines are lines of communications, while the dotted lines indicate the responsibility for construction of the TIT. A context routine is always associated with a unique move routine and a descriptor routine with a unique operator routine (see the pairings in Figure 5).

Any one of three executives can use a TIT: (1) the TIT Executive, (2) the feature test for properties, and (3) the feature test for relations. Figure 5 shows the number and character of the routines that can be incorporated in a TIT.

2.4 Test Item Description

The Test Item Description (TID) is used by the Test Item Taker to communicate its actions both internally and to an observer. The TID allows partial descriptions, sufficient to meet the requirements of the answer form but insufficient to reconstruct the test item. The sequential growth of a partial description reveals the order in which the productions making up a TID are found by the Test Item Taker, and permits comparison of this order with that observed in human eye-motion studies. The eye-movement studies indicate that students do not form a complete description of a test item unless it is required to produce an answer.

The TID was originally developed for the Thurstone letter series test and the Guilford letter analogies test. The information contained in it did not have to be changed when ATT was expanded to include additional tests. However, an addition was made later to describe student behavior in solving the letter series test (see Section 4).

The TID is a list of lists (a tree structure). The main list contains as many entries as the Test Item Taker finds it needs to meet the requirements of the answer form. The particular TID structure illustrated in Figure 6 consists of three sublists, the first of which is shown in detail. We call these sublists productions. The structure of a production is fixed, while the content of its four components (association, start, move, and alphabet) is determined by the Test Item Taker. The *association* list gives the starting symbol and indicates what transformation is to be made in it. *Start*, a number, indicates which symbol measured from the start of a string or group is the first symbol of the production. *Move*, also a number, indicates the number of characters to move from the first symbol in order to reach the second symbol in the production. The *alphabet* is the predefined list of symbols to be used by the

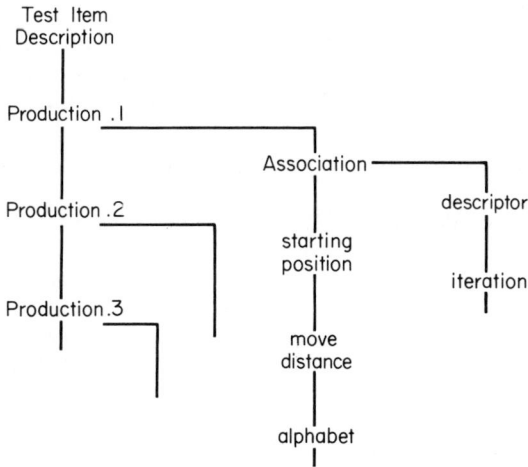

Figure 6 Test Item Description format. The structure used by the Test Item Taker as a log and description of a test item.

association list. The Test Item Taker can use a stored alphabet or create a new alphabet from the test item.

To illustrate the TID, consider the test item:

$$A\ A\ K\ A\ B\ M\ A\ C\ O\ A\ D\ Q\ \_\ \_\ \_\ .$$

Three productions (presented in tabular form) are required to fill in the blanks.

Production	Descriptor	Iteration	Start	Move	Alphabet
1	Same		1	3	
2	Next	1	2	3	English
3	Next	2	3	3	English

Production 1 indicates that starting at the *first* symbol in the test item (A) and moving *three* symbols each time, the *same* symbol or a blank occurs. Production 2 indicates that starting at the *second* symbol in the test item (A) and moving *three* symbols each time, the *next* symbol in the English alphabet (A B C D E) occurs. Production 3 is much like the second except that every other letter (next of next, or iteration = 2) in the English alphabet (K M O Q S) occurs.

The largest start (initial symbol) and the largest start-plus-move (second symbol) are determined from the length of the test item. The maximum iteration of a descriptor is determined by a constant in the Test Item Taker. The presently defined descriptors are listed in Figure 5. The present alphabets are English, backward English, integers, prime numbers, and alphabets constructed from test items.

The TID does not simulate closely the problem-solving techniques used by students for some types of test items, even though these items can be solved by the Test Item Taker. An example of an omission is the idea of triplets in

$$A\ A\ A\ B\ B\ B\ C\ C\ C\ D\ D\ D\ \_\ \_\ \_\ ,$$

which would be handled by the Test Item Taker thus:

Descriptor	Iteration	Start	Move	Alphabet
Next	1	1	3	English
Next	1	2	3	English
Next	1	3	3	English

The TID also lacks a mechanism to handle test items involving alternating descriptors or variable iteration, e.g.,

$$A\ B\ D\ G\ K\ P\ \_ \quad \text{or} \quad 3\ 6\ 3\ 12\ 7\ 42\ \_\ .$$

The obvious next step in the evolution of the TID is to add more operators and descriptors. However, most of the present operators listed in Figure 5 as well as the ones needed to deal with new aptitude tests are based on the concept of Next, using a more refined position reference system than is provided by Move. An example of evolution by improved reference is the additional position control number that was added to the TID in order to describe student eye motions on some of the letter series and number series test items. A satisfactory position reference would eliminate the need for some of the present operators and would extend the coverage of the TID.

SECTION 3
IMPLEMENTATION

The implementation of ATT determines the generality, performance, and efficiency of the program. This section demonstrates the generality of the major elements of ATT; in addition, it shows how the internal representation of a task is constructed and used. In particular, the Test Form Analyzer, the organization of a Test Item Taker from a Task Form Specification, and the elements of the Test Taker are discussed.

ATT has evolved from two previous versions. Version 1 dealt only with the letter series and letter analogies tests, using the English alphabet. The initial form of Version 2 was reported in Williams and Simon (29). The Test Item Description was organized differently from the present version, but contained the same information. Version 2 included more test types and adopted the Task Form Specification, but its Test Form Analyzer was weak and the structure of its Test Item Taker obscure. The present version added the explicit representation of the Test Item Taker and the use of trial Test Item Takers by the Test Form Analyzer. Since the present IPL-V code contains sections from Versions 1 and 2 as well as new code, the program is not to be regarded as a model of good coding.

3.1 Test Form Analyzer

The Test Form Analyzer (TFA), shown in Figure 7, performs the vital function of conceptualizing a task from worked examples. The operation of the TFA in going from these examples to the Task Form Specification is a two-stage process. (1) An example (question-answer pair) is specified, using feature extraction, by a list of features. (2) Each time a feature of the example is found, an attempt is made to refine the Task Form Specification. This process is continued for all of the examples presented.

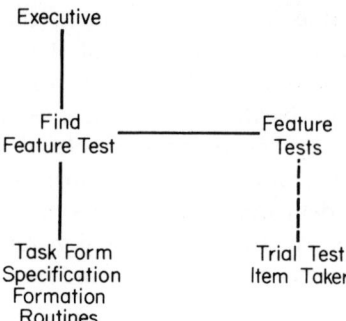

Figure 7 Test Form Analyzer structure. The hierarchy of routines that form the Test Form Analyzer.

Figure 7 also shows the special case (dashed line) of feature tests T6 and T7 that assemble Test Item Takers to check the applicability of relation and property descriptors to the test item. Figure 8 combines the parts of the TFA already discussed to demonstrate a typical operating sequence. The feature tests are executed first, followed by the *add* routines. The Task Form Specification, during its construction, is passed between the routines. In lines 2 and 3, the feature tests use the answer to the test item to discover the answer form. Lines 10 and 11 show the use of the trial Test Item Takers.

3.1.1 Generality. The Task Form Specification, since it controls the assembly of the Test Item Takers, influences the generality of the ATT. Among the eleven aptitude tests shown in Figure 9, eleven of the possible twenty-four combinations of elements of the TFS occur. The remaining combinations represent potential aptitude tests for which there are no examples. All the elements, except descriptors, occur with about equal frequency among the tests. Within the set of aptitude tests selected for study (see Section 4), very few tests use *properties* as their descriptor. As a consequence, the test item description has not been developed to the point where it deals adequately with properties as a descriptor.

3.1.2 Feature List. The feature list is the end result of the first stage of the two-stage process used by the TFA to construct the Task Form Specification. The feature list keeps track of the performance of TFA, governs the selection of features to be tested against the examples, and determines the elements to be added to the Task Form Specification.

At present there are twelve binary features that can be used to describe an example. The features specify the form of the answer (replace, find incorrect symbol or group, or describe), alphabet (letters, digits, or neither), symbol size (constant or variable), format (string or groups), and the success of trial Test Item Takers (relevance of properties or relations).

Input Sequence:

    Problem: A B M C D M E F M G H M _ _ _

    Answer: A B M C D M E F M G H M I J M

Trace of Test Form Analyzer:

  FIND ANSWER FORM
    TEST IF *EXCEPTIONAL ELEMENT* ($\Rightarrow$ NO)
    TEST IF *REPLACE* ($\Rightarrow$ YES)
    ADD *REPLACE* TO TASK FORM SPECIFICATION

  FIND PROBLEM ALPHABET
    TEST IF *CONSTANT SIZE* ($\Rightarrow$ YES)
    TEST IF *LETTERS* ($\Rightarrow$ YES)
    ADD *LETTERS* TO TASK FORM SPECIFICATION

  FIND PROBLEM CONTEXT
    TEST IF *STRING* ($\Rightarrow$ YES)
    TEST IF *GROUP* ($\Rightarrow$ NO)
    ADD *STRING* TO TASK FORM SPECIFICATION

  FIND PROBLEM DESCRIPTORS
    USE TRIAL TEST ITEM TAKER
      TO FIND *PROPERTIES* ($\Rightarrow$ FAILURE)
    USE TRIAL TEST ITEM TAKER
      TO FIND *RELATIONS* ($\Rightarrow$ SUCCESS)
    ADD *RELATIONS* TO TASK FORM SPECIFICATION

Find Feature List:

    not exceptional element
    replace
    constant size
    letters
    string
    not group
    not properties
    relations

Figure 8 Example of operating sequence of Test Form Analyzer.

    Implementing the tests for features is straightforward except for the use of trial Test Item Takers. The question to be answered in that case is: What classes of descriptors are appropriate to the solution of the examples? To answer the question, a few Test Item Takers are assembled using the information already in the Task Form Specification. The applicability of

	Letter analogies	Letter groups	Letter series	Number groups	Number relations	Number series	Number correction	Seeing trends	Word groups	Word relations	Inst. of Living
Descriptor Type											
properties		✓	✓								
relations	✓	✓		✓	✓	✓	✓	✓	✓	✓	✓
Format											
group	✓	✓		✓					✓	✓	✓
string			✓	✓		✓	✓	✓			✓
Symbol Type											
letters	✓	✓	✓						✓	✓	✓
numbers				✓	✓	✓	✓				✓
Answer Form											
replace	✓	✓								✓	✓
exceptional element		✓			✓		✓				
value				✓		✓		✓	✓		

Figure 9 Elements of the Task Form Specification used for typical aptitude tests.

a class of descriptors is determined by examining the productions created by the Test Item Takers.

3.1.3 Task Form Specification. The task form specification is the final result of the work of the TFA. TFA selects features to be tested as they are needed to complete the Task Form Specification. In building the Task Form Specification, the answer form is considered first, then the problem form, starting with the specific (symbol type) and proceeding (through format) to the general (descriptor type). The process advances from one element to the next whenever a feature is found to apply or when no positive features for the element in question can be found. When the TFA has attempted to complete each element of the Task Form Specification, it looks for additional examples, and when it finds one, tries new feature tests as well as tests that were negative on previous examples. A Task Form Specification that was made too specific on an earlier trial can be corrected, because all positive features for a set of examples are listed. When the examples have all been analyzed, the feature list is erased and the Task Form Specification is made available to the Test Item Taker Executive, which then tailor-makes a Test Item Taker for the class of examples presented.

The Task Form Specification can also be derived from the instruction text of the original aptitude test using a key word technique. This simple technique produces correct task form specifications except for (1) a format error in the number grouping, (2) seeing trends and Institute of Living tests, and (3) an operator error in the Institute of Living test. These errors result from the minimal instructions given in the Institute of Living test and the use of the word *group* in the instruction text of the other two tests. A Task Form Specification produced in this alternate manner can be input directly to the Test Item Taker Executive to control the formation of the Test Item Taker.

3.2 Forming the Test Item Taker

A Test Item Taker can be formed within the context of any of three executives. One executive is used when the TIT is operating independently (taking a test). The other two executives are tests for features that are a part of the Test Form Analyzer. From the viewpoint of the TIT it is immaterial which executive is using it.

3.2.1 Generality. ATT seeks to use a few problem-solving processes of wide applicability to each TIT. Thus, the extent to which the processes of TITs are applicable across tasks is important. The processes used to form the TITs are evenly employed among the 11 aptitude tests shown in Figure 10, except for the descriptor and operator processes. Only one or two of the aptitude tests require the four processes: replace (replace a symbol with a new symbol—any position), remove (remove a symbol—any position), double element (same unit of two symbols repeats—any position), and identical elements (same symbol appears more than once—any position). Since, in addition, these four processes can be described in terms of a generalized Next, little attention was paid to them, and they were not recoded for Version 3 of ATT. If these four processes are excluded from consideration, the distribution of processes across tasks is nearly uniform.

3.2.2 Formation. The executive forming a TIT is concerned with selecting the item description routines, with the final evaluation of the test item description and with input and output. Using the information in the Task Form Specification on descriptor type, format, and identified alphabets, a list of relevant descriptor routines is formed. The remaining program organization is delegated to one of three context routines, based on the format of the test item. The context routine in turn picks one of two move routines and one of three action routines using the format and answer form, re-

	Letter analogies	Letter groups	Letter series	Number groups	Number relations	Number series	Number correction	Seeing trends	Word groups	Word relations	Inst. of Living
Context											
group	✓	✓			✓				✓	✓	
string			✓	✓		✓	✓	✓			
group or string											✓
Descriptor											
same, next	✓	✓	✓					✓	✓	✓	✓
add, subtract				✓	✓	✓	✓				
multiply, divide											
replace										✓	✓
remove										✓	✓
double element		✓									
identical elements		✓		✓							
Move											
group	✓	✓			✓				✓	✓	✓
string			✓	✓		✓	✓	✓			✓
Operator											
same, next	✓	✓	✓					✓	✓	✓	✓
mathematical				✓	✓	✓	✓				
replace										✓	✓
remove										✓	✓
double element		✓									
identical elements		✓		✓							
Action											
replace	✓		✓							✓	✓
value				✓		✓		✓	✓		
exceptional element		✓			✓		✓				

Figure 10 Processes used to form the Test Item Takers in solving typical aptitude tests.

spectively, from the Task Form Specification. The information on identified alphabets, also from the Task Form Specification, is used to generate a list of relevant alphabets. Parameters governing movement within a test item are determined from an examination of the test item and the format information. The parameters are used by the move routine in setting up new productions. The descriptor routine picks its own operator routine.

When the form of the TIT has been established, except for an operator routine, and the parameters needed by the TIT have been set, the context routine passes control to the descriptor routine selected by the executive. As attempts are made to complete the TIT, the executive routine has the option of changing the descriptor routine or discontinuing the search. During the search the action routine and (normally) the move routine do not change. As different descriptor routines are used, the operator routines may change.

In the formation of a TIT, the selection of three independent groups of routines is controlled by different parts of the Task Form Specification: the context and move routines are determined by the task format; the descriptor and operator routines are determined by the task operator; the action routine is determined by the answer form.

3.3 Operation of the TIT

The final function, answering the aptitude test item, is executed largely by four processes: descriptor, move, operator, and action. The remaining process, context, serves to start the solution process. This section deals with the function of the four basic processes and the performance of the TIT.

3.3.1 Procedure. An understanding of the operation of the Test Item Taker can be gained by following the actual solution of a test item. Using a letter series test item and a letter analogies test item, protocols of the TIT are shown in Figures 12 and 14. The format of the Test Item Description is the same as in Section 2. Figure 11 explains the notation used in the protocol. The same test items, format, and notation are used in Section 4 (Figures 24 to 27) when the eye motions of students are analyzed.

Each line in the protocol represents one descent from the description process as the operating sequence in Figure 13 indicates. In comparing the TIT protocols and the student protocols (Figures 24 to 27), remember that each line in the student protocol represents ten frames of data rather than a hypothesized human elementary process. In the TIT protocol, each time a trial Test Item Description is accepted as correct (underscored), control returns to the executive routine (lines 3, 8, and 9 in Figure 13) which then has the choice of continuing with a new trial Test Item Description or halting the search.

Symbol	Meaning
A	Alphabet (description)
E	English alphabet
I	Iteration (description)
M	Move (description)
N	Next (operator)
O	Operator (description)
S	Start (description)
S	Same (operator)
TID	Test Item Description

Figure 11 Notation for the Test Item Taker protocol.

	Test Item Taker Moves												Trial Test Item Description				
	A	B	M	C	D	M	E	F	M	G	H	M— — —	O	I	S	M	A
1	A→B→M→C→D→M												S		1	1–5	
2		B———→C→D→M											S		2	2–4	
3			M————→M————→M————→M— — →										S		3	3	
4	A→B→M												N	1	1	1	E
5	A———→M→C→D→M												N	1	1	2–5	E
6		B———→C———→M											N	1	2	2	E
7		B———————→D→M											N	1	2	3–4	E
8	A→B→M→C———— — →E— — —→G— — →												N	2	1	1–2	E
													N	2	1	3	E
9		B———→C→D——— — →F— — →H— — →											N	2	2	2	E
													N	2	2	3	E

Notes: ——— Search
— — — Verify
▲ Match

Figure 12 Test Item Taker protocol with Test Item Description for the letter series test.

```
1                    CONTEXT ROUTINE = STRING . . .
                     DESCRIPTOR ROUTINE = SAME
                        MOVE ROUTINE
                           SET START = 1
                              TEST MOVE = 1 (⇒ NO)
                              . . . . . . . . . .
                              TEST MOVE = 5 (⇒ NO)
2                          SET START = 2
                              TEST MOVE = 2 (⇒ NO)
                              TEST MOVE = 3 (⇒ NO)
3                          SET START = 3
                              TEST MOVE = 3 (⇒ YES)
                     PRODUCE: (S    3  3   )
4                    DESCRIPTOR ROUTINE = NEXT
                        MOVE ROUTINE
                           SET ITERATION = 1
                           SET START = 1
5                             TEST MOVE = 1 (⇒ NO)
                              . . . . . . . . . .
                              TEST MOVE = 5 (⇒ NO)
6                          SET START = 2
                              TEST MOVE = 2 (⇒ NO)
7                             . . . . . . . . . .
                              TEST MOVE = 4 (⇒ NO)
8                          SET ITERATION = 2
                           SET START = 1
                              TEST MOVE = 1 (⇒ NO)
                              TEST MOVE = 2 (⇒ NO)
                              TEST MOVE = 3 (⇒ YES)
                     PRODUCE: (N 2 1 3 E)
9                       MOVE ROUTINE
                           SET ITERATION = 2
                           SET START = 2
                              TEST MOVE = 2 (⇒ NO)
                              TEST MOVE = 3 (⇒ YES)
                     PRODUCE: (N 2 2 3 E)
```

Figure 13 Sample of operating sequence of Test Item Taker.

164 Computer Program Organization Induced from Problem Examples

The TIT starts by counting the number of symbols in the test item. It then looks for a match (line 1) to the letter A (position 1) by moving one to five positions forward. No match is found. The TIT stops at position six because any match found beyond that point could not be confirmed by a second instance. The search proceeds in an orderly manner looking for a match to B (line 2) and M (line 3), with the TIT finding the first correct match in line three. In line four, the TIT finds a match to the sequence A B but fails to get a match to C. A similar situation arises in line six where a failure to get a match to D stops the search. In both lines four and six, the TIT has found a piece of information that could lead to a solution of the problem, but the TIT has no way of using it. The eye-motion films indicate that these two pieces of information are indeed used by the students. The TIT finishes the test item by finding the two remaining matches in lines eight and nine.

In solving a letter analogies test item (Figure 14), the TIT uses group context and group move in place of string context and string move. The TIT starts by determining the group size, and then searches for matches. In line four a match is found that does not contribute to the solution and is subsequently ignored. The TIT will not find the production N 1 3 1 E

	Test Item Taker Moves									Trial Test Item Description				
C	D	G	H	M	N	Q	R	T	U	—	—	O	I	S	M	A
1 C→D→G→H												S		1	1–3	
2 D→G→H												S		2	1–2	
3 G→H												S		3	1	
4 C→D— — — —→M—→N— — — —→T→U												N	1	1	1	E
5 C————→G→H												N	1	1	2–3	E
6 C→D→G→H												N	2–3	1	1–3	E
7 C→D→G— — —→M— — —→Q—→T— — —→												N	4	1	1	E
												N	4	1	2	E
8 D→G→H												N	1–3	2	1–2	E
9 D→G→H— —→N— —→R—→U— — —→												N	4	2	1	E
												N	4	2	2	E

Notes: ———— Search
       — — — Verify
        ▲   Match

Figure 14 Test Item Taker protocol with Test Item Description for the letter analogies test.

because position three is excluded from being a starting position after it has been used by the successful description in line seven.

3.3.2 **Processes.** Four processes (descriptor, move, operator, and action) are responsible for most of the performance shown in Figures 12 to 14 and are explained in the remainder of this section.

The job of a *descriptor routine* is to construct task item descriptions using its particular descriptor. Thus there are separate descriptor routines for most of the descriptors, but due to their similarity, the following descriptors are handled by a single descriptor routine (generalized next) with six entry routines, one for each descriptor: next, add, subtract, multiply, divide, and identical elements. Thus five descriptor routines cover ten possible descriptors. Since three of the descriptor routines (replace, remove, and double element) are required for only a few test items in four aptitude tests, they were not recoded for Version 3.

The descriptor routine starts by setting the operator routine into the TIT structure. Then a description is formed by setting the proper descriptor and descriptor iteration and picking a valid starting position and alphabet from the lists of possible positions and alphabets supplied by the context routine. The production is turned over to the move routine for evaluation. If it is rejected, the descriptor routine will provide additional productions within its capability by altering the starting position, the operator iteration, and the alphabet (if appropriate and if alternatives are available).

The *move* routine finds the starting position specified in the production and the symbol in that position. It applies the operator routine to find the next symbol, and then seeks to match this symbol within the bounds set by the context routine. If a match is found, the move routine sets the move distance in the production. After every move, the move routine executes the action routine to determine if it is to continue. If the action routine indicates that the move routine is to proceed, the production is checked on additional symbols of the test item. If a match is not found, the search is continued. When the move routine has formed a production, the action routine is again executed to determine its acceptabillty.

An *operator* routine is given a symbol and a production. Using the operator iteration and the specified alphabet, the operator routine performs the specified operation on the symbol. Since one operator routine serves for all the mathematical operators, there are seven routines for ten operators. Because four of these routines (replace, remove, double element, and identical elements) apply only in special cases arising in a few aptitude tests, they were not coded for Version 3.

The *action* routines enforce the restrictions imposed by the type of answer expected. Thus in the case of a fill-in test item, a production is accepted by the action routine only if it results in a blank being filled. If, alternatively, the incorrect symbol in a test item is to be identified, in order to be acceptable a production must locate one and only one incorrect symbol. If the answer form specifies that a test item is to be described, a production must correctly describe a feature of the test item. Thus the development of a production is controlled by the three action routines, one for each answer form. Each action routine has its own set of criteria for permitting the development of a production to continue and for accepting it if the development runs to completion.

SECTION 4
COMPARISON

A human being is the most general system that organizes to perform a task. Problems designed for humans were selected as the tasks for ATT, and human performance guided its development. The factors considered in selecting the aptitude tests and the human performance used to evaluate ATT are discussed in this section.

Two systems can be compared at various levels of detail. If general measures of performance are used, such as average score or time per item, little is learned about the intervening processes. On the other hand, if a subject is observed very closely (e.g., eye motions), his accuracy and speed may be affected and his processes may be altered. The present study uses three different kinds of comparison of ATT with humans.

The most aggregate comparison matches the published scores for a test battery, developed as a "study of aptitudes of high level personnel" by J. P. Guilford (12, 15), with the scores obtained by the Test Item Takers. A closer look is taken at the performance of the Test Item Takers on three aptitude tests: letter analogies, letter series, and the Institute of Living intelligence tests. For the letter analogies and letter series tests, comparisons are made between human performance and the Test Item Takers. The Institute of Living test is used to demonstrate the capabilities of the Test Item Takers. Finally, a detailed comparison is made of the test item descriptions generated by the Test Item Takers with the descriptions inferred from the human eye-movement studies.

The performance of ATT can be expected to be broadly similar to human performance, since the techniques used in the program were suggested by the human behavior observed by Kotovsky (unpublished) in the letter series test and the preliminary data from the eye-movement studies. Since the research was aimed at devising a technique for organizing to perform a task, ATT is not necessarily a close model of human behavior (nor is it implied that humans form a Test Item Taker in order to organize their problem-solving activities).

4.1 Test Selection

To insure a representative selection of tasks, aptitude tests were selected from batteries developed by J. P. Guilford. Selection was controlled by Guilford's (8, 9, 10, 11, 14) "structure of intellect" models of abilities.

4.1.1 Structure of Intellect. Guilford's "structure of intellect" is a classification that organizes all kinds of intellectual aptitude factors in a single system. Each factor is cataloged in terms of three basic variables: operation, content, and product. There are five *operations*: cognition (discovery, recognition, or comprehension), memory, convergent thinking (recognized best or conventional answer), divergent thinking (searching), and evaluation (correctness).

Content refers to four types of information: symbolic (conventional signs, usually ordered), semantic, figural, and behavioral. An operation applied to the content of a test item yields one of six kinds of *product*: units (items of information), classes (collection of units), relations (connections between units), systems (organized structures), transformations, and implications.

Taking the basic variables and assigning them to the three dimensions of a cube, as shown in Figure 15, a set of 120 cells is created, each cell supposed to contain a unique ability that is needed for a certain class of tasks. Out of the 120 cells, 82 factors occupying 79 cells have been discussed in the literature and 74 factors have been associated with observed performance. Each cell in the "structure of intellect" carries a three-letter designation indicating the value of the three basic variables it represents: operator first, contents second, and product last. In each case, the designation is the first letter of the variable name, except for convergent thinking (N) and semantic content (M). Thus CSS is cognition of symbolic systems and NSU is convergent production of symbolic units.

4.1.2 Classification. To keep the tests for ATT within bounds, a few variables were chosen from the "structure of intellect." Content was limited to "symbolic" in order to avoid computer input and internal translation difficulties. Operations were limited to "cognition." Products or forms of information were limited to "units," "classes," "relations," and "systems." These restrictions were met by seven tests from the Guilford test battery. An eighth test, word fluency (representing cell CSU), was not used because it requires a large vocabulary and a simple search scheme for solution.

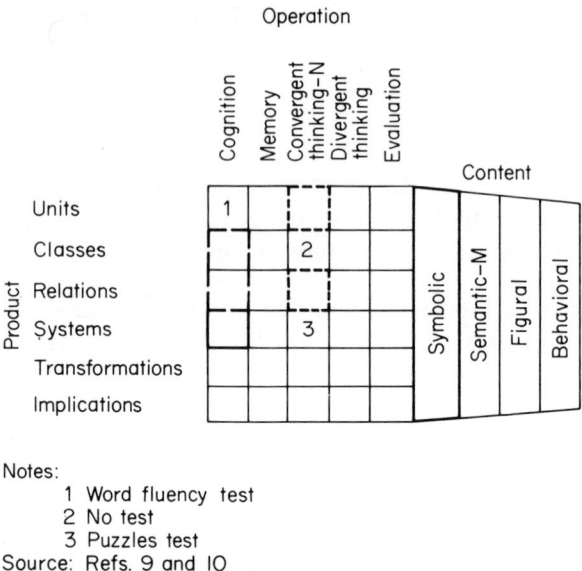

Figure 15 Guilford's Structure of Intellect model. See text for significance of cells enclosed by short-dashed, long-dashed, heavy solid lines.

Thus the tasks used represent the factors enclosed by the solid and long-dashed lines in Figure 15. The L. L. Thurstone letter series test was then added because of its importance in the work of Simon and Kotovsky (24). Guilford [in 1960 (13)] classified the letter series test as NSR, thus suggesting that tests from his collection representing the operation convergent thinking (four additional cells) should be added to the test battery for ATT. Since there is no test for cell NSC and the test for cell NSS, *puzzles*, requires a GPS-like (5, 6) solution strategy, these two cells were not represented in the test battery. Thus tests were added to the battery from the cells bounded by the short-dashed lines, bringing the total to ten tests. The tests and permission to use them were secured from J. P. Guilford. Guilford's classification of the ten tests is shown in Figure 16. The Institute of Living intelligence test, excluding the word-meaning section, was also added to the test battery.

In 1966, Guilford (11) issued a new classification of the tests shown in Figure 16. Five tests used with the Aptitude Test Taker had been dropped from the list because they tested more than one factor. Three other tests were reclassified. As a result of these changes, all the tests left from the original battery were now classified under "cognition," and most were in cell CSS of Figure 15 (solid line). Tests from the original battery that would require changes in the Test Item Taker for solution are in cells CSC and CSR of Figure 15 (long-dashed lines).

| | Classification by Year | |
Test	1960	1966
Letter analogies	CSS	
Letter grouping	CSC	
Letter series	NSR	CSS
Number groups	NSU	CSC
Number relations	CSC	
Number series	CSS	CSS
Number correction	CSS	
Seeing trends	CSR	CSR
Word groups	NSU	CSR
Word relations	CSR	

Source: Refs. 11, 14, and 15.

Figure 16 Guilford's factor classification of the aptitude tests. Cell occupancy in the Structure of Intellect model (Figure 15) of the tests used with the Aptitude Test Taker.

4.2 Test Battery

The comparison of the performance of ATT with the Guilford test data provides an aggregate view of the capability of ATT as well as general ideas for its further evolution. ATT performs comparably with humans on tests classified as CSS but fails on number groups, seeing trends, and word groups which are classified (1966) as CSC and CSR. Remedying this deficiency calls for two extensions of ATT. An easily implemented change would permit intermixing analogy with series patterns by adding another parameter to the Test Item Description. A second possible extension would require a new scheme to designate position and move.

4.2.1 *Comparison.* ATT dealt successfully with seven of the ten tests selected from the Guilford battery. Due to the test conditions used by Guilford, the test scores and test times reported by Guilford (12, 15) cannot be compared directly with ATT. Therefore the tasks were ranked according to difficulty, as shown in Figure 17, using as nearly comparable measures as possible.

The rankings provide little new information. The score ranking based on human subject performance shows no correlation with the other rankings. The two rankings based on the performance of ATT, while not correlated with each other, have an inverse correlation with the time ranking from the human data. Three tests from the original test battery (number groups,

	Ranking			
	Time		Score	
Test	Subjects	ATT	Subjects	ATT
Letter analogies	5	3	7	2
Letter grouping	1	6	2	3
Letter series	7	4	1	1
Number relations	3	2	3	5
Number series	2	5	6	7
Number correction	6	1	5	4
Word relations	4	7	4	6

Source: Refs. 12 and 15.

Figure 17 Comparison of the Aptitude Test Taker and subjects by ranking of test difficulty. The time and score data from J. P. Guilford and the Aptitude Test Taker have been converted to a ranking for comparison where 1 represents the least time per test item and the highest score.

seeing trends, and word groups) are not ranked because the Aptitude Test Taker was unable to solve the problems.

4.2.2 Evaluation. The interesting information from the aggregate comparison of ATT with human performance comes from the unsuccessful aspects of ATT. Three characteristics of the program account for its failures.

First, the Test Item Takers require the move distance to be non-zero. Some properties do not involve associations between symbols of the test item but are properties of individual symbols; "divisible by five" is an example.

Second, there is now no provision to describe a pattern by reference to the end or center of a group. Hence, there is needed a better position and move reference system.

Third, the operator routines for replace, remove, double element, and identical elements were not implemented. These routines are intended to deal with the concept of *same* when the start and move distances are not defined by the test item. This limitation is closely connected with the previous one.

Three modifications were made in the Test Item Description to describe the observed human performance, but no attempt was made to add them to the Test Item Takers.

First, group length was added as an optional item in the Test Item Description. The group length specifies a period within a sequence, as in the Simon and Kotovsky pattern description (24). The use of the group length

```
                length
                ─────────⟶
    A    B    M    C    D    M    E    F    M    —    —    —
         ↑────────⟶
         │   move
        start
```

Sample Test Item

O	I	S	M	L	A
SAME		+3	+3		
NEXT	+1	+1	+1	+3	Eng
NEXT	+1	+2	+2	+3	Eng

L = Group Length

Figure 18 Modified Test Item Description. An example of the use of group length and move to describe a test item.

in a description is illustrated in Figure 18 using the same test item as that shown in Figures 12 and 13.

Second, to describe properties possessed by each symbol of a sequence, the convention was adopted of setting the move distance to zero, and using the group length to drive the Test Item Taker through the sequence.

Third, a sequence of associations in the descriptions was used to describe the cyclic patterns found in the number series test.

An alternate positional reference system suggested by Newell and Simon (22) allows position, move, and group to be expressed by either constants or a simple algebraic formula. For example, if subscripts can be treated as variables so that x_{yz} represents the yth symbol in the zth group or periodic repetition of the pattern, then a concept such as "the TH moves one position to the right in each group" can be expressed as $x_{jj} = T$, $x_{j(j+1)} = H$. The concepts for the last symbol and the next-to-last symbol of a group are still needed since the groups are not always of a uniform length. The concepts of "each group adds one letter" and "the number of I's increase by one in each group" still are not handled by this device.

4.3 Aptitude Tests

The performance of ATT on an item-by-item basis provides a good view of its capability, and demonstrates the effect of the Test Item Description grammar on its power. The performance of ATT is comparable to student performance on analogy tests.

4.3.1 *Student Selection.* To compare student performance with ATT at the item level, an experiment was conducted with twenty-four junior and sophomore college students, using the letter analogies and letter series tests. To determine if measured aptitudes of the students influenced performance and to control the effects of this variable, the students were selected on the basis of their verbal and mathematical scores on the College Entrance Examination. Four groups of subjects represented the four combinations of high and low mathematical and verbal scores. To control for learning during the test session, the order of presentation of the letter analogies and letter series tests was reversed for half of each group. All students were given the same instructions: to work as fast as possible, not to return to a test item, and to take as much time as they needed to complete the test.

4.3.2 Treatment of Data. During the test, the answers and the time per answer were recorded. From these data the average time per correct answer for each subject was subjected to an analysis of variance. The test items were also ranked for each student by time per answer, the incorrectly answered test items being ranked last.

In the analysis of variance, the three control factors were found to be

	Probability of null hypothesis	
Variable	Letter analogies	Letter series
College Board verbal scores	0.45	0.7
College Board math scores	0.4	0.2
Order of presentation	0.01	0.9

Test	Mean time for solution
Letter analogies	
first	21.0 sec/correct ans
second	33.6 sec/correct ans
Letter series	31.0 sec/correct ans

Figure 19 Significance of controlled factors for student performance.

	Rankings				
	Letter series		Letter analogies		
	Aptitude		Aptitude	Students	
Test item	test taker	Students	test taker	first	second
1	1	1	2	11	10
2	5	2	5	3	3
3	19	9	18	19	17
4	2	5	19	20	20
5	10	4	1	4	9
6	11	17	3	1	2
7	16	11	13	12	7
8	15	3	7	2	1
9	18	20	10	5	6
10	14	6	9	10	14
11	3	10	11	16	16
12	20	12	6	13	13
13	9	8	12	6	5
14	12	13	4	7	4
15	7	19	15	8	11
16	4	7	20	15	15
17	8	15	14	17	18
18	13	14	16	14	12
19	17	16	8	9	8
20	6	18	17	18	19

Figure 20 Comparison of the Aptitude Test Taker and students by ranking of item difficulty. The rankings are based on time for solution, with 1 representing the shortest time. The student rankings are the combined rankings of each student's performance. The Kendall coefficients of concordance (0.62 to 0.69) for the combined student rankings are significant at the 0.005 level.

not significant except for the order of presentation of the letter analogies test. The results of the analysis are presented in Figure 19. The slower performance when the letter analogies test is given second might be attributed to this test being the easier of the two and the students having used less than half of the time they had planned to allot for the experiment.

The test item rankings by student were combined into the average rankings shown in Figure 20. The letter analogies test was ranked separately for the two orders of presentation because of the significant difference found in student performance. The Kendall coefficients of concordance (see Siegal, 23) for the three student rankings (letter analogies presented first, 0.69; letter analogies presented second, 0.66; and the letter series, 0.62) are significant at the 0.005 level.

The major changes in the rankings of the letter analogies presented first and second, respectively, can be explained in terms of a change in the students' sophistication about the descriptions required. A student who has already taken the letter series test knows something about the descriptions required for letter analogies, and thus would find some letter analogies test items easier than a less experienced student.

To provide a ranking of the test items to represent the Test Item Takers, the time for solution was used, placing the incorrectly answered items last.

4.3.3 Comparison. For the letter analogies test, the concordance of the rankings by the students and the Test Item Takers is 0.86 and 0.88 for the two orders of presentation, respectively, both significant at the 0.025 level. The concordance of the rankings for the letter series test is 0.66, significant at only the 0.25 level. The difference in concordance is explainable in terms of the solution procedures for letter series used by the students, as indicated by the eye-motion studies and the work of Simon and Kotovsky (24). Both studies indicate that students find a pattern length in the letter series test and then base all their descriptions upon that length. The Test Item Takers do not use a previously defined pattern length in forming a trial description. Moreover, the Test Item Takers do not forget or confuse elements of the Test Item Description when working complex test items. The importance of confusion as a factor in human performance was clear in the verbal protocols from the eye-motion studies.

4.3.4 Intelligence Test. To demonstrate further the characteristics of the Test Item Takers, a series of test items was adapted from the Shipley-Institute of Living test (also known as the Shipley-Hartford Intelligence test). The portion of the intelligence test dealing with word meanings was

Symbol	*Meaning*
A	Alphabet (description)
B	Backward alphabet
E	English alphabet
I	Iteration (description)
M	Move (description)
N	Next (operator)
O	Operator (description)
S	Start (description)
	Same (operator)
V	Vowel alphabet
+	Add (operator)
( )	Relation not found

Figure 21 Notation for the Institute of Living protocol.

	Test	Test item description
		O I S M A
1.	1 2 3 4 5 __	+ 1 1 1
2.	A B B C C D D __	N 1 1 1 E
3.	Z Y X W V U __	N 1 1 1 B
4.	12321 23432 34543 456 __ __	S 1 4
		S 2 2
5.	ESCAPE SCAPE CAPE A __ __	N 1 1 1 *
	* = ESCAPE	N 1 2 1 *
6.	OH HO RAT TAR MOOD __ __ __ __ __	( )
7.	A Z B Y C X D __	N 1 2 2 B
8.	TOT TOT PAR RAP 537 __ __ __	S 1 5
		S 2 3
		S 3 1
9.	MIST IS WASP AS PINT IN TONE __ __	S 2 3
		S 3 3
10.	57326 73265 32657 26573 __ __ __ __ __	S 5 4
		( )
11.	KNIT IN SPUD UP BOTH TO STAY __ __	S 2 4
		S 3 2
12.	SCOTLAND LANDSCAPE SCAPEGOAT __ __ __ __ __	( )
13.	LARGE 12345 REGAL 35421 GLARE __ __ __ __ __	N 5 1 5 *
		N 5 2 5 *
	* = LARGE 12345	N 5 3 5 *
		N 5 4 5 *
		N 5 5 5 *
14.	TAM TAN RIB RID RAT RAW HIP __ __ __ __	S 1 3
		S 2 3
		( )
15.	3124 82 73 154 46 13 __	( )
16.	LAG LEG PEN PIN BIG BOG ROB __ __ __	S 1 3
		S 3 3
		N 1 2 3 V

Figure 22 Shipley-Hartford Intelligence Test (© 1939, The Institute of Living) with Test Item Description.

omitted because ATT is not designed to handle these. The remaining items are shown in Figure 22, along with the test item descriptions produced by the Test Item Takers. The notations used in Figure 22 are listed in Figure 21.

4.3.5 Conclusion. The test items not completed by ATT illustrate four characteristics on which the Test Item Takers fail. Problem 10 of the Institute of Living test as well as problems 16 and 19 of the letter analogies test point up the ease students have with mixed format, whereas the Test Item Takers cannot treat series and analogies interchangeably. Problem 6 of the Institute of Living test requires a more sophisticated grammar than is provided by the Test Item Description to express the concept of symmetry. The inclusion of group length in the Test Item Description is also required to handle position three of problem 14. It is not clear how the students solve problem 15 of the intelligence test, nor how the descriptions of ATT might be enriched to solve it.

The Test Item Takers perform in a manner comparable to students in solving analogy tests, but they fail to use all of the available information in solving series tests. Concepts that cannot be represented in the Test Item Description (e.g., absence of the concept of symmetry) limit the information that the Test Item Takers will enter in the description.

4.4 Test Items.

A detailed comparison of the performance of ATT with the test item descriptions inferred from eye-movement studies substantiates the techniques used to implement ATT and provides specific suggestions for possible improvements.

4.4.1 Experiment. Four eye-movement experiments were run to determine the sequences students used in solving test items. The experiments involved a sophomore and a graduate engineer taking the Thurstone letter series test (used by Simon and Kotovsky, 24), the letter analogies and letter series tests from the experiment reported in the previous section, and the Guilford number series test. The Thurstone letter series test, identified as letter series I in reporting the data, requires one blank to be filled in. The letter series test, identified as letter series II, requires three fill-ins. The items for letter series I are a subset of those for letter series II.

4.4.2 Procedure. The eye movements were filmed by A. Winikoff (30) using the Westgate eye-motion camera and Ampex two-channel audio tape recorder. The visual field of the student is recorded on the eye-camera film together with an eye spot that indicates where the student is looking and a frame count. The student's verbal protocol is recorded on one channel of the audio tape with synchronization information on the other channel. The synchronization normally consists of two tones, one at every tenth frame and the other every hundredth frame. With film in the camera, the spacing of successive tones varies from 2 to 2.5 seconds. Without film in the camera, a situation that occurs during the last test item tried, the tone spacing is 1.4 seconds. Diagrams of the camera can be found in Appendix I of "Eye-Movements as an Aid to Protocol Analysis of Problem Solving Behavior" (Winikoff, 30). The test items were projected one at a time on a screen in front of the student. A special font was selected by the author to improve the clarity of the display.

An experimental session lasts about 40 minutes and produces 5000 frames of data (about 18 minutes). The films and tapes were transcribed by the author. The correspondence between the eye spot and visual field was established by one–three calibration runs recorded during each session. Shifts in calibration between calibration runs were accounted for by plotting all the eye spots for a test item. The plots produced a cluster of points corresponding to each character in the visual field.

4.4.3 **Treatment of Data.** The plots of the eye movements and the verbal protocols, while presented in ten-frame blocks based on the synchronization data, can be aggregated into units that would each result from a specific action relating to the trial of a Test Item Description or a verification. The eye movements and verbal protocol are aggregated independently, and the resulting descriptions are then combined.

A trial Test Item Description from the verbal protocol is accepted for consideration as a part of the combined description if it is correct, even though the student may forget it as he searches for other test item descriptions. A trial Test Item Description from the eye-movement data is accepted for consideration as a part of the combined description if it is correct and the student shows an eye movement based on the description sufficient to complete a part of the test item (verify action).

Illustrative reductions of the eye movements from the letter series II test and the letter analogies test, shown in Figures 24 and 26, and the verbal protocols, shown in Figures 25 and 27, demonstrate the technique. Figure 23 explains the symbols used for all of the Test Item Descriptions. The format is the same as that used in previous figures.

In Figures 24 and 26, each line represents ten frames of data. The trial test item descriptions are placed on the first line that contains part of the corresponding action unit. In the eye-movement data, the verifying action required to accept a description as successful (underscored) usually occurs several lines after the appearance of the trial description.

The sample eye-movement data (Figure 24) show a search strategy slightly different from that used by ATT. Local search is started in lines 1360 and 1400 by looking for simple descriptions that might work; two are found. The third try in line 1400 results in a successful description. Returning (near the end of line 1420) to the start of the test item and remembering the information already discovered (lines 1360 and 1400), the subject develops

Symbol	Meaning
A	Alphabet (description)
B	Backward alphabet
E	English alphabet
I	Iteration (description)
L	Length (description)
M	Move (description)
N	Next (operator)
O	Operator (description)
S	Start (description)
	Same (operator)
	Student
T	Test item number
TID	Test item description
V	Vowel alphabet
I	Letter Series I
II	Letter Series II
+	Add (operator)
−	Subtract (operator)
×	Multiply (operator)
/	Divide (operator)
( )	Relation not found
—	Second solution follows

Notes

Lowercase letters are used for special alphabets.

The word "sounds" indicates that the student used sound patterns to solve the test item.

The word "end" indicates that the student worked from right to left.

Blank entries indicate that the test item was not given to the student.

Figure 23 Notation for eye-movement protocols.

the needed descriptions very rapidly. He does not make the detailed search seen in ATT for *same* associations. More important, his search uses previous information to save rescanning parts of the test item.

The successful trial test item descriptions from the eye-movement data and verbal protocols are checked to insure agreement. A description must appear first in the eye-movement data and then in the verbal protocol to be included in the final protocol. If the descriptions do not appear in the same order in the eye-movement data and the verbal protocol, the order

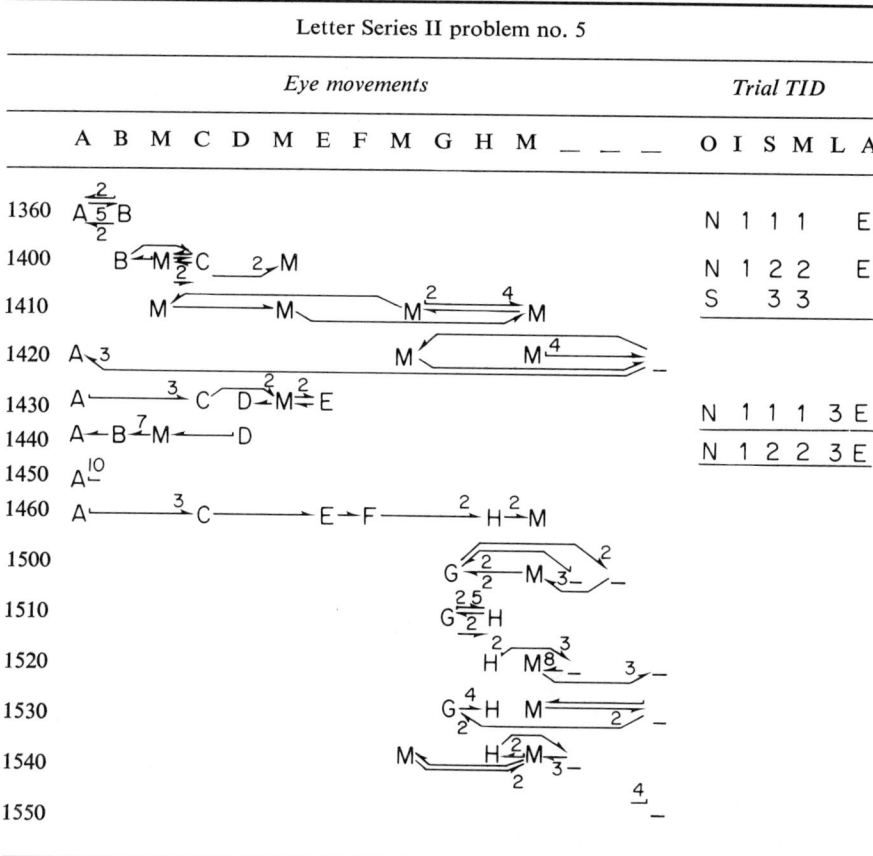

Figure 24 Letter Series. Eye-movement data with Test Item Description. Each line represents ten frames of data. A vertical tail indicates the start of each line. (Film 1054)

is determined by the eye-movement data. The final test item descriptions for the letter analogies, letter series, and number series are presented in Figures 28, 29, and 30, along with the descriptions produced by the Test Item Takers.

To report the performance observed in the eye-movement data for the letter series (Figure 29) and number series (Figure 30) tests, it was necessary to expand the Test Item Description outlined in Section 2. A new attribute, *length*, was added to the description to measure the pattern length from the start position to the next symbol used as a starting symbol (cf. Figure 18). When a length is specified, *move* determines only the second symbol for the association. For the number series test (Figure 30), multiple associa-

A B M C D M E F M G H M _ _ _							
	Verbal protocol			*Trial TID*			
		O	I	S	M	L	A
1360	And here we have						
1400	um						
1410	um looking through this we see a sequence of Ms	S		3	3		
1420	through out the pattern						
1430	and then . .						
1440	we also have interplaced with that	N	1	1	1	3	E
1450	the regular insequence alphabet	N	1	2	2	3	E
1460	So it would be F						
1500	GH then M						
1510	. . .						
1520	it would be IJ						
1530	. . .						
1540	and then another M.						
1550	Experimenter: Okay						

Figure 25 Letter Series. Verbal protocol with Test Item Description. Each line corresponds to ten frames of data. The line number is the frame count to the start of the line. (Tape 1054)

tions indicate a set of operations to be performed cyclically, advancing one for each move. In Figure 30, only the test items for which student protocols exist are presented. Each type of test item description used in the number series test is represented by one of the eight test items presented to the student.

4.4.4 Comparison. Comparing the test item descriptions produced by the student and the Test Item Takers, respectively, for the letter analogies test (Figure 28), six out of 15 descriptions match exactly (test items 1, 5, 6, 10, 14, and 18). The important differences in the remaining descriptions can be explained by three characteristics of the Test Item Takers. The Test Item Takers use the backward alphabet rather than moving in reverse on the forward alphabet as the student does in test items 2 and 17. The Test Item Takers only accept a description that is of immediate value, while the student's patterns in test items 7, 9, 12, and 13 show acceptance and reordering of partial descriptions to produce a solution. In test items 16 and 19 the student treats the analogies as series. The student never recognizes the vowel alphabet in test item 15.

Three additional characteristics account for the differences observed in the test item descriptions for the letter series test. The major difference is

Letter Analogies problem no. 9

	Eye movements	Trial TID
	C D G H M N Q R T U _ _	O I S M A
1170	C →2 D →4 →3 G	N 1 1 1 E
1180	D →3 G →3 M ←N ——2→ T	
1190	C ⇌2 D ⇌3 G	N 1 3 1 E
1200	D ⇌3 G ⇌4 H	N (3) 2 1 E
1210	D ⇌2,5/3 G	
1220	D ⇌2,2 G ——3→ M ⇌2 Q	
1230	M —2→3 Q ← R —5→ T	
1240	N ← Q ←2 T ⇌3/2 U _	
1250	T ⇌6/2 U _	
1260	T ⇌8,2 U	

Figure 26 Letter Analogies. Eye-movement data with Test Item Description. Each line represents ten frames of data. A vertical tail indicates the start of each line. (Film 1046)

	C D G H M N Q R T U _ _	
	Verbal Protocol	Trial TID
		O I S M A
1170	. . .	
1180	Oh boy	
1190	Okay	
1200	Here we have	
1210	uh gaps of two letters	N 1 1 1 E
		N 1 3 1 E
1220	in the alphabet and everything's in order	N 2 2 1 E
1230	. . .	
1240	Should have a UV I mean rather	
1250	. . .	
1260	. . WX	

Figure 27 Letter Analogies. Verbal protocol with Test Item Description. Each line corresponds to ten frames of data. The line number is the frame count to the start of the line. (Tape 1046)

	Student					ATT				
T	O	I	S	M	A	O	I	S	M	A
1	N	3	1	1	E	N	3	1	1	E
2	N	1	2	-1	E	N	1	1	1	B
5	N	1	1	1	E	N	1	1	1	E
6	N	(4)	1	1	E	N	4	1	1	E
7	S		1	1		N	2	1	2	B
	S		3	1		N	2	2	2	B
	N	2	3	-1	E					
8						N	2	1	2	E
						N	2	2	2	E
9	N	1	1	1	E	N	4	1	2	E
	N	1	3	1	E	N	4	2	2	E
	N	(3)	2	1	E					
10	N	1	1	2	E	N	1	1	2	B
	N	1	2	2	B	N	1	2	2	B
11						N	4	1	2	E
						N	4	2	2	E
12	N	1	1	3	E	N	1	1	3	E
	N	1	4	-2	E	N	1	2	1	E
	N	1	2	1	E					
13	N	1	2	2	E	N	1	2	2	E
	N	1	1	1	E	N	3	1	2	E
	N	1	4	-1	E					
14	N	1	1	2	E	N	1	1	2	E
	N	1	2	2	E	N	1	2	2	E
15	S		2	1		S		2	1	
	N	(6)	3	1	E	N	1	1	3	V
16	solved as series item									
	N	1	2	6	E					
	N	1	3	6	E					
	N	1	1	6	E					
	N	1	1	3	E ⎤					
	N	1	2	3	E ⎬ ans					
	N	1	3	3	E ⎦					
17	S		1	2		N	1	1	3	E
	N	1	3	1	E	N	1	3	3	E
	S		4	2		N	1	2	3	B
	N	1	5	-3	E					
18	S		2	3		S		2	3	
	S		3	1		S		3	1	
	N	1	1	5	E	N	1	1	5	E

Figure 28 Letter Analogies Test Item Description. (Film 1046)

	Student					ATT				
T	O	I	S	M	A	O	I	S	M	A
19	solved as series item									
	N	1	1	3	E	N	1	1	3	E
	N	1	3	3	E	N	1	2	3	E
	N	1	2	3	E	N	1	3	3	E
20						S		2	4	
						N	2	1	3	E

Figure 28 (*cont.*)

	I						II						ATT				
T	O	I	S	M	L	A	O	I	S	M	L	A	O	I	S	M	A
1	S		1	2			N	1	1	1		cd	S		1	2	
	S		2	2									S		2	2	
	N	1	1	1		cd											
2	S		1	1	3		S		1	1	3		N	1	1	3	E
	S		2	1	3		S		2	1	3		N	1	2	3	E
	N	1	3	1	3	E	N	1	1	3		E	N	1	3	3	E
3	sounds						S		2	3			S		1	3	
	S		1	3			N	1	3	3		ba	(N	1	3	3	ba)
	S		2	3			N	1	3	1	3	baa					
	N	1	3	3		ba											
4													S		1	2	
													N	1	2	2	E
5	N	1	1	1	3	E	S		3	3			S		3	3	
	S		3	3			N	1	1	1	3	E	N	2	1	3	E
	N	1	2	2	3	E	N	1	2	2	3	E	N	2	2	3	E
6	N	1	1	1	4	E	N	1	1	1	4	E	N	1	1	4	E
	N	1	2	1	4	E	N	1	2	1	4	E	N	1	2	4	E
	N	1	3	1	4	E	N	1	3	1	4	E	N	1	3	4	E
	S		2	3	4		S		2	3	4						
7	S		2	3			S		2	3			S		2	3	
	S		3	6			N	1	3	3		ab	N	2	1	3	qapb
	S		4	6			N	1	4	3		E	N	2	3	3	qapb
8													S		1	4	
													S		2	4	
													N	1	4	4	E

Figure 29 Letter Series Test Item Description. (Films 1053 and 1054)

	I							II							ATT					
T	O	I	S	M	L	A		O	I	S	M	L	A		O	I	S	M	A	
9	S		1	3				S		1	3				S		1	3		
	S		3	3				S		3	3				S		3	3		
	N	1	2	6		E									(N	1	5	6	B)	
	N	1	5	6		B														
10	S		1	3				S		1	3				S		1	3		
	N	1	2	1	3	E		N	1	2	1	3	E		N	1	2	3	E	
	S		3	2	3			S		3	2	3			N	1	3	3	E	
11	S		3	3				S		1	3				S		1	3		
	S		1	3				S		3	3				S		3	3		
	N	1	2	3		E		N	1	2	3		E		N	1	2	3	E	
12															S		2	2		
															(N	1	1	2	B)	
13	S		1	3				S		1	3				S		1	3		
	S		2	3				S		2	3				S		2	3		
	N	1	3	3		B		N	1	3	3		B		N	1	3	4	B	
14	S		2	3	4			N	1	3	1	4	E		N	1	1	4	E	
	S		4	3	4			N	1	1	1	4	E		N	1	2	4	E	
	N	1	1	1	4	E		S		2	3	4			N	1	3	4	E	
	N	1	3	1	4	E		(S		4	3	4	)							
15	N	1	1	3		E		S		3	3				S		3	3		
								N	1	1	3	3	E		N	1	1	3	E	
								N	1	4−2	3	E			N	1	2	3	E	
								N	1	2	3	3	E							
								N	2	1	1	3	E							
16															S		1	3		
															S		3	3		
															N	1	2	3	E	
17	N	1	3	3		E		N	1	3	3		E		N	1	1	3	E	
								S		2	2	3	E		N	1	2	3	E	
								N	1	1	1	3	E		N	1	3	3	E	
								N	1	2	3		E							
18	N	1	1	1	4	E									N	1	1	4	E	
	S		2	3	4										N	1	2	4	E	
	N	1	3	1	4	E									N	1	3	4	E	
	S		4	3	4															
19	S		3	2	3										N	1	1	3	B	
	N	1	2	1	3	B									N	1	2	3	B	
	N	1	1	3		B														
	end																			
20															S		2	2		
															N	1	1	4	E	
															N	1	3	4	E	

Figure 29 (*cont.*)

	Test Item	Student	ATT
		O I S M L	O I S M A
1.	7 13 19 25 31 37	+ 6 1 1	− 6 1 1
2.	729 243 81 27 9 3 1	/ 3 1 1	/ 3 1 1
		× 3 7 −1	
3.	21 23 22 24 23 25	+ 2	+ 1 1 2
		− 1 1 1	+ 1 2 2
4.	2 7 14 19 38 43 86	+ 5 1 1 2	
		× 2 2 1 2	
5.	6 9 13 18 24 31 39	+ 3 + (n − 1)	
		1 1	
8.	27 54 18 36 12 24 8	× 2 1 1 2	
		(/ 3 2 1 2)	
9.	24 25 23 26 22 27 21	+ n	+ 1 2 2
		− n 1 1	− 1 1 2
11.	81 27 32 30 10 15 13	− 2 3 1 3	
		(/ 3 1 1 3)	
		(+ 5 2 1 3)	

Figure 30 Number Series Test with Test Item Descriptions. The number series test requires only a description as an answer. (Film 1047)

caused by the Test Item Taker not using the pattern length to describe a pattern. This discrepancy is seen in test items 2, 5, 10, 14, and 17. Test item 2 requires a more complex pattern length to express the concept of triplets than that provided by the modified Test Item Description. Test item 3 indicates the difficulty the Test Item Takers have with forming special alphabets. Test item 19 shows a student working from right to left in order to find a description.

Finally, the number series test demonstrates that the present Test Item Takers cannot produce compound associations. It should be noted that the student did not find all the compound associations.

SECTION 5
OTHER APPROACHES

Alternate methods to induce pattern transformations from worked examples are suggested by the work of Uhr (27, 28), Solomonoff (25, 26), and Amarel (2). These approaches involve cataloging suitable operations forming an association graph or incremental program organization.

Uhr (27, 28) has constructed three programs that form a memory structure or graph to transform a pattern string. While the programs have been used for natural language translation, Uhr indicates that they could be modified for the kind of tasks the Aptitude Test Taker considers.

Two proposals have been made by Solomonoff (25, 26) for programs that catalog, abstract, and weight transformation rules. The abstractions of the rules, while providing sufficient generality for the arithmetic items considered, do not provide for rules of more general structure.

Amarel (2) has hand-simulated a program that forms transformation programs by assigning weights to partial programs (based on search effort, program complexity, and probable success). The proposed system constructs programs for processing two argument functions in a first-order axiom system such as group theory, number theory, lattice theory, or the propositional calculus. The program can also be viewed as a possible psychological model of insightful processes.

5.1 Transformation Graph

An alternative to the Aptitude Test Taker is a transformation graph for worked examples. The principal functions of the graph are to define the largest familiar patterns and the appropriate response to each pattern. Situations where more than one response is associated with a familiar pattern or where the order of response does not match the order of input are represented by branches in the graph. Classwords and restructuring rules are used to determine which branch to use.

When Uhr's (27, 28) transformation graph is applied to aptitude tests, his restructuring rules represent familiar patterns while his memory represents known operators (e.g., "same," "next"). In the example shown in Figure 31, the graph (which is already built) represents the solution method inferred from the eye-movement study for the test item that was used in previous figures. The intervening variables of Uhr's notation (27) have been omitted for clarity, leaving only the class variables. Given this transformation graph and the input G H M _ _, the system detects the alphabetic sequence, G H, which it replaces with the classwords $C_6 C_7$ (which will be converted to G H I J). It replaces M with C_1 and _ with C_0, producing the composite classword $C_6 C_7 C_1 C_0 C_0$. By the first restructuring rule, this becomes $C_6 C_1 C_7$ (which is converted into G H M I J). Now taking M I J _ as the new input, the system describes this sequence as $C_5 C_1 C_0$. By the second restructuring rule, this becomes $C_1 C_5 C_1$ (or M I J M), completing the sequence.

This account elides some troublesome details—for example, the memory will provide three different classwords for G H M _ _, not just the one that turns out to match a restructuring rule. Moreover, in this example the decisions were made on the basis of the last few characters of the input

Input	Classword	Output
ABMCDMEFMGHM _ _ _		ABMCDMEFMGHM
	$C_6C_7C_1C_0C_0$	ABMCDMEFMGHMIJ_
	$C_1C_5C_0$	ABMCDMEFMGHMIJM

	Memory			
Input		Output	Class	Restructuring rules
A		A	C_1	$C_6C_7C_1C_0C_0 \Rightarrow C_6C_1C_7$
B		B	C_1	$C_1C_5C_0 \Rightarrow C_1C_5C_1$
.		.	.	
.		.	.	
.		.	.	
AB		AB	C_5	
		AB	C_6 ⎤	
		CD	C_7 ⎦	
CD		CD	C_5	
		CD	C_6 ⎤	
		EF	C_7 ⎦	
.		.	.	
.		.	.	
.		.	.	
—			C_0	

Figure 31 Example of transformation by graph. Adaptation of Uhr's graph notation to depict the transformation used by a student. To select among alternative outputs, find a match between the restructuring rules and the classwords representing the input. The brackets indicate multiple outputs from one input.

string, a procedure that would not be useful in the general case. However, even the graph represented in this simple case would require a large number of worked examples to build (because of the complexity of the restructuring rules needed to discriminate between different patterns and the lack of any mechanism to abstract the rules).

The example omits many features of Uhr's scheme. Uhr associates with each familiar pattern the names of all patterns of which the familiar pattern is a part, the class to which the pattern belongs, its contribution to past transformations, and the names of patterns implied by the familiar pattern. The Uhr program starts with the smallest familiar pattern and then, through the associations that are stored with the familiar pattern, finds larger and larger patterns that match the input string. The patterns implied by the familiar patterns are checked against the answer. In this manner the program finds a transformation. If unknown patterns remain in the input string, they are examined to determine if they might belong to existing classes, if some classes should be reshaped, or if new classes should be formed. The major

188 Computer Program Organization Induced from Problem Examples

portion of the program is concerned with a series of learning rules that accommodate the various transformations that may arise.

The Uhr programs do organize on the basis of examples to perform a task. Since each concept must be built up from examples, the graph will be sizable for a task like the ones presented to ATT, and the training sequence would need to be lengthy. The difficulty lies in the limited means of expression in a language that must be built from very elementary concepts. While concepts are originally built from elementary ideas, the power gained from abstracting and including new concepts in the vocabulary has not been realized in the formalization of the task. Amarel (2), as discussed later, has attacked the job of abstracting and adding to the language.

5.2 Catalog of Operations

Pattern transformations can be developed by cataloging the elements of the transformations. The catalog would contain the basic structures of the transformations and the substitutions used to form specific instances.

5.2.1 An Example. The Solomonoff (25, 26) catalog proposal can be applied directly to the letter series task. The basic structures in the catalog represent the familiar pattern constructions while the substitutions represent

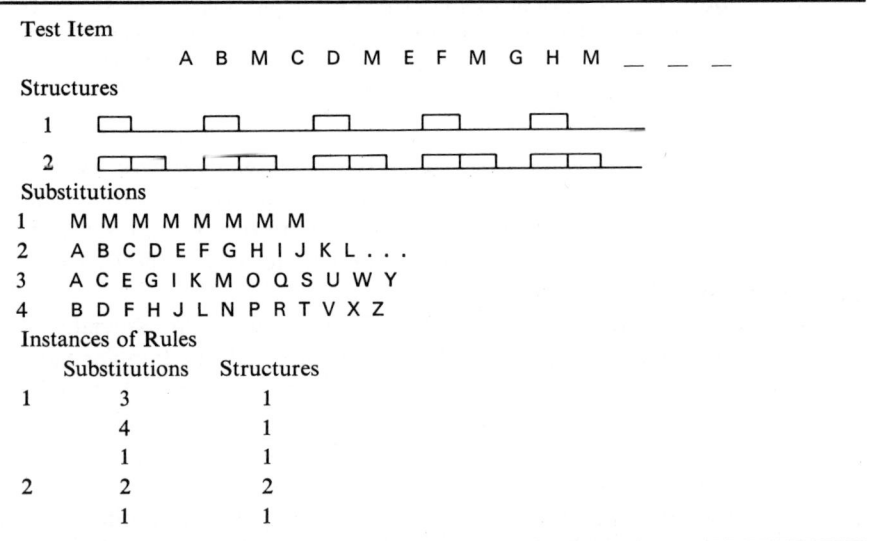

Figure 32 Example of transformation by catalog. Adaptation of Solomonoff's catalog scheme to indicate the rules found by a student (instance 2) and the Aptitude Test Taker (instance 1).

known associations. The sample transformation shown in Figure 32 has sufficient structures and substitutions to demonstrate the Test Item Descriptions from ATT and the descriptions inferred from the eye-motion study.

The first structure represents a periodicity of move of three positions. The second structure represents two characters followed by a skip of one position. The first substitution represents a specific case of the relation *same*. The second substitution is the English alphabet. Substitutions three and four represent the concept of alternate letters of the English alphabet.

The pattern description produced by the Aptitude Test Taker for this item can be duplicated by using substitutions one, three, and four in structure one. The pattern that was inferred from the eye-motion study can be duplicated by combining substitution two in structure two with substitution one in structure one.

5.2.2 Solomonoff's Original Proposals. Solomonoff (25, 26) proposed two programs to catalog the structures and substitutions needed to generate the rules for evaluating arithmetic expressions. In both proposals, rules are generated to solve worked examples. In addition, each rule is weighted according to its success in contributing to the solution of examples. Once a set of rules has proved useful, an attempt is made to find a structure common to several of the rules. Also the substitutions used with each structure are collected, the intention being to build up a set of structures and substitutions that can be combined to solve new test items.

In the original proposal (Solomonoff, 25), an attempt was made to assign weights reflecting the usefulness of the structures and substitutions. Solomonoff (26, p. 426) reports that there was no rigorous way to assign weights to the abstractions. In his newer proposal, weights are not assigned to the structures or substitutions, but it is not stated how these would be selected.

5.2.3 Conclusion. In both proposals, a needed abstraction is missing. While new combinations of structures and substitutions can be tried, there is no way to consider a new variant of a structure. A means of producing new trial structures would have helped in the column arithmetic task considered by Solomonoff, but is not needed for the string arithmetic tasks. However, to expand into other tasks, for example the mathematical aptitude tests used with ATT, the additional abstractions, as well as a way of dealing with them, would be necessary.

Weighting is necessary in catalog schemes for efficiency of operation. In the case of ATT, the order of the descriptors, moves, and alphabets was not changed, but provision was made for program optimization based on past performance. But since the nature of each task clearly indicated the optimum ordering for the Aptitude Test Taker, a weighting scheme was not implemented.

5.3 Program Organization

The Aptitude Test Taker has forms for describing its tasks but does not have specialized languages to describe the operation of the Test Form Analyzer, the Test Item Taker Executive, or the routines that form the Test Item Takers. A specialized language was considered for the routines of the Item Takers but was not implemented because of space restrictions and the diversity of expression required. However, a formal system of languages has been developed by Amarel (2) to describe the procedures for constructing a program from worked examples of two-argument functions.

Amarel's procedure has the most extensive vertical organization of any system considered here. The organization consists of three languages, two of which he describes in detail. At the bottom level is the object language, which is to express the transformation programs. At the second level are programs written in the assembly language, which describes schemes for forming the transformation programs. At the top of the organization is the executive program that expresses in its own language the program formation strategy.

The formation of the programs at the object and assembly language level is controlled by several measures of performance. The most important measure assigns a value to a partial transformation program by estimating from the number of randomly selected problems worked correctly by the partial program, the total number of transformations that would have been accomplished by the partial program. This estimate is converted into a value of the partial program to provide good discrimination among proposed programs. Partial programs are also rated by their complexity, by the amount of search used to develop them (in order to distribute the search evenly over several programs), and by matching their similarity to previously successful programs. The executive uses the weights assigned to the partial programs to optimize the program and to find promising lines for developing the transformation.

The problem domain of two-argument functions in a first-order axiom system is remote from the less formally defined associations found in aptitude tests. However, the concern for developing a program that contains the computer interpretation of a concept is present in both Amarel's program scheme and ATT. The Test Item Taker Executive expresses its program in only one program scheme, whereas Amarel's assembly language is capable of producing a number of program schemes. Of course the application of each scheme requires evaluation.

To enable ATT to operate in a larger problem space and with less direction given by the Test Form Description, local feedback was provided to permit self-modification. The implementation of this feedback is greatly facilitated by using a single program scheme. On the other hand, as sophistication in problem solving is developed, languages at each level of detail will increase the generality and convenience of the problem solver. Amarel has chosen a well-defined problem space and a formally defined set of languages within that space. The Aptitude Test Taker has taken a less sharply defined space and has let the program compensate for the lack or detail in the specification by self-modification.

SECTION 6
PROBLEM SOLVERS

Students, the most general problem solvers available, set a level of achievement that has not been reached in computer programs. To put the performance of ATT in perspective with other computer programs, this section compares ATT with the Simon and Kotovsky (24) Concept Former, the Newell, Shaw, and Simon (5, 6) General Problem Solver, and the Abrahams, Hansen, and Pivar (1) Sequence Prediction Program.

Section 6.1 compares the Simon and Kotovsky model of human performance, the Concept Former, with ATT. Both the difference in the form of the Test Item Descriptions of the two programs and the effects of this difference on the solution techniques are discussed. Then a comparison is made of the two programs' performance on the L. L. Thurstone letter series test.

Section 6.2, using a test item from the letter series test, compares the solution techniques used by the General Problem Solver (Ernst and Newell, 5, pp. 294–310, 338) and ATT. The General Problem Solver (GPS) has been used to model human problem solving and to investigate techniques involved in problem solving. At the time Ernst formulated a representation of the letter series test item for GPS, the concern was with representational issues rather than depth in a particular area. Thus the discussion is concerned with representation and problem solving techniques rather than performance.

Section 6.3 compares an algorithmic series completion program with ATT. The Sequence Prediction Program (Abrahams, Hansen, and Pivar (1) assembles a program that will generate the nth symbol of a series, given n. The consequences of using the symbol position to generate the symbol and the structure of the Sequence Prediction Program are discussed.

6.1 The Concept Former

Simon and Kotovsky (24) have proposed a theory to explain human performance in the induction of a concept from a series test item. The theory is in the form of a computer program, the Concept Former, that simulates the steps involved in finding the concept that describes the sequence of characters.

The Concept Former, while requiring the same problem-solving abilities as ATT, uses a different pattern-generation technique. The Concept Former determines the pattern period by searching for repeating letters or simply-related letters. The program then searches for associations within the period, going outside the predetermined period only as required to complete the pattern description. The Concept Former search within a period is much like the search used by ATT for analogy test items where there are no associations between the groups. The period (move distance) used by ATT is set when a trial production is found to hold. In series test items, ATT finds relations between periods rather than within periods.

It is instructive to compare the Test Item Description of ATT with the system used by the Concept Former. For the letter series test item used in previous examples, the Concept Former description is shown in Figure 33. The first part of the description represents the sequence iteration and the latter represents initialization. Lowercase letters represent characters to be output. M's represent memory cells and their contents represent characters to be output. N(M1) indicates replacement of the contents of M1 by the Next symbol on the sequence indicated by the initialization.

The Concept Former notation describes the test item more parsimoniously than ATT. Consider the sequence

$$A\ B\ C\ D\ B\ C\ D\ E\ C\ D\ E\ F\ \_\ \_\ \_$$

For this sequence, the Concept Former notation describes very well the behavior observed in students, whereas the Test Item Description of ATT has to be expanded to describe the student behavior. The Test Item Description

Test Item
A B M C D M E F M G H M _ _ _

The Concept Former
⟨M1, N(M1), M1, N(M1), m⟩ ⟨M1 = alpha; a⟩

The Aptitude Test Taker

oper	iter	start	move	alpha
Same		3	3	
Next	2	1	3	Eng
Next	2	2	3	Eng

Figure 33 Comparison of the Test Item Descriptions produced by the Aptitude Test Taker and the Concept Former.

produced by ATT does not cover the sequence starting in the fourth position, D E F, since that description is not needed to fill in a blank.

The Concept Former notation can be adapted to describe other tests by introducing new operators and obtaining the initial values from the test item. However, the test item completion sequence specified by the expanded notation would not always match the methods observed in students.

The differences between ATT and the Concept Former are illustrated by the performance of each program in the L. L. Thurstone letter series test. The test items in the letter series test were ranked according to the time each program used for solution. A ranking by student solution time is also included in Figure 34 to provide a basis for comparison. The data on the Concept Former were provided by K. Kotovsky (unpublished). The test item rankings by ATT and the Concept Former are in good agreement as indicated by a Kendall Coefficient of Concordance of 0.87 (significant at the 0.05 level) as shown in Figure 35.

Only two test items ranked by ATT are badly out of line with both the Concept Former and student rankings of the difficulties. Problem 6 is easier for ATT because the ATT finds relations between periods and thus is not

Test item	Aptitude test taker	Ranking Letter Series I Test Concept former	Students
1	1	1	1
2	3	7	2
3	15	14	6
5	7	5	3
6	8	11	13
7	12	4	8
9	14	15	15
10	11	10	4
11	2	2	7
13	6	3	5
14	9	12	9
15	4	6	14
17	5	8	11
18	10	13	10
19	13	9	12

Figure 34 Comparison of the Aptitude Test Taker and the Concept Former by ranking of the test item difficulty. The rankings are based on the time for solution with 1 representing the shortest time. The test item numbers represent the corresponding test items in letter series II test.

	Ranking	Concordance	Level of significance
Aptitude Test Taker	Concept Former	0.87	0.05
Concept Former	Student	0.77	0.1
Student	Aptitude Test Taker	0.66	0.25

Figure 35 Concordance of rankings by the Aptitude Test Taker and the Concept Former. The concordance of the student and Aptitude Test Taker rankings is taken from Section 4.3.2, above.

faced with the difficulty of relating a within-period pattern to the adjoining period. ATT's difficulty with problem 7 can be attributed to not using the period as the basis for finding the pattern. In problem 7, the letter X repeats with a period of three. Since no relation using the English alphabet will work on the remaining positions, a special alphabet needs to be formed. If the period was used, two alphabets (QP and AB) could be formed immediately. The Aptitude Test Taker forms the alphabet QAPB and then finds the AB to be useless for one production and QP useless for the other production.

Some speculation is required to provide reasons for the Concept Former's ranking five test items differently than did ATT and the students. Three reasons appear to cover the five test items. Problems 12 and 13 reflect the fact that the Concept Former deals very easily with the backward alphabet. In problem 2, the Concept Former has difficulties in picking the positions to be used to express the association between sets of triplets, even though the concept of triplets is easily expressed in its notation. In problems 14 and 18 it experiences difficulty in selecting the correct period.

There are two notable discrepancies between student performance and the performance of the two programs. In problems 3 and 10 the students apparently use the overall visual pattern of the test item to detect the pattern size without close inspection of the letters. Problems 15 and 17 indicate that the programs are very good recordkeepers and do not become confused in the face of patterns using closely associated letters.

Problem 9, while rated difficult by both the programs and students, is treated differently by the two programs. In problem 9, the pattern UA repeats with period three. The remaining two patterns repeat with period six. ATT describes the test item using two periods. The Concept Former describes the entire test item using a period of six.

6.2 The General Problem Solver

Ernst and Newell (5, pp. 232–246, 257) posed a letter series test item to the General Problem Solver (GPS). The task is formulated as a search for a suitable test item description in the space of possible descriptions using an approach patterned on that of the ATT. The technique used by ATT is easier to formulate for GPS than the Concept Former technique.

The implementation of ATT strategy within the GPS format is considered somewhat unusual by Ernst and Newell (5, p. 310). The important characteristics of the strategy are handled by careful attention to the details of the task statement to GPS. In order to achieve the goal of filling in the blanks, GPS must be driven to find a complete description of the test item. The requirement for the simplest meaningful description is achieved by providing for communication between sections of the strategy. This communication cannot be directly stated within the GPS format and would normally be considered an incidental result of the task statement chosen. The communication within ATT is provided by self-modification of ATT structure and modification of the Test Item Description.

In the formulation of the letter series task for GPS, the Test Item Description takes a form different from that used by ATT. Figure 36 presents the test item given to GPS, together with the descriptions produced by ATT and by GPS. In GPS, an association exists only between pairs of letters and is assigned to the first letter of the pair. A special association, LAST, is assigned to the final letter of a set of pairs. Because of the method of recordkeeping, there is no need for a starting position nor is there a convenient way to retract a production that subsequently fails.

The comparison of GPS and ATT shows a major difference in the type

Test Item
B C B D B E _ _

The Aptitude Test Taker

oper	iter	start	move	alpha
Same		1	2	Eng
Next	1	2	2	Eng

The General Problem Solver

Letter	Relation	Interval
B	Same	Two
C	Next	Two
B	Same	Two
D	Next	Two
B	Same	Two
E	Next	Two
B	Last	Two
F	Last	Two

Figure 36 Comparison of the Test Item Descriptions produced by the Aptitude Test Taker and the General Problem Solver.

of information required. For GPS, a knowledge of the present status of its work and its goal are normally adequate to determine the next procedure. For ATT, a knowledge of the results of past performance and a test of progress toward its goal are normally adequate to determine the next procedure.

6.3 Sequence Prediction Program

Abrahams, Hansen, and Pivar (1), using a number theoretic approach, have developed an algorithmic series completion program that generalizes Simon and Kotovsky's Concept Former in certain respects. The Sequence Prediction Program assembles a LISP program to generate the nth symbol of a series test item given n, the symbol position number.

The Sequence Prediction Program, like the Concept Former, while requiring the same problem-solving abilities as ATT, uses different pattern generation techniques. The Sequence Prediction Program executive, *predictor*, corresponds in function to the input and output section of the Test Item Taker Executive. Predictor in turn executes *pred 1* which serves the same functions as the descriptor routine and the final acceptance section of the action routine in the Test Item Takers. Pred 1 will accept a two-thirds correct match as correct, which allows it to solve both *replace* and *exceptional element* test items. However, because the program does not discriminate between the two types of test items, it reaches some erroneous solutions.

The problem-solving abilities of the Sequence Prediction Program are contained in the *workers*. From Figure 37, which lists the workers in ATT terms, the extent of the Sequence Prediction Program abilities are apparent as is the confounding of the different program functions. Of course ATT does not translate letter series tests into number series tests and hence has no need for this ability. Nor does ATT have a variable iteration for operators

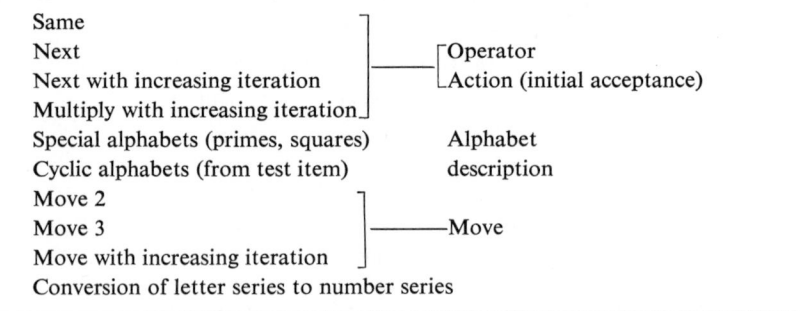

Figure 37 Sequence Prediction Program workers described in Aptitude Test Taker terms. The workers are cataloged by corresponding function in the Test Item Takers.

and moves. A more extensive variable iteration technique, discussed in Section 4, was proposed by Newell and Simon (22).

Variable iteration is a useful technique, required to solve a few test items. However, tying the iteration to the symbol position number, which requires the initialization to be part of the Test Item Description, prevents analogy test items from using the same abilities and generalizes to only a few more series test items. The confounding of different program functions within the workers necessitates the use of recursion and recursion control as well as different routines for variants of an operator or move.

The Sequence Prediction Program has solved some series test items beyond the capabilities of ATT; it also fails on many test items that require the same abilities.

SECTION 7
SUMMARY

The Aptitude Test Taker has demonstrated the computer conceptualization and performance of several inexactly defined tasks.

Using reasoning tasks supplied by J. P. Guilford from test batteries developed for the Naval Air Station (Pensacola, Florida), ATT has demonstrated for several tasks the automatic organization of a computer program to perform a task, using a few worked examples of the task. Previous attempts at developing a performance strategy from worked examples (Amarel, 2; Kilburn, Grimsdale, and Sumner, 19; Solomonoff, 25, 26; Uhr, 27, 28) have required examples of every situation that would be encountered. Previous programs (Ernst and Newell, 5; Evans, 7; Simon and Kotovsky, 24) that·have solved inductive reasoning tasks do not induct a performance strategy from examples. The Aptitude Test Taker, on tasks within its capability, parallels human performance and exceeds the performance of the other computer programs that can deal with one or more of the tasks.

7.1 Method

To guide the evolution of ATT, human performance data were obtained from twenty-four college students working on two tasks, and films of the eye motions of two students working on three tasks. The work of Simon and Kotovsky on the Concept Former (24) also contributed to the evolution of ATT.

Within ATT the functions of conceptualization and performance are executed by the Test Form Analyzer and Test Item Taker. The Test Form Analyzer produces a Task Form Specification from which a computer program, the Test Item Taker, is formed. The Task Form Specification is ATT's conceptualization of the task.

The Test Form Analyzer accepts linear test items as input. With such items, the internal representation and the operations performed on it can easily be described in terms that have clear equivalents in the external test item and the observed human performance.

The Task Form Specification is produced by the Test Form Analyzer by feature extraction, a method that is attractive because of the ease with which either the programmer or a learning routine within the program can add features and change the effect of the occurrence of a feature. The Task Form Specification is easy to expand due to its unitized construction. Any expansion is given meaning by routines added to the available repertoire of the Test Item Taker.

The Test Item Taker Executive using the Task Form Specification assembles a program, the Test Item Taker, designed to handle an inductive reasoning task described by the Task Form specification. Since the Test Item Taker is not organized to handle a specific test item, it adapts to the item by modifying itself. The self-modification along with record modifications are used to implement a simple planning strategy in the Test Item Taker.

7.2 Results

The Aptitude Test Taker has validated the ideas used in its formation. The next step would be the development of a planning strategy that recognizes the value of information that is not immediately useful in the solution of a test item. The planning strategy would call for the extension of the Test Item Description and freer use of associations in the Test Item Description.

The Test Item Taker indicates how a problem solver can evolve. In the present version, if discovered information does not fit the type of information being sought, it is not used effectively or is ignored. Thus, in a more effective problem solver, a production that does not prove to be immediately useful would be retained for future use when other facts may be known (or would be analyzed for information that might be useful in guiding further search). For example, the detection of the period in a series pattern should be used to search for analogy patterns that might be present. Currently, the distinction between series and analogy productions is placed too high in the structure of the Test Item Taker, preventing the mixing of series and analogy productions within a single Test Item Description.

The comparison of human performance with ATT and the discussion of the tests supplied by Guilford underscore the dependence of the sophistication of the Test Item Taker on the richness of the Test Item Description. Thus, further evolution of ATT would include extension of the Test Item Description to include additional concepts involved in the discussion of the human performance. The Test Form Analyzer can presently describe more inductive reasoning problems than the Test Item Taker can solve. Therefore, the most interesting aspect of the evolution of ATT would be to refine the descriptive power of the test item description while reducing the number of descriptors.

APPENDIX
DESCRIPTION OF APTITUDE TESTS USED WITH THE APTITUDE TEST TAKER

Name	Items in test	Original name	Source
Letter analogies	20		L. L. Thurstone
Letter groups	40	Letter grouping	J. P Guilford
Letter series	20		J. P. Guilford
Number groups	15	Number-group naming	J. P. Guilford
Number relations	30		J. P. Guilford
Number series	40		J. P. Guilford
Number correction	20	Number series correction	J. P. Guilford
Seeing trends	24		J. P. Guilford
Word groups	30		J. P. Guilford
Word relations	30		J. P. Guilford
Inst. of Living	20	Shipley-Hartford Intelligence Test	The Institute of Living

LETTER ANALOGIES

This is a test of your ability to see and use relations between pairs of letters. Look at the first sample item.

SAMPLE ITEM I.   m o   f h   j _

You are to select the answer that best fits the relationship in the first two pairs of letters. Notice that in the first two pairs of letters there is one letter of the alphabet missing between "m" and "o" and between "f" and "h." Therefore, you would select "1" as the correct answer because there is one letter missing between "j" and "l." Now try the next item.

SAMPLE ITEM II.   ij ji   po op   ed _ _

Here there are four letters in each group. Notice that in the first two groups of letters the second group is the same as the first spelled backward. Therefore, you would select "de" as the correct answer since it is the same as "ed" spelled backward.

SAMPLE ITEM III. ra se   bo cu   fe _ _

In this sample item, the first letters of each pair are consecutive consonants in the alphabet and the second letters are consecutive vowels. Therefore, the second pair of letters for "fe" would be formed by finding the next consonant and the next vowel in the alphabet. The correct answer is "gi."

The items in this test are similar to these examples, although they may involve other kinds of relationships. You should remember that the relation you discover must fit both given pairs of letters.

There are 20 items to this test. You have 8 minutes to work on the test.

Work as rapidly as you can. Work on each item as it comes, but if you cannot find a solution for an item, go on to the next. Do not spend too much time on any one item. If you have any questions ask them now.

STOP HERE.   WAIT FOR FURTHER INSTRUCTIONS.

1.	r u	c f	f _
2.	v u	q p	d _
3.	k o	g i	t _
4.	b g	l p	t _
5.	h i	t u	n _
6.	e i	a e	o _
7.	tt rr	cc aa	ii _ _
8.	ab cd	lm no	bc _ _
9.	cd gh	mn qr	tu _ _
10.	av bu	dn em	gp _ _
11.	df hj	pr tv	km _ _
12.	gi jh	tv wu	ln _ _
13.	no qp	cd fe	jk _ _
14.	ag bh	ci dj	ek _ _
15.	on nu	ih ho	ed _ _
16.	ace gik	bdf hjl	ceg _ _ _
17.	aza byb	eve fuf	iri _ _ _
18.	apl lpb	gms smh	pde _ _ _
19.	agm bhn	cio djp	ekq _ _ _
20.	pei rae	bou dio	xio _ _ _

Used with the permission of Aptitudes Research Project,
University of Southern California,
J. P. Guilford, Director.

LETTER SERIES

This is a test of your ability to see and use relations in strings of letters. Look at the first sample item

SAMPLE ITEM I.   a b a b a b __

You are to select the answer that best continues the series. Notice that the series is made up of three identical pairs of letters. Therefore, you would select "a" as the correct answer because it is the first letter of the pair "ab." Now try the next item.

SAMPLE ITEM II.   c a d a e a f a __ __

Here the letter "a" occurs in every other position in the series. Notice that the positions not containing an "a" contain consecutive letters in the alphabet. Therefore, you would select "ga" as the correct answer because "g" is the next letter in the alphabet after "f" and "a" is the repeated letter.

SAMPLE ITEM III.   a x b y a x b y a x b y __ __ __

In this sample item, the two letter groups "ax" and "by" alternate. The correct answer is "axb."

The items in this test are similar to these examples, although they may involve other kinds of relationships. You should remember that the relation you discover must fit the series of letters given.

There are 20 items to this test. You have 5 minutes to work on the test.

Work as rapidly as you can. Work on each item as it comes, but if you cannot find a solution for an item, go on to the next. Do not spend too much time on any one item. If you have any questions ask them now.

STOP HERE.   WAIT FOR FURTHER INSTRUCTIONS.

1. c d c d c d __ __ __
2. a a a b b b c c c d d d __ __ __ __
3. a t b a t a a t b a t __ __ __
4. r s r t r u r v r __ __ __
5. a b m c d m e f m g h m __ __ __
6. d e f g e f g h f g h i __ __ __
7. q x a p x b q x a __ __ __
8. a b c d a b c e a b c f a b c __ __ __
9. a d u a c u a e u a b u a f u a __ __ __
10. m a b m b c m c d m __ __ __
11. u r t u s t u t t u __ __ __
12. m n l n k n j n __ __ __

13. a b y a b x a b w a b ___
14. r s c d s t d e t u e f ___
15. n p a o q a p r a q s a ___
16. m n o m o o m p o m ___
17. w x a x y b y z c z a d a b ___
18. j k q r k l r s l m s t ___
19. p o n o n m n m l m l k ___
20. c e g e d e h e e e i e f e ___

Adapted from a test by L. L. Thurstone.

EXAMPLES OF OTHER TESTS

Letter Grouping

1. AABC   ACAD   ACFH   AACG
   ACFH
2. XURM   ABCD   MNOP   EFGH
   XURM
3. KABC   KEFG   LOPQ   KUVN
   LOPQ

Number Groups

1. 35   110   75
   Divisible by 5
2. 676   65   161
   6 appears in each
3. 3   2   17
   Prime numbers

Number Relations

1. 1 5   2 6   5 8   3 7
   5 8
2. 2 6   3 9   4 12   6 15
   6 15
3. 1 3   2 5   3 6   4 9
   3 6

Number Series

1. 15   18   21   24   27   30
   Add 3

2. 24 48 12 24 6 12 3
   Multiply by 2, divide by 4
3. 27 26 24 21 17 12 6
   Subtract 1, subtract 2, subtract 3, . . .

Number Correction
1. 1 2 3 4 5 7
   7
2. 2 4 6 9 10 12
   9
3. 2 4 8 18 32 64
   18

Seeing Trends
1. ANGER BACTERIA CAMEL DEAD EXCITE
   First letters are in alphabetical order
2. RATED CRATE MORNING DEARTH SEPARATE
   The "R" moves one letter to the right in each word

Word Groups
1. READ RETIRE REARMING RESTLESS
   All the words begin with the letters "RE"
2. MAIM TEST GANG LABEL
   The first and last letter of each word are the same

Word Relations
1. ON NO TOP POT PART ____
   ON NO TOP POT PART TRAP
2. OUTSIDE SIDE SLATE LATE FORAGE ____
   OUTSIDE SIDE SLATE LATE FORAGE RAGE
3. REAL SEAL MEAT NEAT BORE ____
   REAL SEAL MEAT NEAT BORE CORE

References

When an article has been reviewed in *Computing Reviews* or *Psychological Abstracts*, a citation is included.

[1] ABRAHAMS, P. W., HANSEN, J. B., and PIVAR, M. *Final Report, Research in Sequence Analysis.* Cambridge, Massachusetts: Information International, April 1965.

[2] AMAREL, S. On the automatic formation of a computer program which represents a theory. *In* M. Yovits, G. T. Jacobi, and A. D. Goldstein (eds.), *Self-Organizing Systems, 1962*. Washington, D.C.: Spartan Books, 1962, 107–175. (See CR 5 (1964), 6, Rev. 6603)

[3] BAKER, F. B. The internal organization of computer models of cognitive behavior. *Behavioral Science* 12, 2, March 1967, 156–161. (CR 8 (1967), 6, Rev. 13119)

[4] CAHILL, H. and HOVLAND, C. E. The role of memory in the acquisition of concepts. *Journal of Experimental Psychology* 59, 1960, 137–144. (PA 35 (1961), 1, Rev. 376)

[5] ERNST, G. W. and NEWELL, A. *GPS: A Case Study in Generality and Problem Solving*. New York: Academic Press, 1969. (CR 11 (1970), 1, Rev. 1823b)

[6] ERNST, G. W. and NEWELL, A. Some issues of representation in a general problem solver. *AFIPS Conference Proceedings* 30, 1967. Washington, D.C.: Thomson Books, 583–600. (CR 8 (1967), 5, Rev. 12694)

[7] EVANS, T. G. A heuristic program to solve geometric-analogy problems. *AFIPS Conference Proceedings* 25, 1964. Baltimore, Maryland: Spartan Books, 327–338. (CR 5 (1964), 5, Rev. 6268) [M]

[8] GUILFORD, J. P. Three faces of intellect. *American Psychologist* 14, 1959, 469–479. (PA 34 (1960), 5, Rev. 7350)

[9] GUILFORD, J. P. A revised structure of intellect. *Reports from the Psychological Laboratory* 19, April 1957, The University of Southern California, Los Angeles.

[10] GUILFORD, J. P. The structure of intellect. *Psychological Bulletin* 53, 1956, 267–293.

[11] GUILFORD, J. P. and HOEPFNER, R. Structure-of-intellect factors and their tests. *Reports from the Psychological Laboratory* 36, June 1966, The University of Southern California, Los Angeles.

[12] GUILFORD, J. P., KETTNER, N. W., and CHRISTENSEN, P. R. A factor-analytic study across the domains of reasoning, creativity, and evaluation, II. Administration of tests and analysis of results. *Reports from the Psychological Laboratory* 16, March 1956, The University of Southern California, Los Angeles.

[13] GUILFORD, J. P., KETTNER, N. W., and CHRISTENSEN, P. R. A factor-analytic study across the domains of reasoning, creativity, and evaluation, I. Hypothesis and description of tests. *Reports from the Psychological Laboratory* 11, July 1954, The University Southern California, Los Angeles.

[14] GUILFORD, J. P. and MERRIFIELD, P. R. The structure of intellect model: its uses and implications. *Reports from the Psychological Laboratory* 24, April 1960, The University of Southern California, Los Angeles.

[15] GUILFORD, J. P., MERRIFIELD, P. R., CHRISTENSEN, P. R., and FRICK J. W. An investigation of symbolic factors of cognition and convergent production. *Reports from the Psychological Laboratory* 23, April 1960, The University of Southern California, Los Angeles.

[16] HUNT, E. B. *Concept Learning: An Information Processing Problem*. New York: John Wiley & Sons, 1962. (CR 6 (1965), 1, Rev. 6872; PA 38 (1964), 1, Rev. 351)

[17] HUNT, E. B. and HOVLAND, C. I. Order of consideration of different types of concepts. *Journal of Experimental Psychology* **59**, 1960, 220–225. (PA 35 (1961), 5, Rev. 5814)
[18] HUNT, E. B., MARIN, J., and STONE, P. J. *Experiments in Induction.* New York: Academic Press, 1966. (CR 7 (1966), 5, Rev. 10345; PA 40 (1966), 8, Rev. 8232)
[19] KILBURN, T., GRIMSDALE, R. L., and SUMNER, F. H. Experiments in machine learning and thinking. *Proceedings of the International Conference on Information Processing.* London: Butterworths (Dist. by: UNESCO, New York), June 1959, 303–309.
[20] NEWELL, A. Some problems of basic organization in problem-solving programs. *In* M. Yovits, G. T. Jacobi, and A. D. Goldstein (eds.), *Self-Organizing Systems, 1962.* Washington, D.C.: Spartan Books, 1962, 393–423. (See CR 5 (1964), 6, Rev. 6603)
[21] NEWELL, A. and KELLEY, H. S. (eds.). *Information Processing Language-V Manual*, 2nd Ed. Englewood Cliffs, New Jersey: Prentice-Hall, 1964. (CR 5 (1964), 6, Rev. 6668)
[22] NEWELL, A. and SIMON, H. A. Simulation of human processing of information. *American Mathematical Monthly* **72**, 2, February 1965, Part 2: Computers and Computing, 111–118.
[23] SIEGAL, S. *Nonparametric Statistics for the Behavioral Sciences.* New York: McGraw-Hill, 1956.
[24] SIMON, H. A. and KOTOVSKY, K. Human acquisition of concepts for sequential patterns. *Psychological Review* **70**, 6, 1963, 534–546. (PA 38 (1964), 4, Rev. 5352)
[25] SOLOMONOFF, R. J. Training sequences for mechanized induction. *In* M. Yovits, G. T. Jacobi, and A. D. Goldstein (eds.), *Self-Organizing Systems, 1962.* Washington, D.C.: Spartan Books, 1962, 425–434. (See CR 5 (1964), 6, Rev. 6603)
[26] SOLOMONOFF, R. J. An inductive inference machine. *IRE National Convention Record* **5**, 2, 1967, 56–62.
[27] UHR, L. Pattern-string learning programs. *Behavioral Science* **9**, 3, July 1964, 258–270. (CR 7 (1966), 1, Rev. 8909)
[28] UHR, L. and INGRAM, G. Language learning, continuous pattern recognition, and class formation. *In* W. A. Kalenich (ed.), *Proceedings of the IFIP Congress 65.* Washington, D.C.: Spartan Books, 1966, 333–334.
[29] WILLIAMS, D. S. and SIMON, H. A. *An example-driven problem solver* (CIP Paper 68), Systems and Communications Sciences. Pittsburgh, Pennsylvania: Carnegie Institute of Technology, May 1964.
[30] WINIKOFF, A. W. Eye-movements as an aid to protocol analysis of problem solving behavior. Pittsburgh: Carnegie Institute of Technology dissertation, 1967.

Part III

USE OF CONTEXT IN DETERMINING MEANING

The two chapters of Part III, by Coles and Siklóssy, explore a different facet of representation and meaning: the relation between natural language sentences and pictorial representations of their meanings.

The sentence "Give me three" is not very meaningful outside the context in which it has been uttered. It could refer to "three of the big apples" or to "three low-priced opera tickets." Unless more context is adjoined—by examining the language stream beyond the sentence boundaries, by looking at the objects denoted by the sentence, or in some other way—the sentence will remain hopelessly ambiguous. Humans can employ such sentences because they embed them in various contexts which are available to the listener. The two chapters of this part investigate the use that information processing systems can make of context—specifically, pictorial context—in interpreting natural language. In both Coles' and Siklóssy's programs, means are provided for translation between information in the form of natural language strings and information describing visual displays.

Coles' system shows how a computer can use pictorial information to help understand a sentence. The computer is given an ambiguous sentence, together with the picture of a situation. The sentence is first analyzed syntactically. If (as is often the case) it is found to be syntactically ambiguous, several parses are produced. The semantic information contained in the picture helps decide which of these parses, if any, are appropriate in the context of the picture. No one of the parses of a sentence is "correct" in general; the particular context in which the sentence appears determines the correct parse.

Siklóssy's system proceeds almost in the reverse order from Coles'. It starts with a structured, contextual description of a situation in what may be looked upon as a picture language. At the same time, the system is given a verbal description of the pictured situation in a natural language—Russian, for example. As more pairs of pictured situations and their corresponding Russian sentences are considered, the system slowly learns to describe situations in Russian—that is, to form a Russian sentence appropriate to each situation.

A striking difference in the organization of these two programs—over and above the difference in the task they perform—is that the syntactic and semantic components remain much more distinct in Coles' program than in Siklóssy's. In the former system, all syntactically acceptable parses are first produced and translated into the first-order predicate calculus before being compared with the pictorial information. This scheme simplifies program organization, but frequently leads to the production of considerable numbers of parses of a single sentence, and would almost certainly have to be modified as the system is extended to more complex situations. If syntactic and semantic processing could be mixed at all stages, a sentence like "All black triangles ... are inside a circle," where the dots stand for some highly ambiguous relative clause, could be found immediately to be vacuously true for a picture that contains no black triangles.

In Siklóssy's system, there is no boundary between the syntactic and semantic components. After the system has learned to "speak" correctly a small subset of Russian, say, nothing can be found in memory that corresponds specifically to a grammer of Russian. The implicit Russian syntactic rules are thoroughly intertwined with semantic rules for translation from the pictorial language to Russian. The system's organization at least raises the possibility that something similar may be true of a human's knowledge of a language: that he may not possess a syntactic grammar that is separated from his semantic knowledge about the relation between the language and its denotations.

Thus we see that both Coles' and Siklóssy's programs suggest novel linguistic hypotheses which deserve exploration as alternatives to some of the standard views about the relations between syntax and semantics which are embedded in contemporary theories of structural linguistics. Because of limits on their structures as well as limitations of computer memory, neither program has advanced beyond relatively simple sentences and situations. Nevertheless, they demonstrate the feasibility of using semantic methods both in receiving communications in natural language and in producing them.

Chapter 5

SYNTAX DIRECTED INTERPRETATION OF NATURAL LANGUAGE

L. Stephen Coles

SECTION 1
INTRODUCTION

1.1 Definition of the Problem

The aim of the research reported here was to investigate how one might construct a computer program capable of communicating with people by means of natural language and elementary pictures taken from a restricted universe of discourse. During the course of this investigation a computer program called GRANIS (GRAphical Natural Inference System) was written. GRANIS accepts a restricted subset of English as input together with elementary line drawings which are input directly to the computer by means of a graphic display console. The problem areas considered for GRANIS were plane geometry, electrical circuits, and organic chemistry; these three diverse areas serve to demonstrate its generality in handling widely varying domains. The example shown in Figure 1 illustrates some of the communication and problem-solving capabilities of GRANIS with electrical circuits.

There are two fundamental problems in constructing a computer model that can make inferences about pictures and natural language. The first is to devise a process to perform a syntactic analysis of the source information, i.e., both for the picture and the natural language text. The second is to find an internal representation for both the picture and text that facilitates problem solving. Although each of these problems is difficult in its own right, the difficulty is further compounded because it is impossible to isolate completely the syntactic from the semantic analysis. This unavoidable interaction between syntax and semantics in natural language is illustrated in the following two sentences suggested by Raphael [63, p. 141]:

(1) Bring me the bottle of milk which is sour.

(2) Bring me the bottle of milk which is cracked.

Our knowledge of bottles and of milk and of what it means to be sour and cracked lead us intuitively to discover the intended parsing of the two sentences. That is to say, we unhesitatingly associate the relative pronoun "which" with its antecedent "milk" in the first case and "bottle" in the second. Indeed, the first example in Figure 1 exhibits this same kind of syntactic ambiguity, since anyone unacquainted with the properties of resistors and capacitors would be tempted to search for ten ohm capacitors in the circuit! The second example, however, does require one to look for

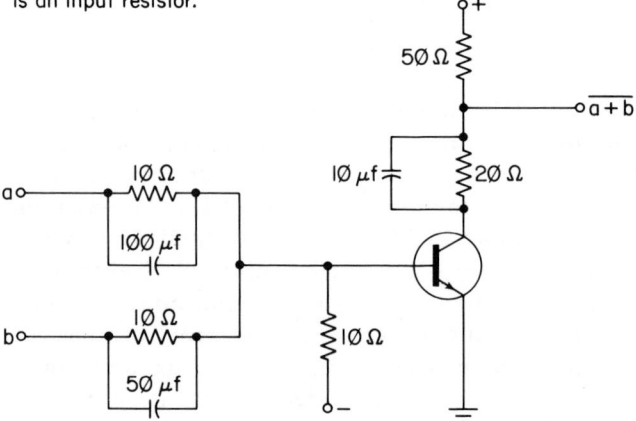

Input sentences:
1. Each resistor in parallel with a capacitor which is ten ohms is an input resistor.
2. Each resistor in parallel with a capacitor which is ten micro farads is an input resistor.

Answers:
Sentence 1 is TRUE for the above circuit.
Sentence 2 is FALSE for the above circuit.

Figure 1

ten microfarad capacitors. We will have more to say about the resolution of ambiguity in Section 2.

In summary, the main concern of this chapter is to explore the relation between syntax and semantics in natural language as it relates to inference-making in some restricted universe of discourse. Pictures provide a context within which the lexical and syntactic ambiguity of input text can be resolved.

1.2 Reasons for Wanting Natural Language and Picture Input

Why would one want to talk with a computer in English? Many formal computer languages such as FORTRAN, ALGOL, LISP, and COBOL already provide a capability for communicating with the computer over a wide variety of problem areas. Indeed, some have even suggested that because of ambiguity, English would be an undesirable language for computer interaction (for example, see Zemanek [90, p. 141] and the discussion in [68]). In addition, the richness of natural language poses enormous memory requirements for the computer. As Paul Garvin recently pointed out[1]

> As far as the structural characteristics of natural language go, perhaps one simple and completely trivial statement can cover it: They are rather complex. They consist of entities of different kinds. To give you a crude example, letters in script are one kind of entity; words with spaces on each side are another kind; sentences are a third kind. All these have describable characteristics, which are rather complex, and which, let us say, make natural language into a system of a much greater complexity than other communication systems, such as gestures or traffic signals.

The complexity of a natural language like English derives from various sources, including syntactic ambiguity, logical ambiguity (amphiboly), suppression of secondary permises (enthymeme), grammatical abbreviation (brachylogy), the fusion of different components of meaning, and the relative abundance of resources for paraphrase. Further complexity results from the fact that, viewed logically, a natural language is not a single system. English, for example, includes both metalinguistic and object language expressions, and even the object language portion does not constitute a single extensional system. In spite of these difficulties, however, there are several important reasons for wanting natural language as a mode of communication.

First, the computer would become immediately accessible as a problem-solving tool for persons not conversant with any computer language appropriate to their needs. In addition, as Halpern [30] points out, the programming community itself would benefit. Since the very beginning of

[1] *IEEE Spectrum*, March 1966, p. 154.

man-computer interaction, there has been a steady movement away from lower-level to higher-level programming languages. The systematic evolution from machine-dependent languages to more sophisticated macro-assembly languages (culminating in machine-independent, compiler, and interpretive languages) points to a definite trend toward the full richness of natural language. It is this evolution which provides the perspective in which to view natural language processing.

A second and equally compelling reason is that certain applications such as text-based information retrieval are best expressed in natural language; other representations require a manual translation process that partially negates the advantage of using a computer in the first place.

Third, today's programming languages are process oriented rather than description oriented. This makes it impossible at present for a human to discuss his problem with a computer in its formative stages, i.e., when it is not yet well defined. Indeed, for most pure mathematicians, a problem which has been sufficiently formalized to permit computer assistance is no longer an interesting problem! With natural language input, on the other hand, it would be possible to engage the computer in a dialog, permitting the user to describe his problem, while the computer questioned assumptions and aided in the process of jointly converging on a mutually acceptable well-defined problem for later solution. Engelbart [22], Licklider [42], and Yershov [89] each give their conception of what such a dialog might be like, and have provided much of the underlying motivation for the work undertaken here. The inherent ambiguity of natural language should not be thought of as a disadvantage in such a dialog. To the contrary, ambiguity that is resolvable within the context of the conversation is a virtue, since it permits greater parsimony in the source statements. Ambiguity is one of the major features that distinguish natural from formal languages, and it actually contributes to the expressive power and flexibility of our language. Even ambiguity that is not currently resolvable can be used to direct the conversation toward the further specification of the problem to be solved.

Finally, natural language can contribute in an important way to the generality of artificially intelligent systems. There is much evidence to indicate that no one global internal representation is suitable for widely varying problem domains (for example, see Newell and Ernst [51]). Thus, rather than continually expanding the problem-solving power of one representation, another approach to generality, sometimes referred to as the "big switch theory" of artificial intelligence, requires some device immediately beneath the surface that will call upon the correct representation once the context has been determined. This approach frequently gives the impression of a system of considerably greater capability than one in which the switching must be done manually by the user. It is suggested that natural language frequently functions in the role of establishing contexts and switching between representations, and therefore can be used to improve the generality of lem-solving systems by providing a framework within which such switching can be performed automatically by the system. Moreover, natural language is essential if we hope ultimately to solve significant artificial intelligence problems such as the "Imitation Game" originally proposed by Turing [80] in 1950, now commonly referred to as the "Turing Test."

Aside from natural language text, what about pictures? The importance of pictorial input is clearly evident in the technical journals that humans use to communicate with each other. Blackboards illustrate the same point. Two important applications of pictorial and natural language input to a computer lie in the areas of information retrieval and automated teaching. Information retrieval on a large pictorial data base is a significant possibility for the future. Four immediate examples of such a large pictorial data base are

(1) a complete set of architectural blueprints for a complex structure.

(2) a set of schematic circuit diagrams for a city-wide electrical power distribution system.

(3) a set of design blueprints for an automobile.

(4) a set of flow charts for a business data-processing program.

Any particular instance may involve a collection of several thousand schematic diagrams. At present, locating a relevant diagram can frequently be an extremely time-consuming process. One can envisage structural design of the future, however, as a large number of engineers creating blueprints on display terminals that are dynamically incorporated into a large body of related design information stored in the mass memory of a computer. This would virtually eliminate the present need for draftsmen. Moreover, the consistency of proposed interfaces and conventions would be established immediately during the design itself, since the system would verify dynamically the consistency with the data base of each proposed increment. In this fashion the design process itself would be considerably accelerated. The ability to interrogate the pictorial data base in terms of simple English sentences means that the designer need not learn a special computer language to operate on the data. This is important for two reasons. First, it is more convenient for designers not already acquainted with appropriate computer languages. Second, for all designers, English would provide a vehicle for interrogating the data superior to any formal computer-oriented language.

In automatic teaching programs the ability of the student to interact with the system in terms of a dialog opens up a host of new possibilities. Most existent automated teaching systems require the student to select from among a small number of prescribed alternatives in replying to any particular question. A static decision about whether to present the next question in the series, return to an earlier question, refresh the student with some previous material, skip to new material, and so on, is made on the basis of the formatted reply given by the student, and no opportunity exists for him to interject qualifications of his own that were not explicitly anticipated by the programmer who originally formulated the programmed text. A future automated teaching system need not be conditioned by such constraints. In teaching an introduction to plane geometry for grade school children, for example, such a future automated teaching system might permit the child to draw his own geometric figures and make simple English statements about them in conjunction with some prompting from the program. Such a system would provide much greater latitude in exploring the ideal environment for individual learning.

Although many arguments to demonstrate the inseparability of natural language text and pictures could be marshaled, no important consequences would follow from this observation if it were not for the fact that, from the point of view of computer processing, these two kinds of information sources can be handled with the same techniques. We will have more to say about this in Section 3.

1.3 Related Systems

Various approaches have been employed in inference making and natural language processing on a computer. An excellent review of techniques for syntactic analysis can be found in Bobrow [6]. Similarly, an extensive survey of question-answering systems can be found in Simmons [71]. A more recent and critical survey of data-retrieval systems, prepared by Kasher [32], points out some of the major weaknesses of previous work, even though it is perhaps unduly pessimistic about future prospects.

As indicated by Bobrow, question-answering systems can be evaluated along several dimensions: syntactic, semantic, and deductive. Along the syntactic dimension one can measure the complexity of the format for acceptable input sentences; along the semantic dimension one can measure the extent to which relations among the defined primitives can be represented in the data structures of the system; along the deductive dimension one can measure the extent to which implicit relations among the inputs can be made explicit upon interrogation by the user. In addition, the ability of the system to interact with the user on a conversational basis and the growth potential of the system are important considerations. We will use these criteria in an evaluation of the work of Kirsch [36] and of Simmons and Londe [72], since both of these systems, like GRANIS, are natural language inference-making systems that operate on a graphic data base.

1.3.1 Graphic Data Base Systems

1.3.1.1 DESCRIPTION OF PLM. In 1963 R. Kirsch, D. Cohen, B. Rankin, and W. Sillars [35] devised a collection of programs called Picture Language Machine (PLM) (which was designed to accept geometric pictures as input) at the National Bureau of Standards. PLM translates both the pictures and an English statement into a common intermediate logical language and determines whether the statement about the picture is true. PLM is composed of three subsystems—a parser, a formalizer, and a predicate evaluator. Its language is limited to a fragment of English suitable for making statements about three geometric figures. The parser is based on an unordered context-free phrase-structure grammar which includes a discontinuous constituent generator. Parsing is accomplished by means of a recognition routine which successively substitutes symbols in the dictionary for words in the sentence or for an intermediate symbol string until the top of the parsing tree is attained.

After the sentence has been parsed, the formalizer, developed by Sillars [69], translates the parsed sentence into the first-order predicate calculus, using a small number of constant predicates. The primitives of the language include brackets, parentheses, the terms "and," "if ... then," "not," "identity," universal and existential quantifiers, variables, and three types of predicates. Typical one-place predicates are

$$\begin{array}{ll} \text{Cir}(x) & x \text{ is a circle} \\ \text{Tri}(x) & x \text{ is a triangle} \\ \text{Bk}(x) & x \text{ is black} \end{array}$$

Examples of two- and three-place predicates are

$$\begin{array}{ll} \text{Bgr}(x,y) & x \text{ is bigger than } y \\ \text{Lf}(x,y) & x \text{ is to the left of } y \\ \text{Smc}(x,y) & x \text{ is the same color as } y \\ \text{Bet}(x,y,z) & x \text{ is between } y \text{ and } z \\ \text{Mort}(x,y,z) & x \text{ is more to the right of } y \text{ than } z \\ \text{Mmid}(x,y,z) & x \text{ is more to the middle of } y \text{ than } z \end{array}$$

The translation process involves substituting formal symbols for grammar symbols beginning at the top of the parsed tree and working down. To each rule in the grammar there corresponds a rule in the formalizer. In the insertion of implication and quantifiers more than a simple substitution is required, but the result is always a unique, unambiguous, well-formed formula. For example, the sentence

(3) Each triangle is to the left of a black circle.

translates into the well-formed formula

(4) $(\forall x)\{Tri(x) \supset (\exists y)\{Bk(y) \wedge Cir(y) \wedge Lf(x, y)\}\}$.

The relations between the geometric variables are well defined and the truth value may be tested by the predicate evaluator.

The predicate evaluator translates from pictures to the formal language. It is designed to accept inputs that have been processed by SADIE, a scanning device used as input to the computer. The inputs are restricted to three sizes of triangle, square, or circle, each of which may be black or white. A technique called *blobbing* is used to distinguish objects resulting from the scan and each such object is then circumscribed within a rectangle. Maximum and minimum x,y coordinates are computed and the ratios of these serve to distinguish triangles from circles or squares. Circles are distinguished from squares on the basis of covering less area. A black figure is one whose area is filled in, while a white figure is just an outline. These relatively simple computations serve to generate the valid predicates from the picture.

1.3.1.2 LIMITATIONS OF PLM. The syntax of PLM is quite restricted, thereby limiting the ability of the user to communicate comfortably with the system, unless he has first become quite familiar with the specification of the grammar. Because the grammar is restricted to a context-free, phrase-structure form, it can be extended only with considerable difficulty. Even if the grammar could be extended with comparative ease, side effects reflected in the semantics, particularly with respect to the scope of quantifiers and the binding of free variables, would continue to present serious problems. The semantics in PLM, however, is probably the more serious limitation. The superficial restrictions, such as limits on the number and range of predicates, are not as serious as the difficulty in initially fitting a wide variety of natural language statements into the predicate calculus format (for example, see Reichenbach [64], Chapter VII). Once the input text has been translated into the predicate calculus, the deductive capabilities of the system are quite powerful, as one might expect.

One of the chief drawbacks of the implementation is lack of conversational capability, preventing a dialog that can be used to help the user converge on a mutually acceptable input statement. In spite of these limitations, and the fact that it never really worked as an integrated operational system, PLM appears to be well conceived and was certainly the first system of this kind to be described in a formal manner. In addition, the possibility for converting to a transformational grammar and the extension to domains other than geometry were so inviting as to provide inspiration for some of the original work on GRANIS.

1.3.2 NAMER

1.3.2.1 DESCRIPTION OF NAMER. In 1964, also inspired by PLM, Simmons and Londe at the System Development Corporation programmed a system called NAMER which could generate natural language sentences from line drawings displayed on a matrix. The primary intent of this research was to demonstrate that pattern recognition programs could be used to identify displayed figures and to identify the relations among them. After this had been established, a language generator was used to generate simple sentences such as "The square is above, to the right of, and larger than the circle." The sentences generated could be construed as answers to the various relational questions that might have been asked.

When a picture is presented on the input matrix, a set of 96 characteristics is computed. The algorithms or operators compute these as functions of the size, shape, and location of the pattern in the matrix. Typical characteristics that are derived include one-bit indications of the presence or absence of parts of the figure in sections of the matrix, of protuberances, of holes in the pattern (as in a circle), and of indentations as in a "u." A first-level learning stage of NAMER selects a small subset of the 96 characteristics—those which correlate most highly with correct recognition of the name by which the experimenter designates the pattern.

The second level of NAMER operates in a comparable fashion to obtain characteristics of the sets of coordinates representing two patterns. At this level the operators generate characteristics of comparative size, separation, density, height, etc. Subsets of these 96 characteristics are learned in the same fashion as at the earlier level to correlate with such relation terms as above, below, thicker than, to the right of, etc.

The language generator uses a very small phrase-structure grammar to generate simple sentences which are true of the picture. Some sample sentences are

(5) The dog is beside and to the right of the boy.

(6) The circle is above the boy.

(7) The boy is to the left of and taller than the dog.

There is a great variety of drawings that can be learned and once a relation is learned between any two figures it usually generalizes successfully to most other pairs of figures.

1.3.2.2 LIMITATIONS OF NAMER. As Simmons admitted, NAMER is not strictly a question answerer. In order to answer English questions selectively, it would be necessary to match the valid statements that can be generated against an analysis of the specific question. Thus, it makes no sense to discuss the syntax of input statements. The generative grammar for the output sentences in NAMER seems to be tacked on as an afterthought, and it shares a difficulty common to all generative grammars—viz., the ability to generate syntactically well-formed sentences which are semantically nonsensical. Thus, significant expansion of NAMER's grammar would probably require further direction from the semantics than is currently provided in order to ensure meaningful sentence generation. NAMER's semantics on the other hand is quite general, since the system is potentially capable of representing arbitrary spatial relationships among an arbitrary collection of primitive objects. This generality derives from NAMER's statistical pattern recognition techniques based on the work of Uhr and Vossler [81]. The inference-making capabilities of NAMER seem mainly inductive rather than deductive, and it is unlikely that deductive machinery could be introduced without extensive reprogramming. NAMER currently has no interactive potential, although it is not inconceivable that this could be added.

1.3.3 Other Systems. In addition to the two graphic data-based systems described above, a number of other programs have been written that, to varying degrees, attempt to answer questions based on natural language inputs. We will mention briefly some of the more important ones but will postpone discussion until the next section.

For his doctoral dissertation at Carnegie Institute of Technology, Robert Lindsay [43] wrote a program called SAD SAM (Syntactic Appraiser and Diagrammer—Semantic Analyzing Machine). The input to the system is a set of sentences taken from Basic English, a subset of English devised by Ogden [54], while the universe of discourse for SAD SAM is the class of family relationships. Bert Green et al. [29] constructed Baseball at the Lincoln Laboratory. Its data base was composed of the month, day, place, teams, and scores for each game in the American League for one year, and it also accepted a limited collection of questions from English. The largest example of a fact retrieval system is the work of Robert Simmons [70] at the System Development Corporation. The Protosynthex I data base is the sixteen volume Golden Book Encyclopedia, and it answers questions as a function of the co-occurrence of content words in the input question with content words in the dictionary.

SIR (Semantic Information Retriever) is a system written by Bertram Raphael [63] in connection with his doctoral thesis at MIT. It is much more independent of a specific data base, but is still limited in the sentence formats that determine what storage and retrieval functions the system will perform. The relations that the system is capable of handling are set inclusion, set membership, equivalence, ownership, part-whole, and left-to-right position. Daniel Bobrow [7] (for his doctoral dissertation at MIT) programmed the STUDENT system which accepts algebra word problems phrased in English similar to that found in high school texts. These problems are translated into equations which can then be evaluated arithmetically. Roger Elliott [21] for his dissertation at the University of Texas programmed the GRAIS System which is an improvement over SIR in that such properties of relations as transitivity, symmetry, and reflexivity can be input by the user. In addition, the system has checks for the redundancy and consistency of input data.

DEACON (Direct English Access and CONtrol) is another large and continuing research project designed originally by Thompson [17] at the TEMPO Facility of the General Electric Company. The data base consists of some operational data on a portion of the naval fleet such as ships, their movements and commanders, etc. DEACON is of special interest because it demonstrates clearly the relation between syntax and semantics using syntax directed techniques, and we will have more to say about this later. Several programs for deductive question-answering have appeared based on the original work of McCarthy [47] with the "Advice Taker." Among them are Fisher Black's work [5] for his doctoral dissertation at Harvard and the work of James Slagle [76] on DEDUCOM (DEDUctive COMmunicator), but neither of these systems has been oriented to natural language input.

Kondô and Murata [37] at Tokyo Metropolitan University describe work toward a natural language inference-making system similar in spirit to the work of Kirsch, but not enough is known about the program to give any definite evaluation at this time. Cooper [16] and Darlington [18] both have programs which translate a subset of English into the propositional calculus. Cooper translates simple English sentences into Aristotelian logic by carefully restricting his grammar, whereas Darlington's program translates certain English riddles into logical form which may then be tested for validity. A program by Ross Quillian [61] in connection with his doctoral dissertation at Carnegie Institute of Technology, although not strong in natural lanauage input, does achieve some general inference-making capabilities by means of a careful structuring of his internal data representation.

1.3.4 Discussion. In the preceding section a number of question-answering systems were mentioned quite briefly. Are there any limitations that all of them share in common? If we disregard for the moment those systems, such as Simmons' Protosynthex, which merely retrieve direct facts from the data base, and concentrate on those which answer questions not explicitly stated in the input, then we observe that they all rely internally upon a formal logical language for obtaining inferences. Now if we further restrict ourselves to that subset which genuinely permits natural language inputs, we discover that the variety of natural language permitted is highly limited. That is to say, although a conversation with the system may "read" like English, even allowing for a restricted vocabulary, it does not "speak" or "write" like English. The reason for this is that in order to get from natural language input into a formal language suitable for inference-making, a translation is required, which in turn, requires as a prerequisite some kind of syntactic analysis of the input. Again, such an analysis requires a grammar, whether explicit or implicit, and getting a grammar sufficiently large to handle more than a mere fragment of natural language seems to be a major stumbling block. But are there any theoretical reasons why this should so, disregarding for the moment the practical problems of handling a large grammar on a computer? Certainly there is evidence to indicate that large grammars can indeed be constructed (for example, see the work of Kuno [38] with the Harvard parser, Lehman and Pendegraft [40] at the University of Texas, the work of Watt [84, 85] at the National Bureau of Standards, Robinson [67] at RAND, the more recent work of Zwicky [91] with transformational grammars, and Clark [10] at IBM).

One theoretical problem that arises with large grammars is the problem of ambiguity. This is evidenced by the large number of parsings produced by the Harvard Multiple Pass Syntactic Analyzer from seemingly innocuous sentences. For example, the sentence

(8) A whip can be a stick with a cord or leather fixed to the end of it, used to give blows in driving animals, etc., or as punishment.

produces over 120 parsings (see Quillian [61], p. 206). And this is not an uncommon occurrence, since similar sentences have been known to generate over one thousand parsings! These large numbers are due to the manner in which the individual ambiguities interact; they combine in a multiplicative rather than an additive manner. The parsings are listed by the program in an essentially random order, while the particular parsing that a human would almost unhesitatingly choose as correct is in no way distinguished from the other, irrelevant, parsings. Occasionally, the natural parsing does not even appear on the list.

Thus before one can provide a genuine deductive, question-answering system with a wide range of natural language input, he must face the problem of ambiguity inherent in English. This entire problem is generally avoided in existing systems by tacitly considering only an unambiguous fragment of natural language which in some sense is isomorphic with the logical language. The problem of translating a possibly ambiguous English sentence into the logical language which does not directly permit the representation of ambiguity is thereby circumvented. But how might one provide a question-answering system with a larger grammar? Before exploring this question and the problem of resolving ambiguity further, we must examine more closely the relation between syntax and semantics in natural language. This is the subject of the next section.

SECTION 2
AN INTEGRATED LINGUISTIC DESCRIPTION

The present section seeks to develop for natural language an integrated conception of the nature of linguistic description suitable for computer modeling. It builds on work accomplished in the area of syntactic analysis, and extends it to include recent work in semantic theory. According to this conception, a linguistic description consists of three components: syntactic, semantic, and pragmatic. The distinction among these three components was first made in the 1930's by Charles Morris [50] when he developed a science of signs which he called "semiotics" based on the earlier work of the American logician Charles Peirce. Morris defined these three terms as follows:

> syntactics— the study of the formal relation of signs to one another without regard to their specific significance;
> semantics— the study of the relation of signs to the objects to which these signs are applicable;
> pragmatics—the study of the origin, uses, and effects of signs within the behavior in which they occur.

To illustrate the distinction between these components, consider the following three sentences:

(1) "It is cold" is a sentence.

(2) "It is cold" is true.

(3) I believe it is cold.

The first is a syntactic assertion; the second a semantic assertion; the third a pragmatic assertion. Indeed, if we assume that it is cold, then by substituting the word "hot" for the word "cold" in each of the above sentences, the first remains true, the second becomes false, while the truth-value of the third cannot be determined.

Katz and Postal [34] have made an important theoretical contribution to our understanding of syntax and semantics. Martin [49] has developed an impressive formalization of pragmatics. In the remainder of this section we will examine how these three components relate in the development of a computer model.

2.1 The Syntactic Component

The syntactic component of a linguistic description of a natural language must be a system of rules that describes the abstract structure underlying the sentences of the language. For the purpose of this chapter a transformational grammar in the sense of Chomsky [11, 12, 13] will be assumed as the form of the syntax.

The initial part of such a grammar is a set of phrase structure rules. The form which such rules take is illustrated in the following oversimplified example:[2]

⟨sentence⟩   ::= ⟨subject⟩⟨predicate⟩
⟨subject⟩   ::= ⟨pronoun⟩|⟨nounphrase⟩
⟨nounphrase⟩ ::= ⟨noun⟩|⟨det⟩⟨adjstring⟩⟨noun⟩
⟨adjstring⟩   ::= ⟨adj⟩|⟨adjstring⟩⟨adj⟩
⟨predicate⟩   ::= ⟨verb⟩⟨nounphrase⟩

⟨pronoun⟩   ::= he | she | they
⟨noun⟩   ::= John | Mary | house
⟨adj⟩   ::= big | small | black | white
⟨verb⟩   ::= love | loves
⟨det⟩   ::= the | a

The above grammar generates such sentences as

(4) John loves Mary.

(5) Mary loves the small white house.

(6) They love a big house.

Conversely, one may view the grammar as a recognizer in which sentences (4)–(6) would be said to be well formed with respect to the grammar, whereas

(7) Mary loves the house.

is not well formed, due to an idiosyncrasy of this particular grammar. For, note that the third rule specifies that at least one adjective must precede the noun in any nounphrase with a determiner. Also observe that a recursive definition (e.g., for adjective string in the fourth rule) is permitted. Such a recursive construction provides for an arbitrary number of adjectives preceding a noun. The *structural diagram* (SD) of a sentence is a tree that exhibits the phrase structure of the sentence. For example, the SD for sentence (5) is as follows:

[2] By using a Backus-Naur Form (BNF) notation we have departed from the standard notation of an immediate constituent grammar generally used by linguists. This has been done for the sake of consistency with the program representation and to emphasize the analytic rather than the generative aspects of the grammar.

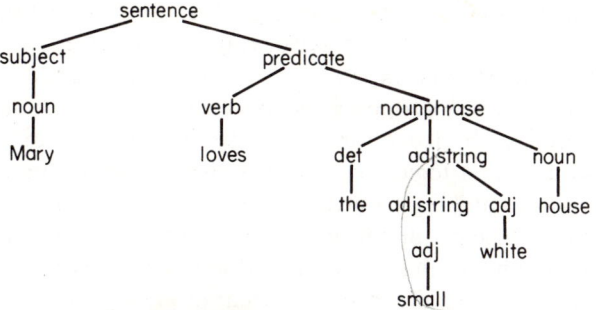

The metasyntactic classes enclosed in angular brackets, such as "sentence," "subject," "nounphrase," and so on are the *non-terminal* symbols of the grammar, whereas "John," "Mary," "house," "big," etc. are the *terminal* symbols associated with the grammar.

The second part of such a grammar is a set of transformations that may be used to convert one sentence in the language to another, where the sentences have a strong intuitive relation. One such transformation is the transformation from active to passive voice: for example, from "John loves Mary" into "Mary is loved by John." Another such transformation is from interrogative to declarative mode, for example, from "Does John love Mary?" into "John loves Mary." Still another important class of transformations maps compound sentences into their simpler kernel sentences and vice versa—for example, from "John loves Mary and Mary loves the small white house" into "John loves Mary" and "Mary loves the small white house." With the introduction of transformation rules, the basic phrase-structure grammar can be simplified. Only a very simple set of "kernel sentences" of a language need be considered. All other complex sentences can first be decomposed into their kernel sentences, and then parsed with respect to the phrase-structure grammar to obtain their structural diagrams.

2.2 The Semantic Component

The semantic component of the linguistic description is taken to be a set of projection rules similar in spirit to that proposed by Katz and Fodor [33]. Such a projective device consists of two parts: first, a *dictionary*, which provides a meaning for each of the terminal symbols in the language, and second, a set of *semantic rules*. The semantic rules assign an interpretation to each source statement in terms of the structural diagram produced by the syntactic component. This interpretation will be an expression in a formal language which expresses the meaning of the source statement.

There has been much discussion as to what kind of formal language, if any, should be used internally to represent the semantic information contained in the source text. If one's goal is merely to extract information directly from the given text, then tree or ring data structures may be adequate. If on the other hand, one expects the system to make deductions about the truth-value of complex propositions concerning varying domains, a general mechanism for such deductions must be independent of any particular domain and a formal logical language is suggested. During the time of the Greeks, linguistics and logic were combined as one general subject. However, in the course of history, linguistics became divorced from logic, particularly in this country. The result of this separation has been extremely unfortunate. As Bar-Hillel [3] has pointed out, a separation of logic from linguistics is inherently wrong. Any attempt to understand even simple inferential mechanisms in natural language requires a recognition of the logical principles that underlie these mechanisms. Consider the following two examples: First, a linguist in attempting to describe the semantics of the phrase "smaller than"—and countless other phrases in English—must account in some way for the conditions that permit one to deduce that "A is smaller than C" given that "A is smaller than B" and "B is smaller than C." A dictionary with entries for "small" and "than" by itself is not sufficient for making such an inference. Some additional semantic rule based on the logic of transitivity is needed.

The second example derives from the relationship between the so-called "deep structure" and "surface structure" distinguished by Chomsky [11]. As Bohnert [9] suggests, the two sentences

(8) Barking dogs don't bite.

(9) Parallel lines don't meet.

have the same surface syntax. Yet the transformation that changes (8) into

(10) No barking dog bites.

when applied to (9) yields

(11) No parallel line meets.

which clearly is unintelligible. This is said to reveal a difference in deep structure between sentences (8) and (9). In order to describe the difference precisely, a systematic way of representing deep structures must be found. The notation of the predicate calculus in symbolic logic provides such a representation in a natural way. Sentence (8) is represented as

(12) $(\forall x)\{Dg(x) \wedge Bk(x) \supset \neg Bt(x)\}$.

That is to say, for every x, if x is a dog and x is barking, then x does not bite. Sentence (9) is represented as

(13) $(\forall x)(\forall y)\{L(x) \wedge L(y) \wedge P(x, y) \subset \neg M(x, y)\}$

or for every x and for every y, if x is a line and y is a line and x is parallel to y, then x does not meet y. This notation reveals, among other things, the different relational demands of "parallel" and "barks," and clearly illustrates the deep structure underlying each term.

For these reasons the predicate calculus has been selected as the formal language to represent the meaning of the source text. The dictionary now takes on the role of a collection of predicates to be used in the construction of expressions in the quantification calculus.

2.3 Relation Between Syntax and Semantics

Before continuing to describe the semantic component, we must examine further the relation between the syntactic and semantic components. First, let us return to the phrase-structure grammar and take note of some of its deficiencies. Some of these deficiencies can be handled in the transformational part, but others cannot. Consider the following two examples. First, the phrase-structure grammar could as easily generate the sentence

(14) They loves Mary.

as "They love Mary." Our intuition tells us that (14) is a grammatical deviation rather than a semantic one, and should be accounted for in the syntactic component. But such a simple rule as "the verb agrees with the subject in gender, person, and number" is not easily expressed in phrase-structure grammar, and such agreement rules abound in natural language. If one were to approach this problem in the phrase-structure grammar, then one would need a separate BNF rule for each agreeing sequence. This particular kind of difficulty, however, can be handled quite well in the transformational part of the grammar.

Now consider a second problem. We can also generate the sentence

(15) The big house loves John.

Now our intuition detects some semantic deviation. The sentence appears to be a reasonably well-formed English sentence. The difficulty is just that it doesn't make any sense. One way of circumventing this problem within the grammar is to refine our notion of what it means to be a noun, i.e., by partitioning nouns into two categories: animate nouns and inanimate nouns. Then we may alter the BNF rule for $\langle$noun$\rangle$ to

$\langle$anoun$\rangle$::= John | Mary | $\cdots$
$\langle$inoun$\rangle$::= house | school | $\cdots$

making appropriate changes in the transformational part to ensure that love and its conjugations are in the class of verbs that permit only animate nouns as subjects. This solution is only temporary, however, since as soon as the grammar grows, a similar problem will arise between abstract and concrete nouns. This will require refining the concept of noun still further.

Still later we will have to deal with such anomalies as "drink concrete" or "eat sincerity." As the grammar continues to grow, where this process will terminate is not clear. Of course, it must ultimately terminate when each lexical item in the general class of nouns forms a syntactic category by itself. But this solution violates our intuitive notion of what it means to be a syntactic category. The distinctions between such one-word categories are semantic and not syntactic. Thus, to approach basic semantic problems through the syntactic component leads to an explosion of the grammar, rendering it unmanageably complex.

On the other hand an attempt to approach essentially syntactic problems via the semantic component is equally doomed to failure. This mistake was first made, it appears, by the medieval grammarians who mechanically postulated a class meaning for each grammatical category. In modern linguistics some grammarians have sought to find a semantic justification to explain why negated verbs in English require the auxiliary verb "do." Such an effort tends to confuse essentially meaningless grammatical transformation with the fundamentally meaningful semantic relations in the language. If these domains are not distinguished, no significant understanding of language can be achieved.

Yet as we observed while discussing ambiguity in the introduction, these two components are highly interactive. At least two kinds of ambiguity can be distinguished: lexical ambiguity and syntactic ambiguity. Lexical ambiguity arises when a particular word in a sentence can give rise to more than one interpretation, such as in

(16) He prefers to wear a light suit.

Here the lexical item *light* can be legitimately construed to mean either light *in weight* or light *in color*. In contrast

(17) He prefers to carry a light suit.

is a lexical ambiguity which can be resolved by the semantic component within the context of the sentence, because it is reasonable to assume that weight is highly correlated with carrying while color is not. Without lexical ambiguity there would be no possibility for puns or euphemisms. Syntactic ambiguity arises when a sentence has multiple parsings each of which can give rise to different interpretations, as in the classic sentence

(18) They are flying planes.

Under one interpretation, they are engaged in flying planes; under another, one observes that those planes are planes that are flying. Another classic

(19) Look at the man on the hill with the telescope.

illustrates a similar phenomenon. Under one interpretation we are exhorted to regard the man who carries a telescope; under another, to look with the aid of a telescope; under still another, our attention is drawn to the man on that hill distingushed by having a telescope mounted on it. Before we can hope to resolve such syntactic ambiguities in a predetermined context, both the syntactic and semantic components must be required to interact with each other.

The syntactic ambiguity above illustrates that, even if the elements of a language description can be partitioned into a terminal and a non-terminal vocabulary, there is no substance to the view that the terminal vocabulary alone is involved in semantic considerations. Such an assumption leads to hopelessly circular, inconclusive arguments as to the borderline between syntactical and semantical deviance. Though claiming the domains of syntax and semantics to be separate, linguists have repeatedly failed to locate any boundary between them. Furthermore, by insisting that semantics does not begin until syntax leaves off most grammarians have claimed too much for syntax. Indeed, one of the principal sources of difficulty for Katz and Postal is this same assumption that semantics begins where syntax ends.

The alternative approach to be presented in a later section makes no attempt to partition syntax and semantics into mutually exclusive domains; on the contrary, we will argue for a deep association. To be sure, the basic parts of the syntactic and semantic components will remain recognizably distinct. At the same time, however, we will integrate the two through a sequential application of syntactic and semantic rules, and in particular, the generation of a semantic representation of the input sentence during the syntactic analysis.

To conclude this section, we have attempted to show

(1) the principal domains of syntax and semantics must remain distinct;

(2) an arbitrary delimitation—whether strongly in favor syntax or semantics—leads to undesirable consequences;

(3) in the general case syntax and semantics must interact in the analysis of sentences.

This interrelation between syntax and semantics is not intended as an apologetic compromise between contending proposals, but as a precise reflection of the facts of lanauage.

2.4 The Pragmatic Component

The role of the pragmatic component is to provide a variable, but well-defined, universe of discourse to control the scope and content of the conversation with the system. The universe of discourse is taken to be a collection of objects, each of which is represented by a description list of attributes and values providing the information relevant to that object. We will show in Section 3 precisely how the system itself may construct automatically such a collection of description lists from a pictorial input, but for the moment, the source of these lists need not concern us.

There are two reasons for restricting the domain of the conversation. First, the large base of knowledge about the world tacitly used by humans in their everyday inference-making must be sampled in an extremely limited way. This is essential in order to fit current computer memories. Second, if we are to avoid making spurious inferences, we must ensure a strict control over the meaning of the individual predicates recognized by the system. Systems that do not appear to have such restrictions but claim to make non-trivial inferences about their subject matter are in reality generating relations mechanically without regard to the meaning of the individual lexical items being manipulated. For example, such a system given

(20) The bottle of ink is in the desk.

may legitimately infer that the ink is in the desk, taking advantage of the transitive properties of "of." Yet, on the other hand, given

(21) The King of France is in the castle.

the system could not avoid making the anomalous inference, "France is in the castle"! This is because "ink" and "France" are merely place holders or dummies in the same dependency analysis. Of course, one could overcome this kind of fallacy with some postediting that takes into consideration the properties of ink and France. But this solution takes us back to description lists and a universe of discourse.

In addition, the universe of discourse provides a context within which the lexical and syntactic ambiguity of natural language input statements may be resolved. Whenever an ambiguous statement is input, at least two distinct well-formed expressions in the quantificational calculus will be constructed. Then by examination of the objects in the universe of discourse, each expression will be evaluated, and the truth-value of each determined. If one of the evaluations is true, while the others are false, then we have a basis for resolving the ambiguity, assuming the speaker intended a true statement. Otherwise, the system must request clarification from the user.

In the event that the ambiguity is resolved, we should not regard it as a source of confusion and something to be avoided. On the contrary, in a sense it is desirable. It gives additional freedom to the user in communicating with the computer by permitting him to concentrate on the problem at hand, rather than on its translation into a formal and unambiguous language. Resolvable ambiguity actually contributes to the expressive power of our language by permitting greater parsimony. What is lost in the input is recovered by relying on the inferential capabilities of the listener. Generally speaking, as long as the listener or the system comprehends the meaning intended, the speaker will seek as much freedom of expression as possible. Of course, inherent in such a scheme is the possibility of being misunderstood. But then, human beings occasionally are misunderstood. In fact, the possibility for misunderstanding increases as the common universe of discourse narrows. The language of treaties and legal documents is seemingly *unnatural* only because one cannot always rely on the inferential capabilities of the parties to resolve ambiguities in the manner in which they were intended.

2.5 Productions

As described, the syntactic component is not yet suitable for computer implementation. We must first obtain a recognizer from the syntactic component which provides convenient interaction with the semantic component within the framework of a computer model. A. Evans [23] and Feldman [25] have described production models for doing precisely this kind of task for compilers. Let us explore the possibility of using the already proven technique of syntax directed compiling in the processing of natural language.[3] In our case, however, instead of using the source language to compile machine code which will be executed later on a particular machine, we will use natural language statements to construct well-formed expressions in the predicate calculus which can be evaluated later with respect to a particular universe of discourse.

The essential ingredient of such recognition models is the production. Basic Floyd-Evans productions are labeled replacement rules for ordered pairs of strings similar to the primary statements in the COMIT and SNOBOL languages. Their crucial feature is the existence of an action field that permits a compile-time action to be associated with the execution of the rule. Generally the action field contains a call on a semantic routine that in turn calls on a collection of run-time routines which are precoded in the compiler and correspond to the primitive operations of the source language. In our application, which is the translation of natural language statements into logical formulae, we propose to replace the action field of the production with an embedded production which we refer to as a semantic production. This innovation permits much greater flexibility in the construction of logical expressions, while still providing close interaction between the syntactic and semantic components.

The notion of using productions in semantic computations rather than in syntactic analysis or generation, however, is not a new concept in itself. Indeed, the notion of syntax-directed computing is descended from the

---

[3] Additional evidence for the value of this approach in natural language is provided by Thompson [79] in connection with his work on DEACON, even though DEACON does not use the predicate calculus as an internal representation.

canonical production systems of Post [57] which were not intentionally oriented to syntax analysis at all. Post [58] proved that any Turing machine calculation can be performed by a production system. The basic idea in the proof was to associate the infinite tape and the current state with the production stack. A one-to-one correspondence between the quintuplets of the Turing machine and the productions could then be established. Markov [48] and Davis [19] further extended the application of productions to logical systems. It was not until the work of Irons [31] and Floyd [26] that productions became an important tool in the parsing of compiler languages on a computer. Thus, as suggested by McCarthy [46], productions are both theoretically and practically a very powerful computing technique.

The translation of natural language statements using syntactic and semantic productions produces an expression in a logical language which is the *interpretation* of the source statement. Thus, this general method will be referred to as *syntax directed interpretation*. This notion must be made more precise, however, if it is to be useful in the construction of a computer model. To this end we will attempt to formalize the ideas presented thus far within the framework of a natural inference system.

2.6 Natural Inference Systems

In this section we will define a type of deductive question-answering system based on natural language input, called a Natural Inference System (NIS). It consists of a triple whose three components are essentially the syntactic, semantic, and pragmatic components discussed earlier. We introduce this formal notion so that we may prove important logical properties of these systems. One such property is completeness. Another is the complementary property of consistency. Both of these properties are shown to hold for natural inference systems.

2.6.1 Definitions. A *natural inference system* is an ordered triple, $\mathfrak{N} = (\mathfrak{H}, \mathfrak{D}, \Omega)$ where $\mathfrak{H}$ is a production system, $\mathfrak{D}$ is a dictionary, and Ω is a universe of discourse.[4]

2.6.1.1 A Production System $\mathfrak{H}$ consists of two components: $\mathfrak{H}_\sigma$ and $\mathfrak{H}_\tau$ where $\mathfrak{H}_\sigma$ is an analytic production system and $\mathfrak{H}_\tau$ is a generative production system.

2.6.1.2 A String is a Finite Sequence of Symbols, including the *empty string*, Λ, which consists of no symbols. For any string s, $\Lambda s = s\Lambda = s$. A *substring* t of a string s ($t \subseteq s$) has the property that $s = \gamma t \rho$ for strings

---

[4] This is analogous to the notion of the environment, η, in the development of Wirth and Weber [88].

γ, ρ (possibly γ, $\rho = \Lambda$). A *proper substring* t of a string s (t $\subset$ s) is a substring such that t $\neq$ s $\neq \Lambda$.

2.6.1.3 A VOCABULARY, $V = \{a_i \mid a_i \text{ is a symbol} \wedge i = 1, 2, \ldots, n < \infty\}$.

2.6.1.4 A PRODUCTION IS AN ORDERED PAIR (φ, ψ) of strings where $\forall a \in \varphi$ and $\forall a \in \psi$, $a \in V$. For some strings χ_1 and χ_2 let

$$\varphi = \chi_1 \omega \chi_2 \quad \text{and} \quad \psi = \chi_1 \omega' \chi_2, \quad \omega \neq \Lambda.$$

A production is *context free* if $\omega \in V$ and $\chi_1 = \chi_2 = \Lambda$; otherwise *context sensitive*.

An *analytic production system* is an ordered pair, $\mathfrak{H}_\sigma = (V_\sigma, P_\sigma)$ where σ, the syntactic stack, designates the stack associated with the analytic productions, $P_\sigma = \{(\varphi, \psi)\}$ is a finite set of productions, and $V_\sigma = V_{\sigma_T} \cup V_{\sigma_N}$ where

$$V_{\sigma_T} = \{a \in V_\sigma \mid \forall (\varphi, \psi) \in P_\sigma, \quad a \notin \omega' \subseteq \psi\}$$

and $V_{\sigma_N} = V_\sigma - V_{\sigma_T}$. V_{σ_T} is called the *analytic terminal vocabulary* and V_{σ_N} is called the *analytic non-terminal vocabulary*.

A *generative production system* is an ordered pair, $\mathfrak{H}_\tau = (V_\tau, P_\tau)$ where τ, the semantic stack, designates the stack associated with the generative productions, $P_\tau = \{(\varphi, \psi)\}$ is a finite set of productions, and $V_\tau = V - V_\sigma = V_{\tau_T} \cup V_{\tau_N}$ where

$$V_{\tau_T} = \{a \in V_\tau \mid \forall (\varphi, \psi) \in P_\tau, \quad a \notin \omega \subseteq \varphi\}$$

and $V_{\tau_N} = V_\tau - V_{\tau_T}$. V_{τ_T} is called the *generative terminal vocabulary* and V_{τ_N} is called the *generative non-terminal vocabulary*.

2.6.1.5 Let $P = \{(\varphi, \psi)\}$ where $\varphi = \chi_1 \omega \chi_2$ and $\psi = \chi_1 \omega' \chi_2$. A *loop* L is a subset of P, $L = \{(\lambda_i, \mu_i)\}$, such that $\lambda_i = \chi_{1_i} \omega_i \chi_{2_i}$ and $\mu_i = \chi_{1_i} \omega'_i \chi_{2_i}$ with $\omega_i \neq \Lambda$ for which the strings $\xi_i \subseteq \omega_i$ and $\eta_i \subseteq \omega_i$ satisfy

$$\eta_i = \xi_{i+1} \quad \text{and} \quad \eta_n = \xi_1 \quad (1 \leq i \leq n).$$

A set of productions is said to be *loop-free* if it contains no occurrence of a loop.

2.6.1.6 A PRODUCTION SYSTEM is said to be *monogenic* if $\forall (\xi, \eta) \in P$ and $\forall (\lambda, \mu) \in P$, $\xi = \lambda$ implies $\eta = \mu$.

Example. A typical labeled production in Formula Algol has the following format:

α: IF $v == [c_1, c_2, \ldots, c_n]$ THEN BEGIN ALTER v TO $[d_1, d_2, \ldots, d_m]$;
GO TO β END;

where α and β are labels, c_i, $d_j \in V$, $i = 1, 2, \ldots, n$; $j = 1, 2, \ldots, m$ are constituents such that $[c_1, c_2, \ldots, c_n] = \varphi$ and $[d_1, d_2, \ldots, d_m] = \psi$, and the double equal sign is a Formula Algol operator that determines if the object on the left-hand side is an instance of the pattern on the right-hand side.

2.6.1.7 A DICTIONARY, $\mathfrak{D} = \{f_i(x_1, x_2, \ldots, x_m) \in V_{\tau\tau} \mid$ the f_i are m-adic predicates $(m \geq 1)$, $i = 1, 2, \ldots, n < \infty$ and the x_j, $j = 1, 2, \ldots, m < \infty$ are free argument variables$\}$.

Example.

1. TRIANGLE(X)
2. BLACK(X)
3. GREATER(X,Y)

2.6.1.8 A UNIVERSE OF DISCOURSE, $\Omega = \{o_k \mid o_k \leftarrow /[A_1 : V_{11}, V_{12}, \ldots, V_{1n_1}] \ldots [A_2 : V_{21}, V_{22}, \ldots, V_{2n_2}] \ldots [A_m : V_{m1}, V_{m2}, \ldots, V_{mn_m}]$, $k = 1, 2, \ldots, 1 < \infty\}$ where the V_{ij} ($i = 1, 2, \ldots, m$ and $j = 1, 2, \ldots, n_i$) are *values* on the *description list* of the object o_k corresponding to the prescribed *attributes* A_i ($i = 1, 2, \ldots, m$).

Example.

1. OBJECT[3]←/[TYPE: POLYGON, TRIANGLE][SIZE: 10000]
   [COLOR: BLACK]
2. OBJECT[4]←/[TYPE: POLYGON, SQUARE][SIZE: 5000]
   [COLOR: WHITE]

2.6.1.9 LET THE PRODUCTION SYSTEM $\mathfrak{H} = (V, P)$ BE GIVEN. We may write $\varphi \to \psi$ when $(\varphi, \psi) \in P$. For each string $v = v_a \varphi v_b$ (v_a, v_b possibly Λ), $v^1 = v_a \psi v_b$ is called a *first transform* of v, and is said to result from the *application* of (φ, ψ) to v. Let $v \Rightarrow v^1$ denote this relation. A string v^k, such that $v \Rightarrow v^1 \Rightarrow \cdots \Rightarrow v^{k-1} \Rightarrow v^k$ is called the *kth transform* of v. Let $v \overset{*}{\Rightarrow} v^k$ denote this relation. For analytic production systems the sequence $v, v^1, v^2, \ldots$ where $v^k \Rightarrow v^{k+1}$ is called a *parse* of v. For generative production systems this sequence is called the *derivation* of v. Note that for a given v, there may be none, one, or many first transforms. If $s \overset{*}{\Rightarrow} t$, we say that s *produces* t, and conversely t is the *reduction* of s.

2.6.1.10 A SEQUENCING FUNCTION IS A METHOD of passing control from one production to the next in an ordered sequence of productions. In a production $\varphi \to \psi$, the elements of φ are said to form a *pattern*. These elements are also called *constituents*. A *match* is an attempt to recognize by means of the pattern φ an exact instance of a configuration of symbols in the stack associated with the production. By convention, the elements of the stack are scanned from right to left. If the contents of the stack, v, is decomposable into $v_a \varphi v_b$ in several ways, then we specify success only for that match which minimizes the length of φv_b while maximizing the length of φ. Thus, a match will be either uniquely successful or unsuccessful. If a match in a production is successful, then a *serial* sequencing function passes control to the labeled production named in the "go to" statement of that production; otherwise it passes control to the next production in the sequence. Using this definition, a Markov Algorithm (cf. Markov [48]) is a set of productions distinguished by a single entry point at the first production, a serial sequencing function, and the condition that all "go to" statements (which are implied in the set) refer to the entry point. A *cluster* of productions is a set of productions distinguished by one entry point, and an error production particular to that set indicating that a certain construction was anticipated in the parse and not found.

2.6.1.11 AN ANALYTIC GRAMMAR, $G_\sigma = (\mathfrak{H}_\sigma, S)$ where $P_\sigma = \{(\varphi, \psi)\}$ is a set of productions and $S \in V_{\sigma_N}$ is a distinguished symbol called the *sentence symbol*. The last production to be executed in an analytic grammar is called a *success* production and must contain an instance of S.

A *generative grammar*, $G_\tau = (\mathfrak{H}_\tau, T)$ where $P_\tau = \{(\varphi, \psi)\}$ is a set of productions and $T \in V_{\tau_N}$ is a distinguished symbol called the *root symbol*. The first production to be executed in a generative grammar must contain an instance of T.

2.6.1.12 AN ANALYTIC LANGUAGE, $L = L(G_\sigma) = \{s = s_1 s_2 \ldots s_n \mid s_i \in V_{\sigma_T}, i = 1, 2, \ldots, n < \infty$ and $s \overset{*}{\Rightarrow} S$ in a finite number of transforms$\}$.

A *generative language*, $L = L(G_\tau) = \{t = t_1 t_2 \ldots t_n \mid t_i \in V_{\tau_T}, i = 1, 2, \ldots, n < \infty$ and $T \overset{*}{\Rightarrow} t$ in a finite number of transforms$\}$.

2.6.1.13 G_{v_1} and G_{v_2} are said to be (weakly) *equivalent* if $L(G_{v_1}) = L(G_{v_2})$.

2.6.1.14 FOR A GIVEN ANALYTIC GRAMMAR a string v is said to be *ambiguously derivable* if there exist two parses of v to S whose associated phrase markers (cf. Chomsky [11, p. 65]) are different. For a given generative grammar a string v is said to be *ambiguously derivable* if there exist two derivations of v from S whose associated phrase markers are different. A grammar is said to be *unambiguous* if $\forall v \in L(G)$ v is not ambiguously derivable.

2.6.1.15 THE GENERATIVE GRAMMAR $G_\tau = (\mathfrak{H}_\tau, T)$ will now be defined more explicitly. The semantic terminal vocabulary V_{τ_T} consists of

(i) a finite set of n-adic predicates $\{F_i\}$, $i = 1, 2, \ldots, m < \infty$ whose members comprise $\mathfrak{D}$
(ii) a finite set of argument variables $\{x_i\}$, $i = 1, 2, \ldots, m < \infty$
(iii) the logical operator "$\neg$"
(iv) the logical connectives "$\vee$", "$\wedge$", "$\supset$", "$\equiv$"
(v) the comma ","
(vi) the two parentheses "(" and ")"
(vii) the universal and existential quantifiers "$\forall$" and "$\exists$."

The semantic non-terminal vocabulary V_{τ_N} consists of a finite set of n-adic predicates $\{F_i\}$, $i = 1, 2, \ldots, m < \infty$.

A *well-formed formula* (wff) in the quantificational calculus is defined recursively as follows:

(i) "$F(x_1, x_2, \ldots, x_n)$" is a wff where $F \in V_{\tau_T}$ is an n-adic predicate ($n \geq 1$) and $x_1, x_2, \ldots, x_n$ are argument variables;
(ii) If φ is a wff then "$(\forall x)\varphi$" and "$(\exists x)\varphi$" are also wff where x is an argument variable;
(iii) If φ is a wff then "$\neg\varphi$" is a wff;
(iv) If φ and ψ are wff then "$(\varphi \vee \psi)$," "$(\varphi \wedge \psi)$," "$(\varphi \supset \psi)$," and "$(\varphi \equiv \psi)$" are also wff.

G_τ is said to be *well formed in the QC* if $L(G_\tau) \subseteq \{\text{wff}\}$.

2.6.1.16 TO DEFINE THE RELATION between $\mathfrak{H}_\sigma$ and $\mathfrak{H}_\tau$ in $\mathfrak{H}$, clusters of productions from $\mathfrak{H}_\sigma$ and $\mathfrak{H}_\tau$ will be interleaved in the general case, although $\mathfrak{H}$ as a whole will be constrained to a serial sequencing function. Thus, associated with each parse in the analytic grammar is a derivation in the generative grammar. In this fashion the analytic productions guide the generation of expressions in the generative language. Even though productions from the analytic and generative grammar are interleaved, the identity of any particular production is always clear, since each production makes explicit reference to either the syntactic stack or the semantic stack. Depending on how the analytic and generative productions are interleaved, each sentence $s \in L(G_\sigma)$ will produce an expression $t \in L(G_\tau)$ called the *interpretation* of s. We will write $\mathfrak{H}(s)$ to denote the interpretation of s.

2.6.1.17 WE SHALL SAY THAT A SENTENCE $s \in L(G_\sigma)$ is *valid* if and only if all instances of the interpretation of s, $\mathfrak{H}(s)$, are true in the universe of discourse, Ω. For any Ω there exists a mechanical procedure for determining whether $s \in L(G_\sigma)$ is valid. Let $t = \mathfrak{H}(s)$ be the interpretation of s. The *evaluation* $\mathfrak{A}$ of t produces a truth-value in the context of the universe of discourse Ω. $\mathfrak{A}_\Omega(t)$ consists of two subprocesses:

1. Apply each of the following productions to t until it is no longer applicable:

(i) $t_1 \equiv t_2 \rightarrow (t_1 \supset t_2) \wedge (t_2 \supset t_1)$
(ii) $t_1 \supset t_2 \rightarrow (\neg t_1 \vee t_2)$
(iii) $\neg \neg t \rightarrow t$
(iv) $(\forall x)t(x) \rightarrow t(o_1) \wedge t(o_2) \wedge \cdots \wedge t(o_n)$
(v) $(\exists x)t(x) \rightarrow t(o_1) \vee t(o_2) \vee \cdots \vee t(o_n)$

where n is the number of objects in Ω. These productions are said to be *elimination* productions, since they each eliminate one terminal symbol from the expression to which they are applicable.[5] Let the resulting schema be t'.

2. Subject t' to the truth table test.

Thus, s is valid if and only if t' is a tautology.

2.6.1.18 THE *negation* OF A SENTENCE s, $\bar{s}$, is the sentence to which has been prefixed the phrase "It is not the case that." In order to operate on the negation of sentences in $L(G_\sigma)$, we require that $\exists \bar{p}_\sigma \in P_\sigma$ and $\bar{p}_\tau \in P_\tau$ such that

$\bar{p}_\sigma$: [It, is, not, the, case, that, ψ] $\rightarrow \psi$ go to $\bar{p}_\tau$;
$\bar{p}_\tau$: $\varphi \rightarrow \neg \varphi$

2.6.1.19 A PRODUCTION SYSTEM $\mathfrak{H}$ is said to be *complete* if $\forall s \in L(G_\sigma)$, either s or the negation of s is valid. A production system is said to be *consistent* if $\forall s \in L(G_\sigma)$, it is not the case that both s and the negation of s are valid.

2.6.2 Properties of Natural Inference Systems

Lemma 1. Let $G_\sigma = (\mathfrak{H}_\sigma, S)$ and $G_\tau = (\mathfrak{H}_\tau, T)$ be given. If P_σ and P_τ are loop free, then $\forall s \in L(G_\sigma)$, $\mathfrak{H}(s)$ exists.

Proof. If no subset of P is a loop, then for $i \neq j$ we must have $s^i \neq s^j$ and $s \overset{*}{\Rightarrow} s^n = S$ for $n < \infty$. Similarly, for $i \neq j$ we must have $t^i \neq t^j$ and $T \overset{*}{\Rightarrow} t^m = t \in L(G_\tau)$ for $m < \infty$. Thus, in the application of $\mathfrak{H}$ to s we obtain an expression $t \in L(G_\tau)$ in a finite number of steps.

There are two principal sources of syntactic ambiguity. One arises if the sequencing function is not unique; another arises if some cluster of productions is not unique. In the latter case the first production is said to *preclude* the second, and the other possible parsing will not be found.

---

[5] See Leblanc [39, pp. 95–98] for *n*-valid evaluation of quantificational schema.

Lemma 2. Let $G_\sigma = (\mathfrak{H}_\sigma, S)$ and $G_\tau = (\mathfrak{H}_\tau, T)$ be given. If each cluster of $\mathfrak{H}_\sigma$ and $\mathfrak{H}_\tau$ is monogenic and $\mathfrak{H}$ is endowed with a serial sequencing function, then $\mathfrak{H}(s)$ is unique.

Proof. Because we have a serial sequencing function, the next production to be executed in the parsing and derivation is unique. If each cluster of $\mathfrak{H}_\sigma$ is monogenic, then there does not exist both $(\varphi, \psi_1) \in P_\sigma$ and $(\varphi, \psi_2) \in P_\sigma$ in the same cluster, $\psi_1 \neq \psi_2$; hence, in $s \Rightarrow s^1$, s^1 is unique. But if s^{k-1} is unique, then s^k is unique, and by induction on k, s has a unique parse $s \overset{*}{\Rightarrow} S$. Similarly, if each cluster in $\mathfrak{H}_\tau$ is monogenic then there does not exist both $(\varphi, \psi_1) \in P_\tau$ and $(\varphi, \psi_2) \in P_\tau$ in the same cluster, $\psi_1 \neq \psi_2$; hence in $T \Rightarrow t^1$, t^1 is unique. But if t^{k-1} is unique, then t^k is unique, and by induction on k, t has a unique derivation $T \overset{*}{\Rightarrow} t$ as a function of s. Thus, $\mathfrak{H}(s) = t$ is a well-defined mapping.

Although the serial sequencing function is given for $\mathfrak{H}$, the sequencing through the productions of $\mathfrak{H}_\tau$ will in general be a function of s. Thus the derivation for any particular $t \in L(G_\tau)$ need not be unique, i.e., $\mathfrak{H}(s)$ is not in general a one-to-one function. The set $PP(t) = \{s \in L(G_\sigma) \mid \mathfrak{H}(s) = t\}$ is called a *paraphrastic* set and consists of all the members of $L(G_\sigma)$ that give rise to the same interpretation.

For the moment we will restrict our attention to the case where $\mathfrak{H}$ has a serial sequencing function and the production systems $\mathfrak{H}_\sigma$ and $\mathfrak{H}_\tau$ are loop-free and have monogenic clusters.

Lemma 3. Let $G_\sigma = (\mathfrak{H}_\sigma, S)$ and $G_\tau = (\mathfrak{H}_\tau, T)$ be given. If G_τ is well formed in the QC then $\mathfrak{H}(s) \in \{\text{wff}\}$.

Proof. By Lemmas 1 and 2, $\mathfrak{H}(s)$ is a well-defined function. $\mathfrak{H}(s) = t \in L(G_\tau)$. But, since G_τ is well formed in the QC, then $t \in \{\text{wff}\}$ and thus $\mathfrak{H}(s) \in \{\text{wff}\}$.

We will now turn our attention to G_τ well formed in the QC.

Lemma 4. $\mathfrak{A}_\Omega(\mathfrak{H}(s)) \in \{0, 1\}$.

Proof. If we associate 0 with false and 1 with true, then it is sufficient to show that for any $t \in \{\text{wff}\}$ the elimination algorithm in $\mathfrak{A}_\Omega$ terminates, since once we have a quantifier-free form of t with no occurrences of "$\equiv$," "$\supset$," and bound variables, the application of truth tables for the logical connectives "$\wedge$," "$\vee$," and "$\neg$" to yield a single truth-value is an easy matter.

Each of the five elimination productions has the form

$$\psi_1 \alpha \psi_2 \rightarrow \beta, \quad \text{where } \alpha \not\subseteq \beta$$

and α takes as value "$\equiv$," "$\supset$," "$\neg\neg$," "$\vee$," and "$\exists$" respectively. Initially t contains a finite number of symbols, thus it contains finitely many occurrences of α. Since $\alpha \not\subseteq \beta$, the number of occurrences of α cannot increase on application of the production. Label each occurrence of α in t. Thus we have α_i, $i = 1, 2, \ldots, n$. By n applications of the production all occurrences of α in t are eliminated, the production is no longer applicable, and control passes to the next production. Since no succeeding production affects the applicability of a preceding production, control will ultimately pass through the fifth production and the algorithm will terminate. The proof depends in an essential way on the finiteness of the universe of discourse, Ω, and it was because of this that it was unnecessary to obtain the Prenex and Skolem Normal Forms.

Theorem 1. $\mathfrak{H}$ is complete.

Proof. From the definition of completeness and Lemma 4 we must show $\forall s \in L(G_\sigma)$ that if $\mathfrak{A}_\Omega(\mathfrak{H}(s)) = 0$ then $\mathfrak{A}_\Omega(\mathfrak{H}(\bar{s})) = 1$. It is sufficient to show $\neg\mathfrak{H}(s) = \mathfrak{H}(\bar{s})$, since $\forall t \in \{\text{wff}\}$ $\mathfrak{A}(t) = 0$ implies $\neg\mathfrak{A}(t) = 1$ implies $\mathfrak{A}(\neg t) = 1$. But the negation transforms in $\mathfrak{H}$ ensure that $\mathfrak{H}(\bar{s}) = \neg\mathfrak{H}(s)$.

Theorem 2. $\mathfrak{H}$ is consistent.

Proof. From the definition of consistency and Lemma 4 we must show, $\forall s \in L(G_\sigma)$, that if $\mathfrak{A}_\Omega(\mathfrak{H}(s)) = 1$ then $\mathfrak{A}_\Omega(\mathfrak{H}(\bar{s})) = 0$. Again it is sufficient to show that $\mathfrak{H}(s) = \neg\mathfrak{H}(\bar{s})$, since $\forall t \in \{\text{wff}\}$ $\mathfrak{A}(t) = 1$ implies $\neg\mathfrak{A}(t) = 0$ implies $\mathfrak{A}(\neg t) = 0$. But again this is assured by the definition of the negation of s.

2.6.3 Ambiguous Grammars.

In the event that all clusters are not monogenic, i.e., the recognizer accepts syntactically ambiguous sentences, then the sequencing function should be modified so that a distinct interpretation is constructed for each legitimate parse of the input sentence. In such a case $\mathfrak{H}(s)$ is no longer a function in the strict sense, but a one-to-many mapping of the input sentence onto the collection of its different interpretations. Thus, the completeness and consistency of $\mathfrak{H}$ no longer hold, since both preceding theorems depend in an essential way on the assumption of a unique interpretation for each input. It is not even clear how to assign a single truth-value to an ambiguous sentence. Although we will not adopt this approach, one method of attack is to use an infinitely many-valued logic. By defining the truth-value ω of a sentence s as

$$\omega(s) = \frac{\text{the number of true interpretations of s}}{\text{the total number of interpretations of s}}$$

we have a method for identifying the truth-value of all sentences. We observe that $\omega \in [0, 1]$ and for $\omega = 1$ we say that s is true, while $\omega = 0$ implies that s is false. $\omega = \frac{1}{2}$ implies that s is ambivalent; $\omega > \frac{1}{2}$ that s is more true than false; and $\omega < \frac{1}{2}$ that s is more false than true. $\omega(s_1) > \omega(s_2)$ suggests that s_1 is more true than s_2, and so on. Note that for the degenerate case of unique interpretations, the definition of ω reduces correctly. In this fashion one might generalize the notion of completeness to say that $\mathfrak{H}$ is complete if s or its negation has an $\omega \geq \frac{1}{2}$. Similarly, consistency might be generalized as it is not the case that both s and its negation have an $\omega > \frac{1}{2}$. Then, with a few additional changes, the theorems would again hold under these generalized definitions.

The difficulty with this approach is that it may violate our intuitive notion of truth and falsity for ambiguous sentences. In the vast majority of cases the speaker intends only one interpretation of his sentence, and frequently is oblivious to any others unless they are explicitly pointed out. Only in the realm of humor does the speaker systematically intend that the listener contrast the varying interpretations of his statement. Any proposal to determine the truth-value of a source statement by weighing the truth-values of the various interpretations and consolidating them all into one global truth-value would seem ludicrous to a serious speaker. But yet, because so much of our language is ambiguous, people must use some method of resolving ambiguity. Otherwise there would be much greater evidence of confusion and misunderstanding than is actually observed. There are at least two reasons why greater misunderstanding does not occur among humans.

First, people tend to order the possible interpretations of a syntactically ambiguous sentence in a natural way. A typical source of syntactic ambiguity is the potentially multiple dependencies that may arise between prepositional phrases or relative phrases and the words or phrases they modify. A heuristic most people observe in finding the preferred interpretation is to let the dependent word or phrase modify its nearest preceding referent. If this first interpretation makes sense, i.e., can be evaluated with respect to the universe of discourse, then the listener will assume that the speaker intended this natural interpretation and immediately proceed to the next statement.

A second reason why there is not more misunderstanding is that unintentional interpretations of ambiguous sentences are generally not false with respect to the universe of discourse, but are vacuous. This provides the listener with another heuristic for making an inference about the likelihood of possible interpretations, since we assume that the serious speaker will tend to form statements that are either true or false, but never vacuous. Both of these heuristics—in direct opposition to the truth-functional computation described above—will be adopted for natural inference systems.

Therefore, our strategy for resolving ambiguity is to evaluate the most natural interpretation first. Only in the case where this natural interpretation is vacuous do we evaluate the next most likely interpretation, and so on until a non-vacuous interpretation is found. And only if each logically possible interpretation is neither true nor false with respect to the universe of discourse do we declare the sentence vacuous. The principal advantage of this strategy is that it minimizes processing time for ambiguous sentences, avoiding a complete evaluation of spurious interpretations. The ordering of possible interpretations, rather than evaluating all logically possible interpretations immediately, eliminates the combinatorial interaction of ambiguities which, although harmless for simple sentences, can be severe for complex sentences. The main disadvantage of this approach, however, is that it will not test explicitly for genuine ambiguity so as to alert the speaker to possibly undesirable consequences. But this is a problem for humans as well.[6]

SECTION 3
GRANIS, A COMPUTER MODEL

A crucial test of any formal mathematical system, like that outlined in Section 2.6, is whether it can be used to guide the design of a running computer program. Such a program immediately provides a demonstration of the feasibility of the ideas upon which it is based. In this section we will see how a natural inference system, like that presented in Section 2, can be implemented.

Formula Algol [56] was selected as the programming language for the implementation. This choice was made because Formula Algol incorporates within the framework of one language a wide variety of formula manipulation and list processing capabilities. Both of these capabilities are essential in our application. Formula Algol extends ALGOL 60 by adding two new types of data structures together with appropriate primitive processes to operate on them. However, the control structure of ALGOL 60 is inherited without change. The two new declaration types are type "FORMULA" and type "SYMBOL."

Because Formula Algol is a compiler rather than an interpretive language it has the advantage of producing highly efficient machine code for later execution. The importance of efficient execution becomes apparent when one attempts to operate with the system in an interactive mode. Experience has shown that if the system takes longer than thirty seconds to

---

[6] In a recent psychological experiment in which humans were presented with the task of completing sentence fragments, MacKay [45] observed that even though subjects consistently took longer to complete ambiguous sentences than unambiguous ones, none of them reported being aware of the ambiguities while completing the sentences.

parse, interpret, and evaluate a simple English sentence, conversation degrades rapidly because the human attention span is exceeded. On any particular machine an interpretive programming language would only make this problem more severe. An undesirable consequence of the fact that Formula Algol is a compiler, however, is the high comparative cost of making even simple structural changes to the program. Recompiling may take as much as four minutes of computer time.

Another important advantage of Formula Algol is its easy readability. Its transparency contrasts sharply with most currently available programming languages. An original design requirement of ALGOL 60 was that it be a language suitable for the communication of algorithms within the programming community, and Formula Algol has inherited the relatively perspicuous notation of its predecessor.

3.1 Program Structure

The three major components of GRANIS—syntactic, semantic, and pragmatic—are readily distinguished in the program. The syntactic component, which comprises the bulk of the program, consists uniformly of clusters of formula productions for the recognition and translation of well-formed English sentences.

3.1.1 The Production System. Given the initial phrase structure grammar, the method used to construct the production recognizer is based on the Earley Algorithm [20]. This algorithm produces a highly efficient one pass, one-push-down-stack, bounded context recognizer which involves no closed subroutines. Two kinds of production clusters called type 0 and type 1 clusters are constructed corresponding to each character in the phrase-structure grammar. A cluster acts as a unit because only its first production has a label to which transfer can be made. The type 0 cluster for a character A (labeled A0) is constructed so as to appear at the point in the parse where an instance of A is expected in the sentence starting with the last symbol scanned. These are constructed only for non-terminals. The type 1 cluster for a character A (labeled A1) is constructed so as to appear at the point in the parse where A is second in the syntax stack, and a decision on the next cluster to be transferred to must be made as a function of context. There are three cases in which type 0 productions are constructed and five cases in which type 1 productions are constructed. These are illustrated in Table 1. A brief outline of the algorithm will be given.

Type 0 Productions. Let A be the non-terminal for which we are constructing type 0 productions. Further, let T(A) be the set of all terminal characters with which A can begin. We will construct a production corresponding to each member of T(A). For each alternative in the definition of

Table 1. BNF Rules to Formula Productions

BNF rules	Formula productions
TYPE 0 PRODUCTIONS	
Context 1. G :: = a | ···	IF S==[$,a] THEN BEGIN ALTER LAST OF S TO [G,NEXT]; GO TO G1 END;
Context 2. G :: = ab ··· | ···	IF S==[$,a] THEN BEGIN INSERT [NEXT] AFTER LAST OF S; GO TO a1 END;
Context 3. G :: = aH ··· | ···	IF S==[$,a] THEN BEGIN INSERT [NEXT] AFTER LAST OF S; GO TO H0 END;
TYPE 1 PRODUCTIONS	
Context 1. G :: = αX | ···	IF S==[$,α,X,SIGMA:$1] THEN BEGIN ALTER LAST 3 OF S TO [G,SIGMA]; GO TO G1 END;
Context 2. G :: = αXH | ···	IF S==[$,α,X,i] THEN GO TO H0;
Context 3. G :: = αXc | ···	IF S==[$,α,X,c] THEN BEGIN ALTER LAST 3 OF S TO [G,NEXT];GO TO G1 END;
Context 4. G :: = αXcd | ···	IF S==[$,α,X,c] THEN BEGIN INSERT [NEXT] AFTER LAST OF S; GO TO c1 END;
Context 5. G :: = αXcH | ···	IF S==[$,α,X,c] THEN BEGIN INSERT [NEXT] AFTER LAST OF S; GO TO H0 END;

Notes: (1) As in COMIT, $ represents an arbitrary number of constituents.
(2) The "SIGMA" is a Formula Algol extractor.
(3) "NEXT" is a parameterless procedure which places the next character from the input string into the stack.

A, if the alternative begins with a terminal, a production is constructed from that string. For terminals, T(a) is defined as T(a) = a. If it begins with a non-terminal B, we determine T(B) from the definition of B and proceed as before with T(A) until we have only alternatives which begin with terminals. The production constructed depends on the context of the initial terminal. The three possible contexts are shown in Table 1. If two of the constructed productions have the same stack element, they should be replaced by one of the form of context 2, since any parsing decision must be postponed until another character has been scanned.

Type 1 *Productions.* Let A be the character for which we are constructing type 1 productions, and let P(A) be the set of all places in the BNF in which A appears. A type 1 production should be constructed for each member of P(A) according to the five cases illustrated in Table 1.

Unlike the type 0 productions, the order of the type 1 productions is important and care should be taken to ensure that no production precludes any other. In the exceptional case where two productions constructed in this fashion mutually preclude each other, we have what is called a "culprit." To delete such a culprit, the grammar must be augmented to increase the context of one of the two culprit alternatives. Since this can always be done without loss of generality, there is no theoretical problem. In any event, for typical natural language grammars such culprit situations are rare. The introduction of metasyntactic class definitions is helpful in consolidating similar type 1 productions, with a significant saving in the total number of productions being realized. Since all of the resulting production clusters are closed with respect to the rest of the productions, their order in the total set of clusters is irrelevant.

To understand better how to construct a recognizer using this algorithm, the BNF grammar given in Section 2 will be taken as an example. When applied to the given grammar of 10 BNF rules, the algorithm produces 46 productions in 15 separate clusters. By defining the following terminal metaclasses:

```
PROCLASS={HE, SHE, THEY}
NOUNCLASS={JOHN, MARY, HOUSE}
ADJCLASS={BIG, SMALL, BLACK, WHITE}
VERBCLASS={LOVE, LOVES}
DETCLASS={THE, A}
```

and by appropriate relabeling, we may delete the redundant clusters for NOUN0 and DET0 to obtain the following 20 formula productions:

```
SENT0:       IF S==[$,PROCLASS] THEN BEGIN ALTER LAST OF S TO
                [PRO,NEXT]; GO TO PRO1 END;
             IF S==[$,DETCLASS] THEN BEGIN ALTER LAST OF S TO
                [DET,NEXT]; GO TO DET1 END;
             IF S==[$,NOUNCLASS] THEN BEGIN ALTER LAST OF S TO
                [NOUN,NEXT] GO TO NOUN1 END
                          ELSE GO TO ERROR SENT0;
SENT1:       IF S==[$,SENT,PERIOD] THEN GO TO SUCCESS
                          ELSE GO TO ERROR SENT1;
SUBJ1:       IF S==[$,SUBJ,VERBCLASS] THEN GO TO VERB0
                          ELSE GO TO ERROR SUBJ1;
NOUNPHRZ1:   IF S==[$, VERB,NOUNPHRZ,SIGMA:$1] THEN BEGIN ALTER LAST
                3 OF S TO [PRED, SIGMA]; GO TO PRED1 END;
             IF S==[$,NOUNPHRZ,SIGMA:$1] THEN BEGIN ALTER LAST 2 OF
                S TO [SUBJ, SIGMA]; GO TO SUBJ1 END
                          ELSE GO TO ERROR NOUNPHRZ1;
ADJST1:      IF S==[$,ADJST,ADJCLASS] THEN GO TO ADJ0;
             IF S==[$,DET,ADJST,NOUNCLASS] THEN GO TO SENT0
                          ELSE GO TO ERROR ADJST1;
```

PRED1:   IF S==[$,SUBJ,PRED,SIGMA:$1] THEN BEGIN ALTER LAST
             3 OF S TO [SENT,SIGMA]; GO TO SENT1 END
                                          ELSE GO TO ERROR PRED1;
PRO1:   IF S==[$,PRO,SIGMA:$1] THEN BEGIN ALTER LAST 2 OF S
             TO [SUBJ,SIGMA]; GO TO SUBJ1 END
                                          ELSE GO TO ERROR PRO1;
NOUN1:   IF S==[$,DET,ADJST,NOUN,SIGMA:$1] THEN BEGIN ALTER LAST
             4 OF S TO [NOUNPHRZ,SIGMA]; GO TO NOUNPHRZ1 END;
             IF S==[$,NOUN,SIGMA:$1] THEN BEGIN ALTER LAST 2 OF S
             TO [NOUNPHRZ,SIGMA]; GO TO NOUNPHRZ1 END
                                          ELSE GO TO ERROR NOUN1;
ADJ0:   IF S==[$,ADJCLASS] THEN BEGIN ALTER LAST OF
             S TO [ADJ,NEXT]; GO TO ADJ1 END
                                          ELSE GO TO ERROR ADJ0;
ADJ1:   IF S==[$,ADJST,ADJ,SIGMA:$1] THEN BEGIN ALTER LAST 3
             OF S TO [ADJST,SIGMA]; GO TO ADJST1 END;
             IF S==[$,ADJ,SICMA:$1] THEN BEGIN ALTER LAST 2 OF S TO
             [ADJST,SIGMA]; GO TO ADJST1 END
                                          ELSE GO TO ERROR ADJ1;
VERB0:   IF S==[$,VERBCLASS] THEN BEGIN ALTER LAST OF S TO
             [VERB,NEXT]; GO TO VERB1 END
                                          ELSE GO TO ERROR VERB0;
VERB1:   IF S==[$,VERB,NOUNCLASS] THEN GO TO SENT0;
             IF S==[$,VERB,DETCLASS] THEN GO TO SENT0
                                          ELSE GO TO ERROR VERB1;
DET1:   IF S==[$,DET,ADJCLASS] THEN GO TO ADJ0
                                          ELSE GO TO ERROR DET1;

It should be emphasized that except for declarations and a few steps for initialization, the above production grammar could be entered directly into the computer and run as a Formula Algol program to parse sentences (4) through (6) in Section 2. Note that sentence (7), "Mary loves the house," would not terminate at the "SUCCESS" exit, but at the "ERROR DET1" exit, since the "DET1" production will attempt to scan for an instance of an adjective when the current entry in the S stack is the terminal "house" and not an adjective.

To illustrate the order sensitivity of certain type 1 productions, observe that interchanging the two productions in the NOUNPHRZ cluster would cause the SUBJECT production to preclude the PREDICATE production, i.e., the grammar would always incorrectly scan predicates as subjects. As seen in this example, the introduction of class definitions for terminals considerably decreases the number of productions required. For example, by introducing the ADJCLASS definition the ADJ0 cluster is reduced from four productions (one for each adjective) to one production for the entire class. A similar saving is realized for the DET1 and ADJST1 clusters. Some of these savings for type 0 productions, however, will be lost with the later introduction of semantic productions. When the BNF grammar is completely partitioned, as in the example given (i.e., there are no occurrences of adjacent terminals and non-terminals in any alternative), the algorithm simplifies (since context 3 for type 0 and contexts 3, 4, and 5 for type 1 productions never occur).

Once the recognizer has been constructed, we must turn our attention to the introduction of semantic productions to cause the source string to be translated into an expression in the predicate calculus. Our policy is to postpone as long as possible the introduction of semantic productions in the parsing, so as to capitalize on as much context as possible. On the other hand, whenever an element of the syntax stack is deleted or replaced in the parsing, some potentially important semantic information may be lost, and a semantic production must appear. Thus, our strategy is to introduce semantic productions at those places and only those places where semantic information may be lost. In terms of the recognition algorithm, provision for semantic productions must always be made for context 1 type 0 and for contexts 1 and 3 type 1 productions. Since the other contexts do not alter the syntax stack, they do not require semantic productions. Taken by themselves, the semantic productions form a generative grammar for expressions in the quantificational calculus. Their form is structurally the same as the syntactic productions. The basic difference is that they operate on an independent semantic stack T. Due to technical constraints in Formula Algol, there are slight differences in appearance. For example, "+" is used as a delimiter for constituents in the stack rather than a comma, and the pattern "ANY" plays a role analogous to the pattern "$."

The combined syntactic and semantic productions are used for the recognition and translation of source statements respectively. For example, upon recognition of the first statement in Figure 1,

> (1) Each resistor in parallel with a capacitor which is ten ohms is an input resistor.

the following wff are constructed:

(2) $(\forall x)\{R(x) \land (\exists y)\{C(y) \land P(x, y) \land \Omega(y, 10)\} \supset I(x) \land R(x)\}$
(3) $(\forall x)\{R(x) \land (\exists y)\{C(y) \land P(x, y)\} \land \Omega(x, 10) \supset I(x) \land R(x)\}$.

The first wff (2) is the natural interpretation of sentence (1), but it incorrectly associates the relative pronoun "which" to the noun resistor; the second wff (3) correctly associates the relative pronoun with the noun capacitor. At this point, however, the correctness of either interpretation has not yet been established.

3.1.2 **The Dictionary.** The terminal vocabulary of the source language is partitioned into two subsets: referent terminals and function terminals. The referent terminals are those words which characterize objects or events. In English, referent words are typically nouns, pronouns, adjectives, adverbs, and most verbs. Function terminals on the other hand are those words which serve to delimit or relate the referent words. In English, function words are typically conjunctions, articles, prepositions, and auxiliary verbs. The semantic meaning of each of the lexical items in the referent terminal vocabulary is provided by the dictionary. The dictionary consists of a collection of boolean procedures for evaluating predicates corresponding to the referent terminals. The arguments of these predicates are variables which take as value objects in the universe of discourse. Nouns and adjectives generally give rise to one-place predicates. Relations such as "greater than" and "to the left of" give rise to two-place predicates. Some typical procedures for the predicates triangle (x), black (x), and greater (x, y) are programmed in Formula Algol as follows:

```
BOOLEAN PROCEDURE TRIANGLEF(X); VALUE X; FORM X;
   BEGIN IF AMONG(TRIANGLE,TYPE(X)) THEN TRIANGLEF←TRUE
                                    ELSE TRIANGLEF←FALSE END;
BOOLEAN PROCEDURE BLACKF(X); VALUE X; FORM X;
   BEGIN IF COLOR(X)=BLACK THEN BLACKF←TRUE
                            ELSE BLACKF←FALSE END;
BOOLEAN PROCEDURE GREATERF(X,Y); VALUE X,Y; FORM X,Y;
   BEGIN IF SIZE(X)<SIZE(Y) THEN GREATERF←TRUE
                             ELSE GREATERF←FALSE END;
```

These procedures of course assume the existence of other numerical and symbolic procedures as well as a set of description lists for the parameters when they are executed. These description lists form the universe of discourse. How they are constructed from a pictorial input will be discussed in the next section.

3.1.3 *The Universe of Discourse.* The universe of discourse for the user of GRANIS is a picture that may be altered dynamically during the course of conversation. It is input directly to the computer on a graphic display console by means of a light pen or cursor. Before the pictorial information can be used to process natural language statements, it must be analyzed and represented in a suitable fashion for later processing.

The fundamental data structure used in the internal representation of pictorial information is the description list. The ring structure described by Sutherland in Sketchpad [78] and by Roberts in CORAL [66] can be simulated as a special case of this general format.

To illustrate the use of description lists, the format of the universe of discourse for the NOR circuit given in Figure 1 is as follows:

$OB_1 \leftarrow$/[TYPE: RESISTOR,INPUT][OHMS: 10][LINK: 1,3];
$OB_2 \leftarrow$/[TYPE: CAPACITOR][UFD: 100][LINK: 1,3];
$OB_3 \leftarrow$/[TYPE: RESISTOR,INPUT][OHMS: 10][LINK: 2,3];
$OB_4 \leftarrow$/[TYPE: CAPACITOR][UFD: 50][LINK: 2,3];
$OB_5 \leftarrow$/[TYPE: RESISTOR,BIAS][OHMS: 10][LINK: 4,3];
$OB_6 \leftarrow$/[TYPE: TRANSISTOR][LINK: 3,5,6];
$OB_7 \leftarrow$/[TYPE: RESISTOR,OUTPUT][OHMS: 20][LINK: 5,7];
$OB_8 \leftarrow$/[TYPE: CAPACITOR][UFD: 10][LINK: 5,7];
$OB_9 \leftarrow$/[TYPE: RESISTOR,OUTPUT][OHMS: 50][LINK: 7,8];

In general, the objects OB can possess arbitrary numbers of attributes, each of which has an associated value list.

But how does one automatically abstract from the two-dimensional information contained in the picture that part which is relevant to the construction of these description lists? Since the basic problem of two-dimensional analysis has not been solved in any general fashion, there is little theoretical knowledge to draw on. On the other hand, the display hardware described by Quatse [60] must itself perform a linearization of the pictorial data, since the regeneration display file for the picture in core memory is in fact a linear array. This is the same file as that used by the hardware to refresh the screen on a continuous basis and thereby maintain a flicker-free display. The file is composed of vector, header, and character string commands. The complete set of display commands and their formats is shown in Table 2. The task of processing a picture then reduces to processing a logic array of display commands and producing as output a set of description lists. This task has considerable structural similarity to the task of parsing a source statement in natural language and producing as output an expression in the predicate calculus. Let us explore the possibility of using the same syntax-directed techniques in this new application, i.e., recognizing and translating pictures rather than text into a suitable internal representation.

First, we observe that because the display file representation is constructed dynamically by the hardware as the user draws the picture, the file contains not only information about what is displayed on the screen at any moment, but also the complete history of the order in which the total picture was drawn. At this point we have a choice. We may choose either to disregard this order information inherent in the hardware representation of the display file or to capitalize on it in some fashion, thereby considerably simplifying the recognition process itself. The disadvantage of this latter choice, however, is that it requires the user to observe certain conventions which specify the manner in which certain parts of the picture are to be drawn in addition to what the picture is to look like when he is done. If these conventions are sufficiently natural, however, so that a user would probably not violate them anyway, then it would be inefficient not to take

Table 2. Display Commands

	31	30	29 24	23		10 9	8 7	4 3	0
Delimit	0	1	011000	///	Address	Page	State	Console	
					20 19				
Header	1	1	///////		Y		X		
Vector string	0	1	010000	S_X S_Y T B	ΔY		ΔX		
Character string	1	0	Char$_1$	T_1 S_1	Char$_2$ T_2 S_2		Char$_3$	T_3	S_3
Compare	0	1	101000	///////		Char	///		
Left margin	0	1	110000	///////			X		
Right margin	0	1	111000	///////			X		
Cycle	0	1	100000	///	Address	//////////			
Store	0	0	////////////////////////////						

Notes: (1) A 13 bit address field is required to locate addresses in the eight thousand word core memory used to hold display files for all consoles.

(2) Ten bit "X" and "Y" coordinates are used to discriminate points in a 1024 × 1024 matrix, the resolving power of the screen.

advantage of the hardware preprocessing. Hence, we have adopted this second choice for GRANIS.

Just how restrictive are these conventions? By way of illustration, the conventions for drawing geometric figures are as follows:

(1) A user must draw figures one at a time, i.e., once having started a figure, he must complete it before going on to the next one, and having completed it, he must never return to it.

(2) Each polygon must be drawn as a sequence of vectors forming a polygonal path.

(3) Upon hitting the last "mark" for the endpoint of the polygon, the user must press the vector function button off, and then on again, before starting a new figure.

The purpose of the first rule is that it guarantees that each figure is distinct and occupies a set of continuous locations in the display file; the second rule guarantees that there is only one header command for each figure; the third rule has the effect of inserting a blanked vector of zero length after the vector string sequence. This operation would be necessary in any event if the user expected to capitalize on the offline translation features inherent in the hardware (cf. Quatse [60, p. 42]). Note that there are no restrictions on the order in which figures are drawn, on overlaying figures, or on the position, size, or orientation of any particular figure. Similar conventions hold for chemistry molecules and electrical circuits.

A consequence of inadvertently violating one of the above rules while drawing a figure is that the figure may not be correctly recognized even though to outward appearances it is identical to one which has already been scanned correctly. However, the introduction of these conventions in drawing figures is merely an expedient to gain more efficiency in the use of memory space and processing time in the picture scanner portion of GRANIS, which has no immediate theoretical interest in itself. There is no reason in principle why these conventions could not be dispensed with by introducing a set of separate preprocessing routines to evaluate absolute coordinates for each vector, and determine the connectivity of the total picture, irrespective of how it was drawn, by means of a set of ϵ-neighborhood computations.

A somewhat related problem is that the picture grammar as constructed may recognize a peculiar object drawn on the screen as a legal figure or symbol even though the peculiar object is only related to the legal figure by way of an extreme topological distortion. In certain situations such recognition is undesirable. For example, GRANIS may identify some object as a "resistor" even though that object bears little outward resemblance (from the human point of view) to the standard resistor symbol. This means that the class of objects the grammar can potentially generate is larger than the intended class of well-formed objects that the grammar is accustomed to recognize. However, in practice this problem has never arisen, since users are inclined to draw only objects they expect to make statements about later. In any event, as the grammar is extended, this problem becomes less severe, since distinguishing between similar equivalence classes then requires finer distinctions, and violations of intuition are less likely.

By means of a simple example let us now see how syntax directed techniques are actually used in the recognition and translation of figures into description lists. For our example we take the four geometric figures shown in Figure 2. The pentagon, triangle, and both squares are represented internally in the computer regeneration memory as a display file of 24 words based on the commands given in Table 2.

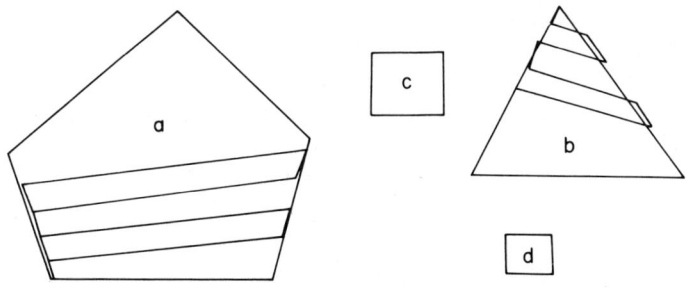

Figure 2

The description lists constructed by the picture scanner for Figure 2 are as follows:

OB_1←/[TYPE: POLYGON,PENTAGON][COLOR: BLACK[7]][SIZE: 18155];
OB_2←/[TYPE: POLYGON,TRIANGLE][COLOR: BLACK][SIZE: 14352];
OB_3←/[TYPE: POLYGON,SQUARE][COLOR: WHITE][SIZE: 5530];
OB_4←/[TYPE: POLYGON,SQUARE][COLOR: WHITE][SIZE: 5022];

How does the program take as input the 24 word logic array and produce the four description lists above? First, some preliminary analysis is performed by appropriately masking each word, determining the number of objects in the picture, and the number of sides in each object. Then in the geometry package, a routine is executed for any particular object to determine whether it is a polygon, as distinct from a mere polygonal path. A polygonal path is a polygon if and only if the end point and the initial point coincide. In terms of the primitive ΔX and ΔY information available to us from the logic array, this condition is satisfied if

$$\sum_{i=1}^{n} \Delta X_i = \sum_{i=1}^{n} \Delta Y_i = 0$$

where n is the number of sides. To allow for human error in drawing, this condition is relaxed to

$$\left|\sum_{i=1}^{n} \Delta X_i\right| < \epsilon \quad \text{and} \quad \left|\sum_{i=1}^{n} \Delta Y_i\right| < \epsilon$$

where the tolerance, ϵ, defines a rectangular neighborhood around the initial point. Coincidence now requires merely that the end point lie in this neighborhood. In practice it has been found that an $\epsilon = 8$ points is adequate.

---

[7] "BLACK" is indicated by crosshatching the figure.

Although the new definition is more relaxed, the concept of polygon is still precisely defined.

If the object is indeed a polygon, then a general area computation is evoked using the cross-product rule for vectors. The area of a triangle with one vertex at the origin and the other two vertices at (x_1, y_1), (x_2, y_2) is given by $|\vec{a} \times \vec{b}|/2$ where $\vec{a} = x_1\vec{i} + y_1\vec{j}$ and $\vec{b} = x_2\vec{i} + y_2\vec{j}$. That is to say, $A = |x_1 y_2 - y_1 x_2|/2$. Then for a polygon of any shape and coordinates (x_i, y_i) given in a counterclockwise direction, if we sum the signed areas of the triangles formed by each side of the polygon and the origin, we obtain for the area of the polygon

$$A = \frac{1}{2} \sum_{i=1}^{n} (x_i y_{i+1} - x_{i+1} y_i)$$

where n is the number of sides.[8]

For actual construction of description lists, we use Formula Algol assignment statements. For example,

```
FOR I←1 STEP 1 UNTIL OBNO DO BEGIN
    IF POLYGONP(OB[I]) THEN BEGIN
        THE TYPE OF OB[I] IS POLYGON;
        THE SIZE OF OB[I] IS AREA;
        IF BLK THEN THE COLOR OF OB[I] IS BLACK
            ELSE THE COLOR OF OB[I] IS WHITE;
        IF SIDES=3 THEN THE TYPE OF OB[I] IS ALSO TRIANGLE;
        IF SIDES=4 THEN THE TYPE OF OB[I] IS ALSO QUADRILATERAL;
        IF SIDES=5 THEN THE TYPE OF OB[I] IS ALSO PENTAGON;
        .
        .
        .
        END;
    END;
```

is taken directly from the program, also illustrating the perspicuity of the language. OBNO is the number of objects in the universe of discourse, and POLYGONP is a boolean procedure that determines whether OB[I] is a polygon and, if so, computes the boolean variable BLK, the integer variable SIDES, and the real variable AREA as described above.

3.1.4 *Evaluation.* Once a well-formed picture has been drawn, the corresponding description lists constructed, a well-formed sentence entered, and the corresponding interpretations built up by the semantic component, we are in a position to determine the truth-value of the input with respect to

---

[8] This result is due to Roberts [65, p. 17]. For a short proof using Stokes' Theorem, see T. Evans [24, p. 47].

the picture. As defined by the system, the truth-value of the input sentence can take on one of three values: valid, invalid, or vacuous. The vacuous case is explicitly distinguished to facilitate the resolution of syntactic ambiguity. The evaluation process takes place in three steps: quantifier elimination, predicate evaluation, and truth-value determination.

First, all occurrences of universal and existential quantifiers are eliminated by generating the objects in the universe of discourse. If $\varphi(x)$ is a wff to be evaluated, the repeated application of the productions

$$(\forall x)\varphi(x) \rightarrow \prod_{i=1}^{n} \varphi(OB_i) = \varphi(OB_1) \wedge \varphi(OB_2) \wedge \cdots \wedge \varphi(OB_n)$$

$$(\exists x)\varphi(x) \rightarrow \sum_{i=1}^{n} \varphi(OB_i) = \varphi(OB_1) \vee \varphi(OB_2) \vee \cdots \vee \varphi(OB_n)$$

will eliminate all occurrences of quantifiers where n is the number of objects in the domain. This process must always terminate, since the universe of discourse contains at most a finite number of distinct objects. In Formula Algol each of the productions is implemented in a formula procedure as follows.

For universal quantifiers:

```
FORM PROCEDURE A(X,SCOPE); VALUE X,SCOPE; FORM X,SCOPE;
  BEGIN INTEGER I; FORM TEMP; TEMP←EVAL(X)SCOPE(O.[1]);
    FOR I←2 STEP 1 UNTIL OBNO DO
      TEMP←TEMP ∧ EVAL(X)SCOPE(O.[I]);
    A←TEMP END;
```

For existential quantifiers:

```
FORM PROCEDURE E(X,SCOPE); VALUE X,SCOPE; FORM X,SCOPE;
  BEGIN INTEGER I; FORM TEMP; TEMP←EVAL(X)SCOPE(O.[1]);
    FOR I←2 STEP 1 UNTIL OBNO DO
      TEMP←TEMP ∨ EVAL(X)SCOPE(O.[I]);
    E←TEMP END;
```

As a specific example of the quantifier elimination process, let us take the statement

(4) Each polygon smaller than a black triangle is a square.

The interpretation of (4) is the wff

(5) $(\forall x)\{P(x) \wedge (\exists y)\{B(y) \wedge T(y) \wedge Sm(x, y)\} \supset Sq(x)\}$[9]

---

[9] (5) is the only interpretation of (4), since (4) is unambiguous with respect to the grammar.

Using the description lists on page 251 derived from Figure 2 as our universe of discourse, if we label the pentagon "a," the triangle "b," the upper square "c," and the lower square "d," then the result of quantifier elimination yields

$\{P(a) \land \{B(a) \land T(a) \land Sm(a, a)$
$\qquad \lor B(b) \land T(b) \land Sm(a, b) \lor B(c) \land T(c) \land Sm(a, c)$
$\qquad \lor B(d) \land T(d) \land Sm(a, d)\} \supset Sq(a)\} \land$
$\{P(b) \land \{B(a) \land T(a) \land Sm(b, a)$
$\qquad \lor B(b) \land T(b) \land Sm(b, b) \lor B(c) \land T(c) \land Sm(b, c)$
$\qquad \lor B(d) \land T(d) \land Sm(b, d)\} \supset Sq(b)\} \land$
$\{P(c) \land \{B(a) \land T(a) \land Sm(c, a)$
$\qquad \lor B(b) \land T(b) \land Sm(c, b) \lor B(c) \land T(c) \land Sm(c, c)$
$\qquad \lor B(d) \land T(d) \land Sm(c, d)\} \supset Sq(c)\} \land$
$\{P(d) \land \{B(a) \land T(a) \land Sm(d, a)$
$\qquad \lor B(b) \land T(b) \land Sm(d, b) \lor B(c) \land T(c) \land Sm(d, c)$
$\qquad \lor B(d) \land T(d) \land Sm(d,d)\} \supset Sq(d)\}$

which is the quantifier-free form of (5) in the given domain.

The second evaluation process evaluates each predicate by determining the truth-value of each of the boolean procedures in the quantifier-free form. Such procedures were illustrated on page 247. In the example above we obtain

$\{T \land \{T \land F \land F \lor T \land T \land F \lor F \land F \land F \lor F \land F \land F\} \supset F\} \land$
$\{T \land \{T \land F \land T \lor T \land T \land F \lor F \land F \land F \lor F \land F \land F\} \supset F\} \land$
$\{T \land \{T \land F \land T \lor T \land T \land T \lor F \land F \land F \lor F \land F \land F\} \supset T\} \land$
$\{T \land \{T \land F \land T \lor T \land T \land T \lor F \land F \land T \lor F \land F \land F\} \supset T\}.$

Finally, knowing the rules of combination for each logical connective, the truth-value of the resulting expression is determined.[10] If the expression is false, then the truth-value "invalid," is assigned. If the expression is true, however, then it must be further verified that it is genuinely rather than vacuously true. For example, sentence (4) would be true at this point even if there were no black polygons in the universe of discourse. This follows from the logic of material implication, and corresponds in a sense to the notion that one can legitimately attribute anything at all to something that does not exist. That is, assuming there were no black polygons on the screen (Figure 7), one might assert that all black polygons were squares, pentagons, circles (or whatever), with impunity. To avoid this sort of anomaly, all occurrences of universal quantification, if any, are replaced by existential quantification and the expression is reevaluated. If the expression is still true upon reevaluation, then "valid" rather than "vacuous" is assigned as the final

---

[10] In practice, the second and third steps cannot be distinguished internally.

truth-value. In the case of our example above, we obtain a "true" for both evaluation and reevaluation, and therefore it follows that the input statement is valid for Figure 2.

In terms of operation, the time to process sentence (4) with respect to Figure 2 on the G-21 computer is about eighteen seconds. In general, processing time increases linearly with the complexity of the picture or the length of the input sentence, but exponentially with the number of nested relative phrases. Processing time at execution, however, has proved less of a problem than exhausting available space. This problem is sometimes referred to as "intermediate expression swell" because even though the initial input data may be modest, and the final output a mere yes or no, the storage requirements for intermediate results may be quite large. A Formula Algol garbage collection routine which returns unnecessary intermediate results to a linked list of available space has reduced this problem to manageable proportions.

3.2 Results

To illustrate the ability of GRANIS to translate simple English sentences into the predicate calculus, Table 3 shows seven representative sentence forms among the many possible forms specified by the grammar. In the domain of geometry, Figures 3 through 7 illustrate typical pictures of geometric figures that can be recognized by GRANIS. The system has

Table 3. Logical Translations

Simple English sentence	Logical translation
1. Positive Universal Every polygon is a triangle.	$(\forall x)\{Poly(x) \supset Tri(x)\}$
2. Negative Universal No resistor is ten ohms.	$(\forall x)\{Res(x) \supset \neg Ohms(10, x)\}$
3. Positive Existential Some atom is carbon.	$(\exists x)\{A(x) \wedge C(x)\}$
4. Negative Existential Some square is not black.	$(\exists x)\{Sq(x) \wedge \neg Bl(x)\}$
5. Relative Phrase Each white polygon bigger than a hexagon is a rectangle.	$(\forall x)\{Wt(x) \wedge Poly(x) \wedge (\exists y)$ $\{Hex(y) \wedge Bg(x, y)\} \supset Rec(x)\}$
6. Compound Phrase Every atom is hydrogen, oxygen, or carbon.	$(\forall x)\{A(x) \supset \{H(x) \vee O(x) \vee C(x)\}\}$
7. Compound Relative Phrase Every PNP transistor connected to an output resistor and connected to a bias resistor is part of a flip-flop	$(\forall x)\{PNP(x) \wedge Trn(x) \wedge (\exists y)$ $\{Out(y) \wedge Res(y) \wedge Con(x, y)\} \wedge$ $(\exists z)\{Bi(z) \wedge Res(z) > Con(x, z)\}$ $\supset (Aw)\{FF(w) \wedge Pt(x, w)\}\}$

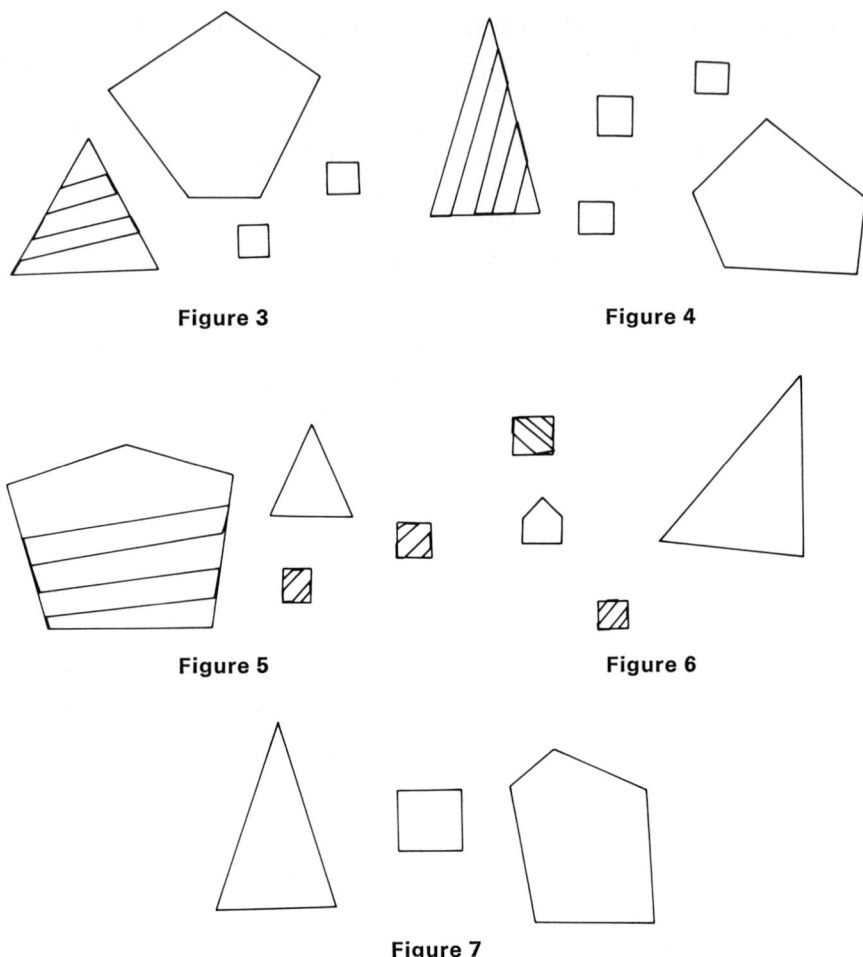

Figure 3

Figure 4

Figure 5

Figure 6

Figure 7

proved sufficiently general in conception to permit a fairly easy conversion from one subject matter to another. To convert from one domain to another, the user need only recompile GRANIS to incorporate the new dictionary and picture recognizer. The dictionary redefines the relevant terms in the referent terminal vocabulary, while the picture scanner permits the recognition of new objects in the new universe of discourse. In the domain of electric circuits, for example, Figures 8 through 12 show typical circuits that can be recognized. In the domain of organic chemistry molecules, Figures 13 through 18 show typical molecules that can be recognized.

To illustrate the power of GRANIS in resolving ambiguity, consider the following three sentences:

(4) Each polygon smaller than a black triangle is a square.

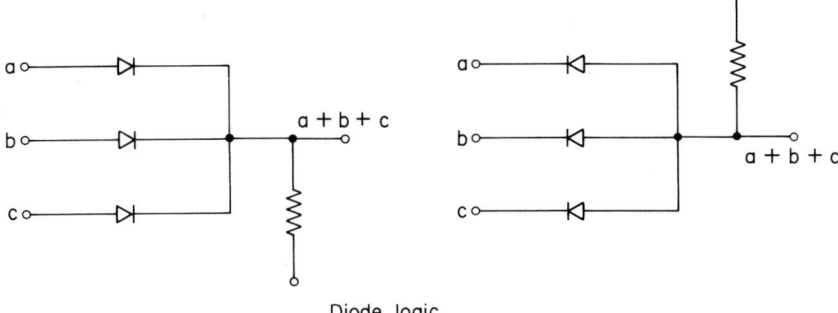

Diode logic

Figure 8

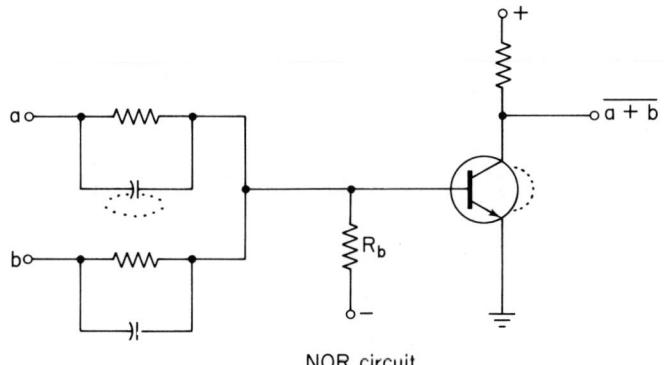

NOR circuit

Figure 9

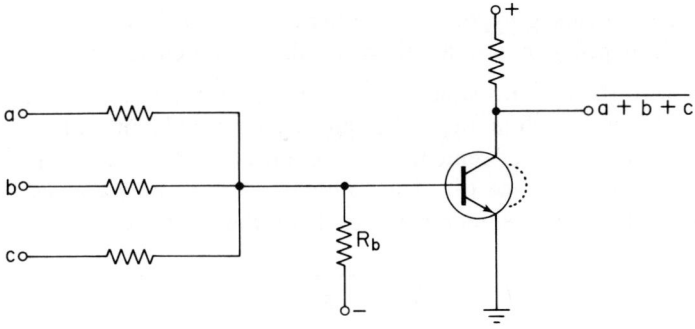

NOR circuit

Figure 10

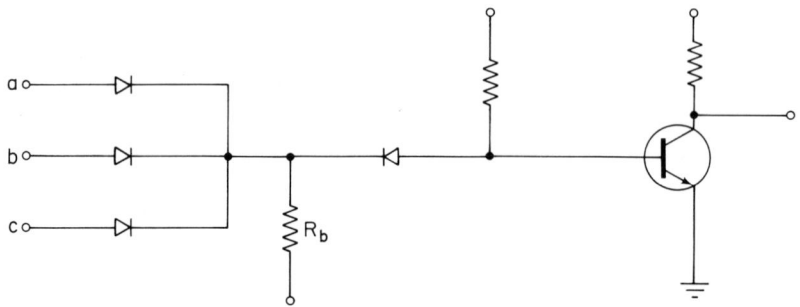

Low level logic

Figure 11

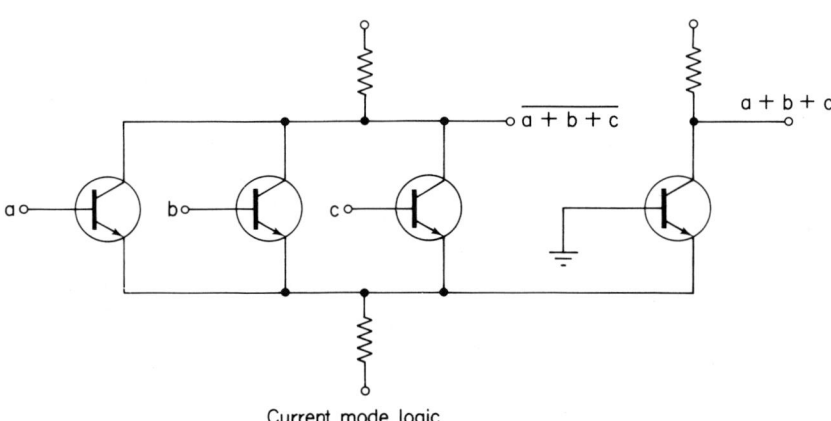

Current mode logic

Figure 12

(6) Each black polygon smaller than a triangle is a square.

(7) Each polygon smaller than a triangle which is black is a square.

together with the nine possible displays in Figure 19. The first two sentences are unambiguous, while the third has two possible interpretations. The natural interpretation of sentence (7) is equivalent to sentence (4); the other is equivalent to sentence (6). The following 3 × 9 matrix gives the truth-value of each of the sentences for each of the nine pictures:

	1	2	3	4	5	6	7	8	9
(4)	Valid	Valid	Valid	Invalid	Invalid	Invalid	Vacuous	Vacuous	Vacuous
(6)	Valid	Invalid	Vacuous	Valid	Invalid	Vacuous	Valid	Invalid	Vacuous
(7)	Valid	Valid	Valid	Invalid	Invalid	Invalid	Valid	Invalid	Vacuous

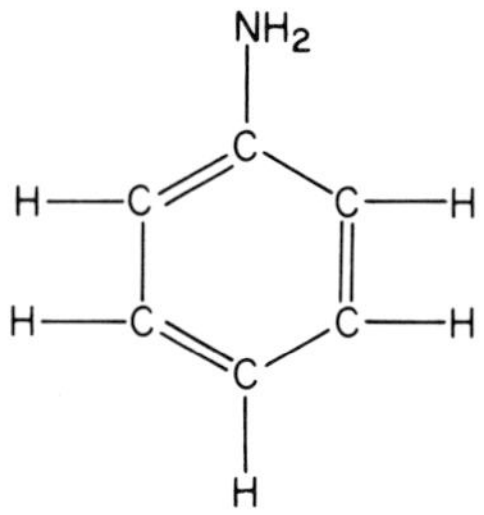

C₆H₅NH₂   Aniline

Figure 13

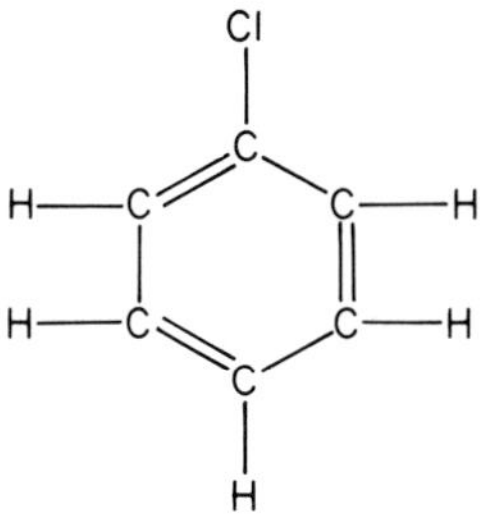

C₆H₅Cl   Chlorobenzene

Figure 14

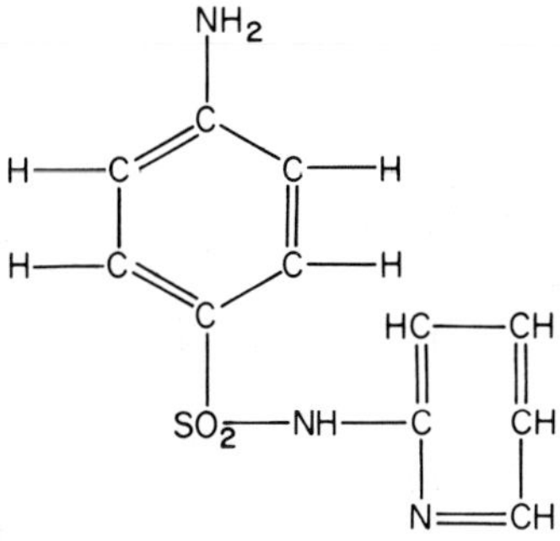

Sulfopyridine

Figure 15

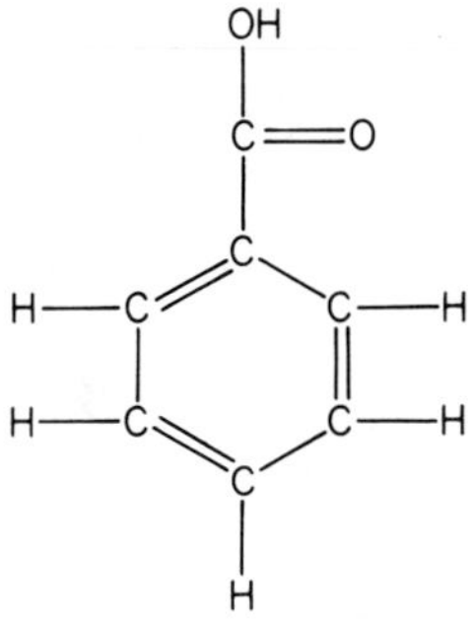

C₆H₅COOH   Benzoic acid

Figure 16

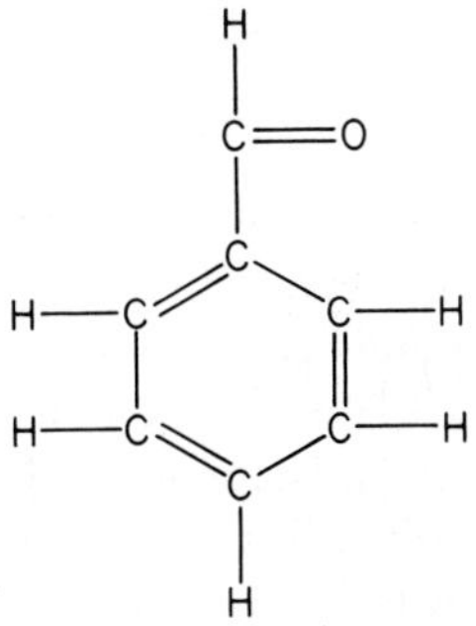

C₆H₅CHO   Benzeldehyde

Figure 17

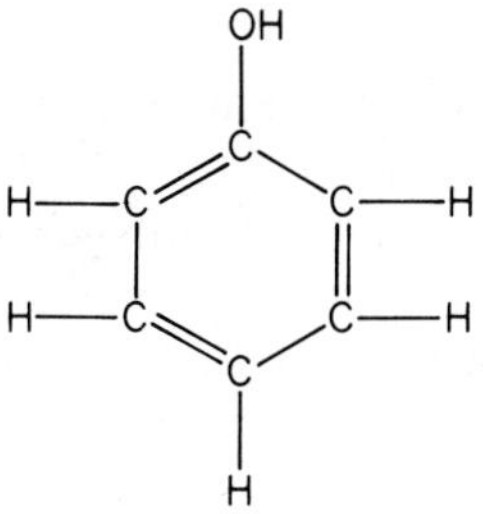

C₆H₅OH   Phenol

Figure 18

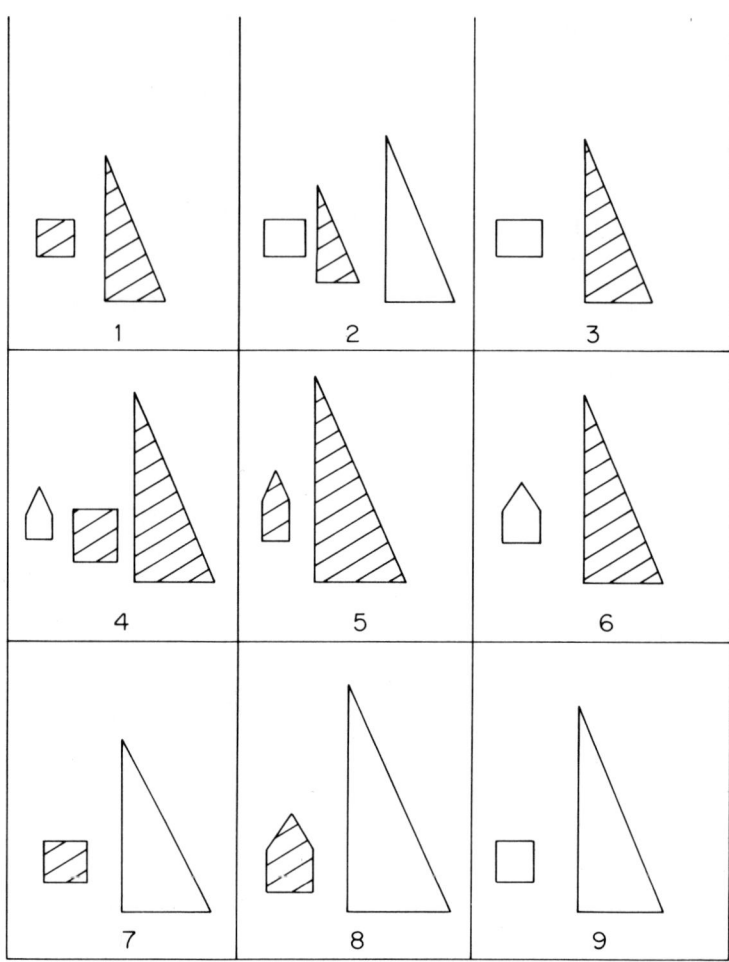

Figure 19

Sentence (4) is vacuous in contexts 7, 8, and 9, since no black triangle occurs in any of these pictures. Similarly, sentence (6) is vacuous in contexts 3, 6, and 9, since no black polygon smaller than a triangle occurs in any of these pictures. In evaluating the truth-value of sentence (7) using the conventions adopted in Section 2.6.3, if the natural interpretation [sentence (4)] is non-vacuous, then the second interpretation [sentence (6)] will not even be evaluated, and the truth-value of sentence (7) is defined to be the same as that of sentence (4). If the natural interpretation is vacuous, however, the second interpretation will be evaluated, and the truth-value of sentence (7) is defined to be the same as that of sentence (6).

SECTION 4
EXTENSIONS

There are a large number of dimensions along which the work described thus far could be expanded. The following four directions will be explored in some detail:

(1) the habitability of the natural language grammar
(2) inferential power
(3) knowledge acquisition
(4) adaptive properties

4.1 Habitability

An extremely difficult problem for question answering systems is the stability of restricted subsets of natural language. As Oettinger [53] pointed out, attempts to define easily manageable fragments of natural language generally fail because the subsets become unstable and drift either in the direction of a formal mathematical notation or in the opposite direction toward a full use of an unrestricted vernacular. In the former case the advantages of natural language are lost, and successful use of the system requires considerable prior indoctrination. In the latter case, the enigmatic problems of unrestricted natural language constantly require extensions to the grammar.

The difficulties of GRANIS—the computer model actually programmed—tend to fall in the latter category. To be sure, several factors tend to constrain the user from casual discourse:

(1) He is seated in front of a computer display console;
(2) He must enter input on a typewriter keyboard;
(3) He is warned in advance that the system comprehends very little English;
(4) He is there to discuss a particular class of pictures;
(5) His referent vocabulary is generally limited to descriptions of objects currently displayed.

Nevertheless, there is an inadvertent tendency to compose phrases that are not acceptable to the grammar as defined by GRANIS. Although error recovery from these situations is adequate, the error messages generally indicate a global difficulty, leaving the user without specific information on how to change his input sentence so that it will be acceptable. This often results in a trial and error interaction that has little of the desirable qualities of genuine conversation.

How might one investigate the stability of a microgrammar for a fragment of natural language? In working on a related problem Watt [83] defined a concept which he called *habitability*. The habitability of a given micro-grammar, according to Watt, is the ability of the grammar to accept elementary lexical and syntactic extrapolations of phrases that are already acceptable to the grammar. To illustrate this definition let us assume that

(1) Is a capacitor here?

is acceptable to the system. Then an elementary syntactic extrapolation might be

(2) Is there a capacitor here?

That is to say, (2) is a strict paraphrase of (1) under identical contextual conditions. Some non-elementary syntactic extrapolations might be

(3) Are there any capacitors here?

(4) Do there happen to be any capacitors here?

(5) Can you find any capacitors here?

(6) Do you see anything in the way of a capacitor here?

Each of the sentences (1) through (6) form an equivalence class which Watt refers to as a *paraphrastic set*. An elementary lexical extrapolation might be

(7) Is a resistor here?

or

(8) Is a diode here?

Non-elementary lexical extrapolations might be

(9) Is a molecule here?

(10) Is a rectangle here?

(11) Is a computer here?

Watt avoids the problem of providing an operational definition of the term "elementary" in the kinds of extrapolations with which he is concerned. Although one might set some arbitrary limits for syntactic extrapolations, saying that elementary syntactic extrapolations are those which require at most the application of two transformations from a given grammar, this sort of distinction is ad hoc and may still violate our intuitive notion of what it means for a micro-grammar to be syntactically habitable. Even though the universe of discourse may be exhibited in the form of a display, a similar criticism may be levied at any attempt to define operationally an elementary lexical extrapolation. In spite of these difficulties in defining an absolute notion of habitability, one can easily compare the relative habitability of two grammars. Thus, the notion of habitability should be useful in approaching the problem of stability in a grammar as it expands or contracts through use.

We have observed that the grammar in our computer model is unstable in the direction of an ever increasing number of productions due to constraints on the flexibility of the input language and a desire to exceed the restrictions on the universe of discourse. Moreover, no absolute boundary can be foreseen beyond which expansion is not required for augmenting the system's usefulness. Indeed, English itself has no absolute boundaries, and is constantly undergoing expansion, albeit at a slow rate. One of the important properties of natural language is the ability to coin a new phrase or term as it becomes useful to do so. Thus, one concludes that the system must incorporate within itself provision for expansion of the grammar, if it is ever to satisfy the requirement of habitability.

How might such expansion take place? Yershov [89] has suggested that

> the system, distinguishing those text fragments which are unclear to it, assign to the user a series of questions on the distinguished fragments. The form and character of the questions is [are] defined by the fragments and the manner in which they are embedded in the overall text. The user's replies to these questions may be regarded as paraphrases of the unclear fragments. The system substitutes them into the initial text and analyzes it again. If necessary, the system again assigns questions to the user, and in this way establishes a dialog between the man and the machine. By means of this dialog the user continually simplifies the formulation of his input statements until they are completely understood by the system.

Once the system and the user have converged on a mutually acceptable paraphrase for a new phrase, this paraphrase will be incorporated into the transformational component of the grammar, and an obligatory transformation will be automatically evoked whenever the new phrase is encountered in all similar future contexts.

And how might one implement such a proposal within the framework of GRANIS? Such a dialog would require in essence changing the binding time of certain system parameters from compile-time to run-time. The productions themselves would have to be treated as formula input data rather than compiled statically into the program. Then for production data structures we would need appropriate primitive operators such as

(1) constructors for new productions,
(2) alteration and deletion operators for existing productions,
(3) extractors for parts of productions,
(4) predicates for determining if a production is an instance of some production schema.

It is not clear how one might drive such primitive operators with commands given in English. The construction of obligatory paraphrastic transformational productions, however, involves only the substitution of terminals for terminals, which can be done before the parsing process begins. If the phrase α in the context ψ_1, ψ_2 is not recognized by the system, then an error recovery procedure initiates a dialog to determine ultimately a paraphrase β, such that $\psi_1 \beta \psi_2$ can be recognized. If the user approves of the paraphrase, then the system constructs a syntactic production of the form

$$\psi_1 \alpha \psi_2 \to \psi_1 \beta \psi_2$$

and places it at the top of the sequence of productions to be executed (if appropriate) before any others. If $\varphi_1 \alpha \varphi_2 \to \varphi_1 \beta \varphi_2$ already exists, then the two productions should be consolidated as $\chi_1 \alpha \chi_2 \to \chi_1 \beta \chi_2$ where $\chi_1 = \varphi_1 \cup \psi_1$ and $\chi_2 = \varphi_2 \cup \psi_2$. If the paraphrase β can be thought of as a definition for α, then of course the production $\alpha \to \beta$ should be constructed, making the transformation context free.

On the other hand, one must pay a price for this systematic escalation of variability in the grammar. The price of generality is inefficiency. If the productions are no longer compiled into the program, they must be executed interpretively, and the parsing and interpretation of input sentences will take longer as a function of the administrative overhead in passing parameters during procedure calls. Each production corresponds to a procedure call and already 90% of the total interpretation time is spent in production processing. (The remainder is taken up mostly in I/O operations with the displays.) Perhaps a compromise can be achieved whereby the base component of the grammar is compiled and the transformational component is executed interpretively. More empirical evidence must be obtained, however, before the proper trade-off between a compiled and an interpretive grammar can be decided upon.

Another interesting problem in regard to the habitability of GRANIS is how to handle the increasing complexity of sentence forms without continually expanding the base component. As suggested on page 225, the basic approach to this problem is to require that the transformational component map the more complex sentences into simpler kernel sentences which are acceptable to the base component. The next question which arises concerns the proper trade-off between the base component and the transformational component.

One extreme position suggested by Simmons [73] is that the base component be restricted to kernel sentences of the form "subject-verb-nominal." For example, given the input sentences

(12) Jack and Jill went up the hill to fetch a pail of water.
(13) The quick brown fox jumped over the lazy dog.

the kernel sentences for (12) would be

(1) Jack went up the hill.
(2) Jill went up the hill.
(3) Jack fetched a pail.
(4) Jill fetched a pail.
(5) Pail (is of) water.

and for (13) would be

(1) The fox is quick.
(2) The fox is brown.
(3) The fox jumped.
(4) The jumping was over.
(5) The dog is lazy.

The difficulty with this approach is that it places too much of the burden of syntactic analysis on the transformational component of the grammar with the undesirable consequence of further isolating syntax from semantics. Moreover, additional ambiguity is introduced in the process of derivation, and therefore reference terms must be added to the kernel sentences to permit one to reconstruct the original input sentence.

In GRANIS, kernel sentences are derived only when the sentence consists of genuinely independent clauses delimited by a conjunction or other punctuation. In such a case, the scope of quantification will not extend across clause boundaries, thereby introducing ambiguity when kernels are derived. Thus, both sentences (12) and (13) are already considered to be kernel sentences, and would be translated directly into the following wff:[11]

(14) $(\exists x_1)\{Jack(x_1) \land (\exists x_2)\{Jill(x_2) \land (\exists x_3)\{Hill(x_3) \land Go(x_1 \land x_2, x_3)\} < (\exists x_4)\{Pail(x_4) \land Fetch(x_1 \land x_2, x_4)\} \land (\exists x_5)\{Water(x_5) \land Of(x_4, x_5)\}\}\}$

(15) $(\exists x_1)\{Quick(x_1) \land Brown(x_1) \land Fox(x_1) \land (\exists x_2)\{Lazy(x_2) \land Dog(x_2) > (\exists x_3)\{Jump(x_1, x_2, x_3) \land Over(x_3)\}\}\}$.

4.2 Inferential Power

Another important avenue for further exploration is the inferential power of GRANIS. There are several aspects to expanding inferential power. First we will discuss some extensions to the predicate calculus notation in order to facilitate operations with factored predicates and additional quantifiers. Second, an extension to enhance the ambiguity-resolving power of GRANIS will be described. Finally, the problems of handling large blocks of input text will be explored briefly.

[11] Parameters which are themselves boolean expressions appear in (14) and (15). We will discuss such parameters in the next section.

4.2.1 Extending the Predicate Calculus.
A major source of abbreviation in natural language derives from the factorization of common predicates governing compound arguments. For example, we say

(16) Draw a rectangle and a triangle.

rather than

(17) Draw a rectangle and draw a triangle.

Now from the point of view of the predicate calculus, the compound object "a rectangle and a triangle" in (16) may be viewed as the result of factoring out the repeated predicate "draw" in (17). Just as the logical translation of (17) is $D(r) \wedge D(t)$, we can imagine a logical notation as suggested by Bohnert [9, p. 16] which permits the representation of sentence (16) as $D(r \wedge t)$. That is, we can construct a "factoring law" which establishes the equivalence

(18) $D(r \wedge t) \equiv D(r) \wedge D(t)$.

Compound subjects or indirect objects, which also occur in English, can be handled in a similar manner. For example, if the immediate logical interpretation of

(19) a goes from b or c to d or e.

is $G(a, (b \vee c), (d \vee e))$ where "G" stands for "goes," then successive distributions would yield the underlying logical translation

(20) $G(a, b, d) \vee G(a, b, e) \vee G(a, c, d) \vee G(a, c, e)$.

To construct a logical notation of this sort in which factoring and distribution would be possible, we must augment the definition of well-formed formula (wff) so as to make compound individual expressions acceptable arguments for predicates. Thus, for example, $P(a \wedge (b \vee c) \wedge d, \neg e \vee f)$ would be a 2-place augmented well-formed formula (awff). In the actual processing of such predicates it may be more desirable to handle them directly rather than expanding them prior to processing.

Another extension of the predicate calculus notation might be to incorporate new quantifier types such as iota quantifiers which correspond to the English definite article "the," or imperative and interrogative quantifiers which correspond to imperative and interrogative statements respectively. In English, when we say "the object" with a certain property, we mean that there exists *one* and *only one* object having that property. Thus, it would be incorrect to say "the black square in Figure 6 is above the pentagon," since there are two black squares. Russell introduced the notation $(\iota x)F(x)$ to mean "the particular thing x having the property F" (cf. Reichenbach [64, p. 258]). The operator in this expression, an inverted Greek "ι," is called the iota operator while x is a bound variable. Imperative and interrogative operators can be introduced in an obvious way. For example, the sentences

(21) Draw a triangle.

(22) Is there a triangle?

might be translated as

(23) (!x){Draw(x) ∧ Triangle(x)}

(24) (?x){Triangle(x)}

What are the rules of inference for these proposed quantifiers? We can write a general definition for the iota quantifier as

(25) $(\iota x)F(x) =_{def} (\exists x)\{F(x) \land (\forall y)\{F(y) \supset (y = x)\}\}$,

although this is probably not the way it should be implemented. The imperative and interrogative quantifiers are not as simple. For elementary imperative statements, i.e., those where the command corresponds to a primitive operation already programmed as a Formula Algol procedure, the procedure should be executed and the expression evaluated after replacing the imperative operator with an existential operator. If the evaluation is true, then the procedure was executed correctly. Otherwise, clarification from the user is necessary. On the other hand, if the operation is not primitive, then some additional inferences must be made by first mapping the imperative statement into its corresponding declarative form, and then decomposing this declarative statement into more elementary kernels each of which can then be mapped back into its corresponding imperative form (cf. Simon [74]).

For interrogative quantifiers, if the question is a simple "yes-no" question, then it can be answered by merely evaluating the truth-value of the expression obtained by replacing the interrogative quantifier with an existential quantifier. Otherwise, the situation is much more complex, and the issue of entailment arises. Most questions make only implicit reference to the class of possible answers which are permissible, and it is a difficult task merely to determine what assumptions are made about the class of legal replies (cf. Belnap [4]).

4.2.2 **Ambiguity Resolution.** At the end of Section 2 we proposed a strategy for resolving syntactic ambiguity that required ordering all logically possible interpretations in a natural way, evaluating the most natural one first, and evaluating the next most likely only in the event this first interpretation was vacuous with respect to the universe of discourse. In GRANIS, this was one of the important ways that feedback of semantic information occurred in the syntactic analysis of input sentences. If we assume that the interpretation can be ordered in a natural way, are there any other reasons for entertaining a second interpretation, aside from the case where the natural interpretation is vacuous? A more useful and general criterion might be that the natural interpretation was not "meaningful" in some fashion, where vacuousness is merely a special case. Without attempting an exhaustive investigation of the concept of "meaning," some brief consideration of the relevant issues should be given.

Both Katz [34] and Chomsky [11] have developed a taxonomy of anomalous sentences. Some of the categories are clearly syntactic, some clearly semantic, and others not easily identifiable along a syntax-semantics continuum. Chomsky specifies two kinds of rules in his syntax to avoid deviant sentences: subcategorization rules and selectional rules.

1. The subcategorization rules prevent improper verb categories as a function of the immediate structure of the phrase marker around the verb. A violation of this type of rule, for example, might result in an intransitive verb being placed in a sentence with a direct object, or a pre-adjectival verb being placed in an intransitive sentence (e.g., "John runs a book" or "John seems quickly").

2. The selectional rules establish agreement requirements among such parts of speech as

   (i) adjectives and the nouns they modify,
   (ii) subjects and their verbs, and
   (iii) verbs and their objects.

These rules would prevent such utterances as "ten ohm capacitors" and "sour bottle" (referred to in the introduction to this chapter), "drink concrete" (referred to in Section 2.3), or such innocent questions as

   (26) What is the temperature of an atom?

It is not clear whether these rules belong in syntax, semantics, or both, but in the realm of syntax, Chomsky [11, p. 83] defines a set of binary selectional features which define subclasses of nouns that demand certain patterns of agreement in corresponding verbs and adjectives. These features are ±common, ±count, ±abstract, ±animate, +human, and are heirarchically organized as follows:

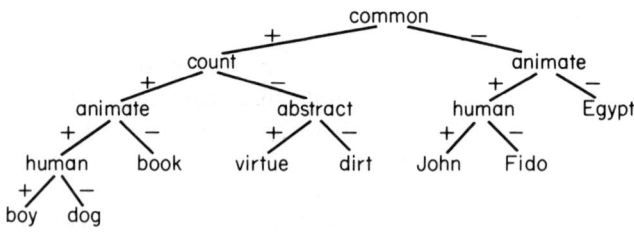

Thus

   (27) The rock admires the scientist.

would be ruled out on syntactic grounds by Chomsky, since "admires" demands a human subject whereas "rock" is inanimate. On the other hand, there is a close correlation between selectional rule violations and contradictions, and a contradiction is certainly a semantic concept. A selectional rule violation is not properly a contradiction in itself, since by definition a contradiction is a statement that is false under all interpretations for any universe of discourse, while a selectional rule violation cannot even be properly said to have a truth-value. However, most selectional rule violations do entail a contradiction. For example,

(28) The married spinster is beautiful.

which is a selectional rule violation, entails the derived assertion

(29) There exists a spinster who is married.

which is a contradiction. Chomsky goes on to discuss whether selectional rules might be more appropriately included in the semantic component [11, pp. 153–160], and Katz accomplishes much the same effect with what he calls "semantic markers" in the semantic component. Katz [34, p. 26] then proceeds to define some clearly semantic categories such as the distinction between contradictory, synthetic, and analytic (tautologous) statements. For example,

(30) Each rectangle is a triangle.

(31) Each rectangle is a square.

(32) Each rectangle is a quadrilateral.

are contradictory, synthetic, and analytic respectively. Later, he even makes a further distinction between statements that are analytic versus statements that are "blatantly true," and correspondingly, statements that are contradictory versus statements that are "blatantly false." For example, an analytic statement might be

(33) My father was a man.

whereas a blatantly true statement might be

(34) Rattlesnakes are poisonous.

If we assume that the user of GRANIS tends to make statements that are not only non-vacuous, but also non-contradictory and non-analytic, and furthermore do not violate selectional rules (hence entailing contradictions)— i.e., if we assume he desires to explore synthetic relations among objects that really exist in the universe of discourse—then we have additional criteria for resolving ambiguity. How might GRANIS be extended to take advantage of these new criteria?

What is called for is more hierarchical structuring in the universe of discourse. At present the description lists are all on one level, i.e., a uniform set of description lists of tokens of objects that appear on the screen of the display. The ability to detect contradictions (as distinct from merely false synthetic statements) or to detect analytic statements (as distinct from merely true statements) or to incorporate selectional features may be easily achieved through description lists of "types" as well as "tokens." To introduce description lists for types, each lexical item would have an associated description list. In particular, for selectional rules each list would contain the selectional features as attributes with the plus or minus as value. In the general case, more complex features would be needed, but these are easily included since Formula Algol provides for a list of values associated with each attribute as an integral part of the language. For example, a part of the description list corresponding to the dictionary entry "triangle" might be

TRIANGLE←/[SHAPE: EQUILATERAL,ISOSCELES,SCALENE, EQUIANGULAR,ACUTE,RIGHT,OBTUSE] ;

indicating seven possible shapes of triangles. Now an interpretation that gave rise to the selectional rule violation "circular triangle," as in the ambiguous sentence

(35) Point to every object next to the triangle which is circular.

would be immediately rejected as anomalous, even though it was the natural interpretation in the sense described earlier; "circular" also was determined to be a conceptually possible value for the attribute shape. The selectional rule violation in this case can be determined easily from the description list of triangle by generating the value list of possible shapes and noting that "circular" is not one of them. The second interpretation of "circular object" would then be evaluated. This process is considerably more efficient than the current mode of operation, which would exhaustively generate the universe of discourse, testing each triangle on the screen for possible "circularity" before concluding that the interpretation was vacuous in the current universe of discourse, and only then going on to look for additional interpretations, if any.

What is proposed, then, is that first a set of global description lists of "types" be added to GRANIS, independent of any local description lists of "tokens" derived from the pictorial universe of discourse on the screen. These global lists should provide information on the intrinsic properties of each type, as well as on the range of possible values over each contingent property. Second, our strategy for resolving syntactic ambiguity should then be refined to use the global lists first to determine whether an interpretation is anomalous (not synthetic), and if it is not, to go on to determine (using the local lists) whether it is vacuous, and proceeding as before. Otherwise, we reject this interpretation out of hand and go on to the next, if any.

To speculate on the distinction between truth-value and meaning in terms of this extension, one may say that the truth-value of a sentence lies in the local lists, while the meaning of a sentence resides in the global lists. These global lists are highly structured, since most values of attributes are themselves types with pointers to other description lists in the set. To recast this list structure in a slightly different perspective, if one were to represent each type as a node in a directed graph where the edges of the graph correspond to the pointers, one begins to approach the kind of model of semantic memory organization described by Quillian [61]. (To carry the analogy still further, the graph may even be said to have "colored" edges to facilitate the construction of legal transitive inferences.) The main distinction from Quillian's work, however, is that this underlying semantic structure would be closely supervised by the syntactic component.

Another interesting possibility for extending the ambiguity-resolving power of GRANIS is to incorporate the basic heuristic of means-ends analysis. This technique has proved successful over a wide class of problem domains in the General Problem Solver (GPS) designed by Newell, Shaw, and Simon (cf. [52]). The "given" is the ambiguous input sentence; the "goal" is a meaningful (synthetic, non-vacuous) interpretation within the universe of discourse; and the "relevant operators" for reducing differences are the productions (syntactic and semantic) applicable to the input sentence. Considerable reprogramming would be needed, however, before GPS techniques could be applied to advantage in the current version of GRANIS.

4.2.3 Multiple Sentences.

Two major limitations on the present version of GRANIS are; (i) it accepts sentences that concern only the current display, thus making it impossible to refer to several different pictures in one statement; and more important, (ii) all record of prior conversation with the system is destroyed once an input statement has been processed correctly. Of course, no great sophistication in language processing can be achieved by analysis of single sentences. To extend the system along this dimension, as a first approximation, a sequence of sentences could be analyzed by taking the logical conjunction of their interpretations, but this solution overlooks some obvious difficulties. Chief among them is the discovery of antecedents of pronominal expressions that cross sentence boundaries. Such expressions have been called "anaphoric" expressions by Olney [55]. Generally, third-person pronouns and possessive adjectives, such as "he" and "his," are anaphoric expressions, as are many other kinds of pronouns. However, in English scientific and technical writing, the most prevalent type of anaphoric expression is exemplified by the following sentences

> (36) Several experiments with college students were performed. The results were encouraging.

"The results" is anaphoric; it stands for an expression that does not actually occur in the text but can be constructed from one that does, namely, "several experiments with college students." Anaphoric expressions play a crucial role in promoting information transfer across sentence boundaries and between parts of complex sentences. In particular, they serve to abbreviate preceding passages, enabling writers and speakers to add to what they have just said without repeating all of it. In English scientific and technical articles about 90 per cent of the sentences contain at least one anaphoric expression [55].

Thus, it becomes clear that a conversation cannot be understood on the basis of an independent analysis of constituent sentences. Indeed, the expressive power of natural language is achieved largely through the abbreviation of complex expressions by means of pronouns. English permits such abbreviation without loss of information by capitalizing on the inferential capability of the listener to resolve ambiguity arising from potentially multiple antecedents associated with anaphoric expressions. The greater the inferential capacity of the listener, the greater parsimony achievable by the speaker without fear of being misunderstood.

Finding the correct antecedents for anaphoric expressions such as "The results" in (36) requires more sophisticated machinery than generating all possible antecedents in the universe of discourse mechanically to determine whether the truth-value of any particular substitution instance is true while others are false. The combinatorial explosion of possible substitutions becomes prohibitive even for small numbers of objects. Clearly, some heuristics are required both to (i) restrict the potential number of antecedents and (ii) order those remaining. For example, heuristics concerning case, gender, and number are obviously important to restrict the potential number of antecedents, whereas an ordering heuristic might be "give first consideration to nearest potential antecedents."

With the introduction of multiple sentence analysis, more general kinds of inference-making such as syllogisms, class inclusion, and transitivity can be considered. For example, given (i) a triangle, a square, and a pentagon, (ii) the knowledge that the relation "to the left of" is transitive, and (iii) the sentences

(37) The triangle is to the left of the square.

(38) The square is to the left of the pentagon.

(39) The triangle is to the left of the pentagon.

then the third sentence is redundant, since it is implied by the first two. Such an inference is not possible in the current version of GRANIS. Based on Figure 7, GRANIS currently would evaluate the truth-value of each of the three sentences independently. In a sense the display serves as a direct model which can be used to test the consistency of all statements made about it. This observation, however, is not especially interesting by itself, since the model is fixed beforehand by the user who draws the display. If, on the other hand, the system could accept imperative statements and modify the display during questioning by the user, it would have much greater inferential capability. Such a capability would entail the construction of a large number of primitive constraint operations for arbitrary displays and would require considerable programming.

4.3 Knowledge Acquisition

In examining the natural language text that accompanied the various pictures of electrical circuits (Figures 8–12) and chemical molecules (Figures 13–18) as possible inputs to GRANIS, it was discovered that invariably the text was inappropriate, not merely because the constructions were too complicated for the grammar, but more basically because the text supplemented the picture by describing that part of the subject matter which was not easily representable in two dimensions rather than by discussing relations of the various subparts of the picture. To illustrate, consider the following two passages, the first from a transistor manual [44, pp. 134–135] which accompanied Figures 8 through 12, and the second from a college chemistry text [27, pp. 504–505] which accompanied Figures 13 through 18.

In the first basic NOR circuit logic is performed by resistors. Any positive input produces an inverted output irrespective of the other inputs. The bias resistor gives temperature stability. The circuit design is straightforward. All logical operations can be performed with only this circuit. Many transistors readily meet the steady state requirements. The second NOR circuit is similar to the first except that capacitors are used to enhance switching speed. The capacitors increase the base current for fast collector current turn-on and minimize storage time by supplying a charge equal to the stored base charge. Thus, it is faster than the first NOR circuit at the expense of additional components and stringent stored charge requirements.

Phenol, benzaldehyde, benzoic acid, and aniline are important industrial derivatives of the benzene series of hydrocarbons. Phenol, commonly called carbolic acid, is a product of the distillation of coal tar. It is a colorless crystalline solid that slowly turns brown when it is exposed to the air. The compound is extremely poisonous. In dilute solution, it is used as a powerful antiseptic. Industrially it is used in the manufacture of explosives, synthetic resins such as bakelite, drugs, and dyes. At the present time, the demand for phenol is so great that synthetic methods of preparation account for better than 75 per cent of the phenol that is used.

Benzaldehyde, another coal-tar product, is used as the raw material for the preparation of many compounds used in industry. It is a liquid that boils at 180°C. It is sold as a perfume and as flavoring material under the name of oil of bitter almonds. Before the development of the coal-tar industry, the compound was obtained from bitter almonds.

Benzoic acid is a white crystalline solid that melts at 122°C. Most of the benzoic acid used in industry is prepared by synthetic methods. Aniline is a colorless liquid that boils at 184°C and also turns brown on continued exposure to the air. Most of the aniline used in industry is prepared from substances that are found in coal tar. Aniline is the starting material for aniline dyes, sometimes called coal-tar dyes. They are made in almost every conceivable shade of color.

As can be seen from the above passages, before GRANIS can be truly useful as a question-answering or information retrieval system, some provision must made for acquiring knowledge about the universe of discourse other than by inspection of pictures. The main implication of this observation is that natural language text in the form of assertions about the universe of discourse must be used to guide either the construction of new description lists or the modification of existing description lists of objects displayed on the screen.

One method of performing this operation without disturbing either the natural language grammar or the expressions in the quantificational calculus output by the semantic productions is to generalize our conception of the evaluation process to include the construction and modification of description lists as well as computations to determine truth-values. That is to say, if the declarative input sentence is an assertion about the universe of discourse rather than a statement to be evaluated with respect to the universe of discourse, then the predicates in the logical expressions should not be construed as boolean procedures, but rather as constructive procedures. In fact, it would be advisable to avoid any a priori assumption that an input statement is an assertion rather than an expression to be evaluated.[12] Thus, each expression should first be evaluated in the conventional manner. To see precisely what this means, let us assume that the input is not anomalous. Then if upon evaluation it is true, the input is *redundant* with respect to the universe of discourse, and processing should terminate. If it is false, then it is *contradictory* with respect to the universe of discourse, and the user should be informed of an inconsistency. Finally, if under all interpretations it is still vacuous, then it can be construed as an *assertion* about the universe of discourse, and this should signal the construction of description lists. This construction, as pointed out by Simon [75] in his work with the Heuristic Compiler, takes place in two stages. First, there is a *selection* stage which locates the place in memory where the new information is to be annexed. Second, there is an *annexing* stage which adds the new descriptive information to the memory structure. The virtue of this entire approach is that it prevents inconsistencies from arising in the data base, even though it may be used by many different people.

---

[12] This is not always clear even in human conversation, and sometimes gives rise to the "Are you asking me or telling me?" phenomenon.

To see how this process might operate in practice, consider the third sentence in the passage on transistor logic.

(40) The bias resistor gives temperature stability.

The logical translation of (40) might be

(41) $(\iota x)\{Bias(x) \land Resistor(x) \land (\exists y)\{Temperaturestability(y) \land Gives(x, y)\}\}$.

Upon evaluation with respect to Figure 1, (41) could then be determined to be a meaningful, synthetic, vacuous interpretation (there don't exist any objects on the screen which are temperatures!). Since (40) is unambiguous, the next step of constructive evaluation is evoked, and by selecting and annexing the fifth description list of the set shown on page 248 would be augmented to

```
OB[5]→/[TYPE: RESISTOR,BIAS][OHMS: 10][LINK: 4,3]
        [GIVES: TEMPERATURESTABILITY];
```

In this manner, the universe of discourse could be systematically expanded to contain information not easily represented in two dimensions.

Description lists might also be used to identify the input assertion for future reference. Williams [87] has suggested that the *documentation* of an input sentence include

⟨Sentence No.⟩←/[STATEMENT:⟨input string⟩][SPEAKER:⟨name⟩]
        [PLACE:⟨console no.⟩][TIME:⟨date⟩,⟨hour⟩,⟨minute⟩]
        [AMBIGUITY:⟨no. of parsings⟩][UNIVERSE OF
        DISCOURSE:⟨display class⟩,⟨display no.⟩];

In this manner, cross-referencing between sentences becomes possible.

4.4 Adaptive Properties

What about the ability of the system to learn from its experience? In Section 4.1 (on habitability), we saw how a limited kind of language learning might take place by means of paraphrastic transformational productions. No mention, however, was made of concept learning or modifying the semantic structure of the model by means of English sentences. This involves much more than the deductive kinds of inference making discussed in Section 4.2. It involves "inductive" rather than "deductive" inference, and such problems of hypothesis formation lie far beyond the scope of the current system. For example, a typical inductive task might be to infer the concept of "square" from several instances of squares displayed on the screen, assuming that the concepts of polygonal figure, side, parallel, and equal in length were either primitive or already inferred from more primitive concepts. The work of T. Evans [24] with geometric analogy problems demonstrates some of the problems and progress in this connection.

A more ambitious goal is to attempt to anticipate what the user will say next by extrapolation of previous conversation together with a knowledge of the subject matter and the properties of the display. A continuous check can then be established between the system's hypothesis of what was expected and what was actually said by the user. In this fashion a measure of the credibility of the conversation is obtained which can be used by GRANIS as a basis for requesting clarification from the user on points of serious disparity.

In an interactive conversation where the user and the system are jointly forming hypotheses and making comparisons, a restriction to the present tense rapidly becomes impractical. The ability to use future and past tenses is therefore imperative. The semantics for various natural language tense constructions is highly complex, and complete analysis of English tense shows the logical existence of tenses that are not even distinguished by special names in English grammar. For a full analysis of tense it is obviously necessary to distinguish between the time of the event (t_e) and the time of speaking or writing (t_s); but as Reichenbach [64, pp. 287–298] has shown, it is also necessary to recognize a third time, the time of reference (t_r). By positioning these times along a temporal continuum we can characterize standard English tenses as in Table 4. It will be noted that more than one tense pattern is possible for future tenses, giving us nine fundamental patterns in all. The terms "past," "present," and "future" are distinguished by the position of t_r relative to t_s. The terms "simple" and "perfect" are distinguished by the position of t_r relative to t_e. Reichenbach distinguishes additional tenses called posterior past and posterior future for which traditional names are non-existent. The posterior past occurs when t_r precedes both t_e and t_s. The posterior future occurs when $t_s < t_r < t_e$. These tenses, for which

Table 4. Structure of English Tenses

Traditional tense name			Tense pattern	Example
1. Past	(a)	Simple	$t_e = t_r < t_s$	went
	(b)	Perfect	$t_e < t_r < t_s$	had gone
2. Present	(a)	Simple	$t_e = t_r = t_s$	goes (go)
	(b)	Perfect	$t_e < t_r = t_s$	has (have) gone
3. Future	(a)	Simple	$t_s < t_e = t_r$	will go
			$t_r = t_s < t_e$	
	(b)	Perfect	$t_s < t_e < t_r$	will have gone
			$t_s = t_e < t_r$	
			$t_e < t_s < t_r$	

our language has no established forms, are expressed by transcriptions. We say, for instance,

(42) I shall be going to see him.

and thus express the posterior future by speaking, not directly of the event at t_e, but of the act of preparation for it. In this fashion we can at least express the time order of events which closely succeed the point of reference.

Once the tense pattern of the sentence has been established, it may be added to the documentation of the sentence. The sentence may then be transformed into a canonical form which deletes all auxiliary verbs and replaces all non-auxiliary verbs with their infinitive form for later parsing. In this fashion no actual tense information is lost, while the kernel grammar may still be restricted to the present tense.

Aside from the four dimensions we have examined thus far, several other avenues along which GRANIS might be expanded present themselves. For the sake of completeness some of these will be mentioned.

1. A demonstration that the linguistic theory proposed applies to natural languages other than English.

2. An exploration of voice input together with the accompanying pattern recognition problems. Such an extension would require the inclusion of a phonological component in our linguistic description.

3. The development of a theory of deviation from well-formedness for each of the components in our linguistic description. Such a theory would explain why some deviations are understood by most listeners while others are not. In the syntactic component we would have to explain why a child who says "gooder" is really understood to mean "better"; in the semantic component why some sentences appear to be anomalous (but in reality are meaningful), and ultimately, why some metaphors are considered poetic while others are merely nonsensical; in the pragmatic component we would be required to investigate the attitudes and beliefs of the speaker together with his memory and perceptual limitations. See Weinreich [86, p. 466] for an approach to a quantitative measure of deviance or Stolz [77] for current work on a psychological approach to deviance.

4. An exploration of natural language generation by GRANIS using an English generative grammar to derive answers to questions. Although the system at present can be said to understand certain English statements, it is itself rather inarticulate, having an extremely limited repertoire of rigidly formatted responses.

5. An extension to permit GRANIS to modify or augment the universe of discourse, i.e., to alter or add to the display which the user has drawn.

6. An exploration of the effect of providing the system with a goal structure which may or may not be in harmony with that of the user.

7. An exploration of the psychological implications of natural inference

models. Note that no claim has been made in this chapter as to how humans process natural language.

Although all of these directions just mentioned represent interesting and challenging avenues for further development, they are largely beyond the scope of the present investigation.

Of the original four directions, the most important is increasing the habitability of GRANIS. Increase in the inferential power, knowledge acquisition, and adaptive properties of GRANIS depend to a large extent on future applications and the needs of individual users.

SECTION 5
CONCLUSION

The purpose of this research was to investigate a unified approach to the processing of English and pictorial input on a computer. Particular emphasis was placed on deductive question answering using syntax directed techniques and the resolution of ambiguity in natural language. A theoretical framework for linguistic description was proposed as the basis for the design of a computer model. Its three components consisted of a production system, a dictionary, and a universe of discourse. Under certain conditions, as described, these components form a natural inference system which is both complete and consistent. The theory was only outlined, and much additional work remains to be done. However, in its present rough form, the theory served as a guide for the implementation of a computer model, GRANIS, which can interact with the user in a limited subset of English concerning restricted pictorial domains.

In this final section we shall summarize the accomplishments of this research, review some of the insights gained, the difficulties encountered, and comment on the practical and theoretical significance of GRANIS as a logic-based question-answering system.

Speaking first in a general way, GRANIS has demonstrated that the same syntax directed techniques which have proved successful in the construction of compilers can be applied to advantage in the efficient processing of both natural language and pictures. Also, it has been demonstrated that a fairly modest extension of the natural language grammar to incorporate some elementary semantic processing is sufficient to resolve many kinds of lexical and syntactic ambiguity. Lexical ambiguity was largely avoided by restricting GRANIS to a specific universe of discourse at any particular time. Thus, each word in the terminal vocabulary was immediately provided with a unique meaning. Syntactic ambiguity was resolved by inspecting the individual objects described in the universe of discourse to determine which interpretation, if any, was meaningful. Thus, the concept of a universe of discourse as a set of description lists was an essential ingredient in resolving constructing ambiguity, and a similar device is probably necessary in constructing a semantic model for any domain. It was in this fashion that the fundamental problem with the Harvard Syntactic Analyzer was avoided, with the conclusion that sentences containing resolvable ambiguity need not be ruled out as inadmissible inputs to a question-answering system. Indeed, resolvable ambiguity has the virtue of permitting greater parsimony by the speaker, since he is able to capitalize on the inferential capability of the system to recover (in the way the speaker intended) information that was lost through ambiguity. Hence, contrary to a commonly held view, some ambiguity is desirable, i.e., ambiguity that can be resolved by simple semantic processing. This is probably the major advantage of incorporating syntax and semantics within the framework of an integrated computer model for processing conversational language.

In the introduction we adopted five criteria for evaluating other pictorial, question-answering systems. Let us now apply these criteria to GRANIS itself.

1. Syntactic—although more sophisticated than the grammar in PLM, the GRANIS syntax is still far too restricted for comfortable use. The underlying theoretical issues were discussed in the previous section on habitability. The greatest practical constraint on the size of the grammar, and thus on the range of acceptable input formats, is the amount of computer memory available. The present version of GRANIS has already reached the maximum allowable size for a Formula Algol program on the G-21 computer. The programming extensions suggested in the preceding section are predicated on a machine with much larger memory facilities embedded within the framework of a genuine time-sharing system.

2. Semantic—the method of syntax directed interpretation in the construction of logical expressions has proved to be extremely general, and has even been applied to the construction of description lists based on the syntactic analysis of pictures.

3. Deductive—the predicate calculus has been a useful tool not only in representing the deep structure of source statements, but also in making inferences about the universe of discourse. It has been learned, however, that attempting to adhere too rigidly to the notation of the predicate calculus leads to undesirable restrictions on the semantic productions and on the class of English sentences that can easily be translated into this notation. Thus, generalizing the notion of well-formed formula, expanding the number of legitimate quantifier types, or increasing the kinds of logical connectives may lead to greater flexibility in making inferences that occur in natural language without sacrificing the significant inferential power of the original notation.

4. Interactive ability—the interactive ability of GRANIS depends strongly on the properties of the G-21 computer and the various underlying systems and monitors with which it must communicate. At present the response time of GRANIS ranges from about five seconds for simple sentences to about twenty seconds for the more complex or ambiguous sentences. The time to change pictures is of the order of ten seconds. This level of performance is barely adequate, and genuine conversation is frequently strained by the sluggishness of the system. Nevertheless, much insight into the problems of establishing a continuing dialog between man and machine was attained in the course of developing a conversational system, and the additional effort in systems programming was judged worthwhile. One such insight was the crucial importance of recoverability from error conditions. Indeed, in retrospect, the embodiment of GRANIS as a running computer program seems almost indispensable. Not only have program runs repeatedly revealed subtle errors in algorithms which appeared only in examples too complex to have been simulated by hand, but also, on occasion, they have provided valuable suggestions for improving the theoretical framework of GRANIS. One such suggestion was the use of vacuous interpretations as a basis for the resolution of syntactic ambiguity.

It has been observed empirically that the response time of GRANIS depends linearly on the number of objects displayed on the screen, linearly on the length of the source string, and exponentially on the depth of nesting of relative phrases. Although these kinds of dependencies are intrinsic to the problem domain, greater efficiency in the evaluation process could be achieved if the algorithms were modified to take greater advantage of the results of successive partial evaluations, since in some circumstances a partial evaluation is sufficient to guarantee a yes or no result regardless of the length of the remaining computation, which may then be dispensed with.

Of course it is realized that natural language communication with computers will come into its own only when supported by a system that permits *voice* communication with the computer. So long as a keyboard stands between man and machine, unpremeditated and informal programming is blocked, and the potential advantage of natural language cannot be wholly realized. Fortunately, projects designed to achieve man-machine voice communication are under way at a number of laboratories, and are sufficiently promising to encourage the parallel pursuit of natural language question-answering systems such as GRANIS.

5. Growth potential—the approach taken in GRANIS of implementing the grammar in terms of a set of syntactic and semantic productions has considerable growth potential for two reasons. First, the productions provide a uniform notational framework for extending both the syntactic and semantic components of the system while simultaneously maintaining a well-defined interface between them. Second, it is a general property of

productions that either an alteration of or an increment to them will generally affect only the local cluster in which the change or addition was made. A single alteration does not have the unfortunate effect of propagating through the entire system, a condition that would require an unknown number of global changes if consistency were to be preserved. As mentioned before, the principal constraint which inhibits the growth and also conditions the performance of GRANIS more than any other single factor is the limited core memory available on the G-21. This factor is far more important at present than the slow processing speed of the G-21, and would probably continue as the dominant constraint if GRANIS were to be implemented on one of the larger and faster third-generation computers now becoming available.

To conclude our evaluation, we have seen that GRANIS represents progress beyond both PLM and NAMER along each of the five dimensions adopted for evaluation. But it should be reemphasized that the fundamental, functional improvement of GRANIS over its predecessors is its unique ability to resolve syntactic ambiguity in a conversational mode while the man and the machine jointly converge on a mutually acceptable form of an input question.

Concerning the practical significance of GRANIS, certain applications in the field of electrical circuits and chemistry can be derived by extension of the results described in Section 3.2. However, in the introduction two possible applications of pictorial, natural language question-answering systems were proposed—viz., pictorial information retrieval and computer aided instruction. What can be said about the use of GRANIS as it now stands in either of these applications? For information retrieval over a large pictorial data base, the current system would require some conceptual modifications in the structuring of the description lists that form the universe of discourse. A hierarchical structuring would be necessary to permit more efficient indexing through the description lists. In automated teaching, several high school plane geometry texts were examined as possible inputs to GRANIS. This project was abandoned when it became apparent that, although the material was coherently organized and fairly self-contained, the required grammatical sophistication was well beyond the limitations of the current system. In searching for more elementary treatments of plane geometry in programmed texts, in the hope that at some point the grammatical constructions would be sufficiently simple to be acceptable to GRANIS, it was observed that increasing appeal is made to the extraordinary "anthropomorphic" data base available to students at that level. Requirements for general knowledge about the world such as "libraries are collections of books" or "screwdrivers are used to screw in screws" abound in such presentations (for example, see Ranucci [62]), and preclude semantic analysis of a large fraction of sentences simply because the lexical definitions are not primitive to the system. Any particular sentence, however, can in principle be understood once the implicit information has been made explicit. Thus, even without extensive reprogramming, the present system could be made to handle most statements about simple geometric pictures, providing there was not too much information tacitly assumed about the real world.

From the linguistic point of view an important theoretical contribution of GRANIS is to the notion of "understanding" in computer systems. Generalizing the operational definition of understanding given by Bobrow [7, p. 7], we say that a computer *understands* a fragment of natural language if it accepts input sentences which are members of this fragment and answers questions based on information contained in a common universe of discourse. GRANIS can be said to understand in this sense. The universe of discourse in the case of GRANIS is a picture that exhibits the relations between the various objects displayed, while the objects in the universe of discourse provide an immediate interpretation of each of the individual lexical items in the referent terminal vocabulary. Although Raphael has said that a system like SIR can be said to "understand" for the class of relations with which it deals [63, p. 9], its "understanding" is in fact restricted to the function words in the terminal vocabulary, i.e., it "understands" the relationships between the referent terms without having any knowledge of the meaning of the referent words themselves. This situation can lead to spurious inferences as was pointed out in Section 2.3. In GRANIS when one says "The triangle is to the left of the square," not only is the relation "to the left of" understood, but also the terms "triangle" and "square." That is, GRANIS really "knows" which objects are triangles and which objects are not, because such basic concepts as "polygon" and "number of sides" are primitive to the system. This elementary notion together with the universe of discourse permit resolution of syntactic ambiguity. Systems like SIR are in principle not capable of such disambiguation without fundamental semantic reorganization.

Another theoretical contribution of GRANIS might be to the field of psychology. In some sense the computer model could be considered a simulation of human processing of linguistic and pictorial information. Of course, psychological experiments would have to be devised to test precisely the similarity between the behavior of the model and human behavior, but in this manner we might obtain useful suggestions for improving GRANIS and at the same time gain valuable insight into human cognitive processes.

To conclude, in 1959 Edmund C. Berkeley said

> Of all the territories of application of computers to human affairs, one that is very likely to have most farreaching effects is the territory in which computers converse and discuss with human beings, using ordinary language,

and handling ideas appropriately. This is a future development which clearly casts its shadow before.[13]

Although most would agree with this statement in spirit, we are still far from writing a program that can understand all, or even a very large segment of, English. However, within its narrow field of competence, GRANIS does serve to demonstrate that computer understanding of limited pictorial and text information is possible. Furthermore, it shows that, using syntax directed interpretation, one could build a system that would communicate well with people both in English and with pictures. Indeed, it is my conviction that ultimate progress in the field of artificial intelligence will depend strongly on the use of on-line graphic display devices and natural language communication. Natural language provides the convenience that permits the user to concentrate on the problem at hand, rather than on a translation into a formal and unambiguous language, while the displays quite literally provide a new dimension in man-machine interaction. Finally, their on-line property provides the necessary responsiveness for genuine conversation.

References

[1] AMAREL, S., Problem solving procedures for efficient syntactic analysis. *20th National Conference of the ACM*, Cleveland, Ohio, August 24–26, 1965.
[2] ARISTOTLE, *De Sophisticis Elenchis* (On Sophistical Refutations).
[3] BAR-HILLEL, Y. The outlook for computational semantics. *Proceedings of the Conference on Computer Related Semantic Analysis.* Las Vegas, Nevada: Wayne State University, December 1965.
[4] BELNAP, N. D., An analysis of questions: preliminary report. TM-1287/000/00. Santa Monica, California: System Development Corporation, June 1963.
[5] BLACK, F. S. A deductive question-answering system. PhD thesis, Harvard University, June 1964. [M]
[6] BOBROW, D. G. Syntactic analysis of English by computer: A survey. *Proceedings of the Fall Joint Computer Conference*, 1963, pp. 365–387.
[7] BOBROW, D. G. Natural language input for a computer problem solving system. MAC-TR-1, MIT, September, 1964. [M]
[8] BOBROW, D. G. Problems in natural language communication with computers. *IEEE Transactions on Human Factors in Electronics* Vol. HFE-8, March 1967, pp. 52–55.
[9] BOHNERT, H. G. and BACKER, P. O. Automatic English-to-logic translation in a simplified model: A study in the logic of grammar. IBM, Yorktown Heights, New York, March 1966.
[10] CLARKE, D. C. and WALL, R. E. An economical program for limited parsing of English. *Proceedings of the Fall Joint Computer Conference*, 1965, pp. 307–316.

[13] Computers and Automation Magazine.

[11] CHOMSKY, N. *Aspects of the Theory of Syntax*. Cambridge, Mass.: MIT Press, 1965.
[12] CHOMSKY, N. *Syntactic Structures*. The Hague: Mouton and Co., 1957.
[13] CHOMSKY, N. and MILLER, G. A. Introduction to the formal analysis of natural languages. *In* Luce, R. D., Bush, R., and Galanter, E., *Handbook of Mathematical Psychology*, Vol. 2. New York: Wiley, 1963, pp. 269–322.
[14] CHOMSKY, N. and SCHUTZENBERGER, M. P. The algebraic theory of context free languages, *In* Braffort, P. and Hirschberg, D., *Computer Programming and Formal Systems, Studies in Logic*. Amsterdam: North-Holland, 1963, pp. 119–161.
[15] COLES, L. S. Scope user's manual for the Carnegie Tech graphical display system. Pittsburgh: Carnegie Institute of Technology, September 1966.
[16] COOPER, W. S. Fact retrieval and deductive question-answering information retrieval systems. *Journal of the ACM* Vol. 11, No. 2, April 1964, pp. 117–137.
[17] CRAIG, J. A., BEREZNER, S. C., CARNEY, H. C., and LONGYEAR, C. R. DEACON: Direct English Access and CONtrol. *Proceedings of the Fall Joint Computer Conference*, 1966, pp. 365–380.
[18] DARLINGTON, J. Translating ordinary language into symbolic logic. Memo MAC-M-149, Project MAC, MIT, March 1964.
[19] DAVIS, M. *Computability and Unsolvability*. New York: McGraw-Hill, 1958.
[20] EARLEY, J. C. Generating a recognizer for a BNF grammar. Pittsburgh: Carnegie Institute of Technology, June 1965.
[21] ELLIOTT, R. W. A model for a fact retrieval system. TNN-42. Austin, Texas: University of Texas, May 1965.
[22] ENGELBART, D. C. Augmenting human intellect: A conceptual framework. Menlo Park, California: Stanford Research Institute, 1963.
[23] EVANS, A. Syntax analysis by a production language. PhD thesis, Carnegie Institute of Technology, 1965.
[24] EVANS, T. G. A program for the solution of geometric-analogy intelligence-test questions. Physical and Mathematical Sciences Research Papers No. 64. Hanscom Field, Massachusetts: Air Force Cambridge Research Laboratories, November 1964. [M]
[25] FELDMAN, J. A. A formal semantics for computer oriented languages. PhD thesis, Carnegie Institute of Technology, May 1964.
[26] FLOYD, R. W. A descriptive language for symbol manipulation. *Journal of the ACM* Vol. 8, No. 4, October 1961, pp. 579–584.
[27] FREY, P. R. *College Chemistry*, 2nd Ed. Englewood Cliffs, N.J.: Prentice-Hall, Inc., 1958.
[28] GILBERT, P. On the syntax of algorithmic languages. *Journal of the ACM* Vol. 13, No. 1, January 1966, pp. 90–107.
[29] GREEN, B. F., et al. BASEBALL: An automatic question-answerer. *In* Feigenbaum and Feldman, *Computers and Thought*. New York: McGraw-Hill, 1963, pp. 207–216. [FF]
[30] HALPERN, M. Foundations for the case for natural language programming. *IEEE Spectrum*, March 1967, pp. 140–149.
[31] IRONS, E. T. A syntax directed compiler for ALGOL 60. *Communications of the ACM* Vol. 4, No. 1, January 1961, pp. 51–55.

[32] KASHER, A. Data-retrival by computer: A critical survey. Technical Report No. 22. Jerusalem, Israel: Hebrew University, January 1966.
[33] KATZ, J. J. and FODOR, J. A. The structure of a semantic theory. *Language* Vol. 39, 1963, pp. 170–210.
[34] KATZ, J. J. and POSTAL, P. M. *An Integrated Theory of Linguistic Description.* Cambridge, Mass.: MIT Press, 1964.
[35] KIRSCH, R. A. Symposium on automated processing of illustrated text. Washington, D. C.: National Bureau of Standards Report No. 8144, December 1963.
[36] KIRSCH, R. A. Computer interpretation of English text and picture patterns. *IEEE Transactions on Electronic Computers* Vol. EC-13, No. 4, August 1964, pp. 363–376.
[37] KONDÔ, M. and MURATA, H. *Problem Solving Machines for Euclidean Geometry.* Setagaya, Tokyo. Tokyo Metropolitan University, 1965.
[38] KUNO, S. The predictive analyzer and a path elimination technique. *Communications of the ACM* Vol. 8, No. 7, July 1965, pp. 453–462.
[39] LEBLANC, H. *An Introduction to Deductive Logic.* New York: Wiley & Sons, 1955.
[40] LEHMAN, W. P. and PENDEGRAFT, E. D. Machine language translation study. Report No. 16, Linguistics Research Center. Austin, Texas: University of Texas, June 1963.
41] LIBERMAN, D. Specification and utilization of a transformational grammar. IBM, Yorktown Heights, New York, March 1966.
[42] LICKLIDER, J. C. R. Man-computer symbiosis. *IRE Transactions on Human Factors in Electronics*, March 1960, pp. 4–11.
[43] LINDSAY, R. K. *Toward the Development of a Machine which Comprehends.* Austin, Texas: University of Texas, May 1961. [FF]
[44] LOWERY, H. R., et al. General electric transistor manual. Semiconductor Department, General Electric Company, Liverpool, New York, 5th edition, 1960.
[45] MACKAY, D. G. To end ambiguous sentences. *Perception and Psychophysics* Vol. 1, No. 12, December 1966, pp. 426–436.
[46] MCCARTHY, J. Problems in the theory of computation. *Proceedings of the IFIP Congress*, May 1965, pp. 221–222.
[47] MCCARTHY, J. Programs with common sense. *Proceedings of the Symposium on Mechanization of Thought Processes*, HMSO, London, 1959. [M]
[48] MARKOV, A. A. Theory of Algorithms. Report 60-51085 Clearinghouse for Federal Scientific and Technical Information, U.S. Department of Commerce, Washington, D.C., 1954.
[49] MARTIN, R. M. Towards a systematic pragmatics, In *Studies in Logic.* Amsterdam: North-Holland, 1959.
[50] MORRIS, C. Foundations of the theory of signs. In *International Encyclopedia of Unified Science* Vol. 1, No. 2. Chicago: University of Chicago Press, 1938.
[51] NEWELL, A. and ERNST, G. W. The search for generality. *Proceedings of the IFIP Congress*, May 1965, pp. 17–24.
[52] NEWELL, A. and ERNST, G. W. *GPS: A Case Study in Generality and Problem Solving.* New York: Academic Press, 1969.

[53] OETTINGER, A. G. Automatic processing of natural and formal languages. *Proceedings of the IFIP Congress*, May 1965, pp. 9–16.
[54] OGDEN, C. K. *A System of Basic English*. New York: Harcourt Brace & Jovanovich, 1934.
[55] OLNEY, J. C. and LONDE, D. L. A research plan for investigating English discourse structure with particular attention to anaphoric relationships. TM(L)-3256, System Development Corporation, Santa Monica, California, November 1966.
[56] PERLIS, A. J., ITURRIAGA, R., and STANDISH, T. A. A definition of formula ALGOL. Pittsburgh: Carnegie Institute of Technology, April 1966.
[57] POST, E. L. Finite Combinatory Processes—Formulation 1. *Journal of Symbolic Logic* Vol. 1, No. 3, September 1936, pp. 103–105.
[58] POST, E. L. Formal reduction of the general combinatorial decision problem. *American Journal of Mathematics* Vol. 65, No. 2, 1943, pp. 197–215.
[59] PUTNAM, H. Some issues in the theory of grammar. In *Structure of Language and its Mathematical Aspects*, Proceedings of Symposia in Applied Mathematics Vol. 12, American Mathematical Society, 1961, pp. 25–42.
[60] QUATSE, J. T. A visual display system suitable for time shared use. Pittsburgh: Carnegie Institute of Technology, June 1965.
[61] QUILLIAN, R. Semantic theory. PhD thesis, Carnegie Institute of Technology, October 1966. [M]
[62] RANUCCI, E. R. *Points, Lines, and Planes: An Introduction to Geometry in Two Dimensions*. Understanding Modern Mathematics Series. New York: Macmillan Co., 1963.
[63] RAPHAEL, B. SIR: A computer program for semantic information retrieval. MAC-TR-2, MIT, June 1964. [M]
[64] REICHENBACH, H. Analysis of conversational language. *In Elements of Symbolic Logic*. New York: Macmillan, 1947, pp. 251–354.
[65] ROBERTS, L. G. Machine perception of three dimensional solids. Technical Report No. 315, Lincoln Laboratory, MIT, May 1963.
[66] ROBERTS, L. G. Graphical communications and control languages. Report MS-1173, Lincoln Laboratory, MIT, September 1964.
[67] ROBINSON, J. J. Automatic parsing and fact retrieval: A comment on grammar, paraphrase, and meaning. Memo RM-5005-PR, The RAND Corporation, Santa Monica, California, February 1964.
[68] SAMMET, J. E. The use of English as a programming language. *Communications of the ACM* Vol. 9, No. 3, March 1966, pp. 228–230.
[69] SILLARS, W. A. An algorithm for representing English sentences in a formal language. National Bureau of Standards Report No. 7884, April 1963.
[70] SIMMONS, R. F. Synthetic language behavior. SP-1245, System Development Corporation, Santa Monica, California, June 1963.
[71] SIMMONS, R. F. Answering English questions by computer: A survey. *Communications of the ACM* Vol. 8, No. 1, January 1965, pp. 53–70.
[72] SIMMONS, R. F. and LONDE, D. L. NAMER: A pattern-recognition system for generating sentences about relations between line drawings. TM-1798, System Development Corporation, Santa Monica, California, June 1963.
[73] SIMMONS, R. F., BURGER, J. F., and LONG, R. E. An approach toward answer-

ing English questions from text. *Proceedings of the Fall Joint Computer Conference*, 1966, pp. 357–363.
[74] SIMON, H. A. The logic of rational decision. *British Journal for the Philosophy of Science* Vol. 16, No. 63, 1965.
[75] SIMON, H. A. The heuristic compiler. Memo RM-3588-PR, The RAND Corporation, Santa Monica, California, May 1963. [SS]
[76] SLAGLE, J. R. Experiments with a deductive question-answering program. *Communications of the ACM* Vol. 8, No. 12, December 1965, pp. 792–798.
[77] STOLZ, W. and MUELLER, L. M. Some experiments with queer sentences: A progress report. Department of Psychology, University of Texas, Austin, Texas.
[78] SUTHERLAND, I. E. Sketchpad: A man-machine graphical communication system. Technical Report No. 296, Lincoln Laboratory, MIT, January 1963.
[79] THOMPSON, F. B. English for the computer. *Proceedings of the Fall Joint Computer Conference*, 1966, pp. 349–356.
[80] TURING, A. M. Computing Machinery and Intelligence. *In* Feigenbaum and Feldman, *Computers and Thought*. New York: McGraw-Hill, 1963, pp. 11–35. [FF]
[81] UHR, L. and VOSSLER, C. A pattern-recognition program that generates, evaluates, and adjusts its own operators. *In* Feigenbaum and Feldman, *Computers and Thought*. New York: McGraw-Hill, 1963, pp. 251–268. [FF]
[82] WANG, H. Toward mechanical mathematics. *IBM Journal of Research and Development*, January 1960, pp. 2–22.
[83] WATT, W. C. A Prerequisite to the Utility of Micro-grammars. Technical Note 258, National Bureau of Standards, Washington, D. C., April 1965.
[84] WATT, W. C. Materials for PLACEBO V. Technical Note 281, National Bureau of Standards, Washington, D. C., January 1966.
[85] WATT, W. C. and ASU, R. W. Concordance to the Rules of PLACEBO V. Report 8934, National Bureau of Standards, Washington, D. C., August 1965.
[86] WEINREICH, U. Explorations in Semantic Theory, *in* Sebeok, T. A., *Current Trends in Linguistics*, Vol. 3. The Hague: Mouton and Co., 1966, pp. 395–477.
[87] WILLIAMS, T. Translating from Ordinary Discourse into Formal Logic: A Preliminary Systems Study. Report No. AFCRC-TN-56-770-AD-98813, ACF Industries, Inc., Alexandria, Virginia, 1956.
[88] WIRTH, N. and WEBER, H. EULER: A Generalization of ALGOL, and its Formal Definition. *Communications of the ACM* Vol. 9, No. 1, January 1966, pp. 13–23.
[89] YERSHOV, A. P. One View of Man-Machine Interaction. *Journal of the ACM* Vol. 12, No. 3, July 1965, pp. 315–325.
[90] ZEMANEK, H. Semiotics and Programming Languages. *Communications of the ACM* Vol. 9, No. 3, March 1966, pp. 139–143.
[91] ZWICKY, A. M., FRIEDMAN, J., HALL, B. C., and WALKER, D. E. The Mitre Syntactic Analysis Procedure for Transformational Grammars. MIP-9, The Mitre Corporation, Bedford, Massachusetts, August 1965.

Chapter 6

NATURAL LANGUAGE LEARNING BY COMPUTER

LAURENT SIKLÓSSY

SECTION 1
INTRODUCTION

Workers in artificial intelligence have, as one of their goals, the writing of sophisticated computer programs that will perform "interesting" and "difficult" tasks. Programs can improve their sophistication by learning, and learning is, indeed, a central problem of artificial intelligence.

One of the first learning tasks that human beings perform is acquiring a natural language (abbreviated NL). Throughout history men have used NL's for communicating among themselves and investigating and interacting with the world. For the past decade, natural language communication of humans with computers has been an active area of interest in artificial intelligence.

Interests in the fields of learning and natural language are combined here in a program called ZBIE that attempts to learn natural languages at an elementary level. The task is considered worthy of investigation in its own right; the program does not try to simulate the learning behavior of human beings.

Natural language learning programs have been few. To the best of the author's knowledge, corroborated by a review of recent work in artificial intelligence (Solomonoff 1966), only one work can qualify: Uhr 1964. By a process of string matching and statistical learning, Uhr's programs attempt to translate strings from one NL (NL1) into strings of another (NL2). The programs are insufficiently documented to explain their structure in detail, but from the output exhibited, several limits appear: the idiosyncrasies of NL1 create difficulties for the program, and cyclical behavior instead of continuous learning sometimes occurs.

A possible cause for the lack of interest in NL learning programs is the feeling, among many linguists, that the language learning task is extremely arduous. Two of the foremost scientists in the field of modern linguistics stated (Chomsky and Miller, 1963):

> To imagine that an adequate grammar could be selected from the infinitude of conceivable alternatives by some process of pure induction on a finite corpus of utterances is to misjudge completely the magnitude of the problem.

Two related areas have received much more attention: the induction of grammars of abstract languages and the extrapolation of sequences. Solomonoff (1958) offered a sketch for the mechanization of linguistic learning, which does not appear to have been programmed, and, later (1964), his formal theory of inductive inference presents various models for extrapolating a long sequence of symbols containing all data to be used in the prediction. A probabilistic approach is used. Simon and Kotovsky (1963) describe programs that induct rules to explain the formation of given serial alphabetic patterns. The rules can then be applied to continue the patterns. Pivar and Finkelstein (1964) report on a similar, performance-oriented program which also handles integer strings. (For a review of recent research, see Solomonoff, 1966.) In either area, the strings considered are "empty"; they lack the means that natural languages possess to express the content of situations in our human evironment.

Before trying to define the learning task, let us consider the technique for teaching languages (to humans) used by I. A. Richards and his co-workers (Richards, 1961). In the language-through-pictures series, pictures are associated with sentences in an NL to be learned. The pictures are to act as a general representation that has uniform meaning for all human beings (*English Through Pictures, Book I* is prefaced in 41 languages). The student is supposed to use the pictures as clues to the meanings of the sentences and, by successive comparisons of the sentences, to infer the vocabulary and grammar of the NL studied.

The student's own mother tongue is bypassed, thereby avoiding problems of translation from one language into another; instead the student learns to translate situations directly from "reality" into a new NL.

(As an aside, the author tried to learn Hebrew, absolutely unknown to him beforehand, from *Hebrew Through Pictures*. He had the advantage of having previously read several other "Language Through Pictures" books in known languages; nevertheless he had great difficulty in determining the meanings of the pictures or the clues to be derived from them, and finally abandoned the endeavor. Several other persons reported identical difficulties.)

The philosophies behind ZBIE and I. A. Richards' booklets are similar. ZBIE uses a functional language (abbreviated FL) to represent situations; FL has the same function in ZBIE as the pictures have in Richards. By successive comparisons of situations, as represented in FL and as expressed in an NL, respectively, ZBIE tries to express other situations represented in FL and, failing that, to use its previous knowledge to learn how to express the other situations. The learning sequence presented to ZBIE is taken from *Russian Through Pictures* with slight modifications.

Section 2 is divided into three parts: in 2.1 we describe FL briefly; in 2.2 we describe the internal representations used by ZBIE: patterns, sets, translation rules, and in-context vocabulary; in 2.3 we describe the organization of ZBIE and the main processor routines. Since Section 2 is rather detailed the reader may wish to come back to it after he has read Section 3.

Section 3 describes ZBIE's learning of Russian.

Section 4 compares ZBIE with Uhr's programs and discusses some of ZBIE's inadequacies.

The Appendix gives a simple example, in German, of ZBIE's "evolutionary learning" capabilities.

ZBIE is coded in IPL-V (Newell, 1964) and has been run on the Carnegie-Mellon University CDC G-21 computer. Since IPL-V code is typically unreadable, the program is not reproduced, but it is described semiformally in Section 2.3.

SECTION 2
THE PROGRAM AND REPRESENTATION

2.1 The Functional Language, FL

The purpose of FL is to represent situations in a way that resembles the pictures (and picture language) of the language-through-pictures series. The main spirit behind FL may be summarized thus: similar situations should have similar representations in FL, where an intuitive feeling for similarity is used. For example, the sentences:

This is a hat.

This is his hat. (referring to a boy)

This is the boy's hat.

should have similar representations in FL. To avoid idiosyncrasies of NL's, FL is not inflected and omits articles. To improve its descriptive power we have added some semantics. For instance, the referent of pronouns is specifically mentioned: he = (man) or you = (spoken boy) if the person spoken to is a boy. This parallels, of course, the way pronouns are represented in pictures.

FL is not unlike the language described by Reichenbach (1947) for his analysis of English. Instead of the usual functional notation f(x1, x2, ..., xn) we use a LISP-like notation (McCarthy 1963), (f x1 x2 ... xn), and also use description lists, enclosed in square brackets ([and]).

Verbs and function words are treated as n-place functions. A few examples should make some of the elementary constructions clear.

FL	NL
(be hat)	This is a hat.
(be hat[of boy])	This is the boy's hat.
(be hat[of (boy)])	This is his hat.
(q be book here)	Is the book here?
(be (on hat table))	The hat is on the table.
(be (on table hat))	The table is on the hat.
(be (on hat[of (boy)] table))	His hat is on the table.
(be (in (and hat book) drawer))	The hat and the book are in the drawer.
(be (in ((and hat book)) (drawer)))	They are in it.

Input to ZBIE takes the form of IPL-V list structures equivalent to the above notation. The most important features of FL seem to be its uniformity and structure: FL sentences are usually trees, not strings.

To make explicit the structure of the trees in FL, it is sufficient to define a recognizer for the terminal nodes of the trees. The following are *terminal nodes:*

—an atomic symbol
　　Example: be, table, boy, 2.
—(⟨atomic symbol⟩)
　　Example: (boy).
—(speaking ⟨any FL construct⟩)
　　Example: (speaking boy).
—(spoken ⟨any FL construct⟩)
　　Example: (spoken boy [numb 2]), where numb = number.
—(⟨atomic symbol⟩[numb ⟨atomic symbol⟩])
　　Example: (man[numb 2]).
—⟨atomic symbol⟩[numb plur], where plur = plural.
　　Example: boy [numb plur].

The terminal nodes in FL are called FL *units*. All other constructs in FL are FL *complex structures*. The program "understands" FL to the extent that it recognizes the FL units of an FL structure.

At this stage FL is a tool, to be modified if necessary. We make no claim that it is "the" representation, or that it is universal. It is equally doubtful that the picture language is universal. For instance, in *German Through Pictures*, p. 239, a German boy plays baseball!

2.2 The Program's Internal Representation

At run-time, ZBIE builds and then uses certain memory structures which will now be described.

2.2.1 The Pattern. The main working structure is the *pattern*, which is used to match FL structures, and then, using the pattern's translation rule, to translate the FL structures into NL. There are two types of patterns, differentiated by a marker on the description list (D.L.) of the pattern. A *top* pattern is used to match FL sentences; a *subpattern* to match FL complex substructures. A pattern is an ordered list of pairs; each pair consists of the *name* of a set and an *extractor*. On the D.L. of the pattern is the *translation rule* of the pattern, and other information.

A more formal description of a pattern can be given in B.N.F.:

⟨pattern⟩ :: = ⟨p-list⟩⟨description list⟩
⟨p-list⟩ :: = ⟨set name⟩⟨extractor⟩ |
　　　　　　　⟨set name⟩⟨extractor⟩⟨p-list⟩
⟨description list⟩:: = ⟨attribute⟩⟨value⟩ |
　　　　　　　⟨attribute⟩⟨value⟩⟨description list⟩
⟨set name⟩ :: = A1 | A2 | A3 . . .
⟨extractor⟩ :: = Y1 | Y2 | Y3 . . .
⟨attribute⟩ :: = ⟨IPL-V regional or internal symbol⟩
⟨value⟩ :: = ⟨IPL-V list structure⟩

In IPL-V, a pattern is represented as a simple describable list. To talk about particular patterns, we shall need some conventions for exhibiting such lists.

$$L2 = S1 \quad S2 \quad S3; \quad A1 = V1, \quad A2 = V2$$

will be taken to represent the list named L2, which is a list whose symbols are S1, S2, and S3, and whose description consists of two attributes, A1 and A2, having values V1 and V2, respectively.

$$L3 = S1 \ (S2 \ S3)$$

represents the list named L3, which is a list of two symbols: S1 and the name of the sublist consisting of (S2 and S3). This use of parentheses eliminates the need for assigning explicit names to all of the sublists, and provides a simple representation for tree structures (nested lists).

With these conventions, a pattern will look like this:

$$P0 = A1\ Y1\ A2\ Y2\ A3\ Y3;\ TR = ((Y1\ Y2)Y3)$$

This reads: the pattern P0 has the pattern list (A1 Y1 A2 Y2 A3 Y3), where the A's are set names and the Y's the corresponding extractors. P0's description list contains the attribute TR (*translation rule*), whose value is the list structure ((Y1 Y2)Y3). By adopting the convention that the Y's and the corresponding A's always have identical subscripts in a given pattern, we can use the simpler notation:

$$P0 = A1\ A2\ A3;\ TR = ((1\ 2)3)$$

which omits explicit mention of the Y's.

A second (simpler) example of a pattern is:

$$P2 = A4\ A3;\ TR = (4\ 3)$$

P2 is the name of the pattern; its p-list is (A4 Y4 A3 Y3); the sets are A4 and A3, the extractors, Y4 and Y3; its translation rule is the list (Y4 Y3). Since, in this and other patterns we shall examine, the translation rule is the only part of the description list with which we shall be concerned, the other attribute-value pairs on that list will be omitted.

The above very compact description for translation rules assumes that the same set name does not occur twice in the p-list of a pattern. This restriction happens to be satisfied by all the examples that we shall describe. However, ZBIE actually uses distinct extractors for each set name in a pattern so that the restriction mentioned is purely for notational convenience.

To understand the function of the extractors, let us describe the process that matches an FL structure to a pattern.

2.2.2 Elementary Description of the Matching Routine. Let us assume that we want to match the FL sentence (be boy) to P2, above. We go down the sentence and the p-list of the pattern in parallel. We check whether the first element of the FL sentence (here, be) is a member of the first set on the p-list of the pattern (here, A4). Since, in our case, "be" is a member of A4, we say that "be" was (successfully) matched to A4. "be" is then placed on the description list of Y4; Y4 has "extracted" the element of the FL sentence which was matched to A4. The matching routine loops back and tests whether the second element of the FL sentence (here, boy) is a member of the second set on the p-list of the pattern (here, A3), and so on.

When we want to translate the matched FL sentence into NL, we use the translation rule of the pattern. The translation rule of P2 is TR(P2) = (Y4 Y3). The meaning of the translation rule is as follows: Take the element extracted by Y4, "be," translate it in the appropriate context (here the context consists of the set A4, of which "be" was a member, and of the pattern P2), then follow this translation (ЭТО) by the translation of the element extracted by Y3, "boy," in the proper context (here, the set A3 and the pattern P2). The second translation is МАЛЬЧИК so that the total translation is ЭТО МАЛЬЧИК. If we cannot find a translation for "boy," we insert a "Z" in the translation, which would become: ЭТО Z.

It may happen, for example, that the second element of FL is not an FL unit, but a complex structure (see sentence 12, Section 3). The matching routine then tries, recursively, to find in A3 a subpattern that can match the second element of FL.

The matching routine uses only set-inclusion tests, but uses them recursively. It is a necessary condition for match that the length of the FL structure at its top level be equal to the number of pairs (set, extractor) in the pattern. The matching routine will be considered in detail in Section 2.3.1 of this chapter.

2.2.3 **The Translation Rule.** The translation rule TR(pattern) is a function from the extractors of the pattern into NL augmented by Z's, where a Z indicates that something was not translated. A few examples follow:

(a) Linear arrangement of the extractors:

$$P37 = A12\ A2\ A3;\ TR = (2\ 12\ 3)$$

The translation rule of P37 is TR(P37) = (2 12 3), and is to be read as follows: Look up in the vocabulary, in the proper context (here, of the set A2 and the pattern P37), the translation of the part of the FL structure that was matched to A2; then follow this translation by the translation, in the proper context, of the part of the FL structure that was matched to A12, etc.

(b) Linear arrangement of some of the extractors:

$$P1 = A1\ A2\ A3;\ TR = (2\ 3)$$

The translation rule of P1 is TR(P1) = (2 3). It is to be read as in case (a) above. Notice that the extractor Y1 is missing in this translation rule. Such an omission occurs when some FL part is not expressed in NL.

(c) Grouping of some extractors:

$$P0 = A1\ A2\ A3;\ TR = ((1\ 2)3)$$

The translation rule is to be read as follows: Take the FL structure that was matched to A1, follow this structure by the FL structure that was matched to A2; then look up this FL complex structure in the vocabulary in the proper context (here, of the pattern P0). The NL string obtained is followed by the translation of the element extracted by Y3, as above, to give the translation of the structure matched to P0.

Example. (Section 3, sentence 1.) If we match (be (man) here) to P0, we shall look up the FL complex (be man)) in the vocabulary, and follow the translation of (be (man)) by the translation of "here" (in the proper context).

The above three functions are now used by ZBIE. Note that since the FL structure matched to A1, say, can be a complex FL part, a recursive translation is implicit in the translation rules. For a detailed example, see Section 3, sentence 12.

The translation rule functions can be generalized immediately. Two examples of different translation rules follow, and many more could be dreamed up. (We assume a pattern with extractors 1 and 2):

(d) Introduction of constants:

$$TR = (2 \text{ NLi } 1)$$

where NLi is some string in NL. Such a rule could be used when some expression in NL has idiomatic fillers.

(e) Disjoint parts:

$$TR = (\text{first}(2) \text{ 1 second}(2))$$

where first and second are functions (which must be defined) on the translation of the FL structure which was extracted by 2. Such a rule could be used to handle separable German verbs.

2.2.4 **The In-Context Vocabulary.** The vocabulary of ZBIE has the two following forms:

(a) FL unit = FL(i), NL string = NL(l), set = (j), pattern = P(k).

To be interpreted: The translation of the FL unit FL(i) when it is a member of the set A(j) and occurs in the context of the pattern P(k) is the string of NL words NL(l).

(b) FL complex = FL(i), NL string = NL(k), pattern = P(j).

To be interpreted: The translation of the FL complex FL(i) in the context of the pattern P(j) is the string NL(k) in NL.

Note that we cannot conclude that some FL unit FL(i) has a translation in the context A(j), P(k) from the knowledge that FL(i) is a member of A(j). We may only have a translation in the context of some other pattern P(k'), or for that matter, none at all.

2.3 The Program's Organization

The control structure of ZBIE consists of two modes. The first initializes the internal structure and constructs a first pattern. The control then passes to a second mode, whereupon new situations are brought in one-by-one and processed.

Mode 1. Initialization

Initially, two situations are presented to ZBIE, each represented in FL and expressed in NL. The situations must be sufficiently similar so that by comparing them ZBIE can deduce its first pattern.

More precisely, ZBIE expects (1) that the two initial FL sentences will be of depth 0, i.e., will have no FL complex substructure; (2) that they will have exactly one element different in the same position in both FL sentences; and (3) that the two corresponding NL sentences will have exactly one element different and in the same position, which must be either at the beginning or at the end of the sentences. The distinct elements in FL and NL are then assumed to correspond to each other; the common parts in FL and NL are also assumed to correspond to each other and a first pattern P0 is set up, with its set and translation rule; the in-context vocabulary is initiated. (See the examples at the beginning of Section 3 and the Appendix.)

Mode 2. Single Sentence Analysis

After initialization, ZBIE operates in the following mode. First, the previously processed FL and NL sentences are erased. Then, the description in FL of a situation is read in, together with its expression in NL which is stored for later use. The FL sentence is then processed following the basic program below (written in an ALGOL-like language, "⟨" and "⟩" delimit blocks):

```
                    SINGLE SENTENCE PROCESSOR
FOR ALL TOP PATTERNS (LAST CREATED, FIRST CONSIDERED) DO
   ⟨MATCH FL TO TOP PATTERN;
```

COMMENT: The matching routine is described Section 2.3.1 below;

```
   IF TOTAL MATCH THEN
      ⟨TRANSLATE;
      IF TRANSLATION HAS NO UNKNOWNS THEN ⟨COMPARE TO INPUT NL;
         IF TRANSLATION=INPUT NL THEN ⟨EXIT AND READ IN THE NEXT SITUATION⟩
         ELSE GO TO ERROR RECOVERY⟩
      ELSE IF TRANSLATION IS CONSISTENT WITH INPUT NL THEN STORE PATTERN
      LIST IN PATTERN LIST HOLDER TO PROCESS ELSE DO NOTHING⟩
```

COMMENT: The consistency test is described in Section 2.3.2;

ELSE STORE PATTERN LIST IN PATTERN LIST HOLDER›
PROCESS ELEMENTS ON THE PATTERN LIST HOLDER;

COMMENT: Processing the pattern lists is described in Section 2.3.3;

‹IF PROCESSING SUCCESSFUL THEN ‹EXIT AND READ IN THE NEXT SITUATION››

COMMENT: Everything failed so far;

CREATE A NEW TOP PATTERN FOR THE SITUATION;

COMMENT: The pattern-creating routine is described in Section 2.3.4,

Before describing how the pattern lists are processed, let us explain some of the terms used.

We saw in Section 2.2 how an FL sentence was matched to a pattern. One of the main routines of ZBIE is the matching routine, which obtains all possible total and partial matches of patterns (and subpatterns) to an FL sentence. Let us consider the matching mechanism again.

2.3.1 The Matching Routine. An FL sentence is a tree structure whose terminal nodes are the FL units. The sets of the p-list of a top pattern can be viewed as the zeroth level of a tree, the pattern tree. The sets themselves contain (sub)patterns; we can think of each subpattern as initiating a new branch of the pattern tree. An instance of a set will be considered a terminal node of the pattern tree if we select an FL unit of the set. If we select a subpattern of the set, the instance of the set will be considered a non-terminal node, and the subpattern will initiate a new subtree. Since a subpattern SP1 may have on its p-list the name of a set which contains a pattern P2 such that P2 is an ancestor of SP1, the system is recursive, and a top pattern can be considered as the head of an infinity of trees of arbitrarily great depth. However, since any given FL sentence is a finite tree, no pattern trees of a depth superior to the depth of the FL sentence need be considered by the matching process.

The pattern trees formed by the patterns resemble a discrimination net. However, a net of depth n cannot distinguish between two trees of depth greater than n that are identical up to and including depth n, while, in some cases, n different patterns could distinguish two such trees thanks to the recursive feature of the patterns. The pattern trees are, therefore, more powerful than a simple discrimination net.

We can view the matching process as a test of whether a given pattern tree is close to being isomorphic to the given FL sentence tree. An FL sentence tree is isomorphic to a pattern tree if the trees can be superimposed, and the terminal nodes (FL units) of the FL sentence are respectively identical to the terminal nodes (FL units of terminal sets) of the pattern tree. Usually we shall have no isomorphism; we then look for as good a fit of a pattern tree to the FL sentence as we can find.

Disregarding the bookkeeping chores involved in backtracking and recursion, it is enough to consider how an FL subtree is matched to an element of a set, a node of the pattern tree. By considering the top patterns as elements of a set, no generality is lost. We treat the special case of an empty set by postulating an empty element for such a set.

2.3.1.1 Outline of the Matching Routine

```
MATCH FL (SUB)TREE TO ELEMENT OF SET;
ELSET := ELEMENT OF SET;
FLTREE := FL SUBTREE;
(IF ELSET IS AN FL WHOLE OR IF ELSET IS EMPTY) THEN ⟨'NO MATCH'; GO TO EXIT⟩;
```

   COMMENT: ELSET is a (sub)pattern;

```
IF LENGTH (P-LIST OF ELSET)≠2 * LENGTH OF FLTREE THEN
                    ⟨'NO MATCH'; GO TO EXIT⟩;
```

   COMMENT: INITIALIZE LOOP;

```
MISTAKE COUNTER := 0;
```

   COMMENT: The mistake counter is associated with this particular level, as are the other identifiers;

```
    I := 0;
    LOOP:
    IF MISTAKE COUNTER > 1 THEN ⟨'NO MATCH'; GO TO EXIT⟩;
    I := I + 1;
    IF I-TH SON OF FLTREE DOES NOT EXIST THEN GO TO EXIT;
    IFLTREE := I-TH SON OF FLTREE;
    IELSET := I-TH SET OF P-LIST OF ELSET;
    IF IFLTREE IS AN FL WHOLE THEN
       ⟨IF IFLTREE IS A MEMBER OF IELSET THEN
          GO TO LOOP
        ELSE ⟨MISTAKE COUNTER := MISTAKE COUNTER + 1; GO TO LOOP⟩⟩
       ELSE ⟨MATCH IFLTREE TO THE ELEMENTS OF IELSET;
```

COMMENT: The match is tried successively on all the elements of IELSET. Thanks to the hidden bookkeeping, we only have to consider the match for one element;

```
         IF RETURN 'NO MATCH' THEN
            ⟨MISTAKE COUNTER := MISTAKE COUNTER + 1; GO TO LOOP⟩
            ELSE GO TO LOOP⟩
```

It is seen that, basically, up to one "mistake" (as defined by the program) is allowed at a given level in a subtree.

2.3.1.2 USE OF THE MATCHING ROUTINE. The matching routine finds pattern lists which it stores in a pattern list holder in decreasing order of match-depth. A pattern list is a list of patterns, headed by a top pattern and containing other (or possibly no) subpatterns which were matched to substructures of the FL sentence. With the pattern list is associated a corresponding list of FL complex structures in one-to-one correspondence with the subpatterns they matched. The matching routine also records the deepest level in the FL sentence to which the match was carried, the match-depth, and whether the match was total or partial. A match is partial if at any point, during the match of a pattern tree to the FL sentence, a mistake counter was incremented. The match-depth is a measure of how good the match of the FL sentence to the pattern list has been, and ZBIE looks at the best matches first.

When the translation of a pattern list is attempted, it may happen that some FL structure cannot be translated. For example, the structure may be an FL unit with no translation in the context considered, or it may be an FL complex part which, for the particular pattern list considered, has no corresponding subpattern to which it was matched. We then insert a Z (Z, Z1, Z2, ...) in the translation. The Z is considered by ZBIE to be the result of an unfulfilled expectation, and ZBIE capitalizes on these expectations for learning. ZBIE checks whether the translation obtained is consistent with the input NL sentence.

2.3.2 The Consistency Test. We can imagine that the translation and the input NL sentence are put side by side. We shall have consistency if we can replace the Z's of the translation by non-empty strings in NL in a unique non-ambiguous way so that the translation becomes identical to the input. Whether this can be done or not is often trivial if no two Z's are adjacent. When two or more Z's are adjacent, ZBIE does not give up but replaces the first Z by an appropriate good guess (if available; see below). The various guesses that will be tried are printed. If progress is made toward consistency, the guess is adopted (we do not have complete backtracking here), and we continue. Otherwise, guesses are tried for the second Z. If this last resort fails, the translation and the input NL sentence are not consistent.

Here we see an example of the caution ZBIE uses in learning. If we want Z Z1 to correspond to the NL string NL1 NL2 NL3, we can make the correspondence in two ways (the Z's must be matched to non-empty strings in NL):

$$Z \leftarrow NL1, Z1 \leftarrow NL2\ NL3;$$
$$Z \leftarrow NL1\ NL2, Z1 \leftarrow NL3;$$

However, if it is a good guess to assume that Z ← NL1, then we can let Z1 ← NL2 NL3.

An example from Section 3 (sentence 4) will illustrate the point. We are testing the consistency of (Z Z1) with (ТЫ ЗДЕСЬ), (Z Z1) is the translation of (be (spoken boy) here). Z comes from the unknown translation of (spoken boy) and "Z1" from the unknown translation of "here." With no additional information, ZBIE refuses to make a correspondence between the Z's and the NL words, and would find the sentence "too hard." (Strictly, we should let Z ← ТЫ, Z1 ← ЗДЕСЬ, for Z's correspond to non-empty strings, but ZBIE is too cautious to do this.) However, it is a "good guess," in this context, to assume that the translation of "here" is "ЗДЕСЬ" so that, as a result, Z ← ТЫ.

If some pattern list completely matches an FL sentence, but we obtain a total translation (without any Z's) that is not identical to the input NL, several possibilities arise:

(1) There was a mistake in the input.

(2) The translation and the input are two different ways of expressing the same situation. Here a teacher (and preferably a time-sharing situation) is needed to convey the information to ZBIE.

(3) ZBIE made an error somewhere and should try to recover from this error; good error recovery is a very difficult problem which will be considered later. At this stage, ZBIE possesses no error recovery mechanism. It was felt that trying to avoid errors was a more fruitful approach than trying to recover from them. The error-avoiding mechanism is powerful enough so that ZBIE actually makes no errors when tested on the simple sentences given as examples.

2.3.3 Processing the Pattern Lists. We now return to the basic program. The processing is slightly different for FL sentences with FL complex parts than for linear FL sentences (of depth 0). Let us describe processing for the former sentences.

2.3.3.1 PATTERN LISTS OF FL SENTENCES WITH COMPLEX PARTS

COMMENT: process pattern lists;

FOR ALL PATTERN LISTS OF THE DEEPEST LEVEL (THEN, DEEPEST LEVEL − 1, ETC...) DO ⟨TRANSLATE PATTERN LISTS;
KEEP ONLY PATTERN LISTS THAT HAVE A TRANSLATION CONSISTENT WITH THE INPUT NL; PROCESS PATTERN LISTS WITH CONSISTENT TRANSLATION, STARTING WITH THE PATTERN LISTS THAT HAVE A TRANSLATION WITH THE GREATEST NUMBER OF ELEMENTS IN COMMON WITH THE INPUT NL SENTENCE⟩

In other words, ZBIE does a translation "in parallel" of all pattern lists that matched the input FL sentence to a given depth, starting with the maximum depth (best matches) first. ZBIE then discards the pattern lists that do not give a consistent translation and starts processing the pattern lists with the best fit to the input, as measured by a set intersection with the input NL sentence.

2.3.3.1.1 Processing the Z's. Processing such a translation is equivalent to processing the Z's. Each Z_i takes the place of some untranslated FL structure, FL_i, and, through the consistency test (2.3.2 above), the Z_i is to be replaced by a non-empty NL string NL_i. From the Z_i we can also obtain such information as: to which set, A_i, did we try to match FL_i; which was the pattern, P_i, to which the father of FL_i (in the FL sentence tree) was being matched.

If FL_i is a unit, we insert FL_i in A_i and set up the in-context vocabulary (FL_i NL_i A_i P_i).

If FL_i is a complex FL, we try to create a list of subpatterns to match FL_i to NL_i (see below). If successful, we would like to insert the top subpattern of the list at the top of A_i.

Before inserting, we check to make sure that the subpattern list will not cause ambiguities. This can happen if there is already in A_i a subpattern list SP1 of which the new subpattern list SP2 is a homomorphic image, i.e., sets of SP2 are subsets of the corresponding sets of SP1 and the translations of the subpatterns in SP1 and SP2 are appropriately identical. If such a condition is satisfied (with some minor additions), no insertion takes place, "not inserted" is printed, and processing of the pattern list ends.

If an FL complex part is to be matched to a set, the backtracking matching routine will search for all the subpatterns (of the set) that will match the FL complex part. If two subpatterns can translate the FL complex part (in different ways), then a potential ambiguity is introduced in the system.

Example. In Section 3, sentence 27, the FL complex (mod this) is translated as ЭТОТ by subpattern P33 and as ЭТА by subpattern P32. The two subpatterns will cause ambiguity if they belong to the same set.

Here is another example of how ZBIE tries to avoid errors. The context in which the subpatterns were originally built was too small, and possibly later, by widening the context, subpatterns can be built without risking subsequent ambiguities.

Note that we insert the head of a subpattern list at the top of A_i so that if the same FL sentence is presented again immediately afterwards, it will be matched without any backtracking, using the subpatterns just created.

2.3.3.2 PATTERN LISTS OF LINEAR FL SENTENCES. When processing linear FL sentences, we are only concerned with top patterns. Because processing all top patterns which give a partial match would be wasteful, we process them as a stack; last-created = first-considered. However, if a pattern is considered, and its translation is just Z (nothing in NL), then "wait" is printed and the pattern is inserted at the bottom of the stack for reconsideration later, if necessary. We do this because we may well find in the stack another more satisfactory pattern with a translation that contains some NL elements and is consistent with the input.

2.3.3.2.1 Match-back. The major difference between processing linear and non-linear FL sentences, respectively, is that if we update the vocabulary by translating an FL complex part in the context of a pattern only, i. e., the translation rule of the pattern was of type (c) (see above, Section 2.2.3), then we try to further analyze and decompose the translation using exactly the same routines that were used for the initialization of the system. If successful, we create a new pattern that will have the same sets and extractors as the pattern considered, but which will have a different (and simpler) translation rule. We call this process MATCH-BACK. For an example, see Section 3, sentence 3; pattern P1 is obtained from pattern P0 by match-back.

Since we try to match an FL sentence to patterns in the reverse order in which they were created (last-pattern-created = first-tried), an FL sentence can be matched and translated by a pattern (obtained by match-back) that is newer than another pattern that would also have matched the sentence. As a result, it can happen that, effectively, some of the older patterns are never reached any more. This result can be beneficial, for some of the earlier patterns may have incorporated mistakes which will not be made again. We have here a rather elementary example of what may be called "evolutionary learning." An example in German appears in the Appendix.

2.3.3.2.2 "Try Learn More". If a linear FL sentence has been translated by a pattern Pi, and if the sentence was completely matched by some other pattern Pj which had been created after Pi, then ZBIE takes the first such pattern Pj that was considered and tries to learn from Pj, as if the sentence had not been translated. ZBIE prints "try learn more" when such a case occurs. It is the simple "try learn more" process that makes "evolutionary learning" possible. We use this process only for linear FL sentences, since, for complex FL sentences, context is essential, and the context exists largely at the level of the in-context translation rather than the level of the set inclusion tests.

2.3.4 The Pattern Creating Routine. Finally, we must consider another very important routine in ZBIE: the pattern-creating routine. Depending on an input parameter, this routine creates either a top pattern or a subpattern. We saw above how the need for new subpatterns arises. ZBIE attempts to create a top pattern when all previously described processing has failed.

The pattern-creating routine is one of the longest and most complicated in the system. Only its main parts will be described. It tries to create a list of patterns that will match the input FL complex structure FLi totally and give as a translation (after such a match) the input NL string NLi, making use of already known information.

The routine makes from one to four passes on FLi. Each pass is first performed on all appropriate elements of FLi before the next pass is begun. The main features of each pass are described next.

2.3.4.1 Outline of Pattern Creating Routine

(1) Find whether an FL unit (not a verb) in FLi already has a translation (in some context A, P) which occurs exactly in NLi. If so, when the patterns are created, associate with the set A (which will occur in some subpattern, Pj, say) the information: To translate an element in A in the context P, guess that the translation is the same as in the context A, Pj and vice versa. This is a case of the "good guess" method mentioned earlier.

(2) Find whether an FL whole (not a verb) in FLi has a translation which "looks like" some string in NLi. The test for similarity uses the first few characters of the print names of the translation and of the element in NLi. For instance, in Russian, the genitive of "boy" looks like the nominative of "boy" (remember that, because of the FL statement, we expect something that has to do with "boy"). Such a test would have to be improved to work for languages (such as Hebrew) where prefixes are added to words.

(3) Treat verbs as in (1). (Verbs vary so much that it is better to postpone guesses about them.)

(4) If some FL whole in FLi had previously been translated as the null symbol (in case of a partial translation rule, of type B, for instance), then assume that again it will be null in the NL.

After each application of the pattern-creating routine to an element of FLi, a check is made for certain terminating conditions: all FL wholes in FLi used up, all NL elements in NLi used up, or only one FL whole left unaccounted for. The system also checks for possible ambiguities. For example, suppose two different FL wholes in FLi have had identical translations, both found in NLi; there is no way to make a correspondence, and the pattern-creating routine exits with "too hard."

The next step is to build translation rules for the subpatterns created.

At this stage, only translation rules of types (a) and (b) (Section 2.2.3) are allowed. The rules are built by considering the NL string input to the routine and making sure that the FL sentence, once matched to the newly built patterns, would in fact be expressed by the given input NL string.

SECTION 3
LEARNING RUSSIAN

We present here the output of a computer run during which ZBIE attempts to learn Russian. The output has been rewritten here in a form that is more readable than the actual printer output.

Comments are given at the right of inputs, or at the end of the processing of a sentence.

Processes and Outputs			*Comments*
LOOKING AT SENTENCES 1 AND 2:			
(BE (MAN) HERE)	ОН ЗДЕСЬ		
(BE (MAN) THERE)	ОН ТАМ		
PROCESS START			The first two sentences to start the initialization.
PUT INTO VOCABULARY			"Be" is put in set A1; "(man)"
(BE (MAN))	ОН	P0	in set A2. Stores FL complex in vocabulary.
PUT INTO VOCABULARY			In-context vocabulary for FL
HERE	ЗДЕСЬ	A3 P0	unit. The FL unit "(here)" is inserted in the set.
PUT INTO VOCABULARY			
THERE	ТАМ	A3 P0	
NEW PATTERN:	P0 = A1 A2 A3; TR = ((1 2)3)		

Comment: The initialization phase is over.
Comment: "Put into vocabulary" has either three or four arguments.

Examples of both cases are illustrated above:

(1) Three arguments. The first argument is an FL complex; the second argument is an NL string; the third argument is a pattern giving the context. The translation of the FL complex in the context of the pattern is the NL string. Example: (be(man)), ОН, P0.

(2) Four arguments. The first argument is an FL unit; the second, an NL string; the third, a set; and the fourth, a pattern. The FL unit is first inserted in the set (the unit may already be in the set). The translation of the FL unit as a member of the set, in the context

of the pattern, is the NL string. We refer to the pair (set, pattern) as the context in which the translation of the FL unit is the NL string. Examples: (here, ЗДЕСЬ, A3, P0), (there, ТАМ, A3, P0).

All additions to the vocabulary are printed as described above.

Processes and Outputs	Comments
LOOKING AT SENTENCE 3:	The inputs are first printed.
(BE (SPEAKING MAN) HERE) Я ЗДЕСЬ	
PROCESS START	Then ZBIE starts processing.
TRY PATTERN P0	"be" is in A1, but
NOT MATCHED.	"(speaking man)" is not in A2.
TRY LEARN PATTERN P0	
(Z ЗДЕСЬ)	"Z" stands for the untranslated
PUT INTO VOCABULARY	FL complex, "(be(speaking man))"
(BE (SPEAKING MAN)) Я P0	
PUT INTO VOCABULARY	Pattern P1 is being built.
(SPEAKING MAN) Я A2 P1	
NEW PATTERN: P1 = A1 A2 A3, TR = (2 3)	

Comment: Pattern P1 has a p-list identical to the p-list of P0. However, the translation rules are different. ZBIE used "(be (man))→OH," and "(be (speaking man))→Я." Both translations are in the context of the pattern P0, for match-back. The comparison of the non-common parts in FL and NL gave "(speaking man)→Я in the context A2, P1." Since the NL strings used for match-back have nothing in common, "be" is assumed not to be translated, and the extractor 1 of the set A1 (which contains "be") is not used in the translation rule TR(P1). It is worth comparing this pattern P1 to the Pattern P1 created by ZBIE when learning the corresponding sentence in German (see the Appendix).

ZBIE also notes that it is a good guess to assume that the translations of a member of A3 in the contexts (A3, P0) and (A3, P1) are the same.

Processes and Outputs	Comments
LOOKING AT SENTENCE 4:	
(BE (SPOKEN BOY) HERE) ТЫ ЗДЕСЬ	
PROCESS START	
TRY PATTERN P1	
NOT MATCHED.	
TRY PATTERN P0	
NOT MATCHED.	
TRY LEARN FROM PATTERN P1	
(Z Z1)	"(spoken-boy)" is not in
GUESS: Z1 = ЗДЕСЬ	set A2, "here" is not known in the context (A3, P1), but is guessed

306 Natural Language Learning by Computer

PUT INTO VOCABULARY
    (SPOKEN BOY)   ТЫ   A2   P1
PUT INTO VOCABULARY
    HERE   ЗДЕСЬ   A3   P1

LOOKING AT SENTENCE 5:
    (BE (MAN) HERE)   ОН ЗДЕСЬ
PROCESS START
TRY PATTERN P1
RESULT: (Z ЗДЕСЬ)

TRY PATTERN P0
RESULT: (ОН ЗДЕСЬ)
TRY LEARN MORE

TRY LEARN FROM PATTERN P1
    (Z ЗДЕСЬ)
PUT IN VOCABULARY
    (MAN)   ОН   A2   P1

LOOKING AT SENTENCE 6:
    (BE (SPEAKING MAN) MAN)   Я МУЖЧИНА
PROCESS START
TRY PATTERN P1
    NOT MATCHED.

TRY PATTERN P0
    NOT MATCHED.
TRY· LEARN FROM PATTERN P1
    (Я Z)
PUT INTO VOCABULARY
    MAN   МУЖЬИНА   A3   P1

LOOKING AT SENTENCE 7:
    (BE (MAN) MAN)   ОН МУЖЧИНА
PROCESS START
TRY PATTERN P1
RESULT: (ОН МУЖЧИНА)

LOOKING AT SENTENCE 8:
    (BE (SPOKEN BOY) BOY)   ТЫ МАЛЬЧИК
PROCESS START
TRY PATTERN P1
    NOT MATCHED.
TRY PATTERN P0
    NOT MATCHED.

to be the same as in the context (A3, P0).
The translation is consistent.

Now "here" is also known in the context (A3, P1).
The first sentence again.

"(man)" is not known in the context (A2, P1).

Pattern P1 was matched entirely.

The sentence will be translated by the pattern P1 from now on.

"man" is not in the set A3. Since P0 has the same p-list as P1, the match on P0 is not attempted

A new sentence.

Translated completely.

```
TRY LEARN FROM PATTERN P1
   (ТЫ Z)
PUT INTO VOCABULARY                          Building up the vocabu-
   BOY     МАЛЬЧИК     A3    P1              lary.

LOOKING AT SENTENCE 9:
   (BE (SPOKEN GIRL) GIRL)    ТЫ ДЕВОЧКА
PROCESS START                                "(spoken girl)" is not in
                                             set A2.
TRY PATTERN P1                               "girl" is not in set A3.
   NOT MATCHED.
TRY PATTERN P0
   NOT MATCHED.
   TOO HARD
```

Two mismatches were found at one level during pattern matching, so that no pattern is close to the FL sentence. The two FL units "(spoken girl)" and "girl" cannot be translated in any context (at this stage), and no new pattern can be built to translate the sentence. Note that if ZBIE had used some of the semantics built into FL to guess that "(spoken girl)" may well have a translation identical to "(spoken boy)" in the same contexts, then the sentence could have been processed successfully at this stage. The guessed translation would have been "ТЫ Z," which is consistent with the input.

We shall hereafter omit the repetitive "try pattern...Pj...not matched...."

Processes and Outputs	*Comments*

LOOKING AT SENTENCE 10:
    (BE BOY)   ЭТО МАЛЬЧИК
 PUT INTO VOCABULARY
    BE   ЭТО   A4   P2
 PUT INTO VOCABULARY
    BOY   МАЛЬЧИК   A3   P2
 	
 NEW PATTERN: P2 = A4 A3; TR = (4 3)
	This sentence matches no previous patterns.
	 Creating pattern P2.
	 A new set.
	
	 The same translation as in the context (A3, P1).

Comments: The sentence in FL has a length of two; previous patterns expect an FL sentence of length three. To build the new pattern, ZBIE tried to find translations for the FL units in the FL sentence, which were identical or close to NL strings in the input NL. "Be" had no translation; however, "boy" had a translation, "МАЛЬЧИК," in the context (A3, P1) (see sentence 8), which is found in the input. The FL unit "be" which had not been accounted for is matched to the remaining parts of the NL input, namely "ЭТО." ZBIE also makes a note that it is a good guess to assume that the translations of an FL unit in the contexts (A3, P2) and (A3, P1) are identical.

```
LOOKING AT SENTENCE 11:
   (BE FOOT)        ЭТО НОГА
```

```
PROCESS START
TRY LEARN FROM PATTERN P2
    (ЭТО Z)
PUT INTO VOCABULARY
     FOOT    НОГА    A3    P2

LOOKING AT SENTENCE 12:                          Not a linear sentence.
    (BE FOOT [OF BOY])        ЭТО НОГА
                              МАЛЬЧИКА
PROCESS START
TRANSLATE P2
    RESULT:   (ЭТО Z)                            Z stands for the translation of the
TRY P2                                           FL complex "foot [of boy]", and, by
                                                 the consistency test, Z is to be
                                                 replaced by "НОГА МАЛЬЧИКА."
PUT INTO VOCABULARY                              Building subpatterns P39 and P38.
     BOY    МАЛЬЧИКА    A6    P38                A different translation, using a
PUT INTO VOCABULARY                              different set.
     FOOT    НОГА    A3    P39                   The same translation as in the con-
                                                 text (A3, P2).
PUT INTO SET                                     The subpattern P38 is inserted at
    P38    A7                                    the top of the set A7.
NEW PATTERN:    P38 = A5 A6; TR = (6)
NEW PATTERN:    P39 = A7 A3; TR = (3 7)
PUT INTO SET
    P39    A3
```

Comment: Let us review carefully our first encounter with a non-linear FL sentence.

At the top level, the FL sentence partly matches the pattern P2: "be" is an element of A4, but the set A3 has no subpattern members. Consequently, the FL complex "foot [of boy]" cannot be matched.

The translations in parallel of pattern lists having matched the FL sentence to the deepest match-depth are tried. This action follows "translate." Here, only one pattern, P2, is found. Then, the pattern lists with a consistent translation are tried. This action follows "try." Here we only try the pattern P2. By the consistency test, the FL complex "foot [of boy]" corresponds to the NL string "НОГА МАЛЬЧИКА" and the pattern creating routine manages to build subpatterns to match the FL complex. Note that previous knowledge has been used to avoid building a whole new top pattern.

When building the subpatterns, the translation of "foot" in the context (A3, P2) is used. The previously encountered translation of "boy" ("МАЛЬЧИК") is not found in the NL string, However, "МАЛЬЧИК" is very close to "МАЛЬЧИКА," so that the translation of "boy," in a new context, is assumed to be "МАЛЬЧИКА." Since all the words in the NL string "НОГА МАЛЬЧИКА" have been accounted for, "of" is assumed not to be translated.

The p-list of the subpattern P39 contains two sets. The set A3 contains foot (and many other FL units); the set A7 contains the subpattern P38. P38 matches the FL complex structure "[of boy]," since "of" is a member of the set A5 and "boy" is a member of the set A6.

Let us visualize the same sentence being matched again to the pattern list (P2 P39 P38). A match of the FL complex structure "foot [of boy]" is attempted against the subpattern P39, a member of A3. A match of the FL complex structure "[of boy]" is attempted against the subpattern P38, member of A7. All matches succeed. The translation rule of P2 calls for the translation of the structure "foot [of boy]" matched against P39. The translation rule of P39 calls for the translation of the element matched to A3, "foot," in the context (A3, P39), which is "НОГА," followed by the translation of the FL complex "[of boy]" matched to P38, (1). The translation rule of P38 calls for the translation of the element matched to A6, "boy," in the context (A6, P38), namely "МАЛЬЧИКА" (2). The translation routine is seen to call on itself recursively.

Note that while the pattern P39 is a member of the set A3, the P-list of P39 contains the same set A3 (i.e., P39 is a noun phrase, containing a noun), so that an infinitely recursive pattern-tree is already possible. When using more than one token of the same pattern, care must be taken to use, also, tokens of the extractors.

Pattern P38, which matches "[of boy]," is a member of the set A7. A7 precedes A3 (which contains "boy") in the P-list of the pattern P39. This peculiarity is due to the IPL-V implementation of the square-bracketed description list in FL.

Processes and Outputs				*Comments*
LOOKING AT SENTENCE 13:				
(BE HAND [OF BOY])	ЭТО РУКА			
	МАЛЬЧИКА			
PROCESS START				
TRANSLATE P2, P39, P38				The pattern list.
RESULT: ЭТО Z МАЛЬЧИКА				"hand" is not in set A3.
TRY P2, P39, P38				
PUT INTO VOCABULARY				
HAND	РУКА	A3	P39	
LOOKING AT SENTENCE 14:				
(BE HAND)	ЭТО РУКА			
PROCESS START				
TRY PATTERN P2				
RESULT: (ЭТО Z)				"hand" is not known in the
TRY LEARN FROM PATTERN P2				context (A3, P2).
(ЭТО Z)				But "hand" can be guessed,

```
GUESS Z = РУКА                            using the similar contexts
                                          (A3, P2) and (A3, P39).
LOOKING AT SENTENCE 15:
   (BE BOOK)          ЭТО КНИГА
PROCESS START
TRY LEARN FROM PATTERN P2
   (ЭТО Z)
PUT INTO VOCABULARY
      BOOK     КНИГА     A3     P2

LOOKING AT SENTENCE 16:
   (Q BE BOOK WHERE)      ГДЕ КНИГА       "Q" means question; it is a
PROCESS START                             marker, not to be translated.
PUT INTO VOCABULARY                       Building pattern P3.
      WHERE    ГДЕ     A10     P3
PUT INTO VOCABULARY
      BOOK     КНИГА     A3     P3
NEW PATTERN:   P3 = A8 A9 A3 A10; TR = (10 3)
```

Comment: Notice the translation rule.

```
LOOKING AT SENTENCE 17:
   (BE (IN (BOOK) HAND))      ОНА В РУКЕ
PROCESS START
TRANSLATE P2
   RESULT:   (ЭТО Z)                      Not consistent.
   TOO HARD
```

Because both "(book)" and "in" are unknown, a new top pattern could not be created. ZBIE will now learn "(book)," then return to the same sentence. "hand" could be guessed from the resemblance of "РУКА" to "РУКЕ."

Processes and Outputs	*Comments*

```
LOOKING AT SENTENCE 18:
   (BE (BOOK) HERE)      ОНА ЗДЕСЬ
PROCESS START
TRY LEARN FROM PATTERN P1
   (Z ЗДЕСЬ)                              Now "(book)" is known as
PUT INTO VOCABULARY                       "ОНА" in the context (A2,
      (BOOK)    ОНА     A2     P1         P1).

LOOKING AT SENTENCE 19:
   (BE (IN (BOOK) HAND))      ОНА В РУКЕ  Identical to sentence 17.
PROCESS START
TRANSLATE P2                              Not consistent.
   RESULT:   (ЭТО Z)                      Building pattern P4.
                                          A newset.
```

```
PUT INTO VOCABULARY
      HAND   РУКЕ    A13    P37
PUT INTO VOCABULARY
      IN     В       A12    P37
PUT INTO VOCABULARY
      (BOOK) ОНА     A2     P37
PUT INTO SET
   P37      A14
NEW PATTERN:    P37 = A12 A2 A13; TR = (2 12 13)
NEW PATTERN:    P4  = A11 A14; TR = (14)
```

Comment: Patterns P2 and P4 both have two sets on their p-lists, but these sets and the translation rules of the patterns are quite different. The translation rule of P37 is worth noting.

```
LOOKING AT SENTENCE 20:
   (BE (IN (BOOK) HAND OF [BOY]))    ОНА В РУКЕ
                                     МАЛЬЧИКА
PROCESS START
TRANSLATE P4, P37
   RESULT:    (ОНА В Z)
TRY P4, P37

PUT INTO VOCABULARY

      HAND   РУКЕ    A13    P36

PUT INTO VOCABULARY
      BOY    МАЛЬЧИКА  A6   P35

PUT INTO SET
   P35      A16
NEW PATTERN:    P35 = A15 A6; TR = (6)
NEW PATTERN:    P36 = A16 A13; TR = (13 16)

LOOKING AT SENTENCE 21:
   (BE PENCIL)     ЭТО КАРАНДАШ
PROCESS START
TRY LEARN FROM PATTERN P4
   (Z)
WAIT


TRY LEARN FROM PATTERN P2
   (ЭТО Z)
PUT INTO VOCABULARY
   PENCIL   КАРАНДАШ    A3    P2
```

A consistent translation. hand [of boy] corresponds to "РУКЕ МАЛЬЧИКА." Building subpatterns P36 and P35.

Not a new set (see sentence 19).

Not a new set (see sentence 12).

When the translation is just Z, we wait the first time around.

Consistent translation.

If we had processed P4 first, we would have obtained:

PUT INTO VOCABULARY
    PENCIL   ЭТО КАРАНДАШ   A14   P4

LOOKING AT SENTENCE 22:
    (Q BE PENCIL WHERE)   ГДЕ КАРАНДАШ
PROCESS START
TRY PATTERN P3   "pencil" is not known in the context (A3, P3).

    (ГДЕ Z)
TRY LEARN FROM PATTERN P3   However, the translation
    (ГДЕ Z)   of "pencil" can be guessed
GUESS Z = КАРАНДАШ   from the context (A3, P2)
                                            to this context, (A3, P3).

PUT INTO VOCABULARY
    PENCIL   КАРАНДАШ   A3   P3

If "good guesses" had been used, this sentence would have been translated.

LOOKING AT SENTENCE 23:
    (BE (PENCIL) THERE)   ОН ТАМ
PROCESS START
TRY LEARN FROM PATTERN P1
    (Z Z1)
GUESS Z1 = ТАМ   The guess makes the translation consistent with the input.

PUT INTO VOCABULARY
    (PENCIL)   ОН   A2   P1   More vocabulary.
PUT INTO VOCABULARY
    THERE   ТАМ   A3   P1

LOOKING AT SENTENCE 24:
    (BE (IN (PENCIL) DRAWER))   ОН В ЯЩИКЕ
PROCESS START
TRANSLATE P4, P37
    RESULT: (Z В Z1)   Even without the guess,
GUESS Z = ОН   the translation is consistent with the NL input.

TRY P4, P37
PUT INTO VOCABULARY
    (PENCIL)   ОН   A2   P37
PUT INTO VOCABULARY
    DRAWER   ЯЩИКЕ   A13   P37

LOOKING AT SENTENCE 25:
    (BE BOY [MOD THIS] HERE)   ЭТОТ МАЛЬЧИК
                                        ЗДЕСЬ

```
PROCESS START
TRANSLATE P1
    RESULT:    (Z ЗДЕСЬ)
TRY P1
PUT INTO VOCABULARY                          Building subpatterns P34
                                             and P33.
        THIS    ЭТОТ     A18      P33
PUT INTO VOCABULARY
        BOY     МАЛЬЧИК  A3       P34
PUT INTO SET
    P33         A19
NEW PATTERN:   P33 = A17 A18; TR = (18)
NEW PATTERN:   P34 = A19 A3; TR = (19 3)
PUT INTO SET
    P34         A2

LOOKING AT SENTENCE 26:
    (BE GIRL)       ЭТО ДЕВОЧКА
PROCESS START
TRY LEARN FROM PATTERN P4
    (Z)
WAIT
TRY LEARN FROM PATTERN P2
    (ЭТО Z)
PUT INTO VOCABULARY
        GIRL    ДЕВОЧКА   A3      P2

LOOKING AT SENTENCE 27:                      This is identical with sen-
                                             tence 9, which had been
                                             found too hard previously.

    (BE (SPOKEN GIRL) GIRL)      ТЫ ДЕВОЧКА
PROCESS START
TRY LEARN FROM PATTERN P1                    Now, we use the transla-
    (Z Z1)                                   tion of "girl" in the con-
GUESS Z1 = ДЕВОЧКА                           text (A3, P2) as a guess
                                             (see sentence 26).
PUT INTO VOCABULARY
        (SPOKEN GIRL)   ТЫ      A2      P1
PUT INTO VOCABULARY
        GIRL    ДЕВОЧКА   A3      P1

LOOKING AT SENTENCE 28:
    (BE GIRL [MOD THIS] HERE)       ЭТА ДЕВОЧКА
                                    ЗДЕСЬ
PROCESS START
MATCHED PATTERN-LIST P1, P34, P33            Pattern-list matching the
                                             FL
    RESULT:    (ЭТОТ Z ЗДЕСЬ)                sentence to a match-depth
                                             of 2. Not consistent.
```

314 Natural Language Learning by Computer

TRANSLATE P1, P34   Pattern list matching the FL

    RESULT: (Z Z1 ЗДЕСЬ)   sentence to a match-depth of 1.

GUESS Z1 = ДЕВОЧКА   With the guess, the translation is consistent with the NL input.

TRY P1, P34
PUT INTO VOCABULARY
     THIS   ЭТА   A21   P32
NEW PATTERN P32 = A20 A21; TR = (21)
    NOT INSERTED   See comments below.
TRANSLATE P1   Pattern-list matching the FL sentence to a match-depth of 0.

    RESULT: (Z ЗДЕСЬ)   Consistent with input. Z takes the place of "girl [mod this]."
TRY P1

PUT INTO VOCABULARY   Building subpatterns P30 and P31.

     GIRL   ДЕВОЧКА   A3   P31
PUT INTO VOCABULARY
     THIS   ЭТА   A21   P30
PUT INTO SET
    P30   A23
NEW PATTERN: P30 = A22 A21; TR = (21)
NEW PATTERN: P31 = A23 A3; TR = (23 3)
PUT INTO SET
   P31 A2

    Here is our first encounter with ZBIE's look-ahead capabilities. The FL sentence is first matched to a match-depth of 2 by the pattern-list (P1 P34 P33) but the translation is not consistent with the NL input, since the first NL words of the translation and input are different. Next, the FL sentence is matched to a match-depth of 1 by the pattern-list (P1 P34). The FL structure "[mod this]" has no corresponding subpattern and therefore contributes the unknown Z(=Z0) to the translation of the FL sentence. "girl" is not known in the context (A3, P34), and contributes the unknown Z1. Since the translation of "girl" can be correctly guessed, the translation of the FL sentence is consistent with the input. The unknown Z takes the place of the FL structure "[mod this]" and, by the consistency test, is to be replaced by "ЭТО." The subpattern P32 is created to match the FL structure "[mod this]," giving as a translation "ЭТО." P32 is to be inserted in the set A19 of the p-list of P34. However, A19 contains the subpattern P33 which is isomorphic to P32. (We would only require that P32 be a homomorphic image of a subpattern in A19.) P32 is not inserted in A19 and the next pattern list is tried. Sentence 30 will provide another example of the same techniques.

Processes and Outputs	*Comments*

```
LOOKING AT SENTENCE 29:
    (BE TREE)    ЭТО ДЕРЕВО
PROCESS START
TRY LEARN FROM PATTERN P4
    (Z)
WAIT
TRY LEARN FROM PATTERN P2
PUT INTO VOCABULARY
        TREE    ДЕРЕВО    A3    P2

LOOKING AT SENTENCE 30:
    (BE TREE [MOD THIS] HERE)    ЭТО ДЕРЕВО
                                 ЗДЕСЬ
PROCESS START
MATCHED PATTERN-LIST P1, P31, P30
    RESULT:    (ЭТО Z ЗДЕСЬ)
```
"tree" is not known in the context (A3, P31), but can be guessed from the context (A3, P2). The result is not consistent.

```
MATCHED PATTERN-LIST P1, P34, P33
```
"tree" is not known in the context (A3, P34), but can be guessed from the context (A3, P2).

```
    RESULT:    (ЭТОТ Z1 ЗДЕСЬ)
TRANSLATE P1, P31
```
Not consistent.
Pattern-list with match-depth of 1.

```
    RESULT: (Z Z1 ЗДЕСЬ)
GUESS Z1 = ДЕРЕВО
TRANSLATE P1, P34
```
Consistent after guess.

Also a pattern-list with match-depth of 1, translated in parallel with the above pattern-list (P1, P31).

```
    RESULT: (Z2 Z3 ЗДЕСЬ)
GUESS Z3 = ДЕРЕВО
TRY P1, P31
```
Consistent after guess.

No preference between the pattern-lists, so try the first one considered.

```
PUT INTO VOCABULARY
        THIS    ЭТО    A25    P29
```
Building subpattern P29.

NEW PATTERN: P29 = A24 A25; TR = (25)
   NOT INSERTED   P29 is isomorphic to P30.
TRY P1, P34   The next pattern-list.
PUT INTO VOCABULARY   Building subpattern P29.
     THIS   ЭТО   A25   P28
NEW PATTERN: P28 = A26 A25; TR = (25)
   NOT INSERTED   P28 is isomorphic to P33.
TRANSLATE P1   Pattern-list with match-
                                         depth of 0.
   RESULT: (Z ЗДЕСЬ)
TRY P1
PUT INTO VOCABULARY   Building subpatterns P27
                                         and P26.
     TREE   ДЕРЕВО   A3   P27
PUT INTO VOCABULARY
     THIS   ЭТО   A25   P26   "ЭТО" was also the trans-
                                         lation of "be" in the
                                         context (A4, P2).
PUT INTO SET
   P26   A28
NEW PATTERN: P26 = A27 A25; TR = (25)
NEW PATTERN: P27 = A28 A3; TR = (28 3)
PUT INTO SET
   P27   A2

LOOKING AT SENTENCE 31:
   (BE BOY [MOD THAT] THERE)   ТОТ МАЛЬЧИК
                                 ТАМ
PROCESS START   Pattern-lists (P1 P27 P26),
TRANSLATE P1, P27, P26   (P1 P31 P30) and (P1 P34
                                         P33) all match the FL
                                         sentence to a match-depth
                                         of 2 and are translated in
                                         parallel.
   RESULT: (Z Z1 ТАМ)   Consistent after guess.
GUESS Z1 = МАЛЬЧИК
TRANSLATE P1, P31, P30
   RESULT: (Z2 Z3 ТАМ)   Consistent after guess.
GUESS Z3 = МАЛЬЧИК
TRANSLATE P1, P34, P33
   RESULT: (Z4 МАЛЬЧИК)   Consistent with input.
TRY P1, P34, P33   The translation of the
                                         pattern-list (P1 P34 P33)
                                         is closest to the NL input,
                                         and (P1 P34 P33) is tried
                                         first.

PUT INTO VOCABULARY
     THAT   ТОТ   A18   P33

If ZBIE had processed the pattern-lists, starting with those of deepest match-depth, in the order in which they are considered, then it would have started processing the pattern-list (P1 P27 P26). ZBIE would then have created the following vocabulary entries:

```
THAT    TOT       A25   P26
BOY     МАЛЬЧИК   A3    P27
```

The last entry would now assure the (incorrect) translation of "(be boy [mod this] here)" as "ЗТО МАЛЬЧИК ЗДЕСЬ." The next example is a slight variation of this one.

LOOKING AT SENTENCE 32:
    (BE GIRL [MOD THAT] THERE)   ТА ДЕВОЧКА
PROCESS START   ТАМ
MATCHED PATTERN LIST P1, P34, P33

"girl" is not known in the context (A3, P34). Not consistent.

    RESULT: (TOT Z TAM)
TRANSLATE P1, P27, P26

Translate pattern-lists (P1 P27 P28) and (P1 P31 P30) in parallel. Consistent after guess.

    RESULT: (Z Z1 TAM)
GUESS Z1 = ДЕВОЧКА
TRANSLATE P1, P31, P30
    RESULT: (Z2 ДЕВОЧКА ТАМ)
TRY P1, P31

Consistent. Pattern-list (P1 P31 P30) gives a translation closest to the NL input.

PUT INTO VOCABULARY
    THAT   TA   A21   P30

LOOKING AT SENTENCE 33:
    (BE HAND [OF (SPEAKING MAN)])   ЭТО МОЯ
    РУКА
PROCESS START
TRANSLATE P2, P39, P38
    RESULT: (ЭТО РУКА Z)

Match-depth of 2. Not consistent.

TRANSLATE P2, P39
    RESULT: (ЭТО РУКА Z)

Match-depth of 1. Not consistent.

TRANSLATE P4

Translate in parallel P4 and P2 (match-depth 0).

    RESULT: (Z)
TRANSLATE P2
    RESULT: (ЭТО Z1)

The translation due to P2 is closest to the NL input. Building subpatterns P25 and P24.

PUT INTO VOCABULARY

    (SPEAKING MAN)   МОЯ   A30   P24

PUT INTO VOCABULARY
    HAND   РУКА   A3   P25
PUT INTO SET
    P24   A31
NEW PATTERN: P24 = A29 A30; TR = (30)
NEW PATTERN;   P25 = A31 A3; TR = (31 3)
PUT INTO SET
    P25   A3

LOOKING AT SENTENCE 34:
    (BE HAND [OF (SPOKEN BOY)])   ЭТО ТВОЯ РУКА
PROCESS START
TRANSLATE P2, P25, P24   Translate in parallel pattern lists (P2 P25 P24) and (P2 P39 P38) which matched the FL sentence to a depth of 2. Consistent.
    RESULT: (ЭТО Z РУКА)
TRANSLATE P2, P39, P38
    RESULT: (ЭТО РУКА Z1)   Not consistent.
TRY P2, P25, P24
PUT INTO VOCABULARY
    (SPOKEN BOY)   ТВОЯ   A30   P24

LOOKING AT SENTENCE 35:
    (BE (ON (BOOK) HAND))   ОНА НА РУКЕ
PROCESS START
TRANSLATE P4, P37
    RESULT: (ОНА Z РУКЕ)
TRY P4, P37
PUT INTO VOCABULARY
    ON   НА   A12   P37

Comment: This slightly unnatural sentence was added to afford a smooth transition toward the next sentence without building a new subpattern. See the comments at the end of sentence 36.

LOOKING AT SENTENCE 36:
    (BE (ON (BOOK) TABLE))   ОНА НА СТОЛЕ
PROCESS START
TRANSLATE P4, P37
    RESULT: (ОНА НА Z)   "table" is not known in the context (A13, P37).
TRY P37
PUT INTO VOCABULARY
    TABLE   СТОЛЕ   A13   P37

Assume that: (a) this sentence had been presented before sentence 35;

(b) "table" was known in some context, for instance as "СТОЛ" (nominative); and (c) "on" was not known (which was the case here). Then ZBIE would have built a new subpattern by: (a) guessing "table" from the previous print-name; by pairing "(book)" with one acceptable translation, "ОНА," of "(book);" (c) assigning "on" to the still unaccounted for NL string "НА." The new subpattern would have been inserted in the set All, on the p-list of P4.

Actually, it is not necessary to build a new subpattern. The new FL sentence fits into the previous pattern structure if we are careful to give enough intermediary sentences, such as sentence 35.

ZBIE tends to generate too many sets and patterns. It would be interesting to give ZBIE the capability to re-organize its structures, for example by merging some sets or some patterns.

Processes and Outputs	Comments
LOOKING AT SENTENCE 37:	
(FUTURE TAKE (SPEAKING MAN) BOOK)	"future" is a marker in
Я ВОЗЬМУ КНИГУ	FL, not to be translated.
PROCESS START	
PUT INTO VOCABULARY	Building pattern P5.
BOOK КНИГУ A34 P5	
PUT INTO VOCABULARY	
TAKE ВОЗЬМУ A33 P5	
PUT INTO VOCABULARY	
(SPEAKING MAN) Я A5 P5	
NEW PATTERN: P5 = A32 A33 A2 A34; TR = (2 33 34)	

SECTION 4
A CRITICAL LOOK AT ZBIE

Uhr's programs (1964) provide an illuminating contrast to some of the mechanisms used by ZBIE. Uhr shows outputs for two programs and describes a planned third program. All his programs learn to translate a natural language, NL1, into another natural language, NL2.

The first program was applied to translate German into English. Words are separated by blanks. The program does not use context and runs into difficulties on that account. For example, "das" in the German "das ist" or "das Glas" is translated "this" or "the," respectively. Uhr's first program cannot handle such a difficulty.

The second program, which was applied to translate English into French, is more powerful in several ways. Words are not separated, and one function of the program is to separate important elements in a continuous flow. For instance, the "s" marking a plural can be separated. It is also more difficult to translate a language with little inflection, such as English, into a more inflected language, such as French, than to translate an inflected language, German, into English. In the latter case, an expanded dictionary often suffices, while in the former case, context is essential.

To obtain context, classes are built on elements of NL2. Class clusters are used to resolve ambiguities and generalize permutations. In the given output, though, the program does not seem to learn the generalized permutation: adjective + noun → noun + adjective.

The third (projected) program is a strengthening of program 2. It can generate classes of classes, i.e., encompass groups of words.

All three programs use statistical weights for learning and unlearning. It appears that some assumptions are made of the corresponding word orders of the languages. In the given example 1, from: "ich bin ein Mann → I am a man," the inferences "ich → I," "bin → am," "ein → a," "Mann → man" seem to be drawn; in example 3, from: "if the boy → si le garçon" and "the → le," the inferences "if → si," "boy → garçon" seem to be drawn.

Let us apply some of the above criteria to ZBIE. Inputs to ZBIE are well separated words, and ZBIE's string manipulating capabilities are limited to checking whether the first few characters of two words are identical or not. ZBIE tries to translate from a non-inflected language (FL) into another language, which will usually be inflected. The classes used by Uhr's programs are built on NL2; the corresponding sets are built on FL, equivalent to NL1, by ZBIE. The classes of classes described by Uhr for the projected program may correspond to the recursive hierarchy (sub)pattern—set—subpattern. ZBIE makes few assumptions about word order, and hence was able to learn the sentences exhibited in Section 3 when the Russian sentences had all been previously inverted, just as readily as when they were given in their natural order. From the examples given by Uhr, it does not appear that either of his two actual programs could learn to translate from NL1 to an inverted NL2.

All the programs build structures at run-time and use these structures for additional learning, which may include building new structures. Using a uniform, structured representation, such as FL, which is in some sense "understood," gives ZBIE a great advantage over a flat string input, but destroys the symmetry that Uhr's programs possess. It may be that structures as powerful as (or even more powerful than) those built in FL can be constructed eventually by programs starting from (unstructured) strings.

We have already encountered various deficiencies in ZBIE. Some of these could be solved by more programming; others necessitate a thorough rethinking of the learning task.

Among remediable deficiencies we should mention:

—The initialization phase is inflexible. Sentences could be stored until two sentences meet the conditions for initializing the first pattern.

—The translation rules should be more general. We mentioned in Section 2.2 two additional kinds of translation rules which are presently not used by ZBIE.

—The methods for obtaining good guesses should be improved. These methods could use, for instance, some of the semantics built into FL (see below).

—The string manipulating capabilities should be more versatile. In particular, prefixes and suffixes should be discovered, thereby allowing generalizations of translations for example, obtaining the translation of an element FLi in some other context Aj, Pj.

—A pattern should admit several translation rules to reflect different ways in which the same situation can be expressed in NL.

—As the number of (sub)patterns increases, heuristics (perhaps of a semantic nature) must be used to speed up search during matching.

—At present, the context of the main verb is the whole pattern, so that, as the same verb (in FL) changes (in NL), a new top pattern is created. In this way, the number of patterns increases much too rapidly.

Besides structure, we tried to build some semantics into FL. We can specify the referent of a pronoun. We can index, if necessary, several persons appearing in a situation to differentiate among them, just as they may be differentiated in a picture. Until now, however, no use has been made of the content of the situations.

A first step, not completely implemented, is to use findings such as: the subject pronouns "(man)" and "(boy)" have identical translations in Russian. We could use this finding to make good guesses on how "man" and "boy" will behave in similar situations. We could also use the functional language description of: "(speaking man [number 2])," "(speaking (and man woman))," and so on, to obtain the notion of "(speaking plural)."

A second step would be to process jointly several situations that are dynamically related. Sequences such as: "the book is on the table, I shall take the book in my hand, I am taking the book, the book is in my hand, it was on the table, etc." are used by I. A. Richards to teach tenses.

A simple scheme of set inclusion tests, as used by ZBIE, is not powerful enough by itself to learn, for example, the Russian reflexive possessive "СВОЙ". A more powerful scheme which looks at correlations among elements in the functional language is needed, i.e., in the FL sentence

(put (personl) (in hat [of (person2)] drawer))

are "personl" and "person2" the same?

The above deficiencies can be overcome by making better use of FL.

The purpose of FL was described in Section 2. Undoubtedly, the "vision of the world" as represented by FL is very close to an Indo-European's "vision of the world." It may be possible that a system could discard the functional language and bootstrap itself to look at the world in the learned natural language.

Programming ZBIE has been a worthwhile experience. The program generated some surprises. The mechanisms for avoiding errors were not very clear at the start. The advantage in translating in parallel pattern lists of a given depth had not been foreseen; it was thought that a simple historic monitor "last-pattern-list-obtained = first-tried" would be adequate.

At present, the pattern-building routines can handle only FL elements that have single NL words as translations. (This limitation can be overcome by additional programming.) Consequently, ZBIE would branch to an empty exit when trying to process, in French, "pencil → LE CRAYON" (two NL words). Dealing with articles, mostly unnecessary but cumbersome symbols, poses some problems. If "pencil → LE CRAYON," and if we also know that "bed → LE LIT" and "wall → LE MUR," we could conclude that "LE" is an unnecessary symbol. Then if we meet "pencil → UN CRAYON" (possibly), we can assume that "UN" is also an unnecessary object. The scheme collapses promptly, though, when we meet "pencil → SON CRAYON" ("his or her pencil"). Here a teacher may well be needed.

A good teaching sequence is probably very important. But even with a good sequence, a time will come when some bad generalizations have been made, and these must be unlearned. ZBIE is careful enough that, at the elementary level considered, error recovery is not needed. We have no exciting scheme to propose. For error recovery, it appears that suitable changes in set memberships may be sufficient in some cases, but additional work at a more advanced level of language proficiency is in order.

SECTION 5
ENVOI

ZBIE is a program of medium length (about 5000 lines of IPL-V code) that tries to solve some aspects of a task that may or may not be very difficult: natural language learning. ZBIE interprets the task as learning to express in a natural language situations as described in a uniform, structured functional language, which may be considered as giving some content to the situations. In the actual program, very little of the power of the functional language is used.

To learn a language, ZBIE builds elementary structures at run-time:

sets, patterns, simple translation rules, an in-context vocabulary. It is capable of improving its structure somewhat, so that a previously learned instance can be learned in a better way. It does not use statistical learning schemes. It has some error-avoiding capability, and has potential error-recovery possibilities that were actually not needed at the modest level considered here. ZBIE uses context both to learn and to avoid errors.

Given situations are parsed in the functional language, not in the natural language; the parsing gives a measure of how close a new situation is to certain classes of previously encountered situations. ZBIE tries to minimize its learning at each stage by trying to capitalize on the maximum amount of information available from previous situations, measured, quite simply, by the depth to which a new situation is parsed by a collection of patterns. In fact, ZBIE abandons the learning task when faced with situations that it considers too difficult to handle at a given stage. Since it can diagnose the particular difficulties it encounters, ZBIE could ask appropriate questions in a time-sharing environment.

It would appear that the functional language should possess in its description all the semantic subtleties of the natural language to be learned, an unappealing notion. A much more powerful system may be able to bootstrap itself and use the natural language it has started to learn as its main representation, with possible references from time to time to the functional language. Semantic subtleties could then be described in the natural language itself.

It appears to be fruitful to look at natural languages as a means for expressing situations with structure and content. Much valuable research can be done in areas touched upon by ZBIE, among which (1) designing more powerful, semantically oriented, functional languages; (2) finding solutions to the problem of error recovery; and (3) implementing the evolutionary reorganization and improvement of structures may well be the most interesting and challenging.

APPENDIX
EVOLUTIONARY LEARNING

We present here a short example, in German, exhibiting an aspect of ZBIE's capabilities. The translation rule for pattern P1 is incorrect. As more examples are given, however, ZBIE builds new patterns P2 and P3. The sentences that were previously translated with P1 are now translated when patterns P2 or P3 are found, so that pattern P1 is not reached any more. Pattern P1 has effectively been washed out.

Processes and Outputs	Comments

LOOKING AT SENTENCE
   (BE (WOMAN) HERE)   SIE IST HIER
   (BE (WOMAN) THERE)   SIE IST DORT

PROCESS START
PUT INTO VOCABULARY
   (BE (WOMAN))   (SIE IST)   P0

PUT INTO VOCABULARY
   HERE   HIER   A3   P0

The first two sentences to start the initialization be is in set A1; "(woman)" in set A2 Context vocabulary for FL complex.

In-context vocabulary for FL unit. The FL unit (in this case, "here") is inserted in the set (in this case, A3).

PUT INTO VOCABULARY
   THERE   DORT   A3   P0
NEW PATTERN: P0 = A1 A2 A3; TR = ((1 2)3)

   Comment: The initialization phase is over.

LOOKING AT SENTENCE
   (BE (MAN [NUMB 2]) THERE)   SIE SIND DORT
PROCESS START

TRY PATTERN P0
   NOT MATCHED.
TRY LEARN FROM PATTERN P0
   (Z DORT)
PUT INTO VOCABULARY
   (BE (MAN [NUMB 2]))   (SIE SIND)   P0
PUT INTO VOCABULARY
   (MAN [NUMB 2])   SIND   A2   P1
PUT INTO VOCABULARY
   BE   SIE   A1   P1
NEW PATTERN: P1 = A1 A2 A3; TR = (1 2 3)

The inputs are first printed.

"(be(man[numb 2])" is the untranslated part, corresponding to Z. Pattern P1 is being built.

   Comment: Pattern P1 has a p-list identical to the p-list of P0. However, the translation rules are different. ZBIE used "(be(woman))→SIE IST," and "(be(man[numb 2]))→SIE SIND," both translations in the context of the pattern P0, for match-back. The common parts in FL and NL, respectively "be" and "SIE," were paired. The comparison of the non-common parts gave "(man[numb 2])→SIND (context A2, P1)." The inference is grammatically incorrect. Note that the translation rule is (1 2 3), in the same order as the sets. It is well worth comparing this pattern P1 to the pattern P1 created by ZBIE when learning Russian (see Section 3).

LOOKING AT SENTENCE		
(BE (WOMAN) HERE)	SIE IST HIER	
PROCESS START		The first sentence again.
TRY PATTERN P1		
RESULT: (SIE Z Z1)		"(woman)" and "here" are not known in the contexts (A2, P1) and (A3, P1) and contribute Z and Z1, respectively.
TRY PATTERN P0		
RESULT: (SIE IST HIER)		
TRY LEARN MORE		The pattern P1 was the first to be totally matched, but was not successfully translated.
TRY LEARN FROM PATTERN P1		
(SIE Z Z1)		
GUESS Z1 = HIER		Z (i.e., "(woman)") is not guessed but Z1 is, giving a translation consistent with the input.
PUT INTO VOCABULARY		
(WOMAN) IST A2 P1		
PUT INTO VOCABULARY		
HERE HIER A3 P1		Now "here" is also known in the context (A3, P1).

Comment: Now (be (woman) here) will be translated by pattern P1.

LOOKING AT SENTENCE		
(BE (MAN) HERE)	ER IST HIER	A new sentence.
PROCESS START		
TRY PATTERN P1		
NOT MATCHED.		"(man)" is not in A2.
TRY PATTERN P0		As the p-lists of P0 and P1 are identical, it is not necessary
NOT MATCHED.		to actually match P0.
TRY LEARN FROM PATTERN P1		
(SIE Z HIER)		Not consistent with input.
TRY LEARN FROM PATTERN P0		
(Z HIER)		Z stands for the unknown translation of "(be(man))"
PUT INTO VOCABULARY		
(BE (MAN)) ER IST P0		
PUT INTO VOCABULARY		Creating pattern P2.
(MAN) ER A2 P2		
PUT INTO VOCABULARY		
BE IST A1 P2		
NEW PATTERN: P2 = A1 A2 A3; TR = (2 1 3)		

Comment: We matched back "(be(man))→ER IST" and "(be(woman))→SIE IST" to obtain a new pattern P2. The translation rule of P2, (2 1 3), is different from the translation rule of P1 and is grammatically correct. Note that the translation rule contains a transformation.

```
LOOKING AT SENTENCE                                        Again the first sentence.
    (BE (WOMAN) HERE)         SIE IST HIER
PROCESS START
TRY PATTERN P2
    RESULT:   (Z IST Z1)
TRY PATTERN P1
    RESULT:   (SIE IST HIER)                               Now translated by P1.
TRY LEARN MORE
TRY LEARN FROM PATTERN P2
    (Z IST Z1)
GUESS Z1 = HIER
PUT INTO VOCABULARY
        HERE     HIER     A3     P2
PUT INTO VOCABULARY
        (WOMAN)     SIE     A2     P2                      Now the sentence will be
                                                           translated by P2.
LOOKING AT SENTENCE                                        A new sentence.

    (BE (SPEAKING MAN [NUMB 2]) HERE)      WIR
                                           SIND
                                           HIER

PROCESS START
TRY PATTERN P3                                             "(speaking man[numb
    NOT MATCHED.                                           2])" is not in A2.
TRY PATTERN P1
    NOT MATCHED.
TRY PATTERN P0
    NOT MATCHED.
TRY LEARN FROM PATTERN P2
    (Z IST HIER)                                           Not consistent with in-
                                                           put.
TRY LEARN FROM PATTERN P1
    (SIE Z HIER)
TRY LEARN FROM PATTERN P0
    (Z HIER)
PUT INTO VOCABULARY
    (BE (SPEAKING MAN [NUMB 2]))      WIR SIND
                                      P0
PUT INTO VOCABULARY                                        Creating pattern P3.
    (SPEAKING MAN [NUMB 2])    WIR     A2     P3
PUT INTO VOCABULARY
    BE     SIND     A1     P3
NEW PATTERN:   P3 = A1 A2 A3; TR = (2 1 3)
```

Comment: The translation rules of P3 and P2 are identical, but "be" is translated differently in the contexts (A1, P2) and (A1, P3).

```
LOOKING AT SENTENCE                                        The third sentence again
    (BE (MAN [NUMB 2]) THERE)      SIE SIND DORT
```

PROCESS START
TRY PATTERN P3
   RESULT: (Z SIND Z1)
TRY PATTERN P2
   RESULT: (Z IST Z1)
TRY PATTERN P1
   RESULT: (SIE SIND Z)
TRY PATTERN P0
   RESULT: (SIE SIND DORT)
TRY LEARN MORE
TRY LEARN FROM PATTERN P3
   (Z SIND Z1)   The translation is con-
GUESS Z1 = DORT   sistent with the input
                                           even without the guess
                                           of Z1.

PUT INTO VOCABULARY
     THERE   DORT   A3   P3
PUT INTO VOCABULARY
     (MAN [NUMB 2])   SIE   A2   P3   Now the sentence will be
                                                     translated by P3.

Comment: We now give sentences one and three again, and show how they are translated by P2 and P3 respectively. The pattern P1 is not reached any more.

LOOKING AT SENTENCE
   (BE (WOMAN) HERE)   SIE IST HIER
PROCESS START
TRY PATTERN P3
   RESULT: (Z SIND Z1)
TRY PATTERN P2
   RESULT: (SIE IST HIER)
TRY LEARN MORE
TRY LEARN FROM PATTERN P3
   (Z SIND Z1)   Not consistent.

LOOKING AT SENTENCE
   (BE (MAN [NUMB 2]) THERE)   SIE SIND DORT
PROCESS START
TRY PATTERN P3
   RESULT: (SIE SIND DORT)

References

CHOMSKY, N. and MILLER, G. A. Introduction the formal analysis of natural languages. *In* Luce, R. D., Bush, R., and Galanter, E. *Handbook of Mathematical Psychology*, Vol. 2. New York: Wiley & Sons, 1963, p. 277.

McCarthy, J., et al. *LISP 1.5 Programmers Manual.* Cambridge, Mass.: MIT Press, 1963.

Newell, A., et al. *Information Processing Language-V Manual.* Englewood Cliffs, N. J.: Prentice-Hall, 1964.

Pivar, M. and Finkelstein, M. Automation, using LISP, of inductive inference on sequences. *The Programming Language LISP,* Information International, Inc., Cambridge, Mass., 1964, pp. 125–136.

Reichenbach, H. *Elements of Symbolic Logic.* New York: Macmillan, 1947.

Richards, I. A., et al. *Russian Through Pictures, Book I.* New York: Washington Square Press, 1961. There are similar books for English, French, Hebrew, Italian, Spanish, and German.

Simon, H. A. and Kotovsky, K. Human acquisition of concepts for sequential patterns. *Psychological Review* Vol. 70, No. 6, 1963, pp. 534–546.

Solomonoff, R. J. The mechanization of linguistic learning. *Proceedings of the Second International Congress on Cybernetics,* Wamur, Belgium, 1960, pp. 180–193.

Solomonoff, R. J. A formal theory of inductive inference. *Information and Control,* 1964, pp. 1–22, 224–254.

Solomonoff, R. J. Some recent work in artificial intelligence. *Proceedings of the IEEE* Vol. 54, No. 12, Dec. 1966, pp. 1687–1697.

Uhr, L. Pattern string learning programs. *Behavioral Science* Vol. 9, July 1964, pp. 258–270.

Part IV

REPRESENTATION BY DESCRIPTION AND MODELING

The two chapters of this part leave linguistic questions to return to more general issues of internal representation. In artificial intelligence approaches to problem solving, two main views have been in evidence. In schemes like the General Problem Solver, and in most extant game-playing schemes, the initial problem situation is represented explicitly—is *modeled*. The operations or moves that are considered alter this situation in order to calculate the consequences of their application, and to discover a sequence of changes that will produce a preferred or goal situation.

The alternative idea in the Advice Taker, first proposed by John McCarthy, was to solve problems by using modal reasoning, that is, a system of logic embodying such concepts as "cause" and "can." (It is unfortunate that the labels for these alternative views—model and modal—should differ by only a single letter, but both terms are solidly established by usage, and we shall have to depend on impeccable proofreading to keep them properly distinguished.) An advice-taking program solves problems by searching for a deduction which proves the existence of a sequence of *possible* actions and their outcomes that will *cause* the desired goal state to be attained.

Pople's *Goal-Oriented Language* (GOL) is a problem-solving language that combines capabilities both of modal reasoning and of search in a model. It provides, therefore, an exceedingly useful environment and piece of machinery for examining the relation between these two approaches, their relative strengths and weaknesses. Simon's chapter, which brings the volume to a close, discusses the theoretical issues surrounding the two approaches. This chapter can profitably be read against the background of John McCarthy's 1958 essay, "Programs With Common Sense," reprinted in Minsky (ed.), *Semantic Information Processing*, pp. 403–418, on which it is a commentary.

A particular virtue of the GOL language for theoretical investigations is that most of the classical problem-solving programs can be represented in it rather simply and directly. Thus, Pople uses as illustrations GOL programs for the Logic Theorist, the General Problem Solver, a Chess Mating Combinations Program, and others.

Both chapters in this part explore the Monkey-and-Banana problem, which has become the stock example for discussions of the model-modal distinction. The problem is borrowed from Köhler's famous experiments on the problem-solving capabilities of apes. A bunch of bananas is hung so that a monkey can reach them only by fitting together two parts of a long stick and knocking them down (alternatively, by putting a stool under them and climbing on it). This deceptively simple (for adult humans!) problem illustrates very clearly what is required in order to model the situation and search in the space of the model, as well as what is required in order to reason, modally, about what is to be done.

In the research reported in this part of the book, as in the earlier parts, we are still in the stage of seeking basic conceptual and theoretical understanding. The computer languages and programs that have been built to explore problems of representation and meaning are still mainly demonstration programs—capable of illuminating issues, but not designed as practical workhorses. Their limited power and generality and the toy problems to which they have been applied should not lead us to dismiss or undervalue the important clarification in the concepts of representation and meaning that have already been attained with their help.

Chapter 7

A GOAL-ORIENTED LANGUAGE FOR THE COMPUTER

Harry E. Pople, Jr.

SECTION 1
INTRODUCTION

Unlike the algebraic computer languages—ALGOL, MAD, FORTRAN, etc.—which are oriented toward numerical computation, GOL is designed to deal with computations involving relations defined on arbitrary symbolic domains. Depending on the interpretations attached to these non-numerical relations, we may think of them as defining concepts, patterns, and other conditions that may characterize some problem, conflict, or other decision-making situation. Such concepts as "checkmate" in chess, "theorem" in a deductive theory, and "goal attainment" in other problem-solving situations are examples of non-numerical relations that are expressible in the GOL language.

Associated with the language is a compiler that maps verbal descriptions of relations, represented by GOL expressions, into algorithms that either *test* or *generate* instances of the described relations. The actions of these GOL evaluation processes may be interpreted in various ways depending on the context and interpretations of the relations involved. For example, a generator process based on a GOL expression of the relation "checkmate" could be thought of as a chess pattern recognizer. On the other hand, a test process based on a description of the *modal* concept, "checkmate is achievable," would be considered a chess problem-solving program. Other processes based on descriptions of other non-numerical relations might be regarded as theorem-provers, general problem solvers, game-players, etc.

In order for compiled GOL processes to engage in the kinds of diverse problem-solving activity suggested above, the compiler must involve something more than a simple translation from one computer language to another. The interpreter of the language must have the capacity to create arbitrary problem-solving processes on call, or must have embedded in it some sort of general heuristic problem-solving procedure. Before discussing the details of the GOL approach to generality in problem solving, we consider in the following section two divergent philosophies that have been most influential in this development—the "descriptive approach" of McCarthy, and the "model approach" of Newell, Shaw, and Simon. We will see later that the GOL philosophy is based on a principle of duality that may be viewed as a synthesis of the two.

1.1 Description vs. Model in Problem Solving[1]

Though similar in purpose, the "advice taker"[2] of McCarthy and the "general problem solver"[3] of Newell, Shaw, and Simon differ in a number of significant ways. Both attempt to provide a computer with commonsensical reasoning and problem-solving capability, and both have been used to analyze a variety of problem situations. However, there is a fundamental difference between these two schemes, both in the representation of elements of a task environment and in the inference and deduction processes available for operating on these representations. In an advice taker the objects and relations that characterize a task environment are *described* verbally in a modal predicate calculus, with deductive inference based on a form of verbal syllogistic reasoning. In GPS, the defining relations are modeled—typically by use of the description list data structure—and "deductive inference" in this context refers to goal-directed search through a sequence of transformations on the data structures of the model.

To illustrate in concrete terms the implications of these differences in representation and process, we consider next a simple task environment as it might be conceived for analysis first by an advice taker and then by a general problem solver. Imagine the following situation:

"A number of boys are playing ball at a baseball field, with George and

---

[1] This section details the historical antecedents of GOL; see Appendix A for relation to current research.
[2] Cf. McCarthy [15] and [17]; see also McCarthy and Hayes [18].
[3] Cf. Newell and Simon [20]; Ernst and Newell [5].

Dick at first and second base, respectively; Harry at the plate; and Charley 'on deck.' Both Harry and Charley are assumed capable of base hits."

One familiar with the game of baseball might make many obvious and immediate deductions about this situation—e.g., that the condition "bases loaded" might occur, a run might score, etc. It is clear that the ability to make such deductions requires more information about the game and the abilities of those who participate than is contained in the description given above. Specifically, certain notions of causality, consistency, and logical consequence are required to perform even the simplest sort of common-sensical reasoning about this environmental description.

1.2 A Descriptive Formulation of the Task

An advice taker is a system of modal logic, consisting of a corpus of axioms and premises, and with inference rules (Modus Ponens and Substitution) that permit the derivation of new facts from those which have been previously established. Certain of the statements in the corpus of an advice taker define relations among objects or individuals of the described situation and are thus particular to the given task. Others are of a more general nature and are intended to reflect "common knowledge." In the current example, we would have among the premises of the corpus the following particular assertions (using integers to indicate field positions, 1 for first base, -1 for on deck, etc.):

P1: at(George, 1)
P2: at(Dick, 2)
P3: at(Harry, 0)
P4: at(Charley, -1),

as well as certain general assertions such as the following sequents:

A1: at(x, y), at(u, v) $\rightarrow$ at(x, y) $\vee$ at(u, v),

and

A2: at(x, y), at(u, v) $\rightarrow$ at(x, y) & at(u, v),

and various other tautologies of propositional logic. In the latter two sequents, x, y, u, and v are all considered to be variables.

The deduction rules of the advice taker permit derivations based on substitution of constants for variables in any axiom (or other statement derived from the axioms) and detachment of any *true* clause in the antecedent (i.e., in the string of expressions to the left of the arrow) of any *true* sequent. Thus, for example, we may particularize axiom A2:

(1) at(Dick, 2), at(Harry, 0) $\rightarrow$ at(Dick, 2) & at(Harry, 0)

and since by premises P2 and P3 we have both:

(2) at(Dick, 2)

and

    (3) at(Harry, 0)

we may conclude:

    (4) at(Dick, 2) & at(Harry, 0).

In order to represent relations among *conditions* (i.e., among assertions such as "at(George, 1)"), we require a set of modal predicates (strictly: modal operators) that admit conditions as arguments. We use the modal predicate "cause," for example, to express relations of cause and effect, where

$$\text{cause}(c1, a, c2)$$

is an assertion that action a, taken in a situation satisfying condition c1, leads to a new situation satisfying condition c2.

To express concepts of feasibility, we use the modal predicate "can," where

$$\text{can}(c, a)$$

states that in a situation satisfying condition c, action a can be taken.

Finally, we have the modal "canult" that expresses concepts of ultimate causality, i.e.,

$$\text{canult}(c)$$

asserts that a situation can ultimately be brought about that satisfies condition c. We can define additional variations on these modalities (see Section 3.2 for a more complete set) but those given above are sufficient for present purposes.

Using the "can" predicate, we express the assumed capabilities of the players by premises:

    P5:   can(at(Harry, 0), hit(Harry, basehit))
    P6:   can(at(Charley, 0), hit(Charley, basehit)),

which assert that either Harry or Charley, if at the plate (position 0), can hit a basehit.

The basic causal relation concerning basehits can be expressed using "cause" as follows:

    P7:   cause(at(s1, p), hit(s2, basehit), at(s1, p+1))

which reflects the assumption that every runner advances one base as a result of a basehit.

The remaining two axioms provide means for derivations of "canult," based on assertions of "cause," "can," and other conditions that may characterize a described situation. The first asserts that if a condition holds, this same condition can ultimately be brought about:

A3:   c → canult(c).

The next axiom is the principal working axiom through which all complex derivations of our advice taker flow.

A4:   cause(c1, a, c), can(c2, a), canult(c1 & c2) → canult(c)

which can be interpreted:

"if, under condition c1, action a causes c, and under condition c2 action a can be undertaken, and a state in which conditions c1 and c2 occur simultaneously can be brought about, then condition c can ultimately be brought about."

This completes, at least for the present, the definition of an information corpus to represent the given task environment. Let us consider now what inferences may be derived as a result of the system's notion of logical consequence; in particular, let us see if the representation is sufficient to permit derivation of

   (a) canult(at(Dick, 3))

and

   (b) canult(at(Dick, 4)),

i.e., can we demonstrate within the system that a run can possibly score in this situation?

Without suggesting the means by which an advice taker might single out the right axioms to try, we give below a possible derivation of condition (a):

First we particularize axiom A4 to get:

   (5) cause(at(Dick, 2), hit(Harry, basehit), at(Dick, 3)), can(at(Harry, 0), hit(Harry, basehit)), canult(at(Dick, 2) & at(Harry, 0)) → canult(at(Dick, 3))

and by substituting in premise P7, we get

   (6) cause(at(Dick, 2), hit(Harry, basehit), at(Dick, 3))

and from P5 we know

   (7) can(at(Harry, 0), hit(Harry, basehit)).

We have already proved (line (4) of page 334)

   (8) at(Dick, 2) & at(Harry, 0)

and with substitution in A3, we find

(9)   at(Dick, 2) & at(Harry, 0) → canult(at(Dick, 2) & at(Harry, 0))

From these we obtain by detachment

(10)   canult(at(Dick, 2) & at(Harry, 0)).

Now (6), (7), and (10) together allow the detachment of all clauses in the antecedent of the sequent (5), yielding

(11)   canult(at(Dick, 3)),

which is the desired result. In the same way, we can show:

(12)   canult(at(George, 2))
(13)   canult(at(Harry, 1))

and

(14)   canult(at(Charley, 0)).

It might appear that another dose of the same medicine will yield condition (b),

$$\text{canult(at(Dick, 4)),}$$

but a complication arises in attempting this derivation that casts serious doubts on the efficacy and generality of the representation and inference procedure being used!

Once again, from axiom A4 we can obtain the working relationship:

(15)   cause(at(Dick, 3), hit(Charley, basehit), at(Dick, 4)), can(at(Charley, 0), hit(Charley, basehit)), canult(at(Dick, 3) & at(Charley, 0))
→ canult(at(Dick, 4))

Again, we know from P7,

(16)   cause(at(Dick, 3), hit(Charley, basehit), at(Dick, 4)) and P6 gives
(17)   can(at(Charley, 0), hit(Charley, basehit)).

The crux of the problem comes when we try to derive

$$\text{canult(at(Dick, 3) & at(Charley, 0)),}$$

since we cannot rely this time on the tautology A2. We have not proved either:

$$\text{at(Dick, 3)}$$

or

$$\text{at(Charley, 0),}$$

and cannot expect to do so since these results would contradict premises P2 and P4. What we *have* proved is:

$$\text{canult}(\text{at}(\text{Dick}, 3))$$

and

$$\text{canult}(\text{at}(\text{Charley}, 0)),$$

modal assertions that the conditions of interest can ultimately be brought about. The crucial question now is the following: Can we, on the basis of these assertions of ultimate derivability, reach the conclusion:

$$\text{canult}(\text{at}(\text{Dick}, 3) \ \& \ \text{at}(\text{Charley}, 0))?$$

Stated more abstractly, should we include in the general corpus of the advice taker some axiom of the form:

A5:   canult(c1), canult(c2) → canult(c1 and c2)?

Without such an axiom, it is impossible to proceed with the derivation of condition (b) (on the basis of the representation which has been adopted). However, if we admit axiom A5, then the way is clear for some seriously erroneous conclusions. For example, from P1 and A3, we can derive

(18)   canult(at(Harry, 0))

which along with

(13)   canult(at(Harry, 1))

and the proposed axiom A5 would permit

$$\text{canult}(\text{at}(\text{Harry}, 0) \ \& \ \text{at}(\text{Harry}, 1)),$$

a clearly unacceptable result.

There are at least two ways to deal with the problem of "conjunctive paradox"—of which the above is just one example.[4] One way we can preserve the conjunction axiom A5 is by attaching expiration dates to any direct assertions involving relations in the described space that are subject to change as a result of applied actions. If, for example, after deciding on the action of a basehit by Harry, we erase the premises P1–P4 and replace them with a new set of "at" statements reflecting the altered situation, the paradox cited above could not arise. This, in essence, is the GOL approach to the problem, which will be discussed in detail later.

An alternative would be to disallow axiom A5 and require that the system corpus be expanded to anticipate all possible conjunctive queries. This is the approach adopted, at least implicitly, in McCarthy's proposals, and in the implementation of an advice taker constructed by Black.[5] To

---

[4] See Simon [22] for various classes of interdependencies giving rise to conjunctive paradoxes.

[5] See Black [3]; cf., also Section 3.2.

provide, in this manner, for an exhaustive set of conjunctive results in the situation described above, we would have to add to the corpus at least the following set of premises:

 P8: cause(at(s0, -1), hit(s1, basehit), at (s0, 0) & at(s1, 1))

 P9: cause(at(s0, -1) & at(s2, p), hit(s1, basehit), at(s0, 0) & at(s1, 1) & at(s2, p $+$ 1))

 P10: cause(at(s0, -1) & at(s2, p1) & at(s3, p2), hit(s1, basehit), at(s0, 0) & at(s1, 1) & at(s2, p1 $+$ 1) & at(s3, p2 $+$ 1))

 P11: cause(at(s0, -1) & at(s2, p1) & at(s3, p2) & at(s4, p3), hit(s1, basehit), at(s0, 0) & at(s1, 1) & at(s2, p1 $+$ 1) & at(s3, p2 $+$ 1) & at(s4, p3 $+$ 1))

This expanded corpus would allow—even without axiom A5—the conclusions "bases loaded," "a run scores," and other conjunctive conditions resulting from a sequence of two basehits. But the cost is high in terms of redundancy in the information corpus—an exorbitant cost when we consider the proliferation and complexity of premises required to represent the more realistic situation in which there may be any number of basehits, outs, sacrifice flies, bases on balls, etc. involved in a derivation. Imagine the problem of trying to represent a game like chess by providing in this explicit manner for all possible conjunctive conditions that one may ever want the advice taker to analyze!

1.3 A Model Formulation of the Task

 Let us now consider the alternate mode of representation referred to earlier—the use of a model, as exemplified by the General Problem Solver of Newell, Shaw, and Simon. The principal advantage of this form of representation is that it permits the very useful tactical heuristic of factoring a conjunctive goal, with attention focusing selectively on one conjunct at a time. As we observed in the previous discussion, such a heuristic often leads to problems in an advice taker formulation, due to interactions caused by interdependencies among the various conjunctive subgoals. However, the issue of conjunctive paradox does not arise in a general problem solver, since the selection of any action as a part of a deduction sequence causes immediate transformation of the data structures comprising the model of the task environment.

 A solution or a derivation of any goal condition is given constructive demonstration in a general problem solver by a sequence of action transformations that lead—from some starting configuration, through perhaps a succession of intermediate states—to an ultimate configuration of the model—the goal state—in which all aspects of the given goal condition are satisfied simultaneously. If there are interactions among the conjunctive conditions—if some action undoes what we thought had already been accomplished by a prior action—these complicating side effects will be reflected in the model. By preventing the actual conjunction in the model of conditions that are mutually exclusive, this constructive procedure prevents any erroneous conjunctive conclusions. If, in the example of the previous section, Harry were to hit a basehit, then in a GPS representation—before any other action is considered—the data structures of the model would be modified to reflect the fact that Harry is now at first base, with all other runners having advanced one base. Selection of any subsequent action would then be predicated on conditions in this newly revised configuration of the model.

1.4 Representation and Process

There are many ways in which the objects and relations characterizing a task environment might be represented in a model. One particularly pervasive representational structure—which shows up in IPL as the description list [21], in LISP as the property list [16], and in SIMSCRIPT as the entity [14]—is the characterization of objects as collections of attribute-value pairs. In the task environment considered previously, we might, for example, use such a structure to represent any of the ballplayers, giving values to the attributes "name," "age," "batting average," etc. as follows:

```
PLAYER1:    (NAME, HARRY)
            (BATTING AVERAGE, .250)
            (AGE, 15)
            (PLAYING POSITION, LEFT FIELD)
            (LINEUP POSITION, 3)
            (PRESENT STATUS, AT BAT)
```
                        etc

Similarly, the current status of play—viewed as an abstract object—might be represented as follows:

```
STATUS:     (TEAM UP, ACES)
            (AT BAT, HARRY)
            (RUNNER AT FIRST, GEORGE)
            (RUNNER AT SECOND, DICK)
            (ONDECK, CHARLEY)
            (OUTS, 0)
```
                        etc

A collection of such data structures, describing individuals, objects, and abstract entities in terms of the properties and attributes they possess, can be constructed to provide as much detail as deemed necessary in the static representation of a task environment.

The dynamics of the situation are then given by a set of transformation processes that represent actions in terms of the changes they bring about in the model. For example, an action such as a basehit would be represented by a process that modifies the status description by advancing every runner, and alters the value associated with the attribute, present status, of each affected player. Similar action processes could be provided to represent sacrifice flies, bases on balls, stolen bases, etc.

In addition to these transformation processes, a general problem solver must be provided with a number of perceptual processes to determine the existence (or non-existence) of certain conditions in the model. It must be possible for GPS to test for the existence of a given set of *goal* conditions, so that the successful derivation of a goal state may be recognized. Moreover, it is often necessary to test for the existence of certain *enabling* conditions that control the application of the transforms. For example, under the enabling condition "next base open" the action "steal base" might be appropriate, otherwise it would not.

In the process of testing for a desired condition of either type (goal or enabling), GPS determines a set of differences, i.e., features of the desired condition that are not satisfied in the current configuration of the model. The basic operational goal of GPS is to eliminate all such differences simultaneously, and this is accomplished through use of the tactical heuristic of selective difference reduction.

Consider again the situation in the running example where we have the goal condition "bases loaded." This might be represented in GPS by the partial status description:

GOAL STATUS: (RUNNER AT FIRST, HARRY)
(RUNNER AT SECOND, GEORGE)
(RUNNER AT THIRD, DICK)

By the process of differencing, GPS would find that this conjunctive goal is unsatisfied on each of the three dimensions (1) runner at first, (2) runner at second, and (3) runner at third. When more than one difference occurs, as in this case, GPS singles out one to attack first on the basis of a difference ordering relation, which is designed to reflect the relative difficulty associated with various possible differences.

Let us assume that reduction of the difference; i.e., runner at third, is selected as the most difficult and therefore the principal objective. There may be any number of actions relevant to this objective, e.g., base on balls, basehit, sacrifice fly, and others. For the sake of argument, let us assume that sacrifice fly has been selected as the action to try. Notice that this action, though relevant to the difference under consideration, would render impossible the attainment of the overall conjunctive goal; i.e., an out for Harry precludes his becoming runner at first, even though it succeeds in attaining the sub-goal: (RUNNER AT THIRD, DICK).

At some point in its deduction process, GPS would have to discover this conflict and cause the model to be brought back to the configuration at this decision point. If any other actions are available (in this case they are), another would be selected and the deduction process continued along some other path of the search tree. Much of the machinery of a general problem solver is devoted to recognizing unpromising directions of search and restoring context in the model to decision points, wherever they may occur in the search tree, at which untried alternative actions remain to be explored. We will consider these issues in more detail later—in the discussion of our version of GPS, the GOL function "ATTAIN."

1.5 A Synthesis of Description and Model

In comparing description with model as modes of representing the elements of a task environment, we have found certain strengths and weaknesses in each approach. As the example of the previous sections shows, there is a distinct advantage in the use of a model to represent problem-solving transformations (actions), since only the immediate effects on the individuals, objects, and abstract entities comprising the model need be represented. The effects of such actions on other conditions that are in some way predicated on these basic elements of the model may be inferred and made explicit at any time by invoking appropriate perceptual processes. In a description representation, however, the effects of all transformations—on all complex conditions that may ever be of interest—must be made explicit in the original structuring of premises for the information corpus of the system.

On the other hand, the process of discovering attainability of some specified goal condition in a description system—assuming that the corpus can be properly structured—is reduced to a matter of theorem proving in a first order modal logic. Thus, if a sequence of deduction steps implies the derivability of a goal, we need not engage in any pattern recognition or other perceptual act to verify this conclusion. This is, of course, not true in a model problem solver, since we must always test a purported goal state to be sure that the final action of a derivation has not inadvertently negated some part of the gains wrought by prior actions of the sequence.

Though the General Problem Solver incorporates a general perceptual process in its differencing operator, one can conceive of many tasks for which the tactical heuristic of difference reduction is ill-suited. In such cases, it is necessary to code special perceptual processes by which the model may be tested for conditions of interest. In the game of chess, for example—where selection of moves is often predicated on such considerations as center control, mobility, potential checks, pins, and forks, etc.—special processes must be created for pattern recognition and move selection on the basis of perceived conditions in the model.

It might appear that a description processor would have the advantage here—since what we would like is the ability to describe the conditions of interest, rather than compose algorithms to test for them. But previous encounters with the description mode of representation have shown that we cannot, in general, deal with the perception of even the simplest of conjunctive conditions that have not been expressly provided for in designing the system.

This brings us to the thesis of this dissertation, which may be put in the form of the following proposition:

Thesis: In order to provide for the perception of described conditions in a model of a task environment, what is required is a synthesis of the description and model modes of representation. The basis for such a synthesis exists in the duality of syntax and semantics, as these terms are understood in a general modal predicate calculus. The formalism of modal logic provides a language in which to describe goals, patterns, concepts, and other conditions of interest in a task environment; the corresponding semantic structures constitute a model in which to test and evaluate such described conditions. Moreover, by allowing use of state variables in expressions of the language, it becomes possible to describe modal concepts and conditions, the evaluation of which requires search through a universe of attainable states of the model structure. Such modal expressions may be used to describe a variety of model-based heuristic problem-solving, game-playing, and decision-making procedures.

In order to test this thesis, we have constructed a language, based on the notation of a general predicate calculus with modal operators and lambda conversion, and have provided for the representation of semantic structures associated with elements of this system. A compiler has been written (embedded in LISP 1.5), which constructs both test and generator processes, based on expressions of the language, that describe conditions and relations of a task environment. A number of modal expressions, defining various heuristic search procedures, have been encoded and tested in the language. Included among these are versions of McCarthy's advice taker, and the General Problem Solver and Logic Theorist of Newell, Shaw, and Simon. The results of these tests are described in detail in Section 3 of this chapter. We devote the following section to some preliminary remarks concerning the syntax, semantics, and pragmatics of the language.

SECTION 2
THE GOL PROGRAMMING SYSTEM

2.1 Overview

The GOL programming system provides for the description of conditions and other relations of interest in a task environment through use of a notation which may be characterized as a many-sorted type theory[6] with state variables. The use of a type theoretic formalism permits quantification and abstraction, subject to certain minimal restrictions, on all types of variables and function letters of the system. That the scheme is many-sorted means simply that there may be different classes of individuals appropriate for different quantified variables; the reason for singling out state variables as a special sort is to suggest that the semantics of GOL involves a model structure—as in the modal semantics of Kripke[7]—that may contain a number of alternate models or states of the universe. By permitting abstraction and quantification on these state variables, as well as on variables defined over classes of propositions, the GOL system admits the introduction of modality as a special case of the predicate expression, described below.

Intuitively, we think of certain symbols and expressions of the GOL language as being n-adic predicates, which determine n-ary relations (subsets of appropriate n-spaces) in each of the alternate states of a GOL model structure. Some predicates are defined only in *extension*, i.e., by an enumeration of n-tuples in the classes with which they are associated in various states of the model structure. A collection of these extensional relations can be viewed as a model (in the sense of the discussion of Section 1) representing certain known characteristics of a given task environment. Other relations of interest may be represented descriptively by *intensional* predicate definitions, which are given by lambda expressions of the language. These are compound expressions involving the abstraction operator (λ),[8] and containing any number of quantifiers and atomic formulae combined by the connectives of propositional logic.

We use the term *semantic evaluation* to refer to the basic GOL computational process, which calls for the generation of n-tuples from the extension, in some given state of the model structure, of an intensionally defined predicate. This process may involve considerable problem-solving activity,

---

[6] The GOL formalism was inspired by the transfinite type theory of Andrews [1].

[7] See Kripke, [11] and [13], for the full development of the model theory. We regret that two terms as similar as "modal" and "model" designate the syntactic and semantic aspects of the situation, respectively. But this usage is now deeply embedded in the literature of symbolic logic and we shall have to live with it.

[8] This is Church's lambda notation, see [4].

particularly in those cases where the intensional predicate definition is recursive, or where it involves quantification on a state variable. In view of this focus on semantic rather than syntactic evaluation, it is perhaps useful to think of GOL not as a system of logic, but rather as a formalism in which to define complex generator processes. Operating on the data structures comprising the model of a task environment, these processes generate instances of described relations, and may be considered to be a set of perceptual processes on that model structure.

2.1.1 A Sample GOL Representation. To illustrate these ideas, we consider next a possible GOL representation for the entities and relations that characterize the game of tic-tac-toe. This is one of the simplest of the board games, played on a 3 × 3 array containing nine squares (S1, S2, ..., S9), arranged as follows:

S1	S2	S3
S4	S5	S6
S7	S8	S9

These squares are organized into eight lines (L1, L2, ..., L8), each of which, containing exactly three squares, can be represented as a ternary relation in extension:

$$
\begin{array}{ll}
L1: & (S1, S2, S3) \\
L2: & (S4, S5, S6) \\
L3: & (S7, S8, S9) \\
L4: & (S1, S4, S7) \\
L5: & (S2, S5, S8) \\
L6: & (S3, S6, S9) \\
L7: & (S1, S5, S9) \\
L8: & (S3, S5, S7)
\end{array}
$$

The monadic predicate *line* can then be represented as the collection of these these triadic predicates, as follows:

$$
\begin{array}{ll}
\text{line:} & (L1) \\
& (L2) \\
& \cdot \\
& \cdot \\
& \cdot \\
& (L8)
\end{array}
$$

In playing this game, the opponents alternate in selecting a blank square on which to place their mark (either X or O); thus in order to represent the status of play, we must give explicit account of the mark (X, O, or – (for blank)) associated with each square. This can be accomplished by means of a "mark" predicate, which has as its extension the set of ordered pairs: (square name, associated mark). For example, we might have:

$$\text{mark:} \quad \begin{array}{l} (S1, X) \\ (S2, -) \\ (S3, O) \\ \text{etc.} \end{array}$$

Using these extensional predicates, we can now describe patterns in this task environment by using the intensional form of predicate definition, the GOL lambda expression. For example, we can express the pattern representing a Win for player X by the following:[9]

$$\lambda(L) \; \exists \; (s1, s2, s3) \; (\text{line } (L) \land L(s1, s2, s3) \land \text{mark}(s1, X) \\ \land \text{mark}(s2, X) \land \text{mark}(s3, X))$$

In evaluating this expression, the GOL processor would generate lines (L), if such can be found, that have all three squares associated with the mark X. In this way, one of the basic conceptual processes required for the intelligent play of this game can be made available to a GOL game-playing program.

One could go on to define a number of other patterns relevant to the play of the game; we give just one more to illustrate the manner in which desirable moves may be associated with perceivable patterns. Any time player X finds, at his move, a line containing two X's and a blank, he can win the game by placing his mark on that blank. Thus it would be good advice to a novice player to look for such patterns and to make the suggested move when possible. To facilitate the description of this pattern (and others based on what are essentially *unordered* triplets of squares) we define first the predicate, permute3, that takes four arguments:

permute3: $\lambda(L, s1, s2, s3) \; (L(s1, s2, s3) \lor L(s1, s3, s2) \lor L(s2, s1, s3) \\ \lor L(s2, s3, s1) \lor L(s3, s1, s2) \lor L(s3, s2, s1))$

Using this predicate, which when evaluated generates all permutations of the squares making up line L, we can write the *winningmove* function, very simply, as follows:

winningmove: $\lambda(s) \; \exists \; (s1, s2, L) \; (\text{line}(L) \land \text{permute3}(L, s1, s2, s) \\ \land \text{mark}(s1, X) \land \text{mark}(s2, X) \land \text{mark}(s, -))$

In a similar manner, we can create intensional predicates that identify

---

[9] Like the LISP M-expression language, the notation used here is an informal transliteration of the actual GOL notation; details of GOL SYNTAX will be presented in the following section.

other suggested moves predicated on other perceivable conditions of the board (such as potential forks, etc.). Given a collection of such pattern-action associations, we can create an advice predicate, in extension, that lists these significant patterns in order of their importance:

$$\text{advice:} \quad \text{(pattern1)} \\ \text{(pattern2)} \\ \text{etc.}$$

Each of the patterns named in the advice extension would be a monadic predicate, of the same general form as winningmove, that defines a generator of suggested moves based on some condition that might obtain in the course of the play.

We are now in a position to write a move selector for player X that embodies the very simple strategy: "either take a winning move if one is available, or else take the best advice that does not lead to a situation in which the opponent has an immediate win on his next move." The ability to look ahead, implied by this strategy, requires some means for altering the status of play—i.e., the *mark* predicate—during the course of an evaluation. We will not here go into the details of state change that the following intensional description entails. For the present, we simply make use of the fact that any sub-formula of a GOL expression of the form:

$$\text{goldig(expr, (trans (a, STATE)))},$$

causes the expression, expr, to be evaluated in a revised state of the model brought about by applying action a to the present state, STATE. (We give details of this syntactic device in the following sections.)

The naive move-selector predicate can now be described as follows:

$$\text{move:} \quad \lambda(s) \text{ (winningmove(s)} \vee \exists \text{ (P) (advice(P)} \wedge \text{P(s)} \\ \wedge \sim \text{goldig(lose, trans(mark(s, X), STATE))))}$$

where "lose" is defined to be the 0-adic predicate:[10]

$$\text{lose:} \quad \lambda \text{ ( )} \exists \text{ (L, s1, s2, s3) (line(L)} \wedge \text{permute3(L, s1, s2, s3)} \\ \wedge \text{ mark(s1, O)} \wedge \text{mark(s2, O)} \wedge \text{mark(s3, --))}.$$

This is not, of course, a complete strategy for intelligent play of the game. Nonetheless, it does illustrate certain features of the GOL philosophy of representation that distinguish it from both the Advice Taker and the General Problem Solver. First, though the GOL formulation involves describing certain conditions that are of interest in the task environment, it does not

---

[10] An "0-adic" predicate is the degenerate case; its evaluation yields a truth value rather than an n-tuple.

provide (as in the Advice Taker) for inferences from a set of premises concerning these conditions. Rather, it provides for perceiving of these conditions in a model of the environment; it can thus deal with partial or even incorrect advice in selecting squares that are to be considered possible moves.

In this sense, the move-selector performs in much the manner of a General Problem Solver, but with an important difference. Where in the General Problem Solver one is constrained by the built-in heuristic procedure of difference reduction—in a GOL representation, we can describe the heuristics of search by the same kinds of language expressions that characterize patterns and other conditions of the environment. Note the difference in purpose underlying a predicate such as *lose* and the move-selector function *move*. Whereas the former describes a possible condition that may occur in the task environment, the latter describes a decision-making procedure, based on the perception of such conditions.

One can describe, in expressions of the GOL language, a wide variety of conditions and search strategies that may be relevant in various problem-solving, game-playing, and decision-making situations. The possible search strategies that may be implemented in GOL range from the simple depth-first and breadth-first schemes to some of the more sophisticated of contemporary designs. We will discuss a number of these techniques in later sections of this chapter. First, we devote the following two sections to a detailed discussion of the syntax and semantics of the language.

2.2 Syntax of GOL Expressions

The set of legal expressions of the GOL language is defined by the syntax given in BNF notation on the following page. The form that heads this list of definitions, the ⟨lambda expression⟩, is the standard means of representing in GOL the intension of a relation. Such an expression denotes a mapping from n-tuples of entities (perhaps of various types) to truth-values, and is thus the definiens of an n-adic predicate. The set of n-tuples of which a given predicate is true constitutes its corresponding extensional form.

To summarize briefly the thrust of this syntax: a predicate or ⟨lambda expression⟩ is formed by prefixing a ⟨lambda body⟩ to a ⟨wff⟩, the latter being a truth-valued proposition built up from ⟨atomic formulae⟩ and ⟨GOLDIG phrases⟩ by use of the connectives (AND, OR, NOT, IMPLIES) and quantifiers (EXISTS, FORALL) of the predicate calculus. Note that the GOL language shares the prefix notation of the programming system in which it is presently implemented, LISP 1.5.[11]

It is important to observe that various of the GOL syntactic types, especially the ⟨predicate variables⟩, ⟨state designators⟩, ⟨transformation

---

[11] The current implementation uses the IBM 7090 computer; a conversion to the IBM 360 is in process.

designators⟩, ⟨arguments⟩, and ⟨identifiers⟩—may be represented by ⟨variables⟩, which are arbitrary LISP atomic symbols. Since these symbols contain no device for identifying the types of entities that the corresponding variables represent, it is possible for certain GOL expressions to be ambiguous, even though well formed according to the rules. For example, an expression of the form:

(LAMBDA (X) (EXISTS (F) (F X)))

(which describes a generator of things, X, for which there is some F such that F(X)), is ambiguous with regard to the types of variables involved. We know from certain contextual cues that F must be a function of the type that takes entities of type X into truth-values, thus that it must be some sort of monadic predicate. But without information about the type of X (and we cannot infer this from context without knowing the type of F), the expression remains ambiguous.

GOL Syntax

```
⟨lambda expression⟩:: = (⟨lambda body⟩⟨wff⟩)
⟨lambda body⟩:: = LAMBDA (⟨variable string⟩)
⟨wff⟩:: = (EXISTS (⟨variable string⟩) ⟨wff⟩)|
         (FORALL (⟨variable string⟩) ⟨implicative expression⟩)|
         (AND ⟨wff string⟩)|
         (OR ⟨wff string⟩)|
         (NOT ⟨atomic formula⟩)| (NOT ⟨goldig phrase⟩)
         (ASSIGN ⟨identifier⟩⟨identifier⟩)|
         ⟨goldig phrase⟩|
         ⟨atomic formula⟩
⟨wff string⟩:: = ⟨wff⟩ | ⟨wff⟩⟨wff string⟩
⟨implicative expression⟩:: = (IMPLIES ⟨atomic formula⟩⟨atomic formula⟩)
              |(IMPLIES ⟨atomic formula⟩⟨goldig phrase⟩)
⟨goldig phrase⟩:: = (GOLDIG ⟨atomic formula⟩⟨state designator⟩)
⟨atomic formula⟩:: = (⟨predicate variable⟩⟨argument string⟩)
⟨state designator⟩:: = STATE | ⟨variable⟩ |
              (⟨transformation designator⟩⟨variable⟩⟨state designator⟩)
⟨variable string⟩:: = ⟨empty⟩ | ⟨variable⟩ | ⟨variable⟩⟨variable string⟩
⟨argument string⟩:: = ⟨empty⟩ | ⟨argument⟩ | ⟨argument⟩⟨argument string⟩
⟨predicate variable⟩:: = ⟨variable⟩
⟨transformation designator⟩:: = ⟨variable⟩
⟨identifier⟩:: = ⟨constant⟩ | ⟨variable⟩
⟨constant⟩:: = STATE | CONTROL
⟨argument⟩:: = ⟨variable⟩
⟨variable⟩:: = ⟨non-reserved atom⟩[12]
```

[12] A "non-reserved atom" is a LISP atomic symbol that is not a member of the ⟨reserved atom⟩ set.

⟨reserved atom⟩:: = STATE | CONTROL | LAMBDA | EXISTS | FORALL | AND |
                    OR | NOT | ASSIGN | GOLDIG | IMPLIES
⟨atom⟩:: = ⟨LISP atomic symbol⟩[13]

There are several ways in which we might revise the language specifications in order to avoid these ambiguities. We might, for example, require that the type of variables be identified syntactically through use of subscripts attached to all variable symbols. This is a technique often used in formulating systems of type theory for purposes of syntactic analysis—i.e., where the objective is to derive results from a set of axioms and rules of inference see [1] and [10]).

In the GOL scheme, however, where we deal with semantic rather than syntactic analyses, it is more convenient to define a set of enrichment rules that allow the disambiguation of GOL expressions on the basis of semantical considerations. In essence, these rules are designed to ensure that the context in which any variable appears is sufficiently rich to permit the inference of its type from knowledge of its domain of definition.

In the case of existential and lambda bound variables, the rule is that any variable that is used as ⟨predicate designator⟩ in some well-formed part, S, of a GOL expression must also appear as ⟨argument⟩ in at least one other well-formed part of the expression that is conjoined to S. If, for example, we were to modify the matrix of the expression given on the previous page, by conjoining the atomic formula, (G F), where G is known (either through extensional or intensional definition) to determine a class of monadic predicate functions—the resulting expression

(LAMBDA (X) (EXISTS (F) (AND (G F) (F X))))

would be both well-formed and unambiguously determined. We can find the type of F, implicitly, by generating an element from the extension of G (recall that such generation is the raison d'être of GOL's evaluation process); on the basis of any such F, we can determine X such that F(X).

The rule for enrichment of context takes a somewhat different form in the case of variables that are universally quantified. As can be seen from the syntax specifications, there is a very limited format for expressions involving the universal quantifier; viz., the underlying expression must be implicative in form, with what are basically atomic formulae as antecedent and consequent.[14] For example, we might write:

(FORALL (X) (IMPLIES (G X) (F X))),

---

[13] A "LISP atomic symbol" is defined in [16].
[14] A GOLDIG phrase (which may appear in the consequent) is to be evaluated in some other state (cf. p. 48).

to express the assertion:

"for every X in the restricted domain determined by G(X), it is also the case that F(X)."

As this suggests, the antecedent of an implicative expression may be used to restrict the domain of definition of variables that appear in the consequent; any universally bound variable that is not so restricted presents an ambiguity that must be resolved. The most obvious technique for accomplishing this resolution is to revise the antecedent expression so that the ambiguous variable becomes included in its set of restrictions. Although both antecedent and consequent of an implicative expression must be essentially atomic formulae, there is no constraint on the type of predicate designators involved. Since these may take any number of arguments, and may be defined either extensionally (by data structures) or intensionally (by other lambda expressions), the limitation to atomic formulae is not as confining as it may at first appear. Nevertheless, in certain situations that may arise in connection with free variables in extensional schemata (these will be discussed in Section 2.4), it may be necessary to fall back on a form of external domain declaration for certain universally quantified variables. The circumstances under which such external declarations are required will be discussed in more detail later.

2.3 Semantics of GOL Expressions

The semantics of modal logic that has been explicated by Kripke provides a useful conceptual framework within which to discuss the semantics of GOL expressions. The discussion of the GOL model structure that follows is patterned on Kripke's description of a normal model structure for quantified modal logics.[15]

We define a GOL model structure to be an ordered triple $\langle G, K, R \rangle$, where K is a non-empty set, G a distinguished element of K, and R a relation on K. Intuitively, we regard K as the set of all possible states of the world; these may be viewed as hypothetical or temporal alternatives to the present state, G. The relation R is, intuitively, the descendant relation on K; thus if S_1 and S_2 are both states, $(R\ S_1\ S_2)$ means that S_2 is a descendant of (or is derivable from) S_1.

An *explicit* model structure is defined as one in which all states of K are specified (as described in the following paragraph)—in advance of any computation. This is rarely the case. More often, we deal with *implicit* model structures where only the present state, G, is defined a priori. Whereas

[15] Kripke [12].

in an explicit model structure the descendant relation may be specified explicitly by a set of ordered pairs, in an implicit structure this relation must be inferred from a set of transformations $\langle t_i \rangle$ which, when applicable, map states of the model structure into their descendants.

By distinguishing states which, though otherwise identical, have been brought about by different sequences of transformations, we can characterize any implicit model structure as a tree, rooted at G, with nodes representing other possible states connected by branches implied by the descendant relation R. For pragmatic reasons, we adopt similar conventions for the relation defined on an explicit model structure; viz., its graph must be representable as a tree structure—directed, connected, and without circuits.

2.3.1 The Interpretation of GOL Expressions. A model of a set Γ of GOL expressions is an assignment $\phi(P, S)$, that defines—for every state S of the model structure and every n-adic predicate variable P that appears *free* in some expression of Γ—a certain set of ordered n-tuples, including exactly those n-tuples of entities (of perhaps various types) of which the predicate P is true in state S. For certain predicate variables, the extensions are given explicitly by enumeration of the sets of n-tuples they contain.[16] Others, however, are described—rather than enumerated—by the lambda expression form of intensional predicate definition. In either case, it is possible, through use of the GOL evaluation process, to access the n-tuples comprising the extension of any predicate in any state and to make inferences therefrom concerning the domains of other variables that appear in Γ.

Observe that in specifying ϕ for all free predicate variables in a set Γ^* of unambiguous GOL expressions, we define implicit restricted domains for all other variables that appear there (including, in particular, other predicate variables that appear bound in some expression of Γ^*, and through these, recursively, all other variables that appear as arguments of these bound predicate variables, etc.). This follows from our earlier considerations of the enrichment rules governing composition of unambiguous GOL expressions.

We now define, inductively, for every formula A that appears in some expression of Γ^*, and every state S in K, a truth-value $\phi(A, S)$ relative to a given assignment of elements (from appropriate domains) to the free variables of A.

(1) For A an atomic formula: (P x1 x2 ... xn), given an assignment of elements a1, a2, ... an to x1, x2, ... xn (where the a_i are drawn from domains inferred for the x_i from $\phi(P, S)$), we define $\phi((P\ x1\ x2\ ...\ xn)\ S) = T$ iff (a1, ... an) is a member of $\phi(P, S)$; otherwise $\phi((P\ x1\ x2\ ...\ xn)\ S) = F$.

---

[16] Such n-tuples may, however, contain free variables, cf. p. 354.

(2) For A of the form (ASSIGN x y), we define $\phi((\text{ASSIGN x y}) S) = T$ for all x, y, and S. Like the pseudo-functions of LISP, this form is used for its effect rather than its value; the effect is to fix variable x to the current value of y.

(3) For A a goldig phrase (GOLDIG B S'), we define $\phi((\text{GOLDIG B S'}) S) = T$ iff $\phi(B, S') = T$; otherwise $\phi((\text{GOLDIG B S'}) S) = F$. This form is used to effect a change of state during the course of a computation (see p. 354).

(4) For A of the form (NOT B), we define $\phi(A, S) = F$ iff $\phi(B, S) = T$; otherwise $\phi(A, S) = T$.

(5) For A of the form (AND A1 A2 ... An), we define $\phi(\text{AND A1 A2 ... An}) S) = T$ iff $\phi(A1, S) = \phi(A2, S) = ... \phi(An, S) = T$; otherwise $\phi((\text{AND A1 A2 ... An}) S) = F$.

(6) For A of the form (OR A1 A2 ... An), we define $\phi((\text{OR A1 A2 ... An}) S) = F$ iff $\phi(A1, S) = \phi(A2, S) = ... \phi(An, S) = F$; otherwise $\phi((\text{OR A1 A2 ...An}) S) = T$.

(7) For A of the form (IMPLIES A1 A2), we define $\phi((\text{IMPLIES A1 A2}) S) = T$ iff $\phi(A1, S) = F$ or $\phi(A2, S) = T$; otherwise $\phi((\text{IMPLIES A1 A2}) S) = F$.

(8) Assume that A is of the form (EXISTS (X1 X2 ... Xn) B), where the free variables of B are included in the set $\{X1, ... Xn, Y1, ..., Ym\}$. Then we define $\phi((\text{EXISTS (X1 ... Xn) B}) S) = T$, relative to some assignment b1, b2, ..., bm to Y1, Y2, ... Ym iff there is some n-tuple of elements a1, a2, ... an such that $\phi(B, S) = T$ under the total assignment a1, ... an, b1, ... bm to X1, ... Xn, Y1, ... Yn; otherwise $\phi((\text{EXISTS (X1 ... Xn) B}) S) = F$.

(9) Assume that A is of the form (FORALL (X1 ... Xn) B), where the free variables of B are included in the set $\{X1, ... Xn, Y1, ... Ym\}$. Then we define $\phi((\text{FORALL (X1 ... Xn) B}) S) = T$, relative to some assignment b1, ... bm to Y1 ... Ym iff, for every combination of elements a1, ... an (where the ai are elements of domains for the X_i inferred from the antecedent of B, an implicative expression) we have $\phi(B, S) = T$ under the total assignment a1, ... an, b1, ... bm to X1, ... Xn, Y1, ... Ym; otherwise $\phi((\text{FORALL (X1 ... Xn) B}) S) = F$.

2.4 Pragmatics of the Language

In this section, we discuss the external command language, by which predicate definitions—both extensional and intensional—are input to the system, and through which the various evaluation processes associated with the intensional predicates become compiled into LISP code and executed. We will not here focus on the details of the GOL compiler, though the essentials of this process will be presented; a more detailed discussion may be found in Appendix B. We consider first the commands required for specification of intensional and extensional predicates, then turn to some pragmatic aspects of the evaluation process. A number of examples of GOL programming will be provided to illustrate the concepts involved.

2.4.1 Intensional Definition; the GOLDEF Command. Predicate variables that appear free in any GOL expression, E, must be assigned to specific extensions in each state of the model structure in order for a computation involving that expression to be well defined. Similar assignments must be provided for all those predicate functors which, through occurrence in some extensional data structure, may fall in the domains of other predicate variables that appear bound in E. These assignments may be made explicitly through use of the GOLSET command (described in the following section) which associates certain specified data structures with the atomic symbols that name the defined predicates. Alternatively, these predicate variables may be assigned to their extensions implicitly—through use of the lambda expression form of intensional description. The latter may be thought of as state independent definitions since, as mentioned previously, a lambda expression may be evaluated to produce elements of the extension of a given predicate in any specified state of the model structure.

Intensional predicate definitions are input to the system by use of the GOLDEF command, which is actually a LISP function similar to the LISP primitive, DEFINE. This function takes a single argument which is a list of definitions, each of the form (⟨predicate name⟩, ⟨defining expression⟩). For every such pair, the defining expression is paired with the indicator, INT (for intensional definition), on the property list of the atomic symbol given as predicate name. To use this command—for example, to specify the MOVE predicate described previously—we would write the following:

```
GOLDEF(( (MOVE (LAMBDA (S) (OR (WINNINGMOVE S)
(EXISTS (P) (AND (ADVICE P) (P S) (NOT (GOLDIG
(LOSE) (TRANS (MARK S X) STATE))))))) ))
```

Any number of defining pairs may be included in the argument list of such a GOLDEF command.

2.4.2 Extensional Definition, The GOLSET Command. The data structures comprising the extensions of predicates are represented in the computer as lists of vectors, which may be input explicitly by a command of the form

GOLSET(((P1 S1) (P2 S2) .. (Pn Sn))).

This command causes the data structures S_i (which are lists of n-tuples) to be paired with the indicator EXT (for extensional definition) on the property list of the atoms P_i which identify the corresponding predicate variables.

As mentioned previously, the data structures representing the extensions of predicates in states other than the initial state (here called EXT) are generally not set up in advance but are constructed, when needed, by applying some state transformation. In this way, we limit the number of states explicitly defined in the model to those actually involved in a computation. This can produce an important saving in problem-solving applications that deal with vast exponential tree structures.

Another way to achieve parsimony in the model is to use free variables in extensional data structures. This is merely a time- and space-saving convention, which does not alter the essential nature of such forms; they are still to be interpreted as naming all n-tuples of entities in the predicate's extension. In the case of these *extensional schemata*, all substitution instances of a given n-tuple, for all combinations of elements from the domains of the free variables involved, are to be considered part of this extension.

To illustrate the use of free variables in extensional data structures, we consider now—a bit prematurely—some of the schemata used in the GOL programs that are described in the following chapter.

The first example is the predicate SAME, which is used in the SOLVMAZE program as an identity relation on a certain finite set S, {A, B, ... J}, representing points in a maze. This predicate could have been defined in extension without use of free variables, as follows:

SAME: ((A A) (B B) .. (J J)).

Our alternative, however, is to use the simpler structure,

SAME: ((P P)),

in which we identify P as a free variable. This use of free variables obviously allows a more compact representation of certain predicates, and in most cases permits more rapid perusal of these data structures by the GOL evaluation process. However, certain complications may be introduced by this abbreviated mode of representation. These issues will be covered in the discussion in the following section.

Another example of an extensional structure containing free variables is the predicate AXIOM used in the GOL THEOREM program to represent a set of axiom schemata for propositional logic. In the following, P, Q, and R are all considered to be free variables.

AXIOM: (((IMPLIES (OR P P) P))
            ((IMPLIES P (OR Q P)))
            ((IMPLIES (OR P Q) (OR Q P)))
            ((IMPLIES (OR P (OR Q R)) (OR Q (OR P R))))

```
((IMPLIES  (IMPLIES P Q)
           (IMPLIES  (OR R P)  (OR R Q )))) )
```

Observe that this is a monadic predicate defined on an infinite domain of sentences of propositional logic; we could not begin to define this relation in extension without use of free variables.

2.4.3 Compilation of Generator Processes. As has been mentioned previously, a lambda expression, which gives the intension of an n-adic predicate, may be converted by the GOL compiler into a generator that produces elements of an appropriate n-dimensional space. As used here, the term "generator" refers to a process that has the following properties:

(1) Given a set of some sort, the generator provides a systematic means of selecting elements one by one from the set. The generator can be re-entered or fired over and over again, always yielding as an output some new member of the set, but

(2) when the distinct elements of the set have been exhausted, the generator indicates this fact and the generation process terminates.

For reasons that will be made clear presently, we call for the compilation of a set of generator processes by a command:

```
GOLPILE((F1 F2  ..  Fn)),
```

where each of the F_i is an expression of the form

⟨predicate variable⟩ ⟨abstract argument string⟩.

Assuming that the predicate variable in this form is n-adic, there will be n symbols—each either a $ or a *—in the corresponding abstract argument string. We regard the $ positions of the string to be *fixed*, meaning that at the time of evaluation, these dimensions will have given arguments specified; conversely, the * positions are considered to be *open*.

On the basis of any given abstract argument string, the compiler can create a generator that will:

(1) Take the actual arguments specified at run time and bind the $ positions of the predicate to these values. For purposes of discussion, we assume that these fixed arguments are actually inserted in the appropriate positions of the string.

(2) Assuming that there are fixed arguments for r of the n dimensions of P, the generator then produces elements from the reduced relation, which we shall call Q, consisting of (n − r)-tuples of entities, which when substituted as arguments in the * positions of the string, are consistent with the other r given arguments, i.e., the total n-tuple that results is in the extension of P.

Elements of the reduced relation Q can be generated from a given *extensional* predicate P in the following way: First, an n-tuple is selected from P and is subjected to a test to determine whether it matches the arguments specified for the $ positions of the string. In performing this test, the system treats any free variable in the extensional schema as a "wild card" that matches anything; once matched, however, such a variable becomes bound throughout the remainder of the computation to that thing with which it was matched.

If the selected n-tuple passes this test, we construct the (n − m)-tuple corresponding to the unconstrained (or *) positions of this n-tuple. Note that in some cases this output-tuple may still contain certain free variables that were left unbound by the match process described above. These variables retain their wild-card status until subsequently matched on input to some other generator process.

If the selected n-tuple from P fails to meet the test, the generation and testing of elements continues until either an element is found that does pass the test—and thus yields an output of the Q generator—or until the P generator is exhausted, in which case the Q generator is also terminated. This process, involving the repetitive selection and processing of elements from a given set generally referred to as "generate and test," is the basic building block of all GOL compiled evaluation processes.

Of the 2^n different abstract argument strings that may be associated with a given n-adic predicate, there is only one for which a generator process is not defined. This corresponds to a string containing no * entries, i.e., a string with no open positions to be filled. In such cases, the evaluation process required is a *test* rather than a generator, yielding the value *true* if the predicate is satisfied on the specified n-tuple of arguments, and *false* otherwise. Notice that this degenerate process is the only one possible in the case of an 0-adic predicate (see footnote 10, above).

2.4.4 Run-Time Evaluation: The GOLDIG Command.

We call for the computation (or firing) of a generator process by a command of the form:

$$\text{GOLDIG}((P\ A1\ A2\ ..\ An)\ S),$$

where

(a) P is a predicate designator that has been defined either extensionally or intensionally.

(b) Each A_i is either an actual argument or the symbol *, and

(c) S is the state in which evaluation is to take place; this is generally given by the symbol EXT which names the state set up by the GOLSET commands.

The GOLDIG command is actually designed to be the GOL compile and execute instruction, but because of space limitations in the present version of the system,[17] we must dispose of the compiler before undertaking any run-time evaluation. This requires advance compilation of all generator processes that will later be required. However, since it is unnecessary, at least in principle, for the user even to be aware of the compiler function, we assume in the following discussion that there is sufficient room in the system for GOLDIG to perform its intended role—first calling the compiler if necessary, then executing the appropriate routines.

2.4.5 Extensional Generators. To illustrate the use of GOLDIG, we consider now an expression involving the extensional predicate schema, IMPARTS, which is used in the THEOREM program to compose and decompose well-formed formulae of propositional logic. The extension of IMPARTS is a ternary relation containing the free variables P and Q:

IMPARTS: (((IMPLIES P Q) P Q))

Though it contains only one explicit triple, this relation is infinite in extent; any pair of expressions substituted for P and Q consistently across the n-tuple leads to an instance of the relation.

To see how this predicate can be used to decompose wff's, consider the following GOLDIG call:

GOLDIG((IMPARTS (IMPLIES A (OR B A)) * *) EXT)

in which we constrain only the leftmost argument position of the predicate. The result of this computation will be the output pair:

(A, (OR B A))

containing respectively the left- and right-hand parts of the input implicative expression. We will see presently how, in a more complex environment, these fragments of the input expression might be processed further.

A number of other generator processes may be compiled on the basis of the given predicate, IMPARTS. In particular, we get a process that will compose rather than decompose wff's by calling for a computation like the following:

GOLDIG((IMPARTS * (OR A B) (OR B A)) EXT),

which leads to a generation of the output 1-tuple:

((IMPLIES (OR A B) (OR B A))).

Observe, for future reference, that this tuple contains, as its only element, an instance of the third axiom schema.

---

[17] That is, the version implemented in 7090 LISP.

2.4.6 Generation from Intensional Relations. We now introduce the computational process involved in more complex generators that are based on intensional predicate definitions. Assume that we have an intensional predicate TEST defined by the following lambda expression:

    TEST: (LAMBDA (X Y) (EXISTS (Z) (AND (IMPARTS Z X Y) (AXIOM Z)))),

and that we call for the following evaluation:

    GOLDIG((TEST (OR A B) (OR B A)) EXT)

The abstract argument string corresponding to this computation contains no * positions; thus we require the compilation of a test process that will determine whether the given pair of arguments constitutes an element in the extension of TEST.

An evaluation process compiled for this expression would first bind those lambda variables in the defining expression of TEST that have specified run-time values. In this example, both X and Y would be so constrained. Next, each existentially bound variable (and any lambda variable that is not bound by input values) becomes associated with the symbol *, indicating that these values are open.

The evaluation process then proceeds to search for feasible values for these open variables that are consistent with all of the constraints imposed by the defining expression. In this example, the first step in this search would be to use the leftmost conjunct as a generator of things, Z, based on the following abstract form

    (IMPARTS * (OR A B) (OR B A)).

As we have seen previously, this generator would yield as output

    ((IMPLIES (OR A B) (OR B A))),

on the basis of which Z would become bound tentatively to:

    (IMPLIES (OR A B) (OR B A)).

A test process based on the rightmost conjunct would then be attempted. This term, with the bound value of Z inserted in place, would appear as:

    (AXIOM (IMPLIES (OR A B) (OR B A))).

Since this is a true expression, and since there are no further conjuncts in the expression to satisfy, a value of true would be returned by this computation.

This process of evaluation described above is, of course, peculiar to the particular lambda expression that was given. However, any process compiled for a conjunctive expression with only existential and lambda bound variables would be essentially similar. The first step in any process is to bind the lambda variables that have arguments supplied at the start; then all other bound variables are treated as open values to be filled by generators based on the various conjunctive expressions. Moving from left to right, these conjunct-generators are used to produce successive bindings of the open variables. The process terminates with the value *true* only if this search is successful; if it is not successful, the generators fire repeatedly until all possible combinations of feasible values of the open variables have been tried. Failure is reported by returning a value of *false* for the computation.

The case of lambda expressions that are basically disjunctive—still involving only lambda and existentially bound variables—is handled in a similar manner. In this case, however, the generators that are produced for the various disjuncts are put in parallel rather than in series. With generators in parallel, the first encountered (moving left to right) fires until it has been exhausted in the search for suitable bindings; then control passes to the generator on its right, which produces until exhaustion; etc. Again, the search continues through successive firings of these generators until a set of bindings for the open variables is found that satisfies the constraints imposed by the overall expression.

Finally, in the case of a universally quantified expression, we have the very restricted structure imposed by the syntax, of an implicative expression with simple left- and right-hand members. Such an expression compiles into an iterative loop that produces all combinations of open variables allowed by the antecedent and tests these in the consequent. A value of *true* is returned only if the consequent test is satisfied for every combination of bindings produced.

A complication sometimes arises in the evaluation of such expressions. If a binding for some universally quantified variable is produced by generating (directly or indirectly) from an extensional schema containing free variables, and if some one or more of these wild-card variables remains free after generation,[18] then it may be meaningless to test this binding in the way described in the previous paragraph. For example, assume that we have the expression:

(FORALL (X) (IMPLIES (F X) (G X))),

where F is defined in extension to be:

F: ((CAN A)),

with A free. (This might paraphrase the line "whatever you can do, I can do, too.")

---

[18] See discussion of wild-card variables, p. 356.

By the nature of the computation defined for such expressions, if there is anything that satisfies G, on the binding (CAN *) to X, the expression is counted *true*. If what we really want is to force an iteration through a set of specified values for A, we have two alternatives. We can require that the extension of F have all such elements explicitly represented; this alternative may be costly in terms of machine space. To provide a more economical representation, we admit the possibility of an outside domain declaration for any symbol used as a free variable in an extensional schema. We can write, for example,

        ATTRIB(A (FEAS (RIDE WALK SING))),

which provides a feasible set of values to be used in iterating on the "can do" loop discussed above.

The problem of wild-card symbols in values used as bindings for quantified variables presents no difficulty with conjunctive or disjunctive expressions. As these symbols are input to successive generators, they take on the values of whatever they match—in these cases, we are interested in finding only that *some* set of feasible bindings satisfies the expression, not that all do so. The wild-card problem can arise, however, in one other context—an expression that is the negation of some other formula. For essentially the same reasons adduced in the previous paragraph, we require that any wild-card symbol bound to a variable that appears in an expression prefixed by the connective NOT must have an outside domain of feasible values specified, as illustrated above. We will see an example in which such domain declaration is required in the ATTAIN program, discussed in Section 4.

2.5 Use of Recursive GOL Expressions

GOL expressions that involve recursive function calls are often used to describe problem-solving and decision-making search activity. Such expressions define what Floyed has called "non-deterministic algorithms,"[19] since they describe paradigms of search without specifying how the search is to be organized and carried out. Consider, for example, the following GOL expression of the predicate SOLVMAZE, which defines the concept, of solvability in a maze. In order to clarify the meaning of this expression the GOL notation is interleaved with an almost literal English translation:[20]

        SOLVMAZE: (LAMBDA (A Z)

---

[19] Cf. Floyd [7].

[20] The predicates SAME and CONNECTED used in this expression would be defined extensionally in the model; SOLVMAZE refers to the expression as a whole, and is intensional.

"a maze is solvable from point A to point Z . .

              (OR (SAME A Z)

if either A is the same as Z . .

              (EXISTS (B)

or there is some point B, . .

              (AND (CONNECTED A B)

connected to A, such that . .

              (SOLVMAZE B Z)))))

the submaze from B to Z is solvable."

It is clear that this expression, by itself, does not define a deterministic search process. It contains no prescription for handling the disjunctive choice implied by the existential quantifier. Nor does it make any provision for recovery from the blind alleys and circuits that may be encountered in the recursion. Nonetheless, the expression conveys a sufficient description of the concept to permit its use by the GOL system in computing the solvability of any given maze. The missing details relating to organization and control of search are supplied by the compiler in the process of structuring a deterministic search algorithm for the concept.

To call for a computation involving the SOLVMAZE test process, we would write the following:

        GOLDIG((SOLVMAZE START EXIT) EXT),

where START and EXIT name two points that appear in the extensional relation, CONNECTED. The evaluation process proceeds from left to right, first testing to see whether the two input symbols are the same; if so, it returns the value, true. If not, it proceeds to search for a binding of B which is paired in the relation CONNECTED with the bound value of A, and which, when treated as a new starting point in the recursive SOLVMAZE call, leads to a true value.

2.5.1 Expression of Modal Concepts.[21]

In any computation involving SOLVMAZE, the context in which evaluation takes place remains constant throughout; the only state referenced is the one specified initially. As

---

[21] We refer to predicates defined on classes of propositions as modal predicates; these may or may not involve quantification on a state variable.

suggested earlier, there are other applications of the language in which this is not the case. In dealing with expressions that define various forms of the modal concept of possibility, for example, the evaluation process may need to search through a number of alternate states of a model structure, seeking one in which some given proposition is satisfied. To permit this kind of search, we must provide for the explicit introduction of state variables in GOL expressions.

To do this, we use a syntactic device called a GOLDIG phrase, which is an expression of the following form that can be used as a constituent sub-formula in any GOL expression:

(GOLDIG ⟨atomic formula⟩ ⟨state designator⟩)

Use of a GOLDIG phrase in an expression indicates that a change of state is to take place before the atomic formula that it contains is evaluated. This method of introducing state variables is a form of management by exception, based on the expectation that most sub-expressions of a predicate definition will be asserted with respect to the present state of the computation. We attach the state variable only to the exceptional case—a sub-formula that expressly calls for evaluation in some other state.

Since the model structure associated with a modal expression may contain a large, perhaps infinite, number of alternate states, we cannot, in general, expect to encode data structures for all of these in advance. Instead, we permit the change of state associated with a GOLDIG phrase to be determined by a process of state transformation. In this way, new—previously unknown—states may be derived by application of transformation operators to the data structures characterizing known states. To indicate state transformation in a GOLDIG phrase, we use a state designator of the following form:

(TRANS ⟨operator⟩ ⟨state designator⟩),

where the operator is typically a bound variable used to convey the changes that are to take place as a result of the transformation, and the usual state designator is either the constant, STATE, that references the present state, or some other symbol that serves as a state variable. The function, TRANS, which denotes a mapping from the designated operator-state pair into a new state, may be designed by the user to effect certain control functions at the time of its evaluation. We will see examples of this use of TRANS at the end of this section.

In order to illustrate the expression of a modal concept calling for state transformation, we consider now a reformulation of the maze-solving algorithm. We assume that the objective in this revised version of the problem is to attain some admissible state of a GOL model structure in which the assertion (AT M EXIT) is true. (M may be thought of as a mouse that is running the maze.) To represent the position of the mouse, we must introduce an extensional relation, AT, which initially has M at some unspecified position outside the maze, and which must be changed in moving from state to state to keep track of M's motions in the model. We must also provide an extensional relation, MOVE, that relates transformation operators with position in the maze.

A modal version of the maze-solving algorithm can then be defined in the following way:

    MODALMAZE: (LAMBDA (GOAL X) (OR

"the goal of a maze is attainable, starting from point X,

        (GOAL)

if either the goal is satisfied in the present state

      (EXISTS (Y A) (AND

or there is some point Y and action A,

       (CONNECTED X Y)

such that Y is connected to X, and

       (MOVE Y A)

A is the action of moving to Y, and

     (GOLDIG (MODALMAZE (GOAL Y)

the goal is attainable, starting from point Y,

      (TRANS A STATE)))))))

in the new state derived by taking action A."

The evaluation of MODALMAZE would be called by a command of the form:

    GOLDIG((MODALMAZE (AT M EXIT) START) EXT).

In this case, the context of evaluation does not remain constant. It progresses through a sequence of transformations, terminating finally with the derivation of a state in which the goal (AT M EXIT) is satisfied, provided of course that it is possible to achieve such a state.[22]

---

[22] Traces of computer runs involving both the SOLVEMAZE and MODALMAZE predicates are given in Section 3.

2.5.2 Heuristic Selection Procedures. The set of alternate states attainable by the process of state transformation can be thought of as forming a tree structure—rooted at the present state, with nodes representing alternate states of the model and branches representing transformations. Any state is attainable from the present state if there is some connected sequence of branches leading to it. Thus attainability or possibility of any goal can be given graphic portrayal as a path, through the tree model structure, that terminates in a state with the desired properties.

The fact that such a state exists does not guarantee that a search procedure will find it in a reasonable amount of computing time. The naive procedure of attempting, in some orderly fashion, all sequences of transformations is in general not an effective strategy of search. The size of a search tree grows at an exponential rate; thus if there are potentially n branches emanating from each node, a tree m deep will contain $\sum_{i=0}^{m} (n^i)$ nodes, all representing attainable states. It does not take very large n or m to make it computationally infeasible to search such a space in an exhaustive manner.[23]

The alternative is to use some selective procedure for restricting the set of transformations that will be attempted at any branch point. In the MODALMAZE example, the choice of transformations attempted from any state is determined by generators based on the conjunctive terms

connected (X, Y) & move (Y, A),

i.e., selected actions are one-step moves to positions Y that are connected to the present location X. This form of legal move selection represents the minimum in search strategy. It is unlikely that any other selection procedure would do better, in general, in dealing with arbitrary maze configurations than this simple legal move selector. However, in many applications, it is possible to define a much more refined concept of desirable move. Indeed, there are some problem areas in which it is possible to narrow the set of desirable operators at each node to a single alternative—the use of the simplex algorithm in linear programming provides a case in point.

In most applications, however, the best we can do is limit the choice, by some heuristic means, to a small set of promising alternatives. The selection of these alternative transformations is often predicated on conditions that exist in the present state of the computation. Thus, the capability of the GOL system to recognize patterns and other conditions in a given state of a model often plays an important role in the implementation of heuristic selection procedures.

---

[23] See [19] for a discussion of the British Museum Algorithm, an exhaustive search procedure.

2.5.3 Search Strategy in GOL.

In much of the contemporary work in heuristic problem solving, search of the problem space is controlled by a strategy that may best be characterized as a branch-and-bound technique. As each state is created at a branch point, an index of merit is computed and used to order that state, along with other unexplored states, on a try list which represents the search tree for the problem space. States are selected for further elaboration and search in the order of their appearance in this list.

This form of search strategy is implemented in GOL through the device of an externally specified ORDER function that is used to evaluate states as they are generated. In any GOL evaluation process, all states created at a GOLDIG branch are given a tentative value and filed in an ordered GOLIST of unexplored states. The ranking of newly created states is carried out by the LISP function, ORDER (which must be designed by the user to compute an integer index that reflects, in some sense, the difficulty of the particular GOLDIG entry under contention). The ranking that this function provides determines whether the given branch will be followed immediately or deferred pending exploration of other alternatives having lower index ratings.

The ORDER function is supplied by a GOL evaluation process with three inputs: one is the difficulty index associated with the present level of the computation, a second is the argument of the predicate in the GOLDIG phrase involved, and the third is the name of the new state to which transfer is contemplated. Any or all of these data may be ignored by the subroutine in computing the rank of a GOLDIG branch. In particular, we get the depth-first search strategy by ignoring the inputs and letting ORDER be the zero function. The breadth-first scheme is obtained almost as simply by letting the value of ORDER be one more than the present-difficulty level.

These two ordering functions give the extremes of search behavior; there are many alternative strategies that fall in between and give superior performance in some applications. By judicious design of the ORDER function, it is possible to have GOL-compiled processes emulate the search behavior of many of these variant schemes. In the following section we outline a possible GOL formulation of the MATER control process, based on the checkmating program of that name designed by G. Baylor and H. Simon [2]. This process exemplifies some of the more interesting notions of contemporary design for search strategy.

2.5.4 The MATER Executive in GOL.

The MATER program is a heuristic problem solver, originally coded in IPL-V, which has had considerable success in the sort of chess situation where one is asked to find a forced mate for one side or the other. The search strategy employed by this program is probably its most powerful feature. Instead of examining moves on the basis of either of the extreme search strategies, the MATER executive selects for further elaboration those branches of the tree that seem most promising, on the basis of a fewest-replies heuristic. There is a small flurry of information-gathering activity as each branch based on a MATER checking move is sprouted. Among other data garnered, a rank index is determined which is simply a count of the number of legal replies open to the opponent at his next move. This integer index is the basis of selecting branches for further search, and may postpone indefinitely exploration of the branch under consideration if the count is greater than those found elsewhere in the search tree.

With this much of an introduction, we can write down a GOL version of this control program. It involves defining two modal expressions, MATER and SUBMATE, that embody the search heuristics. Two other predicates, CHECKING and LEGAL, which are used to define particular classes of moves in the various states, will not be given here, though in order to carry out a computation of MATER, lambda expressions defining these processes would have to be provided as well.

We employ in the following definitions two different transformation functions, TRANS1 and TRANS2, both of which have the business of making a chess move. They differ, however, in the way in which they rank alternatives; i.e., they are associated with different ORDER functions. The operator TRANS1 is associated with the simple zero function mentioned earlier, which carries out a depth-first recursive search. This is overridden, however, by the order function associated with TRANS2, which ranks alternatives on the basis of a count of the extension of the predicate LEGAL in the state under consideration. In attending to alternative branches in the order of this ranking, the GOL executive would make its choices on the basis of the same heuristic criterion as the original MATER program, and should emulate its performance in this task.

The GOL expressions defining MATER and SUBMATE are the following:

        MATER: (LAMBDA ( )

"forced mate is achievable from the present state

        EXISTS (A) (AND (CHECKING A)

if there is some checking move A

        (GOLDIG (SUBMATE)

such that SUBMATE is true

        (TRANS1 A STATE)))))

in the state that results from applying A."

                SUBMATE (LAMBDA ( )

"SUBMATE exists if

                (FORALL (B) (IMPLIES (LEGAL B)

for every legal move B

                (GOLDIG (MATER)

forced mate can be achieved

                (TRANS2 B STATE)))))

in the state that results from applying B."

2.6 Summary

There are many interesting problem-solving, decision-making, and game-playing tasks that involve goals which cannot be expressed conveniently in numerical terms. It is often possible, however, to represent these non-numerical goals as relations defined on suitable symbolic domains. By using forms of notation borrowed from type theory with lambda conversion, we can describe such relations, verbally, in such a way that they may be understood by a machine interpreter. It is thus possible to provide the machine with a measure of perception which can be used both as a guide in the solution of problems and in the perception of solutions, i.e., the act of problem solving itself.

To say that an interpreter understands the intension of a relation means either or both of the following:

(a) the interpreter is able to recognize instances of the pattern or concept denoted by the relation and classify objects as either in or out of the corresponding extension,

(b) the interpreter can generate elements of the extension, i.e., it can produce objects that satisfy all the requisites of the intensional description.

The GOL system can deal with its intensional representation of relations in both of these ways. The compiler has the capacity to produce different segments of code that can either test or generate instances of any relation expressed unambiguously in the language.

In some cases, such computation does nothing more than retrieve information that has been encoded explicitly in the data structures of the

GOL model. The evaluation process simply tests whether a given object is in the known extension of a relation or it produces an element from that known class. More interesting uses of the language involve evaluation of patterns and concepts that are not known a priori in the model. In such cases, the evaluation process may require a certain amount of deductive reasoning in order to respond meaningfully. Where these concepts are defined by recursive GOL expressions, evaluation often takes the form of complex decision-making and problem-solving activity.

Because of space limitations in the present implementation of the GOL system, it has not been possible to experiment with the GOL version of MATER. However, a number of other GOL problem solvers have been tested, including versions of the Advice Taker and General Problem Solver discussed in Section 1. Details of these and other GOL programs are given, along with summaries of computer output, in the following section.

SECTION 3
EXAMPLES OF GOL PROGRAMMING

In this section we discuss a number of programs that have been formulated and tested in the present version of the GOL system. These include the two maze examples discussed previously, (1) a version of the Advice Taker and (2) versions of the General Problem Solver and Logic Theorist of Newell, Shaw, and Simon. For each of these, we give the set of commands necessary to input the expressions and data structures defining the task, and a summary of the computer-generated search process involved in performing the task.

3.1 The Maze Examples Revisited

Since both maze examples have been described in detail in the preceding sections, they need not be elaborated upon here. We give in the following figure (Figure 2) the setup commands and summary of the computer runs of these two processes, operating on the maze configuration illustrated in Figure 1.

The first MAZE example took 26 seconds of 7090 time to compile and execute; the second required almost 53 seconds. It is clear from examining the two trace outputs that both of these processes defined exactly the same search strategy and both traced out the same path through the maze. The reader might wonder at this point whether there is ever reason to employ the more combersome and costly machinery associated with state change and the full GOL model structure. The following two examples, taken

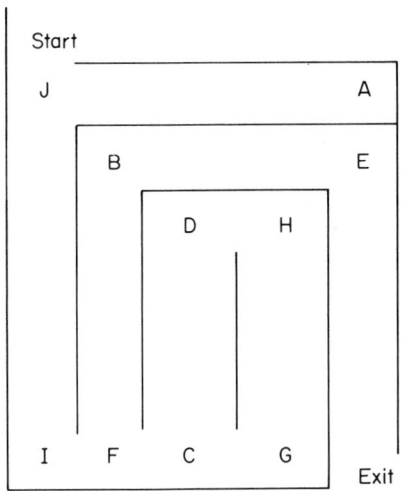

Figure 1 Maze configuration defined by the CONNECTED predicate.

together, constitute our case for problem solvers employing state transformation.

3.2 The GOL Advice Taker

Our version of the Advice Taker is based on Fischer Black's Deductive Question Answering System [3]. In Black's scheme, the universe of discourse is a corpus consisting of a set of axiomatic assertions; inference rules of the system include substitution for free variables and a detachment rule for conditional expressions that is basically equivalent to modus ponens.

In problem-solving situations involving cause and effect reasoning, the corpus of information typically includes several statements predicated on the causal modalities (can, cause, and canult) defined by McCarthy.[24] In Black's system, this set of modal operators is extended to include several special cases of both the cause and can concepts. The following is Black's list of causal operators, with associated meanings:

can(c, s, a):	given that condition c holds, subject s can perform action a.
can2(s, a):	subject s can unconditionally perform action a.
cause(c1, a, c2):	given condition c1, action a causes condition c2.
cause2(a, c):	action a unconditionally causes condition c.

[24] See McCarthy [17].

```
SOLVMAZE
   GOLSET((
      (CONNECTED ( (A J) (B E) (B F) (C D) (C G) (C F) (D H) (D C) (E B) (E EXIT) (F C)
                   (F I) (F B) (G H) (H G) (G C) (H D) (I F) (I J) (J A) (J I) (START J)) )
      (SAME ((P P))) ))
DEFLIST(((SAME (P))) FREVR)       *this identifies P as a free variable in SAME.
   GOLDEF(( (SOLVMAZE (LAMBDA (GOAL X) (OR (SAME GOAL X) (EXISTS (Y) (AND
                  (CONNECTED X Y) (SOLVMAZE GOAL Y))))) ))
   GOLPILE(( (SOLVMAZE $ $) ))    *the $'s indicate specified arguments at run-time
   GOLDIG((SOLVMAZE EXIT START) EXT)
```

                      * * * *   *Output Trace*   * * * *

1(SOLVMAZE EXIT START)
2(SOLVMAZE EXIT J)
  3(SOLVMAZE EXIT A)
  3*VALUE:NIL*
  3(SOLVMAZE EXIT I)
    4(SOLVMAZE EXIT F)
      5(SOLVMAZE EXIT C)
        6(SOLVMAZE EXIT D)
          7(SOLVMAZE EXIT H)
            8(SOLVMAZE EXIT G)
            8*VALUE:NIL*   *recursion terminated because of threatened loop
          7*VALUE:NIL*
        6(SOLVMAZE EXIT G)
          7(SOLVMAZE EXIT H)
            8(SOLVMAZE EXIT D)

Figure 2 The maze examples.

8*VALUE:NIL*
7*VALUE:NIL*
6*VALUE:NIL*
5*VALUE:NIL*
5(SOLVMAZE EXIT B)
6(SOLVMAZE EXIT E)
7(SOLVMAZE EXIT EXIT)
7*VALUE:*T*
6*VALUE:*T*
5*VALUE:*T*
4*VALUE:*T*
3*VALUE:*T*
2*VALUE:*T*
1*VALUE:*T*
END OF COMPUTATION, VALUE = *T*;   Compile & Execute Time (7090) = 26 seconds

MODALMAZE
  GOLSET(((MOVE ((P ((AT ((M Q)) ((M P))))))
              (AT ((M XX)))
              (CONNECTED ((A J) (B E) (B F) (C D) (C G) (C F) (D H) (D C) (E B) (E EXIT) (F C)
              (F I) (F B) (G H) (H G) (G C) (H D) (I F) (I J) (J A) (J I) (START J))))
  DEFLIST(((MOVE (P Q))) FREVR)
  GOLDEF(((MODALMAZE (LAMBDA (GOAL X) (OR (GOAL) (EXISTS (Y A) (AND (CONNECTED X Y)
              (MOVE Y A) (GOLDIG (MODALMAZE GOAL Y) (TRANS A STATE))))))))
  GOLPILE(((MODALMAZE $ $)))
  DEFINE(((ORDER (LAMBDA (X Y Z) 0))))   *This is the zero ORDER function, calling for the depth-first
                                                 recursive mode of search

  GOLDIG((MODALMAZE (AT M EXIT) START) EXT)

Figure 2 (*cont.*)

* * * Output Trace * * *

```
1 (GOLDIG(MODALMAZE (AT M EXIT) START) EXT)
   TRANS(((AT ((M G1)) ((M J))), EXT)  →  S1         *the symbol 'G1' stands for a free variable; 'S1' is the
2 (GOLDIG(MODALMAZE(AT M EXIT) J) S1)                 new state resulting from a transformation on EXT.
   TRANS(((AT ((M G1)) ((M A))), S1)  →  S2
   3 (GOLDIG (MODALMAZE (AT M EXIT) A) S2)           *the system recognizes here that it has created a
      TRANS(((AT ((M G1)) ((M J))), S2)  →  S1        duplicate of an earlier state.
      3*VALUE:NIL*
   TRANS(((AT (M G1)) ((M I))), S1)  →  S3
   3 (GOLDIG (MODALMAZE (AT M EXIT) I) S3)
   TRANS(((AT ((M G1)) ((M F))), S3)  →  S4
   4 (GOLDIG (MODALMAZE (AT M EXIT) F) S4)
      TRANS(((AT ((M G1)) ((M C))), S4)  →  S5
      5 (GOLDIG (MODALMAZE (AT M EXIT) C) S5)
         TRANS(((AT ((M G1)) (M D)))), S5)  →  S6
         6 (GOLDIG (MODALMAZE (AT M EXIT) D) S6)
            TRANS((AT ((M G1)) ((M H))), S6)  →  S7
            7 (GOLDIG (MODALMAZE (AT M EXIT) H) S7)
               TRANS(((AT ((M G1)) ((M G))), S7)  →  S8
               3 (GOLDIG (MODALMAZE (AT M EXIT) G) S8)
                  TRANS(((AT ((M G1)) ((M H))), S8)  →  S7     *duplicate
                  TRANS(((AT ((M G1)) ((M C))), S8)  →  S5     *duplicate
               8*VALUE:NIL*
            TRANS(((AT ((M G1)) ((M D))), S7)  →  S6     *duplicate
            7*VALUE:NIL*
         TRANS(((AT ((M G1)) ((M C))), S6)  →  S5     *duplicate
         6*VALUE:NIL*
      TRANS(((AT ((M G1)) ((M G))), S5)  →  S8
```

Figure 2 (*cont.*)

```
6(GOLDIG (MODALMAZE (AT M EXIT) G) S8)
   TRANS(((AT ((M G1)) ((M H)))), S8) → S7
7(GOLDIG (MODALMAZE (AT M EXIT) H) S7)
   TRANS(((AT ((M G1)) ((M G)))), S7) → S8      *duplicate
   TRANS(((AT ((M G1)) ((M D)))), S7) → S6
8(GOLDIG (MODALMAZE (AT M EXIT) D) S6)
   TRANS(((AT ((M G1)) ((M H)))), S6) → S7      *duplicate
   TRANS(((AT ((M G1)) ((M C)))), S6) → S5      *duplicate
         8*VALUE:NIL*
   TRANS(((AT ((M G1)) ((M C)))), S8) → S5      *duplicate
         7*VALUE:NIL*
   TRANS(((AT ((M G1)) ((M F)))), S5) → S4      *duplicate
         6*VALUE:NIL*
   TRANS(((AT ((M G1)) ((M I)))), S4) → S3      *duplicate
   TRANS(((AT ((M G1)) ((M B)) S4) → S9
5(GOLDIG (MODALMAZE (AT M EXIT) B) S9)
   TRANS(((AT ((M G1)) ((M E)))), S9) → S10
6(GOLDIG (MODALMAZE (AT M EXIT) E) S10)
   TRANS(((AT ((M G1)) ((M B)))), S10) → S9     *again
   TRANS(((AT ((M G1)) ((M EXIT)))), S10) → S11
7(GOLDIG (MODALMAZE (AT M EXIT) EXIT) S11)
         7*VALUE:*T*
      6*VALUE:*T*
    5*VALUE:*T*
   4*VALUE:*T*
  3*VALUE:*T*
 2*VALUE:*T*
1*VALUE:*T*
END OF COMPUTATION, VALUE = *T*;    Compile & Execute Time (7090) = 53 seconds
```

Figure 2 (*cont.*)

canult(s, c): subject s can ultimately bring about condition c.

Certain axioms in the information corpus are of a general nature, not specific to any task. For example, the axioms that define the canult operator are general statements of cause and effect. Consider the following conditional expression that defines a deduction axiom in Black's system:

A1: cause2(a, c), can2(s, a) → canult(s, c)

where a, c, and s are free variables standing for actions, conditions, and subjects, respectively.

The inference rules of Black's system permit detachment of any true clause in the antecedent of a deduction axiom such as A1, above. Thus, if it can be shown that, for some set of values a', c', and s', both cause2(a', c'), and can2(s', a') are derivable from the axioms, we may conclude the true consequent, canult(s', c'). Of course, derivation of the antecedent clauses may require additional deduction steps, application of either substitution or detachment to some other axioms in the corpus.

Successful application of the substitution rule yields an immediate deduction; i.e., if we can show that an asserted clause is a substitution instance of an axiom, no further inference is required. On the other hand, application of the detachment rule typically involves generating and evaluating a conjunctive set of sub-goals. In attempting to apply this rule, the system scans the corpus for some deduction axiom that matches (perhaps with certain substitutions of constants for variables) in its right-hand part the clause that is to be proved. If such an axiom is found, the set of clauses making up its left-hand part then becomes a conjunctive set of sub-goals, all of which must be derivable to permit inference of the given clause.

It happens that in the example given above, the only possible derivation of the antecedent clauses is through substitution, since the corpus contains no deduction axiom with either cause2 or can2 in its right-hand part. The only other deduction axioms are A2 and A3, both of which are concerned with deductions of canult.

A2: cause2(a, c), can(c1, s, a), canult(s, c1) → canult(s, c)

A3: cause(c1, a, c), can2(s, a), canult(s, c1) → canult(s, c)

Since the clause, canult(s, c1), which appears in the antecedent of each of these expressions can be made to match the right-hand parts of all three deduction axioms, we see that there are many alternate ways in which subgoals may be generated in a canult derivation. Thus a search tree involving a canult deduction may be expected to display disjunctive as well as conjunctive branching.

To illustrate the formulation of a problem and its solution in this system, we use the Monkey Problem suggested by McCarthy as being representative of Advice Taker tasks. One of the many variations of the problem is the following:

"A monkey is in a room where a bunch of bananas is hanging from the ceiling too high to reach. In the corner of the room is a chair, and the solution to the monkey's problem is to move the chair under the bananas and climb onto the chair, from which point the bananas can be reached."

The first step in formulating the problem in Advice-Taker terms is simply to recognize the relevant conditions, actions, and actors involved in the scenario. We single out the following list of primitive phrases as descriptors of the actions and conditions that characterize the monkey problem:

moveto(s, o, p):	subject s moves object o to place p.
climb(s, o):	subject s climbs object o.
reach(s, o):	subject s reaches object o.
at(o, p):	object o is at place p.
on(s, o):	subject s is on object o.
has(s, o):	subject s has object o.

The goal of the Advice Taker is to prove:

canult(monkey, (has (monkey, banana))).

It is next necessary to specify the causal laws that relate the actions and conditions of the problem; this is accomplished by annexing a set of cause and can axioms to the information corpus of the system. The following axioms are used to represent the causal relationships in this problem:

C1:	cause2(moveto(s, o, p), at(o, p))
C2:	cause2(reach(s, o), has(s, o))
C3:	cause(at(o, p), climb(s, o), (at(o, p) & on(s, o)))
C4:	can2(M, moveto(M, C, p))
C5:	can2(M, climb(M, C))
C6:	can((at(C, U) & on(M, C)), M, reach(M, B))

In these expressions, the variables s, o, and p are defined respectively over the domains of subjects, objects, and places. The constants B (bananas) and C (chair) are both objects; M (monkey) is a subject, and U (under) is a place.

A particularly useful way to view the distinction between the deduction axioms A1–A3 and the causal axioms C1–C6 is to observe that the deduction axioms are analogous to GOL intensional definitions, while the latter are more like the GOL extensional structures. Consider the difference in the way the concepts can2 and canult are known to the system. The causal axioms

C4 and C5 give an itemized listing of all pairs (s, a) of which the predicate can2 is assumed to be true. This corresponds precisely to what in GOL is called an extensional definition of the concept. Canult, on the other hand, is known through a set of expressions that define a logical complex of relationships, the intension of the concept.

This observation allows us to map any of Black's Advice Taker tasks into a corresponding GOL formulation. The deduction axioms map into intensional GOL predicates; the remaining axioms in the corpus define predicates in extension. The GOL version of the problem then is to GOLDIG the intensional predicate on some given set of arguments; its value is determined by the sort of recursive tree search described in the previous sections, a process very similar to Black's.

In Figure 3 we give the set of commands necessary to define the intensional predicate CANULT and the extensional CAN, CAUSE, CAN2, and CAUSE2 data structures. There follows a trace of the computation of the predicate functor expression (CANULT * (HAS M B)). The reason for evaluating this expression rather than the fully specified sentence (CANULT M (HAS M B)) is to illustrate some of the subtler features of the system. As discussed in Section 2, a predicate functor defines a class in extension and its GOL evaluation involves generation of elements from that class. In this case, the desired computation should yield the name of some member of the class of actors, s, who can ultimately bring about the condition (HAS M B). Had we evaluated the sentence (CANULT M (HAS M B)) instead of the functor, the result of the computation would have been a truth-value rather than a name.

Evaluation of the expression (CANULT * (HAS M B)) requires the compilation of two distinct processes, one a generator based on the abstract argument string (* $), the other a test based on the string ($ $) (cf. discussion, page 356). For discussion purposes, we call these processes CANULT1 and CANULT2, respectively. Note that CANULT1 is to take one argument and return a unit class of names; CANULT2 is to take two arguments and return a truth-value. That this is actually the case can be seen by inspection of the output trace.[25]

3.3 Critique of the Advice Taker

In many problem-solving situations, we must satisfy simultaneously a number of lesser goals, which taken together constitute a *conjunctive main goal*. While the supporting goals may sometimes be dealt with independently, in general we may expect interactions in the task environment to affect the

---

[25] To compile and execute this program required approximately fifteen seconds of 7090 time.

```
GOLSET(( (CAUSE2 (((MOVETO S O P) (AT O P)) ((REACH S O)   (HAS S O))) )
         (CAUSE  (((AT O P) (CLIMB S O) (ATON O P S))) )
         (CAN2  ((M (MOVETO M C P)) (M (CLIMB M C))) )
         (CAN  (((ATON C U M) M (REACH M B))) )) )
DEFLIST(((CAUSE2 (S O P)) (CAUSE (S O P)) (CAN2 (P)) FREVR)
GOLDEF((  (CANULT (LAMBDA (S C) (OR (EXISTS (A) (AND (CAUSE2 A C) (CAN2 S A)))
            (EXISTS (A C1) (AND (CAUSE C1 A C) (CAN2 S A) (CANULT S C1)))
            (EXISTS (A C1) (AND (CAUSE2 A C) (CAN C1 S A) (CANULT S C1))) ))  ))
GOLPILE(( (CANULT * $) (CANULT $ $) ))        *respectively: 'CANULT1' & 'CANULT2'
GOLDIG((CANULT * (HAS M B)) EXT)

                        * * *  Output Trace * * *

1(CANULT1 (HAS M B))
  2(CANULT2 M (ATON C U M)
     3(CANULT2 M (AT C U))
       3*VALUE:*T*
    2*VALUE:*T*
  1*VALUE: (M)
END OF COMPUTATION, VALUE = (M)
```

Figure 3 The Advice Taker in GOL.

simultaneity of the conjunctive goals. In particular, we may find that though each of two sub-goals is separately attainable, their conjunction is not; such goals are said to comprise a mutually exclusive set.

The possibility of separately attainable but mutually exclusive goals presents a difficult choice to the designer of a problem solver based on the inference rules of symbolic logic. Shall the usual rules permitting derivation of a conjunction based on separate derivation of its conjuncts apply? There are clear hazards if they do, but there are equally difficult conceptual problems if they do not, viz., how to deal with the conjunctive main goal?

It may appear at first reading that Black has somehow come to grips with the problem, since one of the sub-goals generated in solving the monkey problem appears conjunctive in form:

$$at(C, U) \& on(M, C)$$

However, as the GOL formulation of the problem shows, the conjunction of primitive conditions implied by this expression is pure illusion, having meaning only to the beholder of the system. The fact that "&" has no real syntactic role to play in the system is evident from our use of the mnemonic ATON(C, U, M) to express the same idea as the expression above.

On closer inspection, we see that none of the primitive phrases characterizing actions and conditions in the problem (see p. 375) has any meaning at all to the system. It is this lack of semantic interpretation that prevents us from dealing effectively with interactions in the problem environment. If actions were treated semantically as operators that transform the environment by modifying primitive conditions, it would be possible to deal with the simultaneity of conjunctive goals by searching through a sequence of action transformations for a state in which all the supporting goals are satisfied simultaneously. This is the purpose of the GOL function ATTAIN, the subject of our next application.

3.4 The GOL General Problem Solver

In the General Problem Solver (GPS) of Newell and Simon [20], the conditions, actions, and causal laws that characterize a task are modeled rather than described. Instead of applying logical inference to an information corpus that describes a task, this system reasons deductively by performing selective transformations on a model of the task.

Objects are represented in a GPS moded by description lists, which are simply conjunctions of attribute-value pairs that tell what conditions the object satisfies. An object is said to exist in the model if all the conditions in its defining conjunction are met there; it is said to be attainable if it can be shown to exist in some derivable state of the model.

In most applications of GPS, the objective is to discover some state of the model in which a given desired object exists. Operationally, this objective translates into a conjunctive main goal of the form considered previously; we seek the simultaneous elimination of all differences—features of the desired object not satisfied in the initial state.

As a tactical heuristic, GPS deals with a conjunction of differences by attacking them one by one in the order of decreasing difficulty, as determined by a user specified difference-ordering relation. Once the most important difference has been detected, a desirable operator relevant to this difference is selected from the table of connections—a relevancy relation on the cross product of difference types and operators. In some cases, the attempt at transformation may fail due to inapplicability of the operator. This can lead to the creation of sub-goals and auxiliary problem-solving activity directed toward derivation of a state to which the desirable operator can be applied. If the criteria of applicability can be met, the selected operator is then used to derive a new state of the model in which, hopefully, the set of differences has been reduced. This process of differencing followed by selection and application of operators is repeated recursively until either some state is found satisfying all aspects of the goal or the program runs out of time, space, or things to try—in which case the process is terminated.

In formulating the GOL version of GPS, we can preserve much of the structure of the Advice Taker by observing that the latter's CAN and CAUSE axioms play essentially the same role as the applicability and desirability relations of the General Problem Solver. It remains to provide a differencing operator that recognizes unsatisfied features of an object and an ordering relation on the set of difference types. All of these can be expressed by the semantical data structures of the GOL system. To this end, we define the following set of extensional relations for the GOL General Problem Solver:

cause2(a, c):	action a is relevant to condition c
can2(a):	a is applicable, unconditionally
can(c, a):	given condition c, a is applicable
ord(d, i):	i is the difficulty of difference d
actab(a, op):	op is the operator form of action a
contains(c, p):	conjunctive condition c contains primitive condition p

The heuristics of GPS are embodied in the GOL function ATTAIN which defines a recursive search process involving state transformation. The expression defining this function is somewhat more complex than any considered previously and in order to explicate the various sub-parts of the expression, we give an annotated version on the next page.

The GOL ATTAIN function interpreted

ATTAIN: (LAMBDA (GOAL D) (OR (AND (FORALL (X)
begin
            (IMPLIES (CONTAINS GOAL X) (X))) (ASSIGN D STATE))
if GOAL is satisfied *then* := ⟨present state⟩ *else*
            (EXISTS (Y COND1 ACTION D1 OP Z) (AND
begin
                    (CONTAINS GOAL Y) (NOT (Y)))
Y := ⟨difference⟩;
            (ORD Y Z) (ASSIGN CONTROL Z)
CONTROL := ⟨difficulty of difference⟩;
            (CAUSE2 ACTION COND1) (CONTAINS COND1 Y)
ACTION := ⟨relevant action⟩;
            (OR (AND (CAN2 ACTION) (ASSIGN D1 STATE))
if ACTION is applicable *then* D1 := ⟨present state⟩ *else*
            (EXISTS (COND2) (AND
begin
                    (CAN COND2 ACTION))
COND2 := ⟨enabling condition⟩;
            (GOLDIG (ATTAIN COND2 D1) STATE))))
D1 := ⟨state in which COND2 is satisfied⟩; *end*;
            (ACTAB ACTION OP)
OP := ⟨transformation operator based on ACTION⟩;
            (GOLDIG (ATTAIN GOAL D) (TRANS OP D1))))))
STATE := ⟨result of applying operator OP to state D1⟩;
D := ⟨state in which GOAL is satisfied⟩; *end*; *end*

The interpretation of the function, in a combined sort of ALGOL—BNF notation, is much more readable than the GOL expression itself and it makes very obvious the nondeterministic character of the algorithm. As discussed in the previous chapter, in order to convert this scheme to a deterministic search process, the compiler must be supplied an ordering function ORDER by which it ranks the disjunctive GOLDIG branches.[26]

In the General Problem Solver, control of branching is based on the relative order of the most difficult difference, as compared to the order of the computation underway. If a sub-goal at a disjunctive branch involves a difference more difficult than the one presently being acted upon, the sub-goal will not be attempted. Instead, the search may ascend to higher levels seeking other alternatives that are consistent with the rule of progression from hard to easy differences.

To achieve this kind of control in the ATTAIN function, we define an

[26] It is to obtain this control that we use the clause (GOLDIG (ATTAIN COND2 D1) STATE) rather than the simpler (ATTAIN COND2 D1) which, though semantically identical, is pragmatically quite different.

auxiliary intensional function TESTR, which—using the difference ordering relation ORD—computes the order of the most difficult difference in any sub-goal. The ORDER subroutine then subtracts from this number the value of CONTROL (to which ATTAIN has assigned the difficulty of the current computation). If this difference is less than or equal to zero, the order of the branch is set to zero (meaning it will be attempted immediately); otherwise the branch is ranked by the positive difference.

3.5 The Revised Monkey Problem

To exemplify the operation of the ATTAIN search process, we consider now a variation on the Monkey Problem, characterized by a conjunctive main goal of a sort that would confound Black's Advice Taker. The problem, suggested by Simon, is characterized by a sequencing interaction in the problem space; see Simon [22] for a discussion of other classes of problems afflicted with semantical interaction. This version of the problem can be stated as follows:

"A monkey is in a room containing at one corner a bowl of cereal and at another a pitcher of cream. The bowl can be carried from place to place but the pitcher is too heavy to do anything with but tip. We assume that if he is grasping both objects the monkey can have breakfast. The solution to his problem therefore is to go first to the bowl and carry this to the corner with the cream."

The goal in this situation can be expressed by the conjunction:

$$grasping(M, BOWL) \& grasping(M, CREAM)$$

which, as observed earlier, can be dealt with by Black's "canult" only if the information corpus contains some causal axiom of the form:

$$cause2(\langle action \rangle, grasping(s, o1) \& grasping(s, o2))$$

or

$$cause(\langle condition \rangle, \langle action \rangle, grasping(s, o1) \& grasping(s, o2))$$

The alternative of including in the corpus the deduction axiom

$$canult(c1), canult(c2) \rightarrow canult(c1 \& c2)$$

is clearly inacceptable as a means of dealing with the problem, since the order in which the two conditions are derived is an important aspect of the solution. Thus, while the derivation of grasping(M, BOWL) followed by grasping(M, CREAM) may permit inference of their conjunction, the opposite sequence of derivations would not. Moreover, if we were to impose the condition that neither object is capable of being moved, the conjunction would not be derivable by any sequence even though both subparts may be met independently.

A problem solver operating in this task environment must be able to keep track of the changes brought about by the monkey's actions and base its decisions concerning the future course of events on information gleaned from changing environment. In short, this requires the mode of operation of a GPS or ATTAIN: a deduction scheme based on a sequence of transformations in a model of the task.

To formulate the problem for solution by ATTAIN, we define a set of extensional data structures based on the following causal relationships:

cause2(carry(s, o, p), at(o, p) & at(s, p))
cause2(moveto(s, p), at(s, p))
cause2(grab(s, o), grasping(s, o))
cause2(release(s, o), ngrasping(s, o))[27]
can2(release(M, o))
can(ngrasping(M, BOWL) & ngrasping(M, CREAM), moveto(M, p))
can(grasping(M, BOWL) & ngrasping(M, CREAM), carry(M, BOWL, p))
can(at(o, p) & at(s, p), grab(s, o))

The initial spatial arrangement of objects is given by the extensional predicate, at, to be:

at(M, P1)
at(CREAM, P2)
at(BOWL, P3)

and the extensional relation, grasping, is initially vacuous. The effects of actions are specified by the extensional actab relation as follows (as interpreted by TRANS):

carry(s, o, p):	remove the present pairs involving s and o from the "at" extension, then add the pairs: (s, p) and (o, p)
moveto(s, p):	remove the present pair involving s from the "at" extension, then add the pair: (s, p)
grab(s, o):	add the pair: (s, o) to the extensional grasping relation
release(s, o):	remove the pair: (s, o) from the grasping extension

[27] The function "ngrasping" is the intensionally defined negation of the extensional "grasping."

Finally we note that the extensional, contains, is used to decompose a conjunction into its component parts; the and2 referred to in this structure is the binary conjunction relation; id is the unary relation, identity.

The commands needed to define the functions and data structures for this application are given in Figure 4. There follows an output trace of two computer runs,[28] one with the conjunctive goal:

$$\text{grasping}(M, BOWL) \ \& \ \text{grasping}(M, CREAM)$$

and the other:

$$\text{grasping}(M, CREAM) \ \& \ \text{grasping}(M, BOWL).$$

The latter is clearly the more difficult phrasing of the problem, since the machine runs out of space before solving it. The problem is that the monkey embarks on a false start, going first to grab the cream—an action that temporarily immobilizes him. After releasing the cream, he goes to the bowl and is on the way back to the cream when the system exhausts available space. It is clear from these two examples that the conjunctive goal can easily be met if both objects are designated as movable. It is still tractable if one object is made stationary. But it is unsolvable if both are considered to be fixed in place. It is hard to conceive of any modification of Black's canult function that would permit this range of deductive reasoning behavior in his system.[29]

As a final example of what can be done in GOL, we consider in the following section a theorem-proving application that resembles in some ways the problem-solving scheme of canult. Here, as there, we have a body of axioms, a set of inference rules, and the objective of proving theorems by a sequence of inferences based ultimately on the axioms. In both cases, we attempt solution by backward search—recursively generating and attempting sub-goals that imply the goal. The analogy fails, however, when we consider the size of the search space generated by these two applications. The simple depth-first search strategy, which proved adequate for the tiny space of the monkey problem, is poorly suited to the potentially infinite search space of the propositional calculus. To get off on a wrong track in this space and continue searching in depth are very likely to produce, as sub-goals, longer and longer sequences of longer and longer meaningless expressions.

A more promising strategy is to minimize this proliferation by dealing first with those sub-goals, at whatever level found, containing the least num-

---

[28] The first of these required 76 seconds to compile and execute on the 7090; the second ran for 123 seconds before exhausting available space.

[29] See, however, Appendix A for an alternative approach to this sequencing paradox, due to Cordell Green [9].

```
GOLSET((
  (CAUSE2 (((CARRY S O P)   (AND2 (AT O P)    (AT S P)))  ((MOVETO S P)  (ID (AT S P)))
          ((GRAB S O)  (ID (GRASPING S O)))  ((RELEASE S O)  (ID (NGRASPING S O))))  )
  (CAN2  (((RELEASE M O)))  )
  (CAN   (((AND2 (NGRASPING M BOWL)     (NGRASPING M CREAM))    (MOVETO M P))
          ((AND2 (GRASPING M BOWL)      (NGRASPING M CREAM))    (CARRY M BOWL P))
          ((AND2 (AT O P)   (AT S P))   (GRAB S O)))  )
  (ORD   ((NGRASPING S O) 0)  ((AT M O) 1)  ((GRASPING S O) 2)  ((AT BOWL O) 2)
          (AT CREAM O) 5)    (S O))  )
  (ACTAB (((CARRY S O P)   ((AT  ((S Q))   (O Q))   ((S P)   (O P))))
          ((MOVETO S P)    ((AT  ((S Q))   ((S P))))
          ((GRAB S O)      ((GRASPING NIL  ((S O))))
          ((RELEASE S O)   ((GRASPING      ((S O))  NIL))))  )
  (CONTAINS (((ID Q) Q)  ((AND2 Q R)  Q)  ((AND2 Q R)  R))  )
  (AT  ((M P1)  (BOWL P3)  (CREAM P2))  )
  (GRASPING ((NIL NIL)))
          ))
DEFLIST(((CAUSE2  (S O P))  (C/N2 (O))  (CAN (S O P))  (CONTAINS  (Q R))  (ACTAB  (S O P Q))
          (ORD  (S O P))) FREVR)
GOLDEF(( (ATTAIN (LAMBDA (GOAL D)  (OR
            (AND (FORALL (X) (IMPLIES  (CONTAINS GOAL X)  (X)))  (ASSIGN D STATE))
          (EXISTS (Y COND1 ACTION D1 OP Z)  (AND
            (CONTAINS GOAL Y) (NOT  (Y))  (ORD Y Z)  (ASSIGN CONTROL Z)
            (CAUSE2 ACTION CCND1)  (CONTAINS COND1 Y)  (OR
              (AND (CAN2 ACTION)  (ASSIGN D1 STATE))
              (EXISTS  (COND2)  (AND  (CAN COND2 ACTION)   (GOLDIG  (ATTAIN COND2 D1)  STATE)))))))
            (ACTAB ACTION OP)  (GOLDIG  (ATTAIN GOAL D)  (TRANS OP D1))))))
          (TESTR (LAMBDA (X Y)  (EXISTS (Z)  (AND (CONTAINS X Z)  (NOT  (Z))  (OPD Z Y))))
          (NGRASPING (LAMBDA  (S O)  (NOT (GRASPING S O))))    ))
(GOLPILE(((ATTAIN $ *)  (NGRASPING $ $)   (TESTR $ *)))
```

Figure 4 The GOL General Problem Solver.

```
DEFINE(((ORDER  (LAMBDA  (X Y Z)   (PROG  (I)   (SETQ  I   (GOLDIG  (LIST  (QUOTE TESTR)X   (QUOTE *))  Y))
                         (COND  ((NULL I)   (RETURN 0)))   (SETQ I   (DIFFERENCE   (CAR I)  Z))
                         (COND  ((MINUSP I)   (RETURN 0)))   (RETURN I))))  ))
ATTRIB   (P   (FEAS   (P1 P2 P3)))
```

The GOL General Problem Solver: Output Trace for two test runs

Test I: GOLDIG ((ATTAIN (AND2 (GRASPING M BOWL)   (GRASPING M CREAM)) *)   EXT)
         1(GOLDIG (ATTAIN (AND2 (GRASPING M BOWL)   (GRASPING M CREAM))) EXT)
          2(GOLDIG (ATTAIN (AND2 (AT BOWL P3)   (AT M P3))) EXT)
            3(GOLDIG (ATTAIN (AND2 (NGRASPING M BOWL)   (NGRASPING M CREAM))) EXT)
            3*VALUE: (EXT)
           TRANS(((AT ((M G1))   ((M P3)))), EXT)   →   S1
            3(GOLDIG (ATTAIN (AND2 (AT BOWL P3)   (AT M P3))) S1)
            3*VALUE: (S1)
          2*VALUE: (S1)
         TRANS(((GRASPING NIL   ((M BOWL)))), S1)   →   S2
          2(GOLDIG (ATTAIN (AND2 (GRASPING M BOWL)   (GRASPING M CREAM))) S2)
            3(GOLDIG (ATTAIN (AND2 (AT CREAM P2)   (AT M P2))) S2)
              4(GOLDIG (ATTAIN (AND2 (GRASPING M BOWL)   (NGRASPING M CREAM))) S2)
              4*VALUE: (S2)
             TRANS(((M G1)   (BOWL G1))   ((M P2)   (BOWL P2)))), S2)   →   S3
              4(GOLDIG (ATTAIN (AND2 (AT CREAM P2)   (AT M P2))) S3)
              4*VALUE: (S3)
            3*VALUE: (S3)
           TRANS(((GRASPING NIL   ((M CREAM)))), S3)   →   S4
            3(GOLDIG (ATTAIN (AND2 (GRASPING M BOWL)   (GRASPING M CREAM))) S4)
            3*VALUE: (S4)

Figure 4 (*cont.*)

```
           2*VALUE:  (S4)
         1*VALUE:  (S4)
         END OF COMPUTATION, VALUE = (S4)

Test II:        GOLDIG  ((ATTAIN  (AND2  (GRASPING M CREAM)   (GRASPING M BOWL))  *)  EXT)
         1(GOLDIG  (ATTAIN  (AND2  (GRASPING M CREAM)  (GRASPING M BOWL)))  EXT)
          2(GOLDIG  (ATTAIN  (AND2  (AT CREAM P2)  (AT M P2)))  EXT)
           3(GOLDIG  (ATTAIN  (AND2  (NGRASPING M BOWL)  (NGRASPING M CREAM)))  EXT)
           3*VALUE:  (EXT)
           TRANS(((AT   ((M G1))   ((M P2))),  EXT)  →  S1
           3(GOLDIG  (ATTAIN  (AND2  (AT CREAM P2)  (AT M P2)))  S1)
           3*VALUE:  (S1)
         2*VALUE:  (S1)
         TRANS(((GRASPING NIL  ((M CREAM)))),  S1)  →  S2
          2(GOLDIG  (ATTAIN  (AND2  (GRASPING M CREAM)  (GRASPING M BOWL)))  S2)
           3(GOLDIG  (ATTAIN  (AND2  (AT BOWL P3)  (AT M P3)))  S2)
            4(GOLDIG  (ATTAIN  (AND2  (NGRASPING M BOWL)  (NGRASPING M CREAM)))  S2)
            TRANS(((GRASPING  ((M CREAM))  NIL),  S2)  →  S1      *recognizes duplicate state
            5(GOLDIG  (ATTAIN  (AND2  (NGRASPING M BOWL)  (NGRASPING M CREAM)))  S1)
            5*VALUE:  (S1)
            4*VALUE: (S1)
            TRANS(((AT   ((M G1))   ((M P3))),  S1)  →  S3
            4(GOLDIG  (ATTAIN  (AND2  (AT BOWL P3)  (AT M P3)))  S3)
            4*VALUE:  (S3)
           3*VALUE:  (S3)
           TRANS(((GRASPING NIL  ((M BOWL))),  S3)  →  S4
           3(GOLDIG  (ATTAIN  (AND2  (GRASPING M CREAM)  (GRASPING M BOWL)))  S4)
            4(GOLDIG  (ATTAIN  (AND2  (AT CREAM P2)  (AT M P2)))  S4)
                  *  *  *  *  *
COMPUTATION TERMINATED AT THIS POINT DUE TO GARBAGE COLLECTOR FAILURE
```

Figure 4 (*cont.*)

ber of symbols. This is the heuristic approach of the GOL version of the Logic Theory Machine described in the following paragraphs.

3.6 The Logic Theorist in GOL

The GOL function THEOREM, which is defined and interpreted by the expressions below, is a modal predicate intended to express the derivability of certain statements of the propositional calculus. The heuristics employed in the search process involve the same three proof procedures articulated in the Logic Theorist (LT) of Newell, Shaw, and Simon [19]. In this scheme the *immediate deduction* method is the one that actually proves theorems; it terminates a search process with a demonstration that the goal or sub-goal is a variation of one of the axioms. The inference at these terminal nodes is based on either *substitution* for free variables or *replacement* of connectives by their definitions. The other two proof procedures are the methods of *detachment* and *chaining*, both of which are used to sprout new branches of the search tree by creating sub-goals which, if provable, imply the validity of the problem expression.

The GOL theoremprover, interpreted

```
              THEOREM:    (LAMBDA  (X) (EXISTS  (Y) (AND
begin
                                      (AXIOM Y)
Y := ⟨axiom⟩;
                (OR  (REPLACES Y X)  (EXISTS  (U V A B W Z)  (AND
if X ≡ Y then *T* else
                (REPLACES X V)  (IMPARTS V A B)  (IMPARTS Y Z W)
V := ⟨implicative equivalent of X⟩;
A := ⟨left hand part of V⟩;
B := ⟨right hand part of V⟩;
Z := ⟨left hand part of Y⟩;
W := ⟨right hand part of Y⟩;
          (OR (AND  (REPLACES A Z)  (REPLACES B W))
if (A ≡ Z) & (B ≡ W) then *T* else
                    (AND  (SIMILAR X Y)  (OR
if X is similar to Y then
              (AND  (REPLACES W B)  (IMPARTS U A Z))
if (W ≡ B) then U := (A ⊃ Z) else
              (AND  (REPLACES Z A)  (IMPARTS U W B))
if (Z ≡ A) then U := (W ⊃ B) else
                          (IMPARTS Y U X))
if X matches W then U := Z;
              (GOLDIG  (THEOREM U)  STATE))))))))
if U is a THEOREM then *T*; end;
```

Four primitive concepts are needed for the definition of the THEOREM predicate: These are:

axiom(x):   x is an axiom
replaces(x, y):   x and y are equivalent, under replacement of principal connective
similar(x, y):   x and y are formulas containing the same number of distinct variables[30]
imparts(x, a, b): x is an implicative expression with a its left- and b its right-hand part

It was pointed out in the previous chapter that, through use of free variables, the extensional relation AXIOM defines an infinite set of axioms including all substitution instances of the five basic schemata. Thus a test process based on the term (AXIOM X) will return the value true if X conforms to any of the infinite variants of any schema. In such a case, we have the immediate deduction that X is a theorem.

Other variations of the axioms, brought about by replacement of connectives, also lead to immediate deductions of THEOREM. For example, if (A ⊃ B) is a substitution instance of a theorem, then its definitional equivalent, (∼ A V B) would also be counted a theorem, and vice versa. The replacement rules used to relate the various syntactic structures of propositional logic are defined by the relation REPLACES given in extension as shown on page 390.

The predicate REPLACES is used in two different ways in the definition of THEOREM. In all occurrences but the second, this term is used to define a test process that yields a value of true if and only if its arguments (both of which are specified) are equivalent under some replacement rule. The only exception is the second occurrence of the term, in the clause (REPLACES X V), which defines a generator of values V that are replacement equivalents of the specified argument X.

The predicate IMPARTS was also described in the previous section; for reference, we repeat the definition here:

    IMPARTS: (((IMPLIES P Q) P Q))

with P and Q free. This function is used in three different ways in the expression defining THEOREM. In each case, the IMPARTS clause defines a generator based on some abstract argument string involving both $'s and *'s. In the first two occurrences, the string is ($ * *); thus, for example, the

---

[30] This predicate is defined by a LISP function, rather than by a GOL intensional form; the GOL compiler can deal with any LISP-defined predicate, provided *all* arguments will be known at run-time.

clause (IMPARTS V A B) becomes a generator of pairs A and B, which are the left-hand and right-hand parts, respectively, of the implicative expression V. As the interpreted version of the expression shows, these clauses have the effect of a set of assignment statements for the variables A, B, Z, and W.

Again referring to the interpreted version of the function, we see that the third and fourth occurrences of the predicate IMPARTS have the effect of assignment statements, setting the variable U to a newly composed implicative expression. This is based on the abstract argument string (* $ $). These clauses are used to create sub-goals U as determined by the forward and reverse chaining methods.

The detachment method is involved in the last occurrence of IMPARTS. With the argument string ($ * $), this clause is used to generate sub-goals U which, if provable, may be detached from an axiom of the form (U $\supset$ X)— yielding thereby the desired theorem X as conclusion.

The sub-goals generated by any of these processes are ranked by the ORDER subroutine on the basis of a symbol count. Those with the smallest number of symbols are the ones attempted first at the recursive GOLDIG branch. As in a number of examples discussed previously, the clause (GOLDIG(THEOREM U) STATE), which does not involve change of state, is used only to invoke the control effected by the ORDER subroutine. If we were to use in its place the simpler, semantically equivalent clause, (THEOREM U), the search strategy would revert to the depth-first recursive mode. For comparison purposes, a version of THEOREM using this simpler clause was tried on some of the theorems of Figure 5. It was unable to prove any theorems requiring either detachment or chaining in their proofs.

Even with the more effective search heuristic, the THEOREM function is at best a mediocre theorem prover. As the output corresponding to Theorem VII shows, even some variants of the axioms receive a null response. The problem in this case is that the search for equivalence under replacement extends only to the top two levels of an expression; Theorem VII requires replacements three levels down.

It is possible to supplant the REPLACES predicate in the definition of THEOREM by an intensionally defined recursive function CORRESPONDS which extends the search for equivalence under replacement as far as necessary in comparing any two expressions. In another version of the theorem prover, using this recursively defined concept of replacement, Theorem VII was recognized after almost two minutes of computer time to be a variant of Axiom IV. Unfortunately, due to additional space requirements imposed by this extra compiled function—none of the other test theorems could be handled by the system. As in the case of the attain function in the second monkey problem, the machine runs out of available space before a deduction can be completed.

```
GOLSET(( (AXIOM  (((IMPLIES  (OR P P)  P))
                  ((IMPLIES  P  (OR Q P)))
                  ((IMPLIES  (OR P Q)  (OR Q P)))
                  ((IMPLIES  (OR P  (OR Q R))  (OR Q  (OR P R))))
                  ((IMPLIES  (IMPLIES P Q)  (IMPLIES  (OR R P)  (OR R Q))))  )
         (REPLACES  ((P P)
                  ((IMPLIES P Q)  (OR  (NOT P)   Q))
                  ((IMPLIES  (NOT P)  Q)  (OR P Q))
                  ((OR P Q)  (IMPLIES  (NOT P)  Q))
                  ((OR  (NOT P)  Q)  (IMPLIES P Q))
                  ((NOT  (NOT P))  P)
                  (P  (NOT  (NOT P))))  )    ))
         (IMPARTS  (((IMPLIES P Q)   P Q))    ))
DEFLIST(((AXIOM  (P Q R))  (REPLACES  (P Q R))  (IMPARTS  (P Q)))  FREVR)
DEFINE((  (ORDER  (LAMBDA  (X Y Z)  (COND  ((ATOM X)  1)  (T  (PLUS  (ORDER  (CAR X)   Y Z)
                  (ORDER  (CDR X)  Y Z))))    ))
GOLDEF((  (THEOREM  (LAMBDA  (X)  (EXISTS  (Y)  (AND  (AXIOM Y)  (OR  (REPLACES Y X)
                  (EXISTS  (U V A B W Z)  (AND  (REPLACES X V)  (IMPARTS V A B)
                  (IMPARTS Y Z W)  (OR  (AND  (REPLACES A Z)  (REPLACES B W))
                  (AND  (SIMILAR X Y)  (OR  (AND  (REPLACES W B)  (IMPARTS U A Z))
                  (AND  (REPLACES Z A)  (IMPARTS U W B))  (IMPARTS Y U X))
                  (GOLDIG  (THEOREM U)  STATE))))))))  ))
GOLPILE((  (THEOREM $)  ))

*THEOREM 1:*      $((A \supset \sim A) \supset \sim A)$
    GOLDIG  ((THEOREM  (IMPLIES  (IMPLIES A  (NOT A))  (NOT A)))  EXT)

                            * * *  *Output Trace*  * * *
```

Figure 5 The GOL Theorem Prover.

```
1(THEOREM (IMPLIES (IMPLIES A (NOT A)) (NOT A)))
1*VALUE:  *T*
END OF COMPUTATION, VALUE IS *T*; 7090 TIME USED = 1.2 seconds.
```

THEOREM II: $(\sim A \supset (A \supset B))$

```
GOLDIG((THEOREM (IMPLIES (NOT A) (IMPLIES A B))) EXT)
 1(THEOREM (IMPLIES (NOT A) (IMPLIES A B)))
   2(THEOREM (IMPLIES (NOT A) B))
     3(THEOREM (IMPLIES (OR G1 (NOT A)) B))
     3*VALUE:  'undecided'
   2*VALUE:  'undecided'
   2(THEOREM (IMPLIES (NOT A) (OR B (NOT A))))
   2*VALUE:  *T*
 1*VALUE:  *T*
END OF COMPUTATION, VALUE IS *T*; 7090 TIME USED = 1 minute, 10 seconds.
```

THEOREM III: $(A \supset (B \supset A))$

```
GOLDIG ((THEOREM (IMPLIES A (IMPLIES B A))) EXT)
 1(THEOREM (IMPLIES A (IMPLIES B A)))
 1*VALUE:  *T*
END OF COMPUTATION, VALUE = *T*; 7090 TIME USED = 4 seconds.
```

THEOREM IV: $(A \supset A)$

```
GOLDIG ((THEOREM (IMPLIES A A)) EXT)
 1(THEOREM (IMPLIES A A))
   2(THEOREM (IMPLIES A (OR A A)))
   2*VALUE:  *T*
 1*VALUE:  *T*
END OF COMPUTATION, VALUE IS *T*; 7090 TIME USED = 25 seconds.
```

*G1 is a 'wild card' variable.

Figure 5 (*cont.*)

THEOREM V: $((A \supset \sim B) \supset (B \supset \sim A))$
GOLDIG ((THEOREM (IMPLIES (IMPLIES A (NOT B)) (IMPLIES B (NOT A)))) EXT)
1*THEOREM (IMPLIES (IMPLIES A (NOT B)) (IMPLIES B (NOT A))))
1*VALUE: *T*
END OF COMPUTATION, VALUE IS *T*; 7090 TIME USED = 10 seconds.

THEOREM VI: $((A \vee A) \supset (A \vee B))$
GOLDIG ((THEOREM (IMPLIES (OR A A) (OR A B))) EXT)
1(THEOREM (IMPLIES (OR A A) (OR A B)))
2(THEOREM (IMPLIES (OR A A) B))
2*VALUE: 'undecided'
2(THEOREM (IMPLIES (OR A A) (OR B A)))
3(THEOREM (IMPLIES (OR A A) A))
3*VALUE: *T*
2*VALUE: *T*
1*VALUE: *T*
END OF COMPUTATION, VALUE IS *T*; 7090 TIME USED = 1 minute, 16 seconds.

THEOREM VII: $((A \supset (B \supset C)) \supset (B \supset (A \supset C)))$
GOLDIG ((THEOREM (IMPLIES A (IMPLIES B C)) (IMPLIES B (IMPLIES A C))) EXT)
1(THEOREM (IMPLIES A (IMPLIES B C)) (IMPLIES B (IMPLIES A C))))
2(THEOREM (IMPLIES (IMPLIES (OR G1 A) (OR G1 (IMPLIES B C))) (IMPLIES B (IMPLIES A C))))
2*VALUE: NIL
1*VALUE: NIL
END OF COMPUTATION, VALUE (erroneously) IS FALSE; 7090 TIME USED = 35 seconds.

Figure 5 (*cont.*)

392

SECTION 4
SUMMARY AND CONCLUSIONS

Our thesis, as stated in Section 1, is that the duality of syntax and semantics—as these terms relate to a modal extension of type theory—provides a dual representation in which both to describe and model various aspects of a problem-solving, decision-making, or game-playing task environment. In order to determine the implications of this proposal, we have devised a computer language, called GOL, with syntax and semantics designed to reflect this duality. Our experience with this new computational facility has shown that both descriptive and model problem solvers may be represented effectively in the expressions and data structures of the system, and that the heuristic search strategies of a variety of problem-solving schemes may be emulated by the associated semantic evaluation processes.

However, certain limitations both in the design of the language and in its present implementation preclude the representation and investigation in GOL of sizable problems: For example, as noted previously, we cannot in the present system do a GOL version of the MATER chess problem-solving program.

In this section we consider some possible revisions in the formulation of the GOL system that might render the latter more efficient in its utilization of computer memory, and propose certain additional features that we feel should be included in the next generation of GOL compilers. We then sketch briefly some of the open questions that have been raised but not answered by this chapter.

4.1 Proposed Revisions and Extensions of the GOL System

4.1.1 Choice of an Embedding Language. The decision to implement an initial version of the GOL compiler in LISP rather than in some lower-level language has probably reduced by several man-years the time required to get a reasonably complete version of the system up and running. LISP is a particularly good language in which to embed other language systems, especially when the language to be implemented resembles LISP in significant respects.

We have now reached the stage of development, however, when it is no longer sufficient to demonstrate feasibility of the GOL philosophy; in the next pass at implementation, our objective will be efficiency of representation and compiled process, rather than expediency in system design and development. It is not clear, at this point, whether the continued use of LISP as an underlying language is compatible with this new objective.

At least a few issues that have emerged from our work cast doubt on the long-run value of LISP as an embedding language for GOL. Consider, for example, the costly business of saving, swapping, and restoring contexts for successive entries into GOL generators. This is a housekeeping chore that one might expect could easily be handled by the built-in LISP pushdown stacks, but which instead requires both extensive LISP code and elaborate use of LISP memory. The problem, briefly, is that ordinary stack operations are designed for use in a depth-first mode of recursive evaluation; in GOL we reject this scheme in favor of a more flexible search strategy controlled by an ordered try-list of sub-generators that are awaiting re-entry at all levels and stages of the computation.

Though generator contexts cannot be stacked, for efficient processing it is clear they must be filed in some reasonably compact and accessible manner. The fact that we have not been able to find a really satisfactory way of managing context within the LISP framework suggests that we should, at least, re-examine the problem the next time around in assembly or machine language terms.

For data representation, too, we have some reservations about the continued use of the LISP format; in this case, it seems that LISP gives perhaps too much flexibility and that, for the most efficient storage of GOL data structures, we should consider specially designed data management routines. GOL data structures are highly structured, containing lists of n-tuples of fixed size. One should be able to obtain much faster access to the data in such structures and at the same time cut significantly the memory requirements by using successive memory locations for the entries in any tuple. We are presently using the LISP array feature to effect this structuring of GOL memory, though there are certain complications involved in attempting dynamic array declarations in this system that greatly add to the cost of storing and accessing data.

4.1.2 Extensions of the Language. In addition to revisions aimed at improved efficiency, we would like to see included in the next version of GOL a number of additional features that would add to the convenience and simplicity of expression. For instance, it would be convenient in many cases to be able to use function designators other than predicates, so that, for example, one would be able to write an assignment statement of the form:

$$(\text{ASSIGN } X \ (F \ Y)),$$

rather than the form now required:

$$(G \ Y \ X),$$

where G is defined to be the binary relation:

$$(T, \ F(T)).$$

Moreover, the use of such functions would greatly simplify certain other expressions, for example those involving the identity or equality predicate. We could write:

EQUAL (F X) (G Y))

in place of the more cumbersome conjunctive expression:

(AND (F1 X Z) (G1 Y W) (EQUAL Z W)),

which is required in the present scheme.

The inclusion of equality as a built-in test process is another extension to be considered in the next version of GOL. This presents some difficulties in view of the diversity of entity types allowed in the system. The meaning of equality must be carefully defined for arguments that are functions of various types. For example, how are we to determine whether two predicates defined by different lambda expressions are equal? Should it be on the basis of some demonstrable mapping of one expression into the other, or on the basis of identical extensions of the two functions? If the latter, must there be identity of extensions in all states of the model structure (i.e., necessary identity) or just in the present state of the computation?

The answers to these questions will necessarily turn on the pragmatic issue: What are the user's needs? At this point, our intuition about eventual uses of the language is not sufficiently developed to engender confidence in providing answers; still it is clear that the next GOL compiler must have some notion of equality built in.

We are on somewhat surer ground in the next proposal: that we make use of the intrinsic ordering (from top to bottom) of the tuples in any extensional predicate. It has been suggested previously that this ordering might sometimes be important—cf. the early discussion of the advice predicate for the tic-tac-toe example (p. 346). Many other examples could be given of extensional relations in which the order of occurrence of tuples could be considered relevant information if only there were some way to take advantage of it. For example, we might want to generate only the top element from some extensional structure, or all tuples between two specified elements, or just the last tuple, and so on. Much can be gained at very little cost by including in the next version of GOL some generating capability that is sensitive to the ordering of data in extensional structures. This will require the addition of a number of built-in processes, associated with such functions as between, first element, first after, and so on, but will not entail any significant revision in the overall structure of the system.

Finally, we note that the next GOL system should have expanded numerical capabilities. While providing functions to be used in assignment statements, we should include also a set of numerical predicates and functions that allow the testing and binding of numerical variables. The lack of such capability is a patent deficiency in the present scheme.

4.2 Areas for Further Research

A number of questions raised during this undertaking have not been answered adequately at this stage of the study; of these, three stand out as areas calling for significant research effort.

The first of these concerns search strategy and the abdication reflected in the requirement that the user specify a function to order states (nodes) in the GOL try list. It is to be hoped that further study will uncover some general principles that will reduce specifying the order function to at most a perfunctory task for the user; ideally, of course, we would like to automate this decision process completely. It is conceivable (though at this point not obvious) that this problem may be formulated for solution in GOL, and that we may devise a GOL strategic process that monitors and controls the problem-solving activity of other lower-level GOL processors. If tractable at all, this promises to be a major undertaking—a task for the revised GOL system when that facility becomes available.

Another area that may usefully find one GOL processor monitoring and influencing the activities of others is inductive learning. The entire research effort to date has been focused on translating from intensional to extensional forms of relations; the process of induction is concerned with movement in the opposite direction. McCarthy has argued[31] that to deal with machine learning, we must first have a formalism in which to express an abstraction; we have such a formalism in GOL. We have the basic tools by which to build new GOL expressions—to generalize and abstract on certain known facts and relations, and thereby to define new abstract patterns and concepts in intension. But to carry out this induction in such a way that the resulting expressions define meaningful relations—that may, for example, relate some perceivable pattern with a desirable move in a given game—requires a measure of sophistication that we do not now possess. Our present thinking is that the most promising avenue of research into this area of inductive reasoning is the paradigm of hypothesis-and-test, whereby newly induced patterns or concepts are treated as mere hypotheses until substantiated in further testing. As additional evidence of relevance is obtained, such induced hypotheses, as they are found adequate to predict or explain subsequent experience, would be retained and added to the system's corpus of knowledge; otherwise they would be modified (if possible) or discarded as irrelevant. The paradigm of hypothesis-and-test reduces the process of inductive learning to a problem-solving search activity, not unlike others that we have considered for formulation in GOL. Again, this promises to be a major undertaking which, if it can be carried out at all, will have to await development of an advanced GOL capability.

[31] See McCarthy [15].

Finally, we must consider another unsettled (and unsettling) question—the organization of sub-formulae within a GOL lambda expression. As we have indicated previously, even the simple interchange of a pair of conjunctive or disjunctive sub-formulae can have considerable effect on the time to solution or even on the attainability of a solution in the evaluation of certain GOL expressions. How are we to teach the user to write good, efficient GOL expressions—how, in particular, are we to get the machine, in making inductive hypotheses, to write good efficient GOL expressions—when so much depends on the pragmatics of the evaluation process?

The only adequate answer to these questions is a reformulation of the GOL evaluation process; we must replace the inherent left-right scan by some other choice process, perhaps ordering the sub-formulae (and their respective generators) on the basis of some heuristic criteria. Again, this problem may map into a heuristic search activity that may itself prove to be tractable as a GOL problem-solving application. If this is true, this problem should be one of the early targets of the ongoing research activity, since its success will have a profound effect on the teachability and usability of the system.

APPENDIX A
RELATION TO CONTEMPORARY WORK

A.1 Green's System QA3

The contemporary work with which our research is most nearly related is that of Cordell Green at Stanford Research Institute. In a paper (see [9]), Green describes a system of first-order logic that serves as the basis of a question-answering system, QA3. This system employs the algorithmic procedures of theorem proving by the resolution method to perform deductive reasoning from a corpus of descriptive information. Like GOL, QA3 deals specifically with a state-space in which the truth-values of assertions are predicated on the states to which these assertions refer. Unlike GOL, however, Green's system does not represent states by collections of semantic data structures; rather, in QA3, states are represented either by given names (e.g., S0, S1, etc.), or by sequences of transformations on states so named. These sequences of transformations can be thought of as complex names for the corresponding derived states.

One result of this difference in conception of the state-space is that all assertions in QA3 must carry state variables, if in fact they are in any way state-dependent. Recall that in GOL it is necessary to attach state variables only to those assertions that are to be evaluated in some state other than the present state, or current context, of the computation. Moreover, since states are known in QA3 only through their names, it is not possible to provide in that system for the sort of perceptual processes that underlie most GOL problem-solving processors. Thus in QA3, as in the other implementations of the Advice Taker discussed previously (cf. p. 369), it is necessary to specify in connection with each state transformation, all those conditions of interest in the state that remain unchanged as a result of the transformation as well as those that change. An example will help clarify these issues.

We previously gave a formulation of the simple monkey problem for the question-answering system of F. Black [3]. This same problem may be formulated for Green's system QA3 as follows:[32]

Axioms:

(1) movable(box)

(2) emptyplace (under-bananas, s0)

(3) at(box, place0, s0)

(4) $\forall$(m, u, b, p, s) (at (b, p, s) $\wedge$ movable (b) $\wedge$ emptyplace (u, s) $\supset$ at(m, u, move(m, b, u, s)) $\wedge$ at(b, u, move(m, b, u, s))))

(5) $\forall$(s) (can(climb(monkey, box, s)))

(6) $\forall$(m, u, b, s) (at(b, u, s) $\wedge$ can (climb(m, b, s) $\supset$ at(b, u, climb (m, b, s) $\wedge$ on(m, b, climb(m, b, s))))

(7) $\forall$(s) (at(box, under-bananas, s) $\wedge$ on (monkey, box, s) $\supset$ can (reach(monkey, bananas, s)))

(8) $\forall$(m, z, s)) $\supset$ has(m, z, reach(m, z, s))

Question:

$\exists$ (sf) (has(monkey, bananas, sf))

The question being asked here can be paraphrased: "Does there exist some state, sf, such that the monkey has the bananas in sf?" In attempting to answer this question, Green's theorem prover—like all schemes based on the resolution principle—first adds the negation of the given question to the corpus of axioms and then attempts to derive a contradiction.

Green has added to the usual machinery of resolution theorem-proving the concept of an answer literal that is "added to each clause in the negation of the question. The arguments of 'answer' are the existentially quantified variables in the question . . . . An answer clause specifies the sets of values that the existentially quantified variables in the question may take in order to preserve the provability of the question."[33]

[32] This formulation of the problem, due to Green, was transmitted in private correspondence.
[33] Green [op. cit.]

In deriving a proof of the question in the example given above, the answer provided by the computation algorithm of QA3 is the following:

sf = reach(monkey, bananas, climb(monkey, box, move(box, box, under, s0))),

which, as mentioned above, is merely a complex way of naming a derivable state that has the desired properties.

Green's problem solver is a powerful and general scheme, clearly set apart from the more restrictive program of Black by virtue of its focus on state-space constructions. One could formulate within QA3 the Simon version of the monkey problem (cf. p. 381), since the conjunctive paradox is dispelled as readily by the state-space of QA3 as by that of GOL.

There are some significant differences between these two approaches to generality in problem solving, however, that suggest a major variance both in representation and performance of the two systems. For one thing, it is necessary in the axioms of QA3 to mention explicitly all those conditions of relevance in the problem that remain unchanged as a result of any state transformation, as well as those that do undergo some change. Thus in Axiom 6, for example, we specify that if b is at u in state s, (i.e., at (b, u, s)), then it continues to be at place u (i.e., at (b, u, climb(m, b, s))) in the revised state that results from the transformation, climb(m, b, s). The situation is not as bad as in some of the cases we have considered previously since, for example, in Axiom 5 we see an illustration of a certain condition (i.e., can(climb(monkey, box, s))) that holds in every state and which can therefore be conjoined to other conditions that may be derived in some state s', without fear of paradoxical results. Nonetheless, it seems clear that in a more complex task environment, such as chess, we would be faced in QA3 with the same sort of axiom proliferation that caused us to despair of the theorem prover approach of the Advice Taker and to advance the GOL thesis in the first place.

It is also worth contemplating, in reciting the differences in approach between QA3 and GOL, the relative advantages of an algorithmic vis-à-vis heuristic search procedure. It is our feeling that the solution procedure of QA3, though algorithmic, may in many cases prove to be much less direct than the corresponding GOL solution process. In particular, we wonder whether there is any likelihood that the algorithm of QA3 could reasonably be modified to utilize advice of the sort that the GOL perceptual processes and heuristic decision procedures provide. Would there for example be any way, in a theorem prover like Green's, to take advantage of the very powerful heuristic of means-ends analysis and difference reduction? At the present state of the art, it seems unlikely.

A.2 Fikes' System REF

Another recent development that has some points of contact with GOL is the REF language and interpreter, which has been designed and implemented at Carnegie-Mellon University by Richard Fikes [6]. This language, formulated as an extension of a procedure language, introduces two new statement types: the select function and the condition. We quote from Fikes [op. cit.]:

> "The 'select' function provides the facility for indicating that a selection is to be made from a space of potential solutions. It requires arguments which define a set and the value of the function is an element of that set. For example, if the base programming language is 'ALGOL' then the statement 'B := SELECT (0, 9)' could mean that B is to be assigned as a value an integer in the range 0 to 9. The 'condition' statement is used to state a Boolean expression which must have 'true' as a value. By using the 'condition' statement one can verify that a selection is a solution to the problem being stated."

With the use of these additional features, it is possible to express in the REF language a wide class of nondeterministic algorithms for constraint-satisfaction and heuristic-programming problems.

There are a number of similarities between the REF and GOL programming systems, also a number of differences. Most obvious is the surface difference in language syntax that arises from the fact that REF is considered an extension of ALGOL, whereas GOL is an extension of LISP. This distinction is more apparent than real; for example, the interpretation of several of the GOL programs given in Section 3 tends to resemble the form and structure of REF programs.

More important than these surface differences are the underlying similarities of purpose and representation of these two systems. Both, for example, provide for the expression of conjunctions and disjunctions of conditions, which are used to control and test the generation of values for variables; both provide means for expressing both universal and existential quantification on these variables; both search through the state-space of possible solutions by performing actual transformations of the data structures defining those states.

Let us consider a simple example that illustrates use of REF in a conjunctive constraint satisfaction problem. Again, quoting from Fikes:

> "Consider the problem of finding two integers in the range 0 to 9 whose sum is 15. Using 'ALGOL' as the base language and the integer valued 'select' function mentioned above, the problem could be stated as follows:

```
BEGIN;
   INTEGER B, C;
   B := SELECT(0, 9);
   C := SELECT(0, 9);
   CONDITION B+C=15;
END; "
```

The procedure (or problem statement) says in effect: "Select integer values in the range 0 to 9 for each of B and C such that their sum is 15."

This same procedure could be represented in GOL (assuming we have added the numerical capabilities required) as follows:

(LAMBDA (B C) (AND (DIGIT B) (DIGIT C) (EQUAL (SUM B C) 15))).

(where DIGIT is an extensionally defined monadic predicate).

What REF provides (and GOL does not) in interpreting such a constraint satisfaction procedure is a mapping of the input constraint set onto an internal structure to which various algorithmic problem-solving techniques can be applied. For example, in this case—the REF condition:

$$B+C=15$$

would be used to eliminate either B or C from the context of the solution, making explicit the reduction in degrees of freedom imposed by this constraint. Thus a determination of value for B would lead to an immediate value for C (without further generation and testing), and vice versa.

GOL has no such constraint manipulation capability. This is true principally because the tools for such manipulation depend on the representation of constraints as systems of simultaneous equations (or inequalities), and this assumes that we are dealing with numerical relations and functions. Certainly, in extending GOL to accommodate numerical relations, we should look to Fikes for techniques to reduce the search involved in the numerical segments of a computation. It is not clear, however, that Fikes' techniques will be of much use in handling such non-numerical relations as have been our concern in the GOL programs discussed previously.

Let us consider now the strategy of heuristic search implemented in the REF interpreter, for it is here that the most significant differences between the GOL and REF problem-solving procedures are found. At any point in the interpretation of a REF program, the internal form of the set of constraints (and other statements) that have been processed up to that point (these may include equations, inequalities, variables, and constants of various types—(i.e., integer, vector, symbol, etc.), constitutes a *context*. This context is constantly changing through the course of a computation, as constraints are simplified, variables are assigned fixed values, and sets of equations are reduced. Finally, upon interpretation of the statement, end, the problem-solving processes of the interpreter complete a backtracking search for values of all variables in the context such that all constraints are satisfied. If these can be found, the computation exits with success; otherwise, the context may be restored to that of some branch point in the program from which the interpreter may develop other contexts, again proceeding line-by-line until interpretation of an end statement causes a re-evaluation of the resulting context.

Branching may occur during a REF interpretation in any of a number of ways. For example, at an *if* statement, where binary branching is controlled by the truth-value of a given Boolean condition, both the assertion and the negation of the given condition may be used at the time of interpretation to establish new contexts. Either of these may be on the path followed directly by the interpreter; the other is then stored as a possible alternative to be explored at some later time, if necessary. Similarly, at a computed-go-to statement, where the controlling variable has not been determined at the time of interpretation, a multiplicity of contexts may be created, one corresponding to each value that variable may take. Again, all but one of these alternate contexts must be filed for future reference, if required later by the interpreter.

The REF interpreter employs a very simple strategy to determine the order in which alternative contexts are to be selected for further elaboration and search. First, for each context, a count is made of the number of elements in the domains associated with each variable in the context; the product of these counts becomes the ordering index for that context. As in GOL, the branch with the lowest index is followed first; in the case of a tie, the selection rule is first-in-first-out. This strategy reverts to a breadth-first scheme in those cases where additional variables are introduced at each branch point (or where the count remains the same). It becomes a depth-first scheme in the converse case of a diminishing number (or diminishing domains) of variables in the context.

The effect of this heuristic rule can be seen in the following example which gives the REF formulation of the ubiquitous monkey problem:

```
          BEGIN;                                              1
              SET. VECTOR X TO X1,X2,UNDER.BANANAS;           2
              SET. VECTOR Y TO ON.FLOOR,ON.BOX;               3
              SET. VECTOR MONKEY TO X1,ON.FLOOR;              4
              SET. VECTOR BOX TO X2,ON.FLOOR;                 5
          WALK: SET MONKEY [1] TO X[SELECT(1,3)];             6
              IF -(MONKEY[1] = BOX[1]) THEN WALK;             7
          L1: SET <M> TO SELECT(1,3);                         8
              GOTO <M> (WALK, CLIMB, MOVE, BOX);              9
          CLIMB: SET MONKEY[2] TO ON.BOX;                     10
```

```
          IF ¬(MONKEY[1] = UNDER.BANANAS) THEN STEP.DOWN;       11
          SET ⟨M⟩ TO SELECT(1,2);                                12
          GOTO ⟨M⟩ (GET.BANANAS,STEP.DOWN);                      13
STEP.DOWN: SET MONKEY[2] TO ON.FLOOR;                            14
          GOTO L1;                                               15
MOVE.BOX: SET MONKEY[1] TO X[SELECT(1,3)];                       16
          SET BOX:1] TO MONKEY[1];                               17
          GOTO L1;                                               18
GET.BANANAS: END;                                                19
```

Disjunctive branching occurs in this procedure as a result of the interpretation of lines 7, 9, 11, and 13. In each case, the number of variables (and the sizes of the corresponding domains) remains unchanged; thus the effective strategy of search is breadth-first. This is, of course, an expensive strategy to employ in this particular problem. However, since there is no way to provide the REF interpreter with a sense of direction [as in the means-end analysis of the GOL ATTAIN function (cf. Section 3.4)], the breadth-first scheme is much safer than a depth-first strategy, since the latter might lead to much aimless wandering—or even disastrous looping.

There is one other important difference between GOL and REF (and other programming languages, too, for that matter); that is the ability provided by the type-theoretic structure of GOL to call subroutines indirectly through quantification or abstraction on either a predicate functor or on a variable defined over the class of wff's of the language. We have used such higher-level binding in almost every program that has been written so far in the language. This is the feature that gives GOL its perceptual power in the selection of transformation operators and we regard it as one of the principal innovations of the system.

APPENDIX B
THE GOL COMPILER AND EVALUATION ROUTINES

B.1 Primitive Generators

The basic component of any GOL-compiled program is the primitive generator (or test process) which is based on an atomic formula of the form:

$$\langle \text{atomic formula} \rangle ::= (\langle \text{predicate variable} \rangle \langle \text{argument string} \rangle)$$

For example: (F X Y), (CAUSE C1 A C2), (ATTAIN A B), ... are all typical instances of atomic formulae that would translate into primitive GOL generator or test processes.

The nature of the process compiled for a given atomic formula is controlled by the run-time status of variables that appear in its argument string. Variables that will have known values at run-time have fixed status; others are open.

An atomic formula involving n arguments has potentially 2^n different generator or test processes that may be compiled, corresponding to the various possible combinations of fixed and open status for variables in the string. To tell the compiler which of these evaluation processes is required, we replace the actual string at compile time by an abstract argument string that depicts the run-time status of variables, using the symbol $ to represent fixed status and the symbol * to represent open.

An atomic formula characterized by an all-$ string will have all arguments fixed at run-time; thus it is translated by the compiler into a *test* routine. At the other extreme, on the basis of an all-* string, the compiler produces a generator that extracts n-tuples from the extension of the designated predicate. Between the extremes of completely fixed and completely open strings are those that have some combination of $'s and *'s. These compile into generators over m space (where $m < n$), yielding m-tuples of values for the open variables that are consistent with the values supplied at run-time for the other $(n - m)$ fixed variables.

In a complex GOL program, a given generator process may be called from various segments of the program. It is essential therefore that all compiled generator processes be re-entrant, i.e., all local variables (and certain global variables as well) that define the context of a computation for some user routine must be passed back to that user for preservation until the next generator call involving the context; otherwise these data might be destroyed by other users of the process. The business of saving, swapping, and restoring generator contexts presents serious bookkeeping problems that are the source of much of the complexity of GOL-compiled programs. These problems, and our solutions to them, will be discussed in detail in Section B. 4, which deals with the GOL executive routines and the structuring of generator contexts on the GOLIST tree.[34]

B.2 Composite Generators

Atomic formulae may be combined in various ways in accordance with the formation rules specified by the GOL syntax (cf. page 00). Three basic structures represented in this syntax control the compilation of complex generator processes; these are the conjunctive, disjunctive, and implicative

---

[34] GOL generators are similar in purpose to those of IPL-V; see [21] for a good discussion of the complexities of generator construction.

forms of expression. Because these involve different segments of the GOL compiler process and because they result in essentially different forms of generator process, we shall discuss these basic structures separately in Sections B.3, B.5, and B.6, respectively. However, because the syntax specifications are recursive, we may expect the compiled processes to exhibit some hierarchical structure in which the basic structures are intermixed in a variety of ways.

We consider first composite generator processes based on conjunctions of atomic formulae. We turn next to generators based on disjunctions of atomic formulae, and consider finally the case of implicative expressions. In all cases, we deal only with situations in which all sub-formula at the top level are atomic. One can then proceed to other expressions that contain complex (i.e., non-atomic) sub-formulae (by reference to the recursive specification of the relevant syntactic forms and the corresponding recursive compiler processes).

B.3 Conjunctive Expressions and Cascaded Generators.

An expression of the following form:

(AND ⟨atomic formula⟩ ⟨atomic formula⟩ ...)

is translated by the compiler into a *cascaded* generator, in which primitive generator and test processes corresponding to the constituent atomic formulae are linked together in such a way that the output of one process becomes the source of inputs to the next. Each simple generator is used to fix certain variables that had appeared in the argument string of the corresponding atomic formula with open status; these bindings are maintained throughout the remaining scope of the computation. For example, a variable that appeared free in the first conjunctive atomic formula would have some feasible value determined by the first of the cascaded generators. It would thereafter be treated as having fixed status in the context of the remaining sub-generators.

In order to communicate variable bindings among the cascaded generators, the compiler must keep track of changes in status that are to take place at run-time and establish the necessary communication links. Thus at every entry to a compiled evaluation process, a set of memory locations (called the ARGVEC) is set aside, with space for each variable bound by a quantifier or lambda in the defining expression. All processes pick up their inputs and deposit their outputs in this array, which is thus the principal communication link among compiled sub-processes. (There is, however, a secondary means of communication called the BDVAR list; this is a structure similar to the LISP A-list, which is used to keep track of bindings for variables that had been free in some extensional structure (cf. Section 2.4). The compiler has no knowledge of such variables (which appear only at run-time) and cannot provide for them in the more efficient and accessible ARGVEC array.)

The general form of a cascaded generator can be represented graphically as follows:

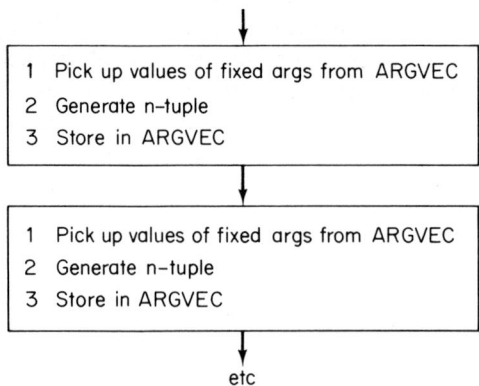

Such a composite generator has much the same effect as the simple generators considered earlier: we enter the routine with a certain set of variables fixed and exit with some larger set fixed, provided, of course, that it is possible to do so.

In the case of a simple generator, when the process is unable to find a new set of values satisfying the given predicate (i.e., a set that has not previously been generated in the context of the particular calling routine), it stops with a special signal indicating failure. Such a failure condition in a simple generator is, in general, not be interpreted as failure of the composite generator process of which it forms a part. Very often, by backing up a more complex generator to some upstream sub-process, it is possible to determine new bindings for certain variables that allow the downstream generator that previously failed to begin producing again.

To handle the recycling of these complex generator processes, we have designed a set of executive routines that become a part of any GOL-compiled process. The purpose of these executive routines is to determine, at any indication of failure of a simple generator, the best way to get the composite generator producing again. This requires that the executive have available the necessary information to re-establish context in any generator, at any level of the computation, to which it might ultimately wish to transfer control. This information is all recorded in a partially ordered list structure referred to as the GOLIST, details of which are described in the following paragraphs.

B.4 The GOL Executive and GOLIST

The GOLIST is a list structure, at the top level of which is an ordered list of entries, each of which contains the necessary summary and control information to restore context for re-entry to some generator in the program. The exact details of these summary and control data depend on the generator involved, and will not be considered in detail here. Some of the standard items on a GOLIST entry include the name of the state in which evaluation is taking place, the relevant argument vector (ARGVEC), the current bound variable list (BDVAR), the set of arguments having fixed status, the location in the program to which control should transfer, and an integer index number which is used to order the entries in the GOLIST.

This last item, the index number, is intended to reflect the difficulty associated with a transfer to the corresponding sub-generator. For example, transfers that involve change of state or recursive function calls may be regarded as more difficult than some others. The exact determination of the difficulty indices is left to the ORDER sub-routine that must be supplied by the user. Lacking any alternative specification, the zero ORDER function is assumed.

By convention, all of the GOLIST entries associated with the simple generators based on atomic formulae have indices of zero (indicating least difficulty) and are filed at the top of the GOLIST. One such entry is created and filed at every successful exit of each simple generator in the program.

The only way non-zero (positive) index numbers may arise is in connection with a non-atomic formula of the following form:

(GOLDIG ⟨atomic formula⟩ ⟨state designator⟩),

the so-called goldig phrase.

Such an expression typically requires that a change of state be carried out before entering the generator process prescribed by its constituent atomic formula. We often choose to consider branches based on goldig phrases to be more difficult than those that operate in the present state of the computation. There may, of course, also be other reasons for classifying one branch as potentially more difficult than others. In these cases, we use the same syntactic structure, i.e., the goldig phrase, but use the constant STATE (which references the present state) in place of some other state designator.

The compiled code corresponding to a goldig phrase includes a function call on the user defined function, ORDER. The three arguments passed by the GOL evaluation program to this ordering routine are the following:

(1) a control number indicating the difficulty of the current computation (i.e., the index number of the most recently selected GOLIST entry).

(2) the new state defined by the state designator in the goldig phrase.

(3) the first argument of the primitive generator that is to be entered.

The result of a computation of the ORDER function becomes the ranking index (of the GOLIST entry) which is used to order the new generator call in the tree of alternatives remaining to be explored. Note that a sub-process based on a goldig phrase differs from others in that it is *never* entered directly; it is evaluated on the basis of the ORDER function and a new call on this sub-process is filed in the GOLIST. Non-zero indices are filed at the end rather than at the beginning of their respective levels of the GOLIST; thus selection is FIFO among these non-zero entries, though as suggested earlier, the selection among zero entries is LIFO (which corresponds to a depth-first recursive mode of search).

When a GOLIST entry is selected (from the top of the GOLIST), the executive alters context and transfers control to the appropriate point in the program. The generation process then continues sequentially until a failure again occurs, causing control to switch back to the executive and the next entry on the GOLIST. The flowchart for our simple cascaded generator needs to be modified to show this provision for cyclical behavior:

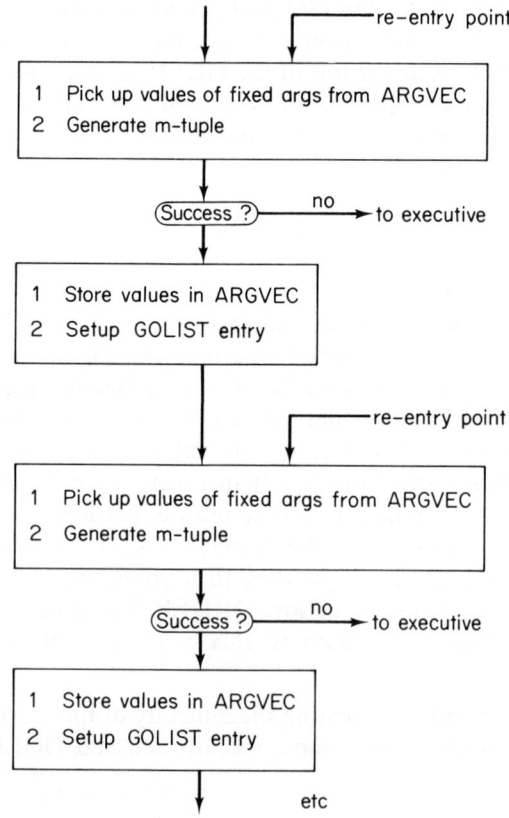

B.5 Disjunctive Expressions and Parallel Generators

A disjunctive expression composed of atomic formulae has the following form:

(OR ⟨atomic formula⟩ ⟨atomic formula⟩ . .)

In this case, the simple generators corresponding to the component subformulae are not cascaded but rather are put in parallel. On successive entries to such a set of parallel generators, the first simple generator keeps producing until it fails, then the next is called and produces until *it* fails, and so on. That all of these primitive generators are equivalent in the sense that all fix the same set of open variables is the implicit assumption made by the compiler.

The mechanism for maintaining context and switching of generators in a disjunctive process is contained in the executive routines and GOLIST conventions that were described in the previous paragraph. For each atomic formula in a disjunctive expression, the compiler creates a primitive generator. Only one of these is inserted in the main stream of the program, but this generator call is preceded in the sequence by a set of GOLIST setup routines, one for each of the other disjuncts. Thus when entering a disjunctive generator, the program first sets up future calls, through the GOLIST, on all of the parallel generators, and then enters the first of these. The process can be charted as follows:

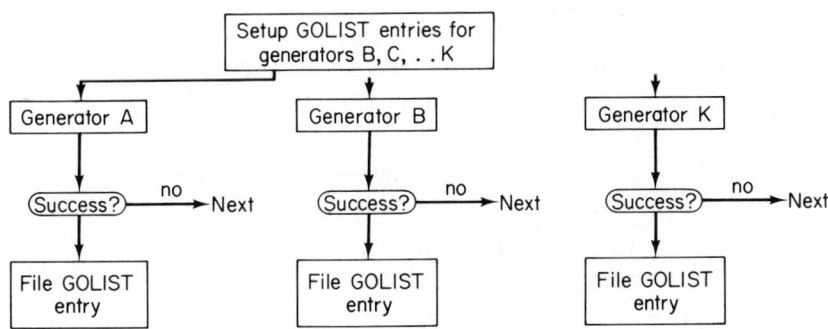

B.6 Implicative Expressions and the Universal Quantifier

The implicative expression, of the form:

(IMPLIES ⟨atomic formula⟩ ⟨atomic formula⟩),

or

(IMPLIES ⟨atomic formula⟩ ⟨goldig phrase⟩)

is used only to describe generators involving universally quantified variables which are restricted by the antecedent phrase to certain m-tuples of values to be tested in the consequent. We have adopted very limited interpretations of the quantifier FORALL and connective IMPLIES, which interpretations do not begin to reflect the usual conception of these symbols. It is expressly not the case that in GOL, an expression of the form:

(FORALL (X1, ... Xn) (IMPLIES A B))

may be considered definitionally equivalent to the form:

(NOT (EXISTS (X1, ... Xn) (AND A (NOT B)))),

as it would be in most systems of logic. (Note that the latter form is not grammatical according to the syntactic rules; the connective NOT may be applied only to atomic sub-formulae.)

The reason for this departure from conventional usage is purely pragmatic. Evaluations involving a universally quantified variable must compile into explicit iterative processes that cannot be dealt with within the framework of the existentially quantified conjunctive expression described above. To define the universal quantifier in terms of existence and negation would complicate unnecessarily the compiler processes associated with those simpler and more frequently encountered forms.

The simplified form of implication considered here can be handled in a very straightforward way by the GOL compiler through an iterative process that links a simple generator and a simple test process according to the following schematic plan:

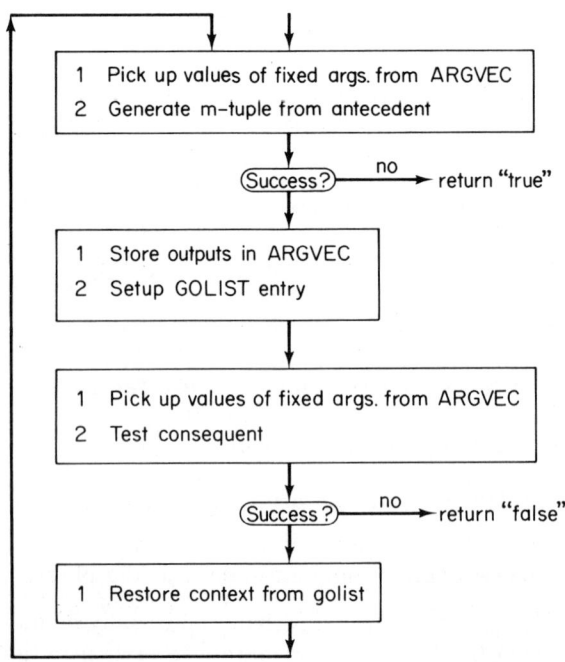

[19] NEWELL, A., SHAW, J. C., and SIMON, H. A. Empirical explorations of the logic theory machine. *Proceedings of the Western Joint Computer Conference*, February 1967, pp. 218–230. Published by the *IRE*. [FF]
[20] NEWELL, A. and SIMON, H. A. GPS—A program that simulates human problem solving. *Proceedings on a Conference on Learning Automata.* Munich: Oldenbourg, 1961. [FF]
[21] NEWELL, A., et al. *Information Processing Language-V Manual.* Englewood Cliffs, New Jersey: Prentice-Hall, 1961.
[22] SIMON, H. A. On reasoning about actions. Carnegie Institute of Technology Complex Information Processing Paper No. 87, 1966. [SS]

Chapter 8

ON REASONING ABOUT ACTIONS

HERBERT A. SIMON

Consider a space in which are represented the possible temporal paths of a system. Each point in the space corresponds to a possible *state* of the system at a particular time. Associated with each path is a sequence of *actions* that will carry the system along that path. Associated with each state is a description, a set of declarative sentences that predicate certain properties of that state. The description is a set of sentences that are true when the system is in that state.

A state description is *complete* if all sentences true in that state (and only such sentences) are contained in it or can be derived from it. A complete state description may be regarded as a basis for the sentences true in that state. The relation between complete state descriptions and states is not one-one. More than one state may have a given description. Moreover, the same state may have several, logically equivalent, complete descriptions. (They must be logically equivalent, since any sentence in the one must be contained in or derivable from the other.)

In the special case where there is a unique original state, and where only a single path leads to any other state, the system takes the form of a tree, and any other state, s, can be designated uniquely by the particular sequence of actions, call it A_s, associated with the path from s_0 to s. We can always represent the part of the system reachable from the original state as a tree by the device of distinguishing two states, even if their descriptions are otherwise identical, when they are reached from the original state by different paths. We shall use this device frequently.

SECTION 1
ACTIONS

A problem of action may be formulated as follows: Given an original state s_0 and a (partial) description d, to find a sequence of actions A_d associated with a path leading from s_0 to a state, call it s_d, whose description implies d. Problems may also be formulated by showing that a state s_d with (partial) description d is *attainable*—that is, that there exists a sequence of actions A_d carrying s_0 into an s_d.

Actions can be combined in classes which are identical with respect to *actor, enabling condition*, and *effect*. In the present discussion, we will concern ourselves only with systems having a single, unique actor, who is the actor for all actions. Hence we will ignore the actor. The enabling condition of an action is a (partial) description that holds for all those states and only those states in which that action can be taken (*initial states* of that action). The effect of an action is a (partial) description that holds for all states produced by the action (*terminal states* of that action).

Let $A(s_1, s_2)$ be an action that transforms state s_1 into state s_2. Let the action belong to the class $A(c_1, c_2)$, that is, the class whose enabling condition is c_1 and whose effect is c_2. Then the description of s_1 implies c_1 and the description of s_2 implies c_2. In what follows, we shall often refer to actions by their class names.

Demonstrations of attainability will generally be recursive in form. For this, it is simplest if we define a state s_2 as being *directly attainable* from another state s_1 if there exists an action $A(s_1, s_2)$. We define a state s_T as being *attainable* from s_I, if s_T is directly attainable from s_I, or if there exists an s_i such that s_T is directly attainable from s_i and s_i is attainable from s_I.

Now we should like to know under what circumstances we can carry out analyses of action by reference purely to the descriptions of states and the class names of the actions, without knowledge of the proper names of states or actions—i.e., without explicit enumeration of the branches of the tree.

SECTION 2
MODELS

In one extreme case this can certainly be done: when (1) the description of each state is complete and (2) the effect of each action contains all differences between the description of the terminal state of the action and its initial state. A set of descriptions of the states and actions of a system satisfying these two conditions will be called a *model* of the system.

In a model, from the complete description of a state and the enabling condition of an action, it can be determined whether that action can be taken in that state; while from the complete description of the initial state and the effect of the action, the complete description of the terminal state can be calculated.

An action problem can be solved in a model by setting the model in the original state s_0, then exploring the tree of paths by applying (and retracting) actions until a path is found leading to the goal state. Before an action is applied, the current state is tested to determine that the enabling condition of the action is satisfied. The action is applied by changing the model in the ways specified by its effect.

The question of whether a state having a particular description is attainable may not be decidable, but if such a state is attainable, an exhaustive breadth-first search will find a path to it in a finite number of steps.

SECTION 3
PROOFS

Since each state is described by a conjunction of sentences, we can metaphorically interpret the (constructive) demonstration that a certain state is attainable as a "derivation" of the sentence describing that state in the following sense: Interpret each action as a rule of inference. Then if action $A(c_1, c_2)$ transforms a state described by c_1 into a state described by c_2, the action may be interpreted as a direct derivation of c_2 from c_1. Since the action will carry *any* state that is partially described by c_1 into a state that is partially described by c_2, it is clear that c_1 contains the only "relevant" premises for the derivation among all the sentences contained in the description of the initial state.

Consider, now, the case where the admissible actions do, literally, correspond with applications of the legitimate rules of inference in some system of logic. We take as the complete description of a state the conjunction of the axioms together with all sentences produced by the sequence of actions leading to that state. For example, if the state is reached after the kth step in a proof, then the state description is the conjunction of the axioms with the first k expressions in the proof.

Notice that the actions in fact only change state descriptions, not states, because all of the sentences written down in a proof are derivable from the premises, hence are true of the original state. Nevertheless, we shall find it convenient to identify states with their descriptions, hence to treat as distinct two different descriptions, even if they belong to the same state.

Under these assumptions, if s_2 is a state attainable from state s_1 (i.e., there exists a proof in which s_1 is the state reached after a certain step and s_2 is the state reached after some subsequent step), then the description of s_2 contains the description of s_1. Hence, if any action A is directly applicable to s_1 it is also directly applicable to s_2, but the converse does not hold.

It follows that if a state containing c_1 is attainable, and a state containing c_2 is attainable, then a state containing $c_1 \cdot c_2$ is attainable. For let A_{21}, $A_{22}, \ldots, A_{2N}$ be the sequence of actions that transforms the original state into c_2. Since the state containing c_1 also satisfies all the conditions of the original state, and since A_{21} is applicable in the latter state, it is also applicable in the former. By the same reasoning, A_{22} is again applicable to the terminal state of A_{21}, and so on. Hence c_2 is attainable from c_1, and the state in which c_2 is attained also contains c_1. Hence this state contains $c_1 \cdot c_2$.

SECTION 4
INCOMPLETE DESCRIPTIONS

We may wish to handle action problems without making explicit the complete descriptions of states. We must make them explicit in manipulating models. Consider the following kind of "real-life" problem:

> I wish to read a certain book. I recall that it lies on the desk of my study. In order to read it, therefore, I must fetch it. However, I cannot read without my glasses. These are on my bedside table. I must fetch them also and put them on. Now I can open the book and read it.

The actions are A1 "fetch the book," A2 "fetch the glasses," A3 "put on the glasses," A4 "open the book," A5 "read the book." The first two (it is assumed) have no enabling conditions; their effects are C1 "I have the book" and C2 "I have the glasses," respectively. The enabling condition for putting on the glasses is C2 "I have the glasses" and its effect is C3 "I am wearing the glasses." The enabling condition for opening the book is C1 "I have the book" and its effect is C4 "The book is open." The enabling conditions for reading the book are C4 "The book is open" and C3 "I am wearing glasses," and their effect is C5 "The book has been read." Now consider the attainment of the goal of reading the book, that is, of the state "The book has been read." By "ordinary reasoning," which we shall examine in a moment, I might work out a plan as follows:

> In order to read the book, it must be open and I must wear my glasses. In order for it to be open I must have it, and to have it I must fetch it. To wear my glasses, I must put them on, and to put them on, I must fetch them. Therefore, I shall attain my end by fetching the glasses, putting them on, fetching the book, opening it, and reading.

Now McCarthy has shown how this "ordinary reasoning" could be carried out making use of modal operators he calls "can," "cause," and "can ultimately." By combining his operators "can" and "cause" into a single operator, which we shall call "can," we are able to simplify matters considerably without changing the scheme in any essential way. $CAN(c_1, c_2)$ is interpreted to mean that a state with description c_2 is attainable from a state with description c_1. If we designate by ϕ the condition satisfied by the original state s_0, then $CAN(\phi, c_1)$ which we shall abbreviate $CAN(c_1)$ means that c_1 is attainable from the original state. Now we introduce two axioms:

(1) $\qquad CAN(c_1, c_2), CAN(c_2, c_3) \rightarrow CAN(c_1, c_3)$

This axiom states that CAN is transitive; it is the analogue of syllogism for "implies" in the propositional calculus.

(2) $\qquad CAN(c_1), CAN(c_1 \cdot c_2, c_3) \rightarrow CAN(c_2, c_3)$

This axiom is the analog of Peano's Principle of Exportation: $((A \& B)$ implies $C) \rightarrow (A$ implies $(B$ implies $C))$. From (2) and the additional "Axiom of Tautology," $CAN(c_1, c_1)$ (i.e., the null action is always possible), we can derive the closely related Principle of Composition as follows:

From Axiom (2), letting $c_3 = c_2 \cdot c_1$, we obtain

(3) $\qquad CAN(c_1), CAN(c_1 \cdot c_2, c_1 \cdot c_2) \rightarrow CAN(c_2, c_1 \cdot c_2)$,

which, by $CAN(c, c)$, reduces to:

(4) $\qquad CAN(c_1) \rightarrow CAN(c_2, c_1 \cdot c_2)$.

From Axiom (1), we derive the principle:

(5) $\qquad CAN(c_1), CAN(c_1, c_2) \rightarrow CAN(c_2)$,

hence,

(6) $\qquad CAN(c_2), CAN(c_2, c_1 \cdot c_2) \rightarrow CAN(c_1 \cdot c_2)$.

Combining (4) and (6), we finally obtain:

(7) $\qquad CAN(c_1), CAN(c_2) \rightarrow CAN(c_1 \cdot c_2)$,

which is the analog of the Principle of Composition.

In our example, the available actions are $A1(\phi, C1)$, $A2(\phi, C2)$, $A3(C2, C3)$, $A4(C1, C4)$, and $A5(C4 \cdot C3, C5)$. Since the enabling conditions for A1 and A2 are null, we may assert: $CAN(C1)$ and $CAN(C2)$. From the other three actions, we get $CAN(C2, C3)$, $CAN(C1, C4)$, and $CAN(C4 \cdot C3, C5)$.

Applying (5) to CAN(C1) and CAN(C1, C4), we get CAN(C4). Applying (2) to CAN(C4) and CAN(C4·C3, C5), we get CAN(C3, C5). Next, by (5), from CAN(C2) and CAN(C2, C3) we get CAN(C3). Finally, by (5), CAN(C3) and CAN(C3, C5) yield CAN(C5). (The reader can easily verify that CAN(C5) is also derivable using (7) in place of (2)).

Alternatively, both the Principle of Exportation, (2), and the Principle of Composition, (7), can be derived from the axiom:

(8) $$CAN(c_1) \to CAN(c_2, c_1 \cdot c_2).$$

To prove (2), from (8), we get:

(9) $$CAN(c_1), CAN(c_1 \cdot c_2, c_3) \to CAN(c_2, c_1 \cdot c_2), CAN(c_1 \cdot c_2, c_3).$$

and by (1), expression (2) follows immediately.

To prove (7), from (8), we get:

(10) $$CAN(c_1), CAN(c_2) \to CAN(c_2), CAN(c_2, c_1 \cdot c_2)$$

and applying (5) to the second expression on the right-hand side of (10), expression (7) results.

Returning to our earlier theorem-proving example, we can interpret $CAN(c_1, c_2)$ as meaning that c_2 is derivable (by the rules of inference) from c_1 and $CAN(c_1)$ as meaning that c_1 is derivable from the premises. Then our two axioms are standard rules of inference—Axiom (1) states the transitivity of the relation of derivability, while Axiom (2) states that if c_1 is derivable and c_3 is derivable from c_1 and c_2, then c_3 is derivable from c_2. Hence this scheme of "ordinary reasoning" is valid for a space of proofs.

However, it is easy to construct an example of a space in which the second axiom is not valid. (In our interpretation of CAN, the definition of attainability guarantees the validity of the first axiom.) Let us see how this difficulty can arise.

First, an abstract example. We consider a space in which c_2 is attainable along one particular path, and c_3 only along another particular path, disjunct from the first. Then $CAN(c_2)$ and $CAN(c_3)$ but not $CAN(c_2, c_3)$.

Next, a concrete example. John is enamoured of a blonde actress. If he had a luxurious car, costing $15,000, and a yacht, also costing $15,000, he could seduce the actress. His assets total $15,000, and he is a poor credit risk. Can he seduce the actress? From the facts given, CAN(own the car) and CAN(own the yacht). Then, by application of (7) and (5), CAN(seduce the actress) follows immediately.

This kind of difficulty will arise in all problems where actions entail the expenditure of scarce resources. Under these circumstances, none of the axioms (2), (7), or (8) is admissible. More generally, these axioms can be expected to fail whenever there is any significant interdependence among actions. These axioms might well be labeled "Axioms of Independence" in analogy to the axiom of multiplication of independent probabilities.

The same difficulty arises (in several guises but for the same reasons) in some well-known "paradoxes" of modal logic. Does "I want a cat" and "I want a dog" imply "I want a cat and dog"? Does "I want cigarette and matches" imply "I want matches"? In both cases, the air of paradox stems from the nonindependence of the terms of the conjunction.

The only known general way out of the difficulty (i.e., the only way to handle the most general action spaces) appears to be to abandon the modal logic—in particular, the Axiom of Independence—and carry out the analysis with a model, in which only the Axiom of Transitivity is assumed.

Now we could construct a heuristic problem solver by designing it to behave *as if* the Axiom of Independence held, but to test the actual attainability of its goals by trying out actions in a model. In fact, the main heuristics of most problem-solving systems that operate by selective search can be interpreted in exactly this way.

In the General Problem Solver, the condition to be attained may be represented as a conjunction of differences between an initial state of the system and the goal state. A succession of actions is then sought that will remove these differences in turn—i.e., a path through the states: $c_1, c_1 \cdot c_2, c_1 \cdot c_2 \cdot c_3, \ldots$, where the c's are sentences stating that the corresponding differences are absent. If Axiom (8) were valid, and if there were at least one action for removing each difference, then this scheme would be a straightforward algorithm. If differences are not always mutually independent, however, then removal of one difference may introduce another, and the scheme is only a heuristic.

The planning heuristic for GPS similarly makes the implicit assumption that if a path can be found for eliminating the "essential" differences between two expressions, then sub-paths can be found that will deal with the "inessential" differences without reintroducing essential differences.

SECTION 5
THE MONKEY-BANANA PROBLEM

Since discussions of the monkey-banana problem provided much of the original motivation for this analysis, the problem will be outlined briefly here. We shall see that most of the issues have already been discussed in the previous section.

The problem has been formulated in Saul Amarel's paper: A room contains a bunch of bananas, a monkey, and a chair. The bananas are hung out of reach of the monkey; but if the chair is under the bananas and the monkey is on the chair, then the monkey can reach and get them. What should the monkey do to get the bananas? (In some versions, the monkey must use a stick to reach the bananas, even if he is on the chair.)

As the problem is stated, the several actions are independent. Hence the *Principle of Composition* may be assumed in its original form. The monkey can place the chair under the bananas. This satisfies the condition for his climbing on the chair, which he then does. The chair being under the bananas and the monkey being on the chair satisfy the conditions for his reaching the bananas, which he at last does. It is not hard to change the problem to introduce interdependencies.

1. Time is limited. The monkey has not time *first* to fetch the chair, then to climb on it.

2. The chair and bananas are connected by a rope over a couple of pulleys. When the monkey pulls the chair under the bananas, the bananas ascend out of reach.

3. Instead of the action of "standing on the chair," we can consider the monkey as "standing two feet above the floor." With this change in formulation, the latter action is only performable after the chair has been moved under the bananas.

Going a little further afield for a final example, we pose a classical task that has been used (with human subjects) in research on problem solving. Two strings are suspended, more than two arms' length apart, from the ceiling of a room. The monkey is to tie them together. He can reach either string and bring its end to the center of the room, but he cannot reach both simultaneously.

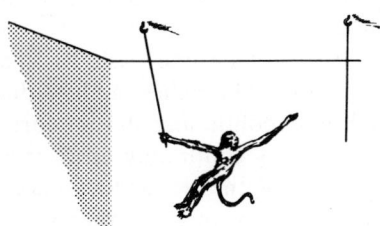

SECTION 6
COMMENTS ON MODELS

For the purposes of this analysis, I have taken the completeness of its state descriptions as the distinguishing characteristic of a model. "Complete" should not be confused with "explicit." From an information processing standpoint, the workability of a model may depend crucially on how much of the information must be made explicit and how much can be held implicitly.

Consider a representation of a board for playing chess. A model could be constructed by stating, for each square, the list of pieces standing on that square and the list of pieces not standing on it. Of course this representation would be highly redundant. If the list of pieces not standing on each square were simply omitted, the remaining set of sentences would still be a complete description of the board, as we have defined that term. An even briefer description would only name the men actually on the board, with their squares, omitting mention of the unoccupied squares.

Economy in its state description is, of course, not the only criterion for determining the suitability of a representation. (If it were, we would never index a book or write down a theorem in mathematics, for the index and the theorem are redundant.) Other criteria include efficiency in updating when actions change the state of the system and efficiency in calculating the available actions and the consequences of taking particular actions. A discussion of the design of models would take us beyond the scope of this paper.

SECTION 7
SYMMETRIES

A serious disadvantage of working with a model is that proofs of attainability—and especially proofs of non-attainability—may require exploration of the entire tree of attainable states. If there were some way of mapping the model by a many-one transformation onto a smaller space, such proofs might be greatly simplified.

Symmetries in the tree provide one basis for mapping. In tic-tac-toe, for example, the number of initial branches can be reduced from nine to three by observing that the sub-trees continuing all four corner moves are mutually isomorphic, as are the sub-trees continuing all four side moves. This symmetry alone reduces the size of the tic-tac-toe space by a factor of three. If advantage is taken of all other symmetries, the total tree is reduced to a few thousand branches.

Gelernter and Rochester's theorem on syntactic symmetry (Gelernter and Rochester, 1958, pp. 339–340) has a similar motivation. A syntactic symmetry is, essentially, an automorphism of a set of axioms and hypotheses, under a permutation of the names of the constants. Translating this concept and its consequence in terms of a search tree, we may regard conditions c_1 and c_2 as syntactically symmetric with respect to c_3 if $CAN(c_2, c_3)$ is equivalent to $CAN(c_1, c_3)$ in the strong sense that every path from c_2 to c_3 is isomorphic to a path from c_1 to c_3, and conversely.

By transitivity,

$$\text{CAN}(c_1, c_2), \text{CAN}(c_2, c_3) \to \text{CAN}(c_1, c_3)$$

But from syntactic symmetry we can draw a stronger conclusion:

If c_1 and c_2 are syntactically symmetric, and $\text{CAN}(c_1, c_3)$, then there must exist at least one path from c_1 to c_3 that does not pass through c_2. Suppose the contrary, i.e., that all paths from c_1 to c_3 pass through c_2. Then there must be a shortest such path, $P_1: c_1 \to c_2 \to c_3$. Now the sub-path in P_1 from c_2 to c_3 cannot pass through c_1, else P_1 would not be the shortest path from c_1 to c_3. Therefore there is a path from c_2 to c_3 that does not pass through c_1; and hence, by syntactic symmetry, a path from $c'_2 = c_1$ to c_3 that does not pass through $c'_1 = c_2$. Q.E.D.

By similar reasoning we reach the strong conclusion that, for every path from c_1 to c_3 through c_2, there must exist a sub-path from c_1 to c_3 not passing through c_2 or from c_2 to c_3 not passing through c_1 (and in the latter case, an isomorphic path from c_1 to c_3 not passing through c_2). Hence any proof of $\text{CAN}(c_1, c_3)$ that uses $\text{CAN}(c_1, c_2)$ can be replaced by a shorter proof that does not use $\text{CAN}(c_1, c_2)$. Hence proving $\text{CAN}(c_1, c_2)$ is always useless.

SECTION 8
HEREDITARY PROPERTIES

Another technique for reducing the search space while retaining a model is called by Newell (1965) "integrating the equations of motion." Consider the checkerboard-domino problem. A checkerboard is mutilated by removing two diagonally opposite corner squares. The task is to cover the board exactly by dominoes, each domino covering precisely two squares (i.e., each domino is 2×1 in size). This task is impossible, and the problem is to prove its impossibility.

One approach to the problem is to map the search space (in which a move consists in placing one more domino on the board) on a smaller space in which a move consists in reducing by unity the number of uncovered black squares and the number of uncovered white squares (since each domino covers one of each). A state in this latter space is described by a pair of integers: the numbers of uncovered black and white squares respectively.

In the compressed space (which is still a model), the initial state is (32, 30) and the desired final state (0, 0). Since each move subtracts from the state vector the unit vector (1, 1), N moves will subtract (N, N). Therefore, to reduce the second component to zero, we must make exactly N moves. But N moves will produce the vector (2, 0) and not the desired vector (0, 0).

There is another approach to the checkerboard-domino problem, however, that dispenses with "integrating" the moves or running the model explicitly. It depends on the concept of *hereditary property* (Newell, *op. cit.*, p. 206).

A property of states of a model is *hereditary* if, for all actions A and for all states s_i and s_j,

$$H(s_i) \text{ and } A(s_i, s_j) \text{ implies } H(s_j).$$

If such a property exists, and we can show that a particular state possesses the property, then, by transitivity, all states attainable from that state possess the property.

Now consider, in the checkerboard-domino problem, the difference between the number of uncovered black squares and uncovered white squares. Since all moves cover exactly one square of each color, they do not alter this difference, which is, therefore, a hereditary property. Since the initial state has value $+2$ for this difference, and the desired terminal state has value 0, the terminal state is not attainable. Thus, the discovery of hereditary properties may be a powerful means for investigating the attainability of states. To show that this particular swallow is not solitary, we shall sketch out three other examples of the application of hereditary properties in solving such problems.

8.1 Cube-brick Problem

Can a $6 \times 6 \times 6$ cube be constructed from bricks that are uniformly $1 \times 2 \times 4$ in size?

A. First hereditary property: Every structure built from such bricks must have a volume divisible by 8 (the volume of a single brick). But the $6 \times 6 \times 6$ cube has this property, hence the property cannot be used to prove impossibility.

B. Second hereditary property: Imagine the cube to be made up of 27 $2 \times 2 \times 2$ cubes. Give each such cube the coordinates i, j, k ($1 \leq i, j, k \leq 3$), in the usual way. Color black the cubes whose coordinates sum to an odd number; color the remaining cubes white. There will then be 14 black cubes and 13 white cubes.

Each move consists in adding a $1 \times 2 \times 4$ brick to the structure. Consider a lengthwise half of such a brick, $1 \times 1 \times 4$ in size. When placed in the structure this half-brick must form part of a column—a $1 \times 1 \times 6$ "pencil" in the whole structure. Now such a structure will be colored either:

B B W W B B

or

W W B B W W

In either case, a connected segment of length 4 must fill exactly two black squares and two white, for the possible cases are: B B W W, B W W B, W W B B, and W B B W. Hence, any move (the addition of two half-bricks) will reduce the number of unoccupied black spaces and white spaces each by four. Hence, the difference between the number of unoccupied spaces of the two colors is a hereditary property and equals zero.

In the initial state, with the proposed coloring, the vector of black and white unoccupied spaces is (56, 52); in the desired final state it is (0, 0). Hence the construction is impossible.

It should be noted that the proof of the hereditary property involved handling several cases. The number of cases was greatly reduced by introducing the notion of "pencil," thus taking advantage of the symmetries of rotation of the cube. Thus, this example illustrates how a problem can be simplified by joint use of symmetry and induction on a hereditary property.

8.2 Rule of the Square

In chess, the so-called "rule of the square" is used to determine whether Black's King can prevent White's pawn from Queening. Number the ranks from 1 to 8 (Queening rank) and the files from 1 (QR) to 8 (KR). Let the pawn initially have coordinates (m, n) and the King be on file k, with Black to move. Then Black can prevent Queening or capture the pawn on Queening if and only if $|k - n| \leq (9 - m)$.

To prove this, we need to consider pairs of moves, a Black move M_B followed by a White move M_W. We show that there exists an M_B such that for all M_B, if the inequality of the theorem holds *before* this pair of moves, it holds afterwards. Proof: Any M_W increases m by one, at most, but there always exists an M_B (move of the King toward the pawn's file) that decreases $|k - n|$ by one. Hence, with good play, the inequality is hereditary.

Conversely, for every M_B there exists an M_W (an advance of the pawn) such that, if the inequality *does not* hold before the moves are made, it will not hold afterwards. Hence non-satisfaction of the inequality is also hereditary with good play.

8.3 NIM

In the game of NIM, as in chess, we must consider a sequence of two moves, one by each player. The "hereditary" property is cyclical over such a pair of moves. The starting position in NIM consists of m rows of $n_i (i - 1, \ldots, m)$ counters each. A move consists of removing any number, k $(1 \leq k \leq m_i)$, of counters from any single row. The player who removes the last counter wins.

Positions in NIM can be separated into two classes, P_W and P_L, with the following properties:

1. The position after all counters have been removed (where the player who has moved last wins) belongs to P_L.

2. If the current position belongs to P_W (and is not the winning position), then there exists a move that changes it to a position in P_L.

3. If the current position belongs to P_L, every move changes it to a position in P_W.

Hence, when the current position is in P_W, the player whose turn it is can always assure that it will again be in that set on his next turn by choosing a move that puts it in P_L.

The concept illustrated by the Rule of the Square and NIM generalizes to the concept of *forcing position* in a two-person game. Suppose that *won position* has been defined. Then P is a forcing position for the player whose turn it is if it is either a won position or there exists a move such that after any legal reply the position again becomes a forcing position. Thus, in the game of chess, a player who is a Queen ahead of his opponent is, with rare exceptions, in a forcing position.

In the checkerboard-domino and cube-brick examples, a hereditary property was used to show the unattainability of a goal. In the chess and NIM examples, a property was used to characterize a path to a goal. We may generalize these latter examples to one-person problems by introducing the notion of *transmissible* property.

A property T is *transmissible* if for every S_i such that $T(S_i)$, there exists an action $A(S_i, S_j)$ such that $T(S_j)$.

Now if all branches terminate and if goal states, and no other terminal states, have a transmissible property T, to reach a goal state it is only necessary to find a state with T, then select a sequence of actions that keeps the system in states with T. If the presence or absence of T in a state can be determined by examining the state, then once in a state with T we can replace dynamic analysis in searching for a goal state by static evaluation. Hence there is a close relation between hereditary and transmissible properties and the use of static evaluation in heuristic search.

SECTION 9
MODEL SUBSPACES

In addition to, or in combination with, symmetries, hereditary properties, and transmissible properties, a problem space may possess other special properties that allow transformation to a smaller space, which may still constitute a model. The technique that is known as linear programming provides an important example.

Consider the problem of finding the maximum of a linear form in N variables subject to a set of constraints in the form of linear equalities and inequalities on subsets of the variables. Consider the sets of values of the variables (feasible points) that satisfy all the constraints. The boundary of the set of feasible points is a polygon in the appropriate hyperspace.

It can be shown that the maximum occurs at one or more extreme points of the boundary of the space of feasible points. Therefore, in searching for the maximum, only extreme points need be examined (rather than all feasible points).

As a matter of fact a search algorithm (simplex algorithm) exists that conducts an even more efficient search. At each step, the algorithm examines an extreme point and discovers an adjacent extreme point (if any) having a higher value of the criterion function. (If there is none, the problem is solved, for it can be shown that there is a monotonic increasing path of values from any extreme point, through a succession of adjacent extreme points, to the maximum.) Since the number of extreme points is finite, the algorithm is guaranteed to terminate, and since the path always moves upward (in terms of the criterion), only a minute fraction of all extreme points will usually have to be examined.

In the simplex algorithm, the monotonic upward trend of the search path and the guarantee that a local maximum is the global maximum provide a property closely resembling, and in a sense stronger than, transmissibility.

There is no known efficient algorithm for solving linear programming problems without conducting a search at least in the model space of extreme points, and good reason to suppose that no general algorithm of this kind exists.

SECTION 10
NON-INDEPENDENCE

In a previous section it was shown that non-independence among actions is the central source of difficulty in replacing models with modal procedures for causal reasoning. This section develops a number of schemes for handling important special cases of non-independence.

10.1 Resource Limitation

Suppose that each action A consumes or produces some quantity r_A of a scarce resource, of which the actor possessed, at the outset, the quantity r_0. Then we include the resource consumption (or production) in the effect of each action. The resource effect of a sequence of actions will simply be the algebraic sum of the resource effects of the individual actions comprising the sequence. We assume independence among actions, *except* for the resource limitation.

Then we can formulate a new *Axiom of Composition:*

(11) $\text{CAN}(r_0 \geq r_1, c_1), \text{CAN}(r_0 \geq r_2, c_2) \rightarrow \text{CAN}(r_0 \geq r_1 + r_2, c_1 \cdot c_2).$

This axiom deals, of course, with the Seducer's Paradox illustrated earlier, for if c_1 is car ownership, and c_2 is yacht ownership, then CAN(\$15,000, c_1) and CAN(\$15,000, c_2) imply CAN(\$30,000, $c_1 \cdot c_2$) but not CAN(\$15,000, $c_1 \cdot c_2$).

Many economic models, in particular the so-called *activity analysis* and *input-output* models, fall within the present scheme, with the important generalization that there may be several scarce resources instead of just one. Let the performance of the ith activity consume (produce) a_{ij} units of the jth resource, and let the vector with components b_j represent the initial resource availability. Then we wish to know whether, by carrying out the various activities with different intensities (specified by the vector with components $x_i \geq 0$), we can produce the vector of resources with components c_j.

Here the problem reduces to a question of the existence of non-negative solutions to systems of linear equations, and a search through the space of actions is not necessary.

10.2 Specific Requirements

The modified Axiom of Composition, proposed for the case of resource limitation, can be further amended to handle situations where particular actions may consume specific unique resources. Suppose a cabinet is to be built with pieces of wood already on hand. Then if a piece is used for one part, it is not available for another. If a_i means that the ith piece is available, then we can introduce an *Axiom of Composition* of the form:

(12) $\text{CAN}(a_{1i}(i = 1, \ldots, k_1), c_1), \text{CAN}(a_{2i}(i = 1, \ldots, k_2), c_2)$
$\rightarrow \text{CAN} (\prod_{i,j} a_{1i} \cdot a_{2j}, c_1 \cdot c_2).$

Then the feasibility of a conjunction of two actions can be determined by checking off the list of raw materials initially available the particular ones consumed by each action. If there is no overlap, the actions can be treated as independent.

This kind of interdependence leads to a phenomenon that has been called *functional fixity* in psychology. The standard experiment runs as follows: A subject is provided with two objects and given a task that requires him, temporarily, to use one of them. He is then given a second task for which either object would seem equally appropriate. With frequency greater than chance, subjects use for the second task the object *not* used for the first, even though the latter is now free.

An algorithm that would check each object off the list of available objects as it was used would exhibit functional fixity. The advantage of such an algorithm (which may outweigh its disadvantages in particular applications) is that it avoids the need for detailed temporal scheduling of actions. Its disadvantage is that it may declare impossible conjoint actions that are perfectly feasible if scheduled properly.

A common difficulty in chess analysis is the interdependence that arises from a piece performing multiple functions—guarding several other pieces, for example. An analysis assuming independence may allocate the piece to one function after it has already been committed to another. On the other hand, functional fixity in analyzing a chess position may blind a player to the possibility of using a piece for one function after it has been relieved of another.

10.3 Temporal Interdependence

Another form of temporal interdependence arises when an action can be performed, provided it is performed in the right sequence. That is to say, $CAN(c_1)$ and $CAN(c_1, c_2)$ imply $CAN(c_2)$ but not $CAN(c_2, c_1)$.

In the monkey-banana problem, suppose we put a partition in the room, having a door that swings shut and opens from only one side, with the monkey and stick initially on one side (the side from which the door can be opened), and the box and bananas on the other. The monkey can fetch the stick, carry it through the door, put the box under the bananas, climb up and reach them. But if, forgetting the stick, he gets the box first, he will be out of luck.

A possible "checkoff" procedure in such situations is to associate with the problem a directed graph that expresses the precedence conditions. Then a plan is viable if no action is performed until all predecessors on the graph have been performed. Whether it will be easy or difficult to construct the directed graph will depend, of course, on the nature of the constraints and the form in which the problem is given.

Overdependence on a unique resource has played a major role in a number of historical military debacles. Military forces are, in general, only partially "consumed" by an action, but are incapable of acting at two places at once. Thus d'Erlon's Corps, during the Waterloo Campaign, could probably have decided the issue at either Quatre Bras or Ligny, but in fact spent the day marching and countermarching between those two fields. Or to take an even more global example, Germany, in World War II, almost succeeded in solving its resource-commitment problem by a one-at-a-time strategy of consuming Poland, then France, then the USSR.

10.4 Analysis in Chess

All of these kinds of interdependencies appear, in one form or another, in the game of chess. For this reason, chess analysis is usually carried on in a composite, heuristic fashion making use both of functional analysis—resembling our use of CAN with transitivity and composition—and concrete dynamic analysis by searching the model space of the tree of chess positions. The former is used largely to discover possible sequences of actions; the latter to check them for interactions. Since the analysis must be carried out mentally, even the dynamic analysis often overlooks interactions through failure to update the model completely or accurately.

References

BLACK, FISCHER. A deductive question answering system. Unpublished doctoral dissertation, Harvard University, 1964. [M]

GELERNTER, H., and ROCHESTER, N. Intelligent behavior in problem-solving machines. *IBM Research and Development Journal*, October 1958, pp. 336–345.

MCCARTHY, JOHN. Situations, actions, and causal laws. Stanford University, Artificial Intelligence Project, Memo No. 2, 1963. [M]

NEWELL, ALLEN. Limitations of the current stock of ideas about problem solving. *In* A. Kent and O. E. Taulbee (eds.), *Electronic Information Handling*, Washington, D.C.: Spartan Books, 1965, Chapter 17.

AUTHOR INDEX

A

Abrahams, P. W., 145, 191, 196, 203
Amarel, S., 144–45, 185–86, 188, 190–91, 197, 204, 283, 420
Andrews, P. B., 343, 412
Aristotle, 283
Asu, R. W., 287

B

Backer, P. O. 50, 65, 283
Baker, F. B., 204
Bar-Hillel, Y., 226, 283
Baumert, L. D., 412
Baylor, G. W., 41, 365
Belnap, N. D., 267, 283
Berezner, S. C., 284
Berkeley, E. C., 282
Black, F. S., 221, 283, 337, 369, 374, 376, 378, 381, 383, 398, 399, 412, 430
Bobrow, D. G., 50–54, 56, 59–60, 65, 216, 220, 282–83
Bohnert, H. G., 50, 65, 266, 283
Burger, J. F., 286

C

Cahill, H., 204
Carney, H. C., 284
Chomsky, C., 66, 224
Chomsky, N., 45, 65, 224, 268, 284, 289, 327
Christensen, P. R., 204
Church, A., 343, 412
Clarke, D. C., 222, 283
Cohen, D., 217
Colby, K. M., 50, 65
Coles, L. S., 3, 50–54, 58–61, 65, 207–9, 211–87
Cooper, W. S., 221, 284
Craig, J. A., 284

D

Darlington, J. L., 50, 53–54, 59–61, 65, 221, 284
Davis, M., 232, 284

E

Earley, J. C., 284
Elliott, R. W., 221, 284
Enea, H., 50, 65
Engelbart, D. C., 214, 284
Ernst, G. W., 145, 148, 194–95, 197, 204, 214, 285, 332, 412

Evans, A., 231, 284
Evans, T. G., 148, 197, 204, 252, 276, 284

F

Feigenbaum, E. A., 43, 65, 142
Feldman, J., 43, 65, 142
Feldman, J. A., 231, 284
Fikes, R. E., 400–403, 412
Finkelstein, M., 289, 328
Floyd, R., 68, 231–32, 284, 360, 412
Fodor, J. A., 225, 285
Frey, P. R., 284
Frick, J. W., 204
Friedman, J., 287

G

Galler, B. A., 8
Garber, M., 142
Garvin, P., 213
Gelernter, H., 2, 422, 430
Gilbert, P., 284
Golomb, S. W., 412
Green, B. F., 50–51, 53–54, 59, 61, 65, 220, 284
Green, C., 383, 397–99, 412
Grimsdale, R. L., 144, 197, 205
Guilford, J. P., 145, 153, 166–70, 197, 204

H

Hall, B. C., 287
Halpern, M., 213, 284
Hansen, J. B., 145, 191, 196, 203
Hayes, P., 332, 412
Henkin, L., 412
Hoepfner, R., 204
Hovland, C. I., 144, 204–5
Hunt, E. B., 144–45, 204–5

I

Ingram, G., 205
Irons, E. T., 232, 284

Iturriaga, R., 286

K

Kasher, A., 51, 66, 216, 285
Katz, J. J., 223, 225, 229, 269, 285
Kelley, H. S., 205
Kettner, N. W., 204
Kilburn, T., 144, 197, 205
Kirsch, R. A., 50, 66, 216–17, 221, 285
Kondô, M., 221, 285
Kotovsky, K., 145, 166, 168, 170, 174, 191, 193, 196, 197, 205, 289, 328
Kripke S., 343, 350, 412
Kuno, S., 222, 285

L

Laughery, K., 66
Leblanc, H., 237, 285
Lehman, W. P., 222, 285
Liberman, D., 285
Licklider, J. C. R., 214, 285
Lindsay, R. K., 50–53, 55, 59, 61, 66, 220, 285
Londe, D. L., 50–51, 62–63, 66, 216, 219, 286
Long, R. E., 286
Longyear, C. R., 284
Lowery, H. R., 285

M

McCarthy, J., 123, 142, 221, 232, 285, 291, 328, 329, 330, 332, 337, 342, 369, 374, 396, 412, 418, 430
MacKay, D. G., 241, 285
Marin, J., 144, 205
Markov, A. A., 232, 235, 285
Markowitz, R., 412
Martin, R. M., 223, 285
Merrifield, P. R., 204
Miller, G. A., 284, 289, 327
Minsky, M., 66, 142
Morehead, A. H., 142
Morris, C., 223, 285
Mott-Smith, G., 142
Mueller, L. M., 287

Murata, H., 221, 285

N

Newell, A., 42–43, 72, 123, 142, 145, 148, 171, 191, 194–95, 197, 204, 205, 214, 271, 285, 328, 332, 338, 342, 368, 378, 387, 412–13, 423, 430

O

Oettinger, A. G., 261, 286
Ogden, C. K., 220, 286
Olney, J. C., 271, 286

P

Peano, G., 418
Peirce, C. S., 223
Pendegraft, E. D., 222, 285
Perlis, A. J., 8, 286
Pivar, M., 145, 191, 196, 203, 289, 328
Pople, H. E., 330–413
Post, E. L., 232, 286
Postal, P. M., 223, 229, 285
Putnam, H., 286

Q

Quatse, J. T., 248, 250, 286
Quillian, R., 50–51, 59, 62, 66, 221–22, 271, 286

R

Rankin, B., 217
Ranucci, E. R., 286
Raphael, B., 50–52, 55–56, 59–61, 66, 212, 220, 282, 286
Reichenbach, H., 218, 266, 276, 286, 291, 328
Richards, I. A., 49, 289, 290, 321, 328
Roberts, L. G., 247, 252, 286
Robinson, J. J., 222, 286
Rochester, N., 2, 422, 430
Russell, B., 266

S

Sammet, J. E., 286
Samuel, A. L., 72, 142
Schutzenberger, M. P., 284
Shaw, J. C., 42, 72, 142, 191, 271, 332, 338, 342, 368, 378, 387, 413
Siegal S., 205
Siklóssy, L., 3, 8, 44–66, 207–9, 288–327
Sillars, W. E., 217, 286
Simmons, R. F., 49, 66, 216, 219–21, 264, 286
Simon, H. A., 7–43, 44–66, 72, 142, 145, 168, 170, 171, 174, 191, 196–97, 205, 271, 274, 287, 289, 328, 330, 332, 337, 338, 342, 365, 368, 378, 381, 387, 399, 412–13, 414–30
Slagle, J. R., 221, 287
Solomonoff, R. J., 185–86, 188–89, 197, 205, 289, 328
Standish, T. A., 286
Stolz, W., 287
Stone, P. J., 144, 205
Sumner, F. H., 144, 197, 205
Sutherland, I. E., 247, 287

T

Thompson, F. B., 221, 231, 287
Thurstone, L. L., 148, 168, 193, 202
Turing, A. M., 215, 287

U

Uhr, L., 144, 185–88, 197, 205, 220, 287, 289, 319, 328

V

Vossler, C., 220, 287

W

Walker, D. E., 287
Wall, R. E., 283
Wang, H., 287
Watt, W. C., 222, 262, 287

Weber, H., 287
Weinreich, U., 287
Weizenbaum, J., 50, 52, 54, 59–60, 62, 66
Williams, D. S., 3, 8, 67–69, 143–205
Williams, T., 275, 287
Williams, T. G., 8, 67–69, 71–142
Winikoff, A., 145, 176–77, 205
Wirth, N., 287
Wolf, A. K., 66

Y

Yershov, A. P., 214, 263, 287

Z

Zemanek, H., 213–287
Zwicky, A. M., 222, 287

SUBJECT INDEX

A

Action, 414–15
Adaptive properties (*see* Learning)
Advice predicate, 346
Advice taker, 221, 329, 332–33, 337–38, 346–47, 368, 375–76, 398–99
  in GOL, 369, 374–78
Alphabets, 147
Ambiguity, 47–48, 55, 57, 62, 64, 201, 207–8, 213, 214, 222, 228–30, 235–41, 256–60, 303, 320, 348–50
  resolution of, 265, 267–71, 282;
  use of sensory information to remove, 58–59
  use of stored information to remove, 57–58
Ambiguous grammar, 239–41
Analogy problems, 148, 153, 164, 166, 171–76, 181–82, 199–200, 276
Analysis by synthesis, 54
Anaphoric expressions, 271–73 (*see also* Context)
Annexing information, 38–42, 55–59, 273–75
Aptitude Test Taker (ATT), 143–205
  comparison with human performance, 166–85
  comparison with other programs, 185–97

Aptitude Test Taker (ATT) (*Cont.*)
  implementation of, 155–66
Aptitude tests, 68, 167, 171–76, 199–203
Artificial intelligence, 214, 288–90
  history of, 1–2, 7, 9–10, 143–45
Associative memory, 62
ATTAIN (GOL function), 341, 379–82
Attainability, 329, 334, 364, 415–19, 424
Axiom of independence, 420

B

Backtracking, 402
Backus-Naur (BNF) notation, 224
BASEBALL program, 220
Basic English, 220
"Big switch theory," 214
Branch-and-bound algorithm, 365
British Museum Algorithm, 364

C

"Can" (*see* Feasibility)
Canonical forms, 58
Canult, 334, 369, 374–77, 418 (*see also* Cause, Attainability)
Cascaded generators, 405–6
Cause, 329, 334–35, 369, 374–75, 418

436 Subject Index

Cell test unit (CTU), 84–87, 90–94, 101, 103, 120–21, 126, 130–31, 134
Checkers, 103–10
Cognitive processes, simulation of, 1 (*see also* Human Problem Solving)
Compiler:
   design of, 7, 12–21
   for GOL, 403–12
   general, 12, 18–21 (*see also* Heuristic Compiler)
Complexity, 4–5
Composition, principle of, 418–21, 428
Computer aided instruction, 215–16
Concept Former Program, 191–94, 197
Conjunctive goal, 376–77, 383
Conjunctive paradox, 337–39, 381–83, 420
Consistency test in ZBIE, 299–300
Constraint manipulation, 401
Context, 55–57, 207–9, 230, 271–73, 295, 302, 320, 349, 401–2

D

Data (*see* Pictorial information; Representation of data)
DEACON (Direct English Access and Control) program, 221, 231
DEDUCOM program, 221
Deep structure, 45, 48, 51–54, 65, 226 (*see also* Linguistics)
Definite descriptions, 37–40
Definition, compiling routine from, 35–36
Description list, 13, 27–30, 229–30, 248, 251–52, 269–70, 275, 292–93, 339, 378
Descriptions, 74, 79, 92, 96–99, 119
   incomplete, 417 (*see also* Partial descriptions)
   of test items, 152–55, 164–66
   of board for game, 96–98
Dictionary (*see* Lexicon)
Difference reduction, 340, 379
Dynamic analysis, 430

E

Earley Algorithm, 242
Eights, 107–14

Enabling conditions, 415, 417
Equality test, 395
Error avoidance, 299, 301, 322
Error recovery, 300, 322–27
Evaluation, in GOL, 331, 343, 358–59, 367–68, 397, 403–12
   in GRANIS, 252–55
   of sentence, 236–37, 241
Evaluation functions, 124–25
Evaluation processes, 274–75
Experience, applied to new situation, 72, 74
Extensional generators, 357
Extensional predicates, 343, 345, 351–56, 376
Extractors, 292–94
Eye movements, 161, 166, 176–85, 197

F

Feasibility, 329, 334–35, 369
Feature extraction, 155–56
Fewest replies heuristic, 366
"Find" processes, 32–34, 138 (*see also* Search)
Flexibility of representations, 27
Flow diagrams, 19, 21–24
Floyd-Evans productions, 231
Forcing position, 426
Formula ALGOL, 241, 245–46, 267, 270
Function designators, 394
Functional analysis, 430
Functional description compiler, 12, 16–19
Functional descriptions, 26–27
Functional fixity, 428–29
Functional language (FL), 290–92, 321–22
Functional languages, recursive, 36–37

G

Game-playing programs, 68, 71–142, 329
Games, examples of, 99–117
General Game Playing Language (GGPL) syntax, 76–81
General Game Playing Program (GGPP), 71–142
   and human behavior, 73–75

General Game Playing Program (*Cont.*)
  flow of control in, 81–82
  generality of, 127–33
  primitive routines for 134–42
Generality, 73, 117, 127–33, 156–59
General Problem Solver (GPS), 2, 4, 9–11, 21, 123, 148, 191, 194–96, 271, 329–32, 338–42, 346–47, 368, 378–86, 420
  relation of to Heuristic Compiler, 21, 24
Generative grammar, 235–36
Generators, context sensitive, 395
  in GGPP, 87–89
  in GOL, 355–60, 403–9
Goal-Oriented Language (GOL), 330–413 (*see also* GOL Programming System)
GOL programming system, 343–68
  applications of, 368–92
  extensions of, 393–97
GOLDEF command, 353
GOLDIG command, 346–49, 352, 356–60, 362–63, 380, 389, 407
"Good guess" method, 300, 303, 305, 321
GRAIS program, 221
Grammaticality (*see* Syntax)
GRANIS (Graphical Natural Inference System) program, 211–87
  program structure of, 242–55 (*see also* Natural Inference System)

H

Habitability, 261–65
Hearer programs, 47, 51–61
Hearts, 115–16
Hereditary properties, 423–26
Heuristic Compiler (HC), 3, 7–43, 274
Heuristic search, 347, 364–65, 389, 396–99, 401–2 (*see also* Problem solving)
Hoyle's *Book of Games,* 67–68, 107, 127–28, 142
Human problem solving, 9, 40–41, 73–75, 166–85, 282 (*see also* Natural language)

I

Imperatives, formalization of, 267, 272–73

Induction, 3–4
  from examples, 36, 68, 143–205
  of grammars, 289
Inductive learning, 396
Inductive reasoning, 143 (*see also* Induction from examples)
Inference making, 55, 216, 222, 230, 272
Inferential power, 265–73
Information, amount of, 73
Information retrieval, 55, 214, 220–21 (*see also* Inference Making, Question-answering programs)
Initialization, 296, 304, 321, 324
Input to language processor, structuring, 52–54
Institute of Living Test, 159, 166, 174–75
Intelligence tests (*see* Aptitude tests)
Intension, representation of, 347, 367
Intensional generators, 358–60, 367–68
Intensional predicates, 343, 345, 351, 353, 376, 411
Interactive conversation, 276, 280
Interpretation of GOL expressions, 351
Interrogatives, formalization of, 267
IPL-V, 13, 27–28, 75–76, 122–23, 147, 291–92, 322
Isomorphism and representation, 30–31

K

Kernel sentences, 264–65
Knowledge, stored, 59–60
Knowledge acquisition (*see* Annexing information)

L

Lambda expression, 343, 345, 347, 355, 358–59
Language (*see* Linguistics, Natural language)
  semantic processing of, 42–66
  through pictures, 289–90
Language competence, 45–46
Language learning, 208, 288–327 (*see also* Learning)
Language performance, 45–46
Language translation (*see* Translation of languages)

Learner programs, 47, 63–64
Learning, 275–78, 288
  in game playing programs, 124–27
  German, 323–27
  natural language, 288–327
  Russian, 304–19
  in ZBIE, 302
Letter analogies (*see* Analogy problems)
Letter series test, 148, 153, 166, 168, 173, 176, 179–80, 183–85, 188, 193, 196, 201–2
Lexicon, 42, 45, 48, 53, 62, 64, 225–28, 234, 246–47, 295
Linguistic description, 223–41
Linguistics, 8, 31, 60, 207–9, 226 (*see also* Language)
LISP 1.5, 342, 345–48, 393–94
List structures, 76–79, 118–19
Lists, 76, 78
Logic Theorist (LT), 2, 330, 342, 368
  in GOL, 387–92
Look-ahead, 314

M

Markov Algorithm, 235
Match-back, 302, 305, 325
Match depth, 299
Match process, 4, 42, 52–54, 64, 164 (*see also* Patterns)
  in ZBIE, 293–94, 297–99, 301
MATER program, 330, 365–67
Maze-solving algorithm, 363, 364, 368–73
Meaning, 207–9 (*see also* Semantics)
Meaning and truth-value, 270
Means-end analysis, 9, 11, 16, 20 (see *also* General Problem Solver)
Modal concepts, expression of in GOL, 361–63
Modal logic, 329, 332–34, 341–43, 350, 361–63, 374–78, 418, 420
Model, 329–30, 341–43, 415–16, 421–22
Model structure, 350, 362
Model subspace, 427
Monkey-and-banana problem, 330, 374–77, 381–86, 398–99, 420–21, 429
Moves, in games, 94–96, 139–40

N

NAMER program, 219–20

Natural Inference System, 232–41
Natural language, 2, 8–9, 25–28, 31–32, 40–42, 207, 211–87 (*see also* Language)
  learning of, 288–327
  representation of, 25–28
Non-deterministic algorithm, 68, 360, 380, 400
Non-independence among actions, 427–30
Non-linear FL sentence, 308

O

Objects, representation of, 74–75 (*see also* Description list, List structures)
Organization of ZBIE program, 296–304

P

Paraphrastic set, 228, 262
Parsing, 208, 217–18, 222, 236–37, 239, 245, 248 (*see also* Syntax, Semantics)
Partial descriptions, compiling routines from, 40–42
Pattern creation process in ZBIE, 302–304
Pattern language, 120–21
Pattern list (p-list), 292, **297**, 299, 300–304
Pattern recognition, 74, 84–94, 127, 155–58, 164, 218–20 (*see also* Induction from examples, Match processes)
Patterns, 234–35, 345
  in GGPP, 84–92
  in TAT (*see* Test Item Description)
  in ZBIE, 292–93
Perceptual processes, 240–42
Phrase marker, 52–53, 55
Phrase-structure grammar, 219
Pictorial information, 207, 213–19, 247–52, 274, 289–92
Picture grammar, 250
Picture Language Machine (PLM), 217–18
Pictures, representation of, 63
Planning heuristic, 420
Pragmatics, 223, 229–31
  of GOL, 352–60
Predicate calculus, 123, 217–18, 226–27, 231, 246–47, 255–62, 279
  extending, 265–67

Predicates (see Extensional predicates, Intensional predicates)
Problem, 10–11
Problem solving, 7, 9–12, 329, 332, 341, 420 (see also Heuristic search)
 programs, 191–97
Process language, 10–11
Processes, generalized, 32–37
Production system, 232–34, 237
 of GRANIS, 242–46
Productions, 75, 79–80, 119, 154, 231–33, 244–45, 280–81
Program, for Checkers, 105–10
 for Eights, 112–14
 for Hearts, 115–16
 for Tic-Tac-Toe, 103
 syntax of in GGPL, 79–81
Programming, computer, 7–9
 as problem solving, 11–12
Programming languages, higher-level, 214 (see also IPL-V, LISP 1.5)
Projection rules, 45, 51–52, 60
Proofs, 416–17 (see also Theorem proving)
Propositional calculus, 221
Protocols (see Verbal protocols, Eye movements)
Protosynthex, 220–21
Pushdown stacks, 82–83, 119–20, 235, 242, 246, 394

Q

Quantifiers, 266
 in GOL, 409–10
Question-answering programs, 51–52, 216, 221, 274

R

Reasoning about actions, 414–30
Recursive GOL expressions, 360–61
Redundancy, 4, 422
REF problem solving system, 400–403
Representation, 1–2, 9, 25–42, 67–69, 74–75, 94–117
 alternative, 123
 of board games, 121–22, 133
 of card games, 122, 128–33

Representation (Cont.)
 of data, 394
 of data, in ATT, 147–55
 by description, 329–38, 341–42 (see also Modal logic)
 design of, 28–31, 67–69
 experiments with, 31–42
 in GOL, 344–47
 of input to GGPP, 83–84, 100–101, 103–105, 115
 internal, 67–69, 117–23, 212, 221
 internal, of ZBIE, 292–95, 329
 by modeling, 329–33, 341–42, 378
 and process, 339–41
 of test items, 147–48
Resolution method, 397–98
Resource limitation, 419–20, 427–30

S

SAD SAM program, 220
Scare resources, 419–20
Search, efficiency of, 93–94
 selective, 9, 124
 termination of, 411–12
Search processes in GGPP, 84–94, 102, 106, 121, 130, 141
Search space, reducing, 423, 426–27
 size of, 383
Search strategy, 427
Selective search (see Search, Problem solving)
Semantic component, 252
Semantic data structures, 379
Semantic description, 36, 38
Semantic evaluation, 343, 349
Semantic markers, 269
Semantic productions, 231, 246–47
Semantics, 2–3, 7–8, 45–47, 56, 60, 64–65, 208, 223–24, 279, 321, 378
 in FL, 291
 of GOL expressions, 350–51
 of PLM, 218
 (see also, Language, semantic processing of)
Sentences, multiple, 271–73
Sequence extrapolation, 289
Sequence Prediction Program, 191, 196–97
Sequencing function, 234–35

Shipley-Hartford Intelligence Test (*see* Institute of Living Test)
Simulation of human information processing (*see* Human problem solving, Natural language)
SIR (Semantic Information Retriever) program, 220
"Sort" processes, 34–36
Speaker programs, 47, 61–62
State description compiler, 12–16, 41
State descriptions, 14, 19, 27–28, 414–16, 421–22
State designator in GOL, 348
State language, 10–11
State space, 397
State transformation, 362, 364, 398, 407–408
Statistics, 3
Strategy, 68, 346–47, 365, 389, 396
  in Hearts, 111–12
  in Tic-Tac-Toe, 103
Structure of intellect, 145, 167–69
STUDENT program, 221
Subgoal generation, 125–27
Surface structure, 226
Symbol structures, 1
Symbols, 76–78
Symmetry, 176, 422–25
Synonymy, 47–48, 57–58
Syntactic description, 36–37
Syntactic symmetry, 422–23
Syntax, 45–47, 63–64, 208, 212, 216, 223–29
  and generality, 48–49
  of GOL expressions, 347–50
  of GGPL, 77
  of GRANIS, 279
  and semantics, 46, 49, 227–29, 393
Syntax-directed interpretation, 211–87

T

Task domain, 1–2
Teaching sequence, 322
Template matching, 60
Temporal interdependence, 429–30
Tense logic, 276–77
Test Form Analyzer (TFA), 143–45, 148, 150, 155–59, 198
Test Form Specification (TFS), 144–45, 148–51, 158–59, 198
Test Item Description (TID), 152–55, 177, 181–85, 192, 195
Test Item Taker (TIT), 144–46, 149, 151–52, 159–66, 196, 198
  operation of, 161–66
  process of forming, 159–61
Theorem proving, 387–92, 397–99
Tic-Tac-Toe, 74–75, 88–89, 99–103, 126
  data description, 100–101
  GOL representation of, 344–46
  program, 102–4
Topic of understanding (*see* Universe of discourse)
Transformation by catalog, 188–89
Transformation graph, 186–88
Transformational grammar, 224–25, 263–65, 293, 295 (*see also* Linguistics)
Translation of languages, 2, 49, 63, 289–90, 319–22
Translation rule, 292–95, 304–5, 321
Transmissible property, 426–27
Tree structures, 291
Try list, 365
Turing machine, 232
Turing Test, 215
Type theory, many-sorted, 343

U

Understanding, 367
Universe of discourse, 54, 211, 229–31, 234, 240, 262–69, 274–77, 281–82
  of GRANIS, 247–52

V

Verbal protocols, 176–81
Visual displays, 207 (*see also* Pictorial information)
Vocabulary, 295 (*see also* Lexicon)

W

"Wild-card" variable, 356, 359–60
Won position, 426
Word order in language translation, 320

Z

ZBIE program, 288–327